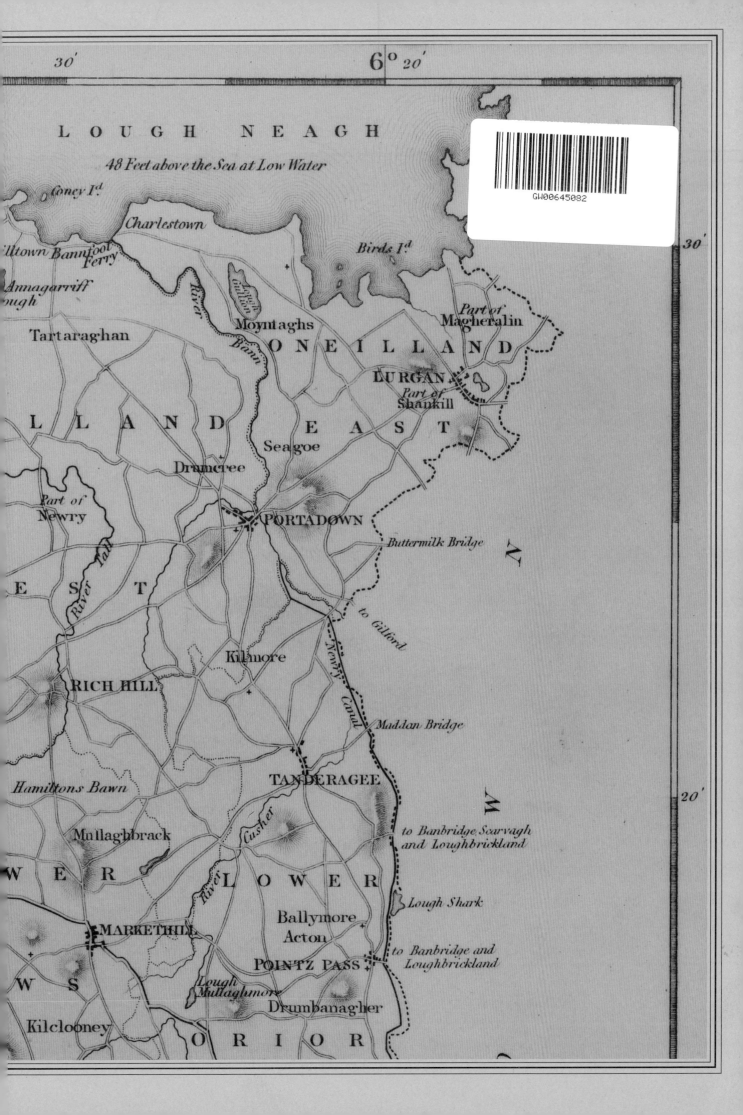

BUILDINGS OF COUNTY ARMAGH

BUILDINGS
OF
COUNTY ARMAGH

by

C E B BRETT

with photographs by

MICHAEL O'CONNELL

A publication of the
ULSTER ARCHITECTURAL HERITAGE SOCIETY

BELFAST
1999

First published 1999
by the
Ulster Architectural Heritage Society
66 Donegall Pass, Belfast BT7 1BU

Edited by Gordon Wheeler
Designed by Della Varilly
Printed by Nicholson & Bass, Ltd

ISBN 0 900457 54 6

A catalogue record for this book
is available from the British Library

Frontispiece: The Callan River, with disused beetling mill and Tassagh railway viaduct (200)
Photograph: Michael O'Connell
End-papers: Map of County Armagh, 1837 (from S Lewis: *Topographical dictionary*)

DEDICATED

to

Hugh Dixon and Dick Oram

who have done so much
to record and preserve
the built heritage of County Armagh

CONTENTS

... From where I lived
We might watch Long Bullets being played,
Follow the course of a pair of whippets,
Try to keep in time with a Lambeg Drum.

There'd be Derryscollop, and Cloveneden,
The parish where W R Rodgers held sway.
And where the first Orange Lodge was founded,
An orchard full of No Surrenders.

We could always go closer if you wanted,
To where Macha had challenged the charioteer
And Swift the Houyhnhnm,
The open field where her twins were whelped.
Then, the scene of the Armagh Rail Disaster.
Why not brave the Planetarium?

Paul Muldoon

from 'Armageddon, Armageddon',
in 'Mules', London, 1977, p 55.

ACKNOWLEDGEMENTS

I owe thanks to the very many people who have helped, over a period of nearly three years, in the compilation of this book. I do not live, and have never lived, in County Armagh; my only family connection with the county is that in 1795 my great-great-great-grandfather, Charles Brett of Belfast, wine merchant, married "a fair Black with fifteen hundred", Matilda Black being a daughter of the Armagh wine merchants who lived at Blamount or, as it is now called, Ballintaggart (126). In this book, therefore, I have been much more dependent on the help of the natives of the county than was the case in County Antrim.

My particular thanks are due to Dr Noel and Mrs Rosemary Marshall of Salter's Grange; to John MacEvoy of Meigh; to Anthony Cranney and Michelle Boyle of RoSA (Regeneration of South Armagh), Crossmaglen; and to Harvey Bicker, formerly of Poyntzpass: all of whom took me to see many buildings I might otherwise have missed. I also thank Catherine McCullough and Greer Ramsey of the Armagh County Museum; Mary McVeigh of the SELB Irish and Local Studies Library, Armagh; Harry Carson of Archbishop Robinson's Library, Armagh; Philip Wilson of the Craigavon Museum Project; and Joe Canning, acting librarian of the Cardinal Tomás O Fiaich Memorial Library, Armagh.

In Belfast, I am especially grateful to John Killen, Gerry Healey and Mary Delargy of the Linen Hall Library, to the staff of the Public Record Office of Northern Ireland, to Terence Reeves-Smyth of the Monuments and Buildings Record, to Peter and Belinda Jupp, to Karen Latimer of the Architecture and Planning Library of the Queen's University, to Cormac Bourke, W A Maguire and Trevor Parkhill of the Ulster Museum, to Sally Skillen of the Ulster Folk and Transport Museum, to Peter Marlow and Frances Bailey of the National Trust, and to Ann Hamlin, lately of the Environment and Heritage Service; and in Dublin, to Ann-Martha Rowan, and David Griffin, of the Irish Architectural Archive, to Maurice Craig and to Edward McParland.

I am particularly appreciative of the meticulous professionalism of Gordon Wheeler, who has not only edited this book, but also undertaken the laborious tasks of compiling the Bibliography and checking all the footnotes; and of that of Della Varilly, its flexible and ingenious designer. As to the typing, Eileen Barrett typed the drafts of the earlier pages for me, but when she had to give up for reasons of health, my family told me that I must learn to use my own personal computer. Not without difficulty, and with much help from Dianne Williams, I have more or less managed to do so: so I have nobody to blame for errors but myself!

I have to thank the following for permission to make use of illustrations, of which they are respectively the copyright-holders: the National Museums of Scotland for the photograph at page xiv; the Department of Archaeology, QUB, for those at pages 4 and 13; the National Museums and Galleries of Northern Ireland for those at pages 8, 9, 89, 100 and 281 (Ulster Museum), 19, 20, 21, 75, 155, 190, 199, 238 (Ulster Folk Museum), 103 (Armagh County Museum); Archbishop Robinson's Library, Armagh for those at pages 23 and 25; The Representative Church Body, Dublin, for those at pages 53 and 54; the Irish Architectural Archive, Dublin, for those at pages 48, 62, 94, 109, 220, 235-6, 251, 266 and 268; the SELB Irish and Local Studies Library, Armagh, for those at pages 92, 206, 221, 222, 254 and 277; the Public Record Office of Northern Ireland for those at pages 22, 101, 102, 133, 159, 178, 182 and 195; and The Monuments and Buildings Record of Northern Ireland for those on pages 2, 3, 72, 76, 90, 93, 94, 99, 102, 103, 104, 105, 153, 170, 176, 229 and 233; and to the Trustees of Sir John Soane's Museum for the drawing on page 266. My thanks are due also to other owners who allowed me to reproduce old photographs.

I am quite exceptionally grateful to my friend and colleague, Michael O'Connell, for the time and pains he has devoted to taking a very large proportion of the photographs with which this book is illustrated. Without them, it would be a poor thing indeed. All the colour photographs are his, with the exception of the interior picture of the staircase hall in the Argory, which is reproduced by courtesy of the National Trust Picture Library, and is by Andreas von Einsiedel.

My especial thanks are due to Paul Muldoon, now Professor of Poetry at the University of Oxford, for permitting me to quote an admirably apposite passage from his poem 'Armageddon, Armageddon' published in 'Mules' in 1977.

I must also express my gratitude and appreciation to the several charities and other bodies which have accorded financial support to this publication: in particular,

Armagh City and District Council.
The Belfast Society
Craigavon Borough Council
Department of the Environment for Northern Ireland
The Dufferin Foundation
Esmé Mitchell Trust
The Marc Fitch Fund
School of Irish Studies Foundation

And last but not least, I must express my gratitude to all of the people of County Armagh who showed me their homes, or the buildings for which they were responsible, or who went to trouble to turn up title-deeds, family papers, or pictures which threw light on the history of the buildings here described.

C E B B

INTRODUCTION

As with the companion volume for County Antrim, published in 1996, my main purpose has been the filling of gaps. I find it extraordinary that those in the Department of the Environment responsible for historic monuments and buildings in Northern Ireland should have done so little towards the publication of highly valuable but not easily accessible information. It is true that a start was made by Hugh Dixon on a volume for county Armagh, but he had many other duties, and when he left to join the staff of the National Trust, the project seems just to have been dropped. I have had access to his notes, and very helpful they were - so far as they went. I understand that it is hoped to publish quite soon a volume on the archaeology of county Armagh, but that it will have a cut-off date of 1550 AD. There appears still to be no proposal for any publication covering later buildings.

So far as the voluntary sector is concerned, there is, of course, the excellent and authoritative gazetteer, The Buildings of Armagh, compiled in 1992 by Robert McKinstry, Richard Oram, Roger Weatherup and Primrose Wilson for the Ulster Architectural Heritage Society: but, despite its title, it deals only with buildings within the city of Armagh. This faced me with a dilemma: what to do about the city? If I excluded it, on grounds of duplication, I risked disappointing purchasers of this book, who might very reasonably expect to be provided with information about, at the very least, the city's two cathedrals. On the other hand, it would have been perverse to reproduce all the entries over again, with or without laboriously putting the same facts into different words. In the end, and after discussion with the authors of the earlier gazetteer, I have adopted a middle course: I have very much restricted the number of entries for buildings within the city; I have quoted fairly extensively, with the authors' permission, from their descriptions and comments; but I have on occasion expanded them, and in a few instances felt myself at liberty to disagree with them.

I hope the resulting balance between town and country buildings will justify any lack of completeness. And here I must emphasise that, like that for County Antrim, this book is a selective personal anthology, and makes no attempt to pass itself off as an inventory. I have tried to include all the most important buildings, using the aesthetic standards of an architectural historian; and such others as took my fancy for one reason or another. As before, I have used the word "building" broadly to embrace everything from a dolmen to an obelisk, from a cannon to a cottage, from a cathedral to a gospel hall. To some extent, I have given preference to the respectable middling-sized farm-houses or mill-owners' houses in which the county is still quite rich - though much less so

than was the case a few years ago: "improvements", plastic windows and doors, above all replacement dwellings, have wrought havoc with the dwindling stock: not to mention the intermittent Troubles of the years from 1921 up to the very recent past.

Armagh is in many respects a county of very different character from Antrim. It is predominantly an inland county, constrained between Lough Neagh to the north, the river Bann to the east, and the river Blackwater to the west: and with a wavering boundary to the south, running from Carlingford Lough to the high ground of the Fews. (The erratic course of this southern boundary through the town of Newry is particularly confusing).

The county can be divided into three very distinct areas. To the north, the flat expanse bordering Lough Neagh, with its peatland, drains, reeds and birch trees, has been rendered only marginally prosperous by successive lowerings of the level of the lough. South of this, there is a wide extent of rich, rolling, agricultural countryside, attractively wooded and orcharded, which over the years has produced fecund crops of corn, flax, apples, and (today's crop) mushrooms. This is the heartland of the 17th-century English plantation. South of this again, the land begins to rise; the rocky hills of the Fews lead to the, very beautiful, volcanic mini-mountains of the Ring of Gullion; in this comparatively barren countryside took refuge those who had been evicted by the planters.

Here, the uneasy relationship between the Planter and the Gael reaches its climax: Armagh is the historic heartland of the political and religious Troubles of Ulster. Drumcree in the north, Crossmaglen in the south, symbolise the two extremes of passionately held beliefs and convictions. This book is not about politics, but about buildings. I have for the most part sought to exclude buildings with strong political associations, be they Orange halls or the British army's watch-towers or the numerous IRA memorials of south Armagh. (I could not resist, though, including Colonel Saunderson (216) wearing his sash on the Twelfth of July, a statue come to life like the Commendatore in Don Giovanni). But buildings are very much affected by politics: not just by bunting, graffiti, and wall-paintings, but by bombs and bullets. Every town and village in the county has suffered their ravages: the most important buildings have, for the most part, been laboriously restored; but the lesser shops, pubs and homes that line so many main streets have mostly lost the details that gave them their character. That is one reason why there are fewer urban than rural buildings in this book.

Because of the defensive (and understandable) security-consciousness of many householders, I had a good many difficulties with access, except where I enjoyed local sponsorship: not always the case. For the same reason, there are very few interior photographs or ground plans in this book. I succeeded in getting inside about two-thirds of the buildings described, but, where I was evidently unwelcome, I preferred not to insist. I was refused access in one instance, and Michael O'Connell and I were more than once refused permission to photograph private houses. But most people, however suspicious initially, became friendly and helpful once they understood the nature of the book. I cannot say the same for some of their dogs. Fierce dogs are the bane not only of the postman, but also of the architectural historian; and a high proportion of the dogs of County Armagh are imbued either with the spirit of Drumcree, or that of Crossmaglen.

I have tried to provide the basic information on address, townland, parish, District Council area, and grid reference, which a researcher is likely to need; but it should be remembered that boundaries can be moved, and parishes restructured over the years. The grid references represent my own estimates based on the 1:50,000 Ordnance Survey maps. I am afraid that some mistakes will inevitably have crept into these geographical particulars.

I have sought to indicate whether a building is listed and, if so, in which category; and whether a building lies within the boundaries of a conservation area. But these things can change, and any reader with a special interest in a particular building would be wise to check its current status with the Environment and Heritage Service, especially in view of the ward-by-ward Second Survey on the ground which is currently taking place.

The system of grading employed is, at present, confusing. It is said that the grading system used in Northern Ireland is similar to the Scottish system, though different from that used in England and Wales. The Information Guide for the Second Survey of Historic Buildings, issued in 1999, does nothing to elucidate the categorisation. Annex C to Planning Policy Statement 6, issued in March 1999, helps a bit:[1] grade A denotes "buildings of greatest importance to Northern Ireland including both outstanding architectural set-pieces and the least altered examples of each representative style, period and grouping"; Grade B+, "buildings which might have merited grade A status but for detracting features such as incomplete design, lower quality additions, or alterations"; Grade B, "buildings of local importance and good examples of a particular period or style". But then the issue is clouded: "Since 1987 the Department has been banding Grade B buildings into two groups, namely B1 and B2. Generally B1 is chosen for buildings that qualify for listing by virtue of a relatively wide selection of attributes ... B2 is chosen for buildings that qualify for listing by virtue of only a few attributes". In practice, it is almost impossible to work out why very similar buildings may be designated in one case B+, in another B1. In addition, it seems that Q is used to identify a particular kind of thatched property for grant purposes; IA is used to indicate significance in terms of industrial archaeology.

My primary concern has been, throughout, with the external appearance of the buildings recorded; my next concern with their history, owners and occupiers, and associations. I have, of course, recorded internal features

of particular interest when I stumbled upon them, but have not gone out of my way to search for them. It must be said, however, that the county boasts some very fine interior detailing: not only in the three National Trust houses open to the public - Ardress (60), The Argory (66), and Derrymore House (106) - but also in buildings such as Primate Robinson's chapel (22), the Armagh court-house (169), the two cathedrals (39 and 47), and one or two other churches. Some of these are open to the public; most private houses are not; I must beg readers of this book to respect the privacy of those who find visitors unwelcome.

The arrangement of the eight chapters, and of the entries within each chapter, is broadly consistent with Buildings of County Antrim. Within each section, buildings are mostly arranged in approximate order of date, unless considerations of contrast, comparison, or layout, suggest otherwise. But it must be noted that the dating of Irish buildings is still a somewhat inexact science: documentary evidence is rare, except in the case of the more important (or more recent) buildings. I have tried to be as scholarly as possible in my researches, but there is still a lot of guesswork in this book, and inevitably some of my guesses will turn out to have been wrong. I shall welcome correction from those who can adduce evidence to show that I have been mistaken.

Indeed, the matter of evidence is very relevant, for it can be very difficult indeed to track down reliable information and documents for old buildings. In the first place, maps: John Rocque's county map, published in 1760, is not really all that useful, though often cited: for it is almost always impossible to tell whether the houses he marks are the same as those now standing. Besides, as Sir Charles Coote judiciously remarked in 1804, it "was not considered correct". Tantalisingly, Coote adds that "another map of the county, from actual survey, was presented to the Grand Jury in the year 1778, by Messrs William and Conyngham M'Crea, which was the labour of three years. This map, and also Rocque's, hang in the Grand Jury Room".[2] Alas, the members of the Grand Jury were too parsimonious to bear the cost of engraving the M'Creas' map, and the original has disappeared: it would have been an invaluable tool in the preparation of this book. Apart from Daniel Beaufort's map of Ireland of 1792, at too small a scale to be much help, and Taylor and Skinner's very useful road books of 1778 and 1783, there are no reliable maps for the county earlier than the first Ordnance Survey sheets of 1836.

Three other important sources, upon which I relied greatly for Buildings of County Antrim, are for Armagh either wanting altogether, or very scanty. There are no surviving Ordnance Survey memoirs for the city or parish of Armagh; and the skimpy records that do survive for other parishes in the county have been collected into a single slim volume by Angélique Day and Patrick McWilliams: whereas the memoirs for county Antrim occupied fourteen volumes. Dr O'Laverty's invaluable history of the Diocese of Down and Connor has never had a counterpart for the parishes of either the county or the diocese of Armagh, nor have I succeeded in discovering, amongst the memoirs of travellers, any book half as informative about Armagh as Atkinson's Ireland Exhibited to England of 1823 is about County Antrim.

On the positive side, the existence of no less than three excellent libraries in Armagh city, all provided with helpful and knowledgeable librarians, proved a great asset; as did the existence of a number of good local histories and directories, listed in the Bibliography on page 278, of which Coote, Stuart, Rogers, and Bassett proved the most useful. Once again I have made extensive use of the manuscript Valuation books of the 1830s calendared as 1B in the Public Record Office. They are not easy to work with: unless the researcher knows beforehand the parish and townland, and the name of the occupier, of the building he seeks, he may be forced to retire defeated. Their system of categorisation is highly confusing, and does not seem to have been consistently applied. Some volumes, and some of the key-numbered maps, are missing, as are (quite often) page numbers and exact dates. Nevertheless, once again, I believe that, by collating information derived from the first valuation with information derived from the Ordance Survey maps and memoirs, I have been able to put together quite a lot of hitherto unfamiliar facts.

The later, so-called 'Griffith' valuation of 1859-60, calendared in the Public record office as 2B, and the still later series running on into the 1930s, calendared as 12B, have also provided much useful information. It may be remarked that the Valuation books are more helpful for large houses, less helpful for cottages, shops, or terrace houses in towns and villages, unless independent evidence of identification exists: for street numbers did not exist, and house names are rarely given.[3]

During the interval between the valuations of 1830 and of 1860, a number of useful books appeared: in particular, Samuel Lewis's two-volume Topographical Dictionary of Ireland (in editions of 1837, 1838, and 1847) and the three-volume Parliamentary Gazetteer of Ireland, published in 1845-6, both of which are generally informative about certain kinds of buildings - especially churches and glebe-houses, since the information was largely collected from the clergy - and reliable.

The enormous store of typed Armachiana, and other manuscripts and transcriptions, compiled by Mr T G F Paterson (with whom I served on the Northern Ireland Committee of the National Trust, and whom I greatly respected) in the Armagh County Museum was sometimes useful, but his interests were primarily genealogical and he did not devote much attention to architects or architecture. His cuttings, and copies of extracts from local newspapers, proved invaluable. The statutory lists maintained by the Historic Monuments and Buildings Service of the Department of the Environment provided a starting-point for research, and the files in the Monuments and Buildings Record, sometimes including notes by Hugh Dixon, Dick Oram or Belinda Jupp, were often helpful. However, it still requires a stroke of good luck to discover clear evidence of the architect of most Ulster buildings.

The three principal architects of County Armagh were, of course, Thomas Cooley, his pupil Francis Johnston, and (a long way behind) the latter's nephew, William Murray. Amongst the runners-up were George Ensor (at Ardress, 60); the Williamsons (at the Argory, 66); Thomas Duff and W J Barre, both of Newry; J J McCarthy and J J McDonnell; and the various imported country house architects - Thomas Hopper, William Playfair, perhaps John Nash. But there is surpringly little which can be firmly attributed to leading Belfast or Dublin architects. I have tried hard to resist the temptation to make attributions on purely stylistic grounds. I suspect that, locally, much has been attributed to Francis Johnston, in particular, which was not his at all. As usual, the most important local architect was Anon.

One interesting feature of Armagh is the very high quality of much of the carved stone-work. This is perhaps not surprising, considering the qualities of the stone from the local quarries - on which subject, see the instructive article by Philip Doughty, Keeper of Geology at the Ulster Museum, on 'The stones of Armagh' in the introductory pages to the UAHS Buildings of Armagh of 1992. As he remarks, "These rocks give a character, sometimes craggy, often noble, which seems entirely suited to this ancient ecclesiastical market town and its people". And: "In fact the refined buildings of the city show all the elaborations of the finest West Country eighteenth and nineteenth century architecture, reminiscent of Pulteney Street and the other principal terraces of Bath. There are elaborate plinths, mouldings, cornices, pilasters, pillars and shafts and finishes ranging from rough pitched, through plain ashlars to rustications, with faces boasted, furrowed, broached and pick panelled".[4] What holds good for the city holds good also for the county, where, however, there is sometimes a degree of incongruity between the elegance and clarity of stone door-case, and the ordinariness of the wall to which it is attached.

I cannot prove it, but I strongly suspect that, somewhere in the counties of Armagh, Louth or Monaghan, between around 1775 and 1835, there was a specialist factory turning out both carved door-cases and carved mantelpieces to customers' specifications: and that the owner of a very plain house might decide to embellish it by glueing a new door-case onto his front wall. Bradshaw's General Directory of 1819 shows no less than fourteen masons resident in the city of Armagh; also James Nugent's stone and marble yard in Abbey Street: but I have been unable to discover anything more. If anyone can throw light on this, I shall be glad to hear from them.

I started this book on New Year's Day 1997, and finished it in June 1999. Inevitably, changes will have taken place on the ground between these dates; and indeed more may take place between June and the date of actual publication. Not only will there be unavoidable changes in the field, there will no doubt be mistakes which I could and should have avoided: for these, I accept full responsibility; but I will welcome corrections in the hope that it may prove possible to incorporate them in any new edition.

I have enjoyed the preparation of this book, and the discoveries both on the ground, and amongst the documents; though I have become very tired of travelling the weary road from my home in Greenisland to Armagh. Many people showed me much kindness and, indeed, hospitality: a few were suspicious and unhelpful. I visited for the first time many delightful and interesting places, and got one or two surprises. Behind one castellated wall, I found a deserted castle out of fairyland; behind another, a wealthy smuggler's exotic hacienda. At the end of one avenue I was greeted by a nice young lady still in her nightie at noon; at the end of another, by a savage pack of dogs and goats. On balance, the satisfaction and enjoyment easily outweighed the disappointments, though I cannot say that the nice surprises outnumbered the nasty ones.

C E B B
June 1999

References: 1. Planning Service 'Planning policy statement', 6, 1999, pp 48-49. 2. Coote, 'Armagh', 1804, p 284. 3. T Parkhill, 'Valuation records in the Public Record Office of Northern Ireland', in 'Ulster local studies', XVI, 1994, pp 45-58. 4. P S Doughty in 'Buildings of Armagh', UAHS, 1992, p 27.

ABBREVIATIONS

BNL	*Belfast Newsletter*
C of I	Church of Ireland
CSPI	*Calendar of State papers relating to Ireland*
DB	*Dublin builder*
DPJ	*Dublin penny journal*
GJ	Grand Jury
HEARTH	Hearth Housing Association and Revolving Fund
HMNI	*Historic monuments of Northern Ireland*
HMSO	Her Majesty's Stationery Office
IAA	Irish Architectural Archive
IB	*Irish builder*
IGS	Irish Georgian Society
JCLAS	*Journal of the County Louth Archaeological Society*
JIA	*Journal of Irish archaeology*
JRSAI	*Journal of the Royal Society of Antiquaries of Ireland*
MBR	Monuments and Buildings Record of Northern Ireland, Belfast
NLI	National Library of Ireland, Dublin
NT	National Trust
OS	Ordnance Survey
OSM	*Ordnance Survey memoirs*
PBNHPS	*Proceedings of the Belfast Natural History and Philosophical Society*
PG	*Parliamentary gazetteer of Ireland*
PRO	Public Record Office, Kew
PRONI	Public Record Office of Northern Ireland, Belfast
PSAMNI	*Preliminary survey of the ancient monuments of Northern Ireland*
QUB	Queen's University, Belfast
RC	Roman Catholic
RCB	Representative Church Body of the Church of Ireland, Dublin
RHA	Royal Hibernian Academy, Dublin
RIA	Royal Irish Academy, Dublin
RIBA	Royal Institute of British Architects, London
RIAI	Royal Institution of the Architects of Ireland, Dublin
RoSA	Regeneration of South Armagh
SARC	South Armagh Ramblers' Club
SELB	Southern Education and Library Board
TCD	Trinity College, Dublin
td	Townland
TD	Lewis's *Topographical dictionary of Ireland*
UAHS	Ulster Architectural Heritage Society
UCD	University College, Dublin
UJA	*Ulster journal of archaeology*
VAL	Valuation books

Throughout the text, figures appearing in parentheses
refer to the entry numbers for other buildings discussed

Bronze 12th-century crucifixion plaque found in Marrassit or College Hall townland, Tynan. Photograph: National Museums of Scotland
(Original size: 8.2 cm x 8.7 cm)

CHAPTER ONE

ANTIQUITIES, FORTIFICATIONS AND RUINS

Although the county of Armagh is extremely rich in literary, historic, and indeed pre-historic associations, it has surprisingly little to show for it. There are only eighteen scheduled monuments in state care, of which no less than eight are cairns. Of the monuments not in state care, the major, if enigmatic, earthworks of the Dane's Cast and the Dorsey are comparatively incomplete, and visually less impressive than an abandoned railway embankment. Navan Fort (3) is really something of a disappointment, as well as much of a puzzle. There is no holestone; though I must admit that there is an intriguing stone with a hole in it - the tombstone of Bryan McCabe, obiit 1796, in Creggan churchyard (17), through which somebody, at some date, has seen fit to drill a neat hole. There is not so much as a stump of a round tower (that at Killevy, 12, was blown down by a gale in 1768). The few early monastic remains are not in a good state of preservation. There is not a single tower-house with its roof on. The county has raths aplenty, cashels a few, crannogs a mere handful; but not many of these are well-preserved; and, for some reason, few are as picturesque as examples to be found in other Ulster counties. Armagh lacks Norman castles comparable to those at Carrickfergus and Dundrum; it lacks even the more modest mottes, with or without baileys (except for traces of a motte on Coney Island in Lough Neagh). Charlemont Fort was for many years an important military stronghold and artillery barracks, but almost everything has gone, leaving only the gatehouse (15), and that in deplorable condition. One is left with the feeling that most of the antiquities of this contentious county, especially the more martial ones, have been quite worn out by constant use.

Nevertheless, it is not wholly devoid of interesting places to visit: and I have included descriptions of a handful of antiquities worth seeing. I should draw attention also to the fact that the museums of Ireland - in particular, the Ulster Museum in Belfast; the National Museum of Ireland in Dublin; and the Armagh County Museum - own a considerable number of ancient artefacts found within the boundaries of the county. One of these, an exquisite piece, I illustrate opposite; the original, a bronze 12th-century (or perhaps earlier) crucifixion plaque found in College Hall townland near Tynan in 1844, now belonging to the National Museums of Scotland, is on loan to, and on display at, the Ulster Museum, Belfast;[1] a reproduction has been incorporated into the tabernacle door in St John's Roman Catholic church, Middletown (30).

Reference: 1. A Hamlin and R G Haworth, in JRSAI, CXII, 1982, pp 112-116.

Clontygora Court-Tomb, Meigh

1. An unexpectedly impressive, and unexpectedly extensive, Neolithic burial-place, locally known as "the King's Ring", originally having three chambers, but now somewhat incomplete. It appears that, some 200 years ago, stone-seekers took stones from the cairn for use in the construction of the first lock of the Newry canal; and a century later, the rebuilders of a quay for Narrow Water ferry obtained leave to help themselves, and sought to break up several of the larger stones; whilst, in between times, the local farmers used this as a quarry for field-wall-building.

This cairn seems to mark the transition between court tomb and portal tomb, though T G F Paterson calls it "a very imposing horned cairn with façade stones eight and a half feet high ... the covering stone of the first chamber is about eleven feet long by six feet wide". HMNI says "Court and chambers are built of very large stones with some roofing slabs still in position, but little cairn material survives. Finds from the excavation" - in 1937 - "included cremated bone, flints, and Neolithic pottery".

A surprisingly attractive and moving place, considering how boring some cairns can be.

Photograph: MBR.

Situation: Off Flagstaff Road; td, Clontygora; Parish, Killevy; District Council, Newry & Mourne; Grid ref. J 098 194.

References: Monument in state care. O Davies and T G F Paterson, in PBNHPS, 2nd series, I, 1936/37, pp 20-42; HMNI, 1983, p 79; Mallory and McNeill, 'Archaeology of Ulster', 1991, p 65.

Ballykeel Dolmen, Camlough

2. An exceptionally slim, sharply-shaped and elegant dolmen, sited on a hummock in the saucer created by the surrounding low, but steep, hills. This is a remarkable example of prehistoric craftsmanship in its own right (albeit restored).

"SW of Camlough at the W foot of Slieve Gullion. Portal (or tripod) dolmen stands at the S end of a long cairn, now 0.6 to 0.9 m high, with a stone cist (not now visible) near the N end. The dolmen is formed of two tall portal stones, with a high sill between, and a lower backstone, supporting a huge capstone, reinstated from a slipped position after excavation in 1963. Bone did not survive but there were plentiful finds of Neolithic pottery" (HMNI).

"A striking megalithic chamber with high portals supporting a great slab (10 ft by 8 ft) which appears to have slipped owing to the collapse of a third stone set behind. It is set at the southern edge of a wedge-shaped cairn, 94 ft long by 30 ft at the widest, which is retained in place by a peristalith"(a surrounding kerb of stone). "There are indications of small cist-like graves elsewhere in the cairn" (T G F Paterson in PSAMNI). "A late Neolithic date is clearly established for this monument"(Evans).

The site was excavated by A E P Collins in the summer of 1963, and written up by him in the Ulster Journal of Archaeology. "Many hundred sherds were recovered in the chamber area as well as three worked flints. No trace of bone, whether burned or unburned, was found ... After

excavation of the dolmen conservation measures were undertaken. The fallen closing slab was pulled back into its original vertical position. The split backstone was reunited with a special cement and pinned with bronze dowels set in lead before being re-erected on top of a low concrete bench and concrete was poured round the bases of portal stones and door-slab. Finally, the capstone was lifted back in position on the three supports". What these archaeologists do be up to in the interests of historical authenticity! But it must be said that the work was very well done, and is now almost impossible to detect.

"One of the richer tombs, Ballykeel, Co. Armagh, yielded a number of fine decorated bowls and flint tools. As is often the case in the acidic Ulster soils, there was no trace of a burial" ... "while some sites produce only a single type of pot, others, such as Ballykeel ... produce examples of nearly every form of Neolithic pot"(Mallory and McNeill).

Photograph: MBR.
Situation: 300 yds south of Ballykeel bridge, 4 miles south-west of Camlough; td, Ballykeel; Parish, Forkhill; District Council, Newry & Mourne; Grid ref. H 995 213.
References: Monument in state care. PSAMNI, 1940, p 76,pl 16; A E P Collins, in UJA, 3rd series, XXVIII, 1965, pp 47-70; Evans, 'Guide', 1966, p 56; 'Creggan: journal of the Creggan Local History Society', I, No 4, 1990, p 25; HMNI, 1983, pp 5, 78; Mallory and McNeill, 'Archaeology of Ulster', 1991, pp 54, 64.

Navan Fort, Armagh

3. There are many different ways of looking at Navan. The visible remains amount to little more than a pair of pimples on a grassy drumlin; yet this may be viewed as the most important archaeological site in Ulster. It may be considered in isolation; or it may be considered as part of a much larger, and largely unexplored, group, including Loughnashade, Haughey's Fort, Creeveroe, and the Dorsey. The site may be viewed romantically as that of the royal palace of Emain Macha, seat of Conchubar, Deirdre and Cuchulain, and the Red Branch knights of the Táin; or it may be analysed clinically and analytically. Last but not least, it can be regarded as just a tourist trap, the rather boring real-life pendant to the excitingly expensive grass-roofed Visitors' Centre near by.

An area of some 12 acres is surrounded by an earthwork and ditch, the ditch being on the inside, so it seems unlikely to have been intended for defence: however, Estyn Evans mischievously observes "Though defensively unorthodox, this could merely reflect the Irishman's perverseness - or his laziness in preferring to shovel earth downhill". Although it bears some of the features of a henge like Avebury or Stonehenge, the dates are wrong by some 2000 years, for they are believed to date from about 2000 B C, whilst Navan is dated at around 95 B C. Parts of the site were very exhaustively excavated by the late Dudley Waterman between 1961 and 1971; the conclusions have at last been published in an authoritative work "completed and edited" by C J Lynn, with contributions from other scholars. They are complex, peculiar, and strain credibility to the utmost. Further excavation in 1998

has confirmed that "the enclosure of Navan was undertaken at approximately the same time as the erection of its most substantial monument... and they are both part of a single horizon of construction"; but otherwise has thrown little new light on the enigmatic features of the site.

To borrow a very terse summary by Cooney, Site A "is a ring-barrow built over an area used for circular-plan buildings, dating from the Late Bronze Age or Iron Age". Site B "is a complex site with activity starting in the Neolithic, the construction of a circular ditched enclosure in the Late Bronze Age, and within this a very complex series of ring-slot buildings and enclosures" - (a ring-slot building seems to mean one whose walls can be replaced without first removing the roof) - "which were replaced by a multi-ring timber structure ... with a massive central post felled in 95 BC. This structure was filled with a large flat-topped cairn of limestone and then burned. The cairn and burned remains of the timber structure were covered immediately by a mound of turves and sods." But why, why, why? No wonder that in the 8th or 9th century AD, the site seems to have been referred to as the sidbruig ('elf-mount' or 'fairy hill') of Emain.

Scholars in general, and Mallory in particular, are persuaded that the identification of Navan with the Emain Macha of the Táin can be sustained. For my part, I am sceptical. It is possible to argue the contrary view: that, like King Arthur's Camelot, Conchubar's Emain Macha is best viewed as a purely imaginary and romantic palace.

The (no doubt highly imaginative) descriptions in the Táin of the Great Hall at Emain Macha assert that it had bronze partitions, a ceiling of silver, with pillars of bronze, whose "head-pieces glittered with gold and were set with carbuncles, so that night and day were equally light therein" ... "In it were held great and numerous gatherings of every kind, and wonderful pastimes. Games and music and singing there, heroes performing their feats, poets singing, harpers and players on the timpan striking up their sounds".

Lady Gregory, purporting to provide a translation "in plain and simple words", comes up with the following description:

"It was at Emain Macha, that was sometimes called Macha of the Spears, Conchubar, the High King, had the Eachrais Uladh, the Assembly House of Ulster, and it was there he had his chief palace. A fine palace it was, having three houses in it, the Royal House, and the Speckled House, and the House of the Red Branch. In the Royal House there were three times fifty rooms, and the walls were made of red yew, with copper rivets. And Conchubar's own room was on the ground, and the walls of it faced with bronze, and silver up above, with gold birds on it, and their heads set with shining carbuncles; and there were nine partitions from the fire to the wall, and thirty feet the height of each partition. And there was a silver rod before Conchubar with three golden apples on it, and when he shook the rod or struck it, all the house would be silent. It was in the House of the Red Branch were kept the heads and weapons of beaten enemies, and in the Speckled House were kept the swords and the shields and the spears of the heroes of Ulster. And it was called the Speckled House because of the brightness and the colours of the hilts of the swords, and the bright spears, green or grey, with rings and bands of silver and gold about them, and the gold and silver that were on the rims and bosses of the shields, and the brightness of the drinking-cups and the horns".

The traces of buildings on the site fail to match up to any such description. Certainly, no signs have been found of any palace remotely comparable to Thebes, Knossos, or even Troy. The archaeological finds at the site seem miserably scanty if this is to be accepted as the centre of wealth and power in Ireland, second only to the palace of the Ard Rí at Tara. True, four large and ornate bronze horns were found in the water at Loughnashade in 1798. But neither earlier nor later has there come to light even one of those extraordinary gold torcs and ornaments to be seen in such abundance in the National Museum in Dublin; only one gold item, and that long since lost. No silver; no jewels; no carbuncles; no jade; little enough pottery and glass; a variety of spear-heads, arrow-heads, and cutting tools. Two human skeletons, one with vestiges of iron nails from its coffin, were found; the skull of a barbary ape; and numerous food bones, many of them from pigs, also. From these last bizarre discoveries, it seems to have been accepted that the occupiers of the site enjoyed wealth and princely status. Only the important could afford a diet of pork chops (or Ulster fry). Raftery finds it "tempting to think of a Phoenician ship, drawn by a rumour of Irish mineral wealth, sailing up the Irish Sea with a Barbary ape on board some time around the middle or

end of the last pre-Christian millennium". Just how convincing is all this? I fail to be persuaded.

However, Waterman and Lynn conclude that "the population ... in later prehistory may have seen Navan as a regional ceremonial centre. The purpose of the mound cannot be deduced in a wholly logical or convincing way"; and Lynn has speculated that "the Navan mound was purpose-built for kingly inauguration and ceremonies of regional importance" ... "employing in its design and materials cosmological beliefs associated with kingship". And: "Whether the sanctuary was also a residence of kings, as distinct from a place where kingship could be bestowed, is another matter. It cannot be assumed, however, that the sanctuary suddenly became a place of kingship with the construction of the mound in 95/4 BC. The question of the social position of the high-status residents of site B..., immediately pre-dating the mound, remains. Were they kings or the priestly keepers of the sacred site?"

George Petrie visited the site in 1838: "You will be able to imagine the delight I felt in walking over, and examining in detail, this most interesting and, in its way, magnificent capital of a semi-barbarous people ... Here it was that the four Dacian shaped trumpets of the most exquisite beauty were found ... The spot in which they were discovered was shown to me by the son of the man who found them."

On a fine day, a visit to Navan is rewarding. Despite the past ravages of the nearby quarry, clearly visible in aerial photographs, and closed down in 1986 by a brave decision of Richard Needham MP contrary to the advice of some of his civil servants. "'What the hell is the point of having a Minister,' I exploded. 'I shall inform the world that I am no better than a eunuch at the court of the Chinese Emperor!'" - the hill is neatly presented. Whilst utterly unacropolitan, it enjoys a spectacular view over the surrounding countryside. The merits of the Visitors' Centre established by Needham are more debatable. Certainly it presents, in somewhat gimmicky form, much information (and many speculations) about the site and its associations; but it is not a museum, and contains no authentic material artefacts. There are some stuffed figures, reproductions of the trumpets and the ape's skull, and a most uneirenical audio-visual display of the barbarous conduct of Cuchulain and his gang. This is perhaps a pity, for the Centre was conceived as a place which might bring together those devoted to the Celtic tradition, and those devoted to the separatism of Ulster. Whether it achieves this aim must be open to doubt.

Photograph: QUB Department of Archaeology.
Situation: Just off Armagh-Killylea Road; td, Navan; Parish, Eglish; District Council, Armagh; Grid ref. H 847 452.
References: Monument in state care. Stokes, 'Life of G Petrie', 1868, p 123; 1868, p 123; Lady Gregory, 'Cuchulain of Muirthemne' 1902, p 43; Leslie, 'Armagh clergy', 1911, p 296; PSAMNI, 1941, p 65; Evans, 'Guide', 1966, p 23; HMNI, 1983, p 80; Mallory and McNeill, 'Archaeology of Ulster', 1991, pp 146-150; Waterman and Lynn, 'Excavations at Navan", 1997, passim; G Cooney, in 'Archaeology Ireland', II, No 3, Autumn 1997, p 32; Needham, 'Battling for peace', 1998, p 248.

Cashel, Cashel Hill, Seagahan, Lisnadill

4. Cashel Hill is an extraordinary place, half-way between Markethill and Keady, a northern outcrop of the mountains of the Fews, with spectacular views over south and central Ulster; well worth a visit, even if there is not much left of the cashel which crowns it. Indeed, it is now hard to be sure that it is more than a sheep-fold. Little as there is to see, it is practically impossible to photograph: yet it is a very numinous place, which irresistibly reminds me of Kuno Meyer's translation from Selections from Ancient Irish Poetry:

> The fort over against the oak-wood,
> Once it was Bruidge's, it was Cathal's,
> It was Aed's, it was Ailill's,
> It was Conaing's, it was Cuiline's,
> And it was Maelduin's:
> The fort remains after each in his turn -
> And the kings asleep in the ground.

T G F Paterson, in PSAMNI, says "A very large cashel which gives its name to this townland. Locally the enclosure is known as 'The Relig'. It contains a souterrain now closed and is approximately 36 yds in diam. The largest amber bead ever found in Ireland was discovered here ... A fallen pillar-stone, partly buried on the N E side, is said "to mark the burial-place of an ancient king." In his notes in Armagh County Museum, Mr Paterson adds - "The wall of the cashel has been greatly reduced within living memory both in height and width". Mary Delargy, of the Linen Hall Library, tells me that reilig is Irish Gaelic for graveyard. It is interesting that the royal burial ground on Iona, said to hold the bones of sixty kings, including Macduff and Macbeth, is known as the 'Relig Oran'.

An unsigned field report of 1971 in the MBR says: "Very fine hill-top site, level falls to east and south, flatter to north. Very extensive views. Walls seem intact in lower courses, 5 - 6 feet thick, upper parts field stones. Is fairly circular but somewhat squared off to the east where field boundaries impinge. Interior featureless and nothing specifically ecclesiastical except the name 'Relig', and burial traditions. Diameter about 130 feet".

This has potential as a tourist attraction; yet it is not even in state charge.

Photograph: Michael O'Connell.
Situation: Just off Cashel Road, Seagahan; td, Cashel; Parish, Lisnadill; District Council, Armagh; Grid ref. H 904 367.
References: Scheduled monument. Meyer, 'Selections from ancient Irish poetry', 1928, p 93; PSAMNI, 1940, p 71; T G F Paterson, Ms 135 in Armagh County Museum; unsigned notes in MBR; information from Mary Delargy.

Creggan Old Church (?)

5. On the face of it, and so labelled, this is the early 19th-century 'Eastwood Vault', in the graveyard of Creggan church (17). Indeed, it may well be the burial place of Mary Tinley, née Eastwood, who died in 1815, according to a memorial plaque inside Creggan church. But Dr Geraldine Carville, who describes herself as "an historical geographer", has argued quite persuasively, if not by any means incontrovertibly, that the Eastwood family may have adopted this "old stone church" as their burial vault in favour of "holy ground"; and that it is in fact a very early Christian church.

Her first argument is that "the architecture, the walls of stone, the stone roof, aumbrey, splayed window, a (now blocked up) circular window on the east front, a vaulted roof, the imprint of osiers on the ceiling, a recessed entrance, a building of low elevation, of low roof pitch is reminiscent of old churches such as that of Ardmore county Wexford, Rahan county Offaly, Innisfallen county Kerry or Mochta's county Louth". The external measurements are 20 feet six inches by twelve feet ten inches by nine feet five inches; the walls are four feet thick; the interior is spanned by a barrel vault; "obviously these dimensions were governed by the limitations imposed by the barrel vault type of stone roof". "Another remarkable feature of the north and south walls are the buttresses of the type usually found on ancient churches". There is, she argues, evidence of alterations to doorway and windows.

Secondly, the use of the words "stone house" in the parish records - "like the damliag (Duleek) - the first stone house or church built in 489 carries a similar inference. Duleek was the prototype built by St Cianan who was *prayerfully assisted by Mochua of Derrynoose when he asked the Lord to provide good weather whilst the masons were building it*".

Thirdly, Dr Carville argues, perhaps a little on the model of Newgrange, that the orientation of the church could have been such as to allow the dawn light to shine through a small window upon the altar on a particular day of the year. She asserts that the orientation of "churches associated with a local saint was aligned according to the position of the sun on the day the saint died. A window on the east gable of the church allowed the light to shine upon the altar". The evidence for this does not seem to me entirely convincing. However, she had the novel idea of asking the Armagh Observatory to compute the date upon which the sun would have so shone into this little church. "In due course a reply was received and the day upon which the sun would have shone into the stone building along the direction 120 degrees west of north, 4 degrees altitude, was 11th February. Consultation of the martyrology of the saints revealed that this is the feast day of Jarlath (Mac Tréna), the third Archbishop of Armagh who died 481 AD."

Fourthly, she asserts that Tréna was head of a ruling sept, who lived in a three-ring rath: Rathtrillick (9), only ten miles from the Fews, which St Patrick is known to have visited, and which became a monument associated with a struggle between a Christian and a druid. Patrick predicted that, unless Tréna changed his ways "no king of his posterity should succeed him": and this came true; for his twin sons, Setna and Jarlath, both became ecclesiastics.

This is all quite revolutionary stuff, enough to make the hairs on a more conventional scholar's neck stiffen. As Dr Carville remarks of her investigation of the orientation, "this is the first time that this method has been used in Ireland and the scholarship is now open for it to be used on other unknown and indeed known sites in Ireland". Her arguments were rubbished with great academic sniffiness in a review by Con Manning, an archaeologist of standing, in the Journal of the County Louth Archaeological and Historical Society: "One of the dating methods used is as novel as it is invalid ... It has to be stated clearly that this building is not a church and never was a church ...The building is ordinary rubble masonry, which judging from the photographs, would appear to be of 18th or 19th century date..." (Is this an admission that the reviewer has never seen the building? If so, that greatly weakens his case). "The author does not have an up-to-date knowledge or competence in either early Irish history (ecclesiastical or otherwise) or archaeology, the main topics of the book". Whew!

For my part, having looked at the building, read the book, read the review, and looked yet again at the building, I am persuaded, not without some misgivings, that Dr Carville deserves the benefit of the doubt. If so, this neglected little structure is one of the most important in the county. If not, it is no more than a triviality of purely local interest. But this fine, swingeing academic controversy, worthy of the correspondence column of the Times Literary Supplement, does lend it, at any rate, curiosity value; and a thrill for tourists too - for every visitor is at liberty to back one horse or the other.

Photograph: Michael O'Connell.
Situation: In Creggan churchyard; td, Creggan Bane Glebe; Parish, Creggan; District Council, Newry & Mourne; Grid ref. H 923 159.
References: Not separately listed. Leslie, 'Armagh Clergy', 1911, p 207; Carville, 'Creggan', 1996, passim; C Manning, in JCLAS, XXIII, 4, 1996, p 512.

Kilnasaggart Pillar Stone, Jonesborough

6. "A tall granite pillar marks the site of an early cemetery on one of Early Christian Ireland's great 'main roads', the *Slighe Miodhluachra,* running from Drogheda N through the Moyry Pass to Dunseverick in N Antrim" (HMNI). Dr John O'Donovan, in his letters, records the belief of the country people that a crock of gold was buried at its foot, and his fear that it would be overturned by treasure-seekers; which apparently it was, soon after, but reset. Lewis says only "a little south of the village stands an upright single stone with an illegible inscription". A very early example of Christian stone-carving. Bishop Reeves, who described it very thoroughly in 1853, thought it "one of the most interesting Christian monuments now existing in Ireland".

Described by Hamlin in 1976 as "A tall pillar, seven feet visible above ground, one foot eight inches to one foot five inches wide, and six to seven inches thick; face to the south-east flattish, to the north-west convex. Angle to north battered, with knife-sharpening scores low down, once thought to be Ogam (Macalister 1949 refutes this)". Excavations in 1968 had revealed some two feet more below ground. The stone stands near the edge of a small enclosure, reached by crossing two fields and two stiles. It has a rugged and weather-beaten look. The cracks in the stone harbour a golden lichen; but it is in very good order, even if its surroundings are somewhat neglected.

One face has one very large and ornate cross, and two smaller crosses; the other, ten more crosses; and on the former, a long datable inscription, Hamlin says in Irish, Mallory and MacNeill say in Latin; perhaps Reeves gave rise to the confusion by translating the Irish into parallel Latin text: the inscription appears to read: IN LOC SO TANIMMAIRNI (Hamlin) or THIMMAERNI (Reeves) TERNOHC MAC CERAN BIC ER CUL PETER APSTEL. This is taken by everyone to record the dedication of the place by Ternohc, son of Ceran Bic, under the patronage of Peter the Apostle. Most conveniently, Ternohc's obituary occurs in the Annals of the Four Masters for either 714 or 716: so "the pillar can reasonably be dated to about 700" (Hamlin).

All the scholars concerned seem to have been too embarrassed to have noticed, or at any rate to have mentioned, the remarkably phallic shape of this somewhat peculiar monument. Could it have been, like the holestone at Layde, a more ancient piece re-used for Christian purposes?

Photographs: R J Welch, Ulster Museum, W02/17/1-2. Wood-engraving: Doyle, 'Tours in Ulster', 1854.

Situation: In fields south-west of Jonesborough, off Kilnasaggart Road, very close to the border with Co. Louth; td, Edenappa; Parish, Jonesborough; District Council, Newry & Mourne; Grid ref. J 063 150.

References: Monument in state care. O'Donovan, 'Letters ... 1835', 1927, p 2; Lewis, TD, II, 1837, p 32; W Reeves in UJA, 1st series, I, 1853, p 221; JCLAS, I, 1904/07, p 92; ; Macalister, Corpus inscriptionum', II, 1949, p 114; A E Hamlin, QUB thesis in MBR, 1976, p 518; HMNI, 1983, p 82; Mallory and McNeill, 'Archaeology of Ulster', 1991, p 214.

Tynan High Crosses

7. The small village of Tynan boasts no less than four High Crosses, of which two appear to be indigenous, possibly associated with the early Christian monastery believed to have existed on the site of the parish church (21); and two were imported from County Tyrone as garden ornaments (!) by Sir James M Stronge in either 1840 or 1844 (accounts differ).

First, 'the Village Cross': its broken components were noted in 1804 as a "relick of antiquity" by Sir Charles Coote. It seems to have "suffered either from the Puritans or from the weather" (Paterson); or from the activities of Cromwell's soldiery (Leslie). In 1835, Lt Bailey of the Ordnance Survey wrote "there is a remnant of antiquity consisting of an oblong stone standing on a large black stone. The characters on the oblong stone are nearly effaced ... At the foot of the black stone lies another stone which appears to have been part of a cross much mutilated. This stone formerly stood on the top of the oblong stone mentioned before, but was maliciously thrown down a few years ago". His colleague Mr Williamson, in 1838, took a more jaundiced view: "The remains of an old stone cross formerly used as a market cross are still visible. The inscription is defaced but 2 hideous little figures resembling idols may still be discerned".

HMNI says that it "is not in its original position, having been moved at least twice. It is composite, made up of two different crosses, the base and lower shaft of one being matched with the upper shaft and head of another. The lower shaft on the E side has a rectangular panel with Adam and Eve and on the W side is another panel with a large figure and smaller figures behind. The head is mended and partly reconstructed, of open ringed form decorated with tall bosses. The shaft has panels of interlaced decoration". Harbison identifies the subject as 'Adam and Eve knowing their nakedness'. "Two figures stand beneath the tree, up the stems of which the serpent crawls ... The figure on the left hides its nakedness with both hands. That on the right with only the left hand." And, on the west face of the shaft, "a tall figure flanked by tiers of much smaller figures" which, because of its similarity to panels on the crosses at Kells and Monasterboice, he tentatively identifies as 'David being acclaimed King by his people'. T G F Paterson says "No certain date can be ascribed to this cross which, with its base, is about 13$^{1}/_{2}$ ft high and 4 ft wide across the arms; but from its comparatively rude appearance it may be assigned to at least the 8th or 9th century". Ann Hamlin has, however, with the benefit of modern scholarship, proposed a 10th-century date. Despite its chequered history, a remarkably impressive monument, well sited, well cared for, and well presented.

'The Terrace Cross' - "eleven feet high, on the terrace at the south side of the house, with pierced ring, raised mouldings and circular and diamond-shaped patterns in low relief, partly restored" (Leslie). "A tall and graceful specimen of its type" (Hayward). Formerly in or near the churchyard, removed to its present site, below and in front of the house, about 1840. Now somewhat overshadowed by the ancient yew trees amongst which it was planted. The interlace ornament on the side facing away from the house is particularly impressive.

'The Well Cross' - "eight feet six inches high, over a well, beside the avenue, with solid ring, raised and incised lines, and traces of central figure" (Leslie). On the west face, Harbison thinks he detects Saints Paul and Anthony breaking bread in the desert; and, above them, a much-worn crucifixion scene. Near the northern entrance to Tynan Abbey, this is one of the two "brought by Sir James Stronge from the townland of Glenarb in the parish of Aghaloo and placed in their present situation as ornaments" (Lt Bailey). The well at its foot has unhappily run dry as a result of the ill-judged River Blackwater drainage scheme, and at least one of the great oak trees in the parkland nearby has died from the same cause.

'The Island Cross' is the other cross transported from Glenarb, and "placed in a small flower garden near the lake" (Bailey); "on an island in a lake on the demesne, seven feet six inches high, with pierced ring, mouldings along angles, and carved boss in centre of each side" (Leslie). Now in close proximity to an abandoned wooden boatshed, the bridge to the island likewise victim of decay.

The noted antiquary and historian Bishop Reeves was Prebendary of Tynan from 1865 to 1875, combining this appointment for some years with those of Dean of Armagh, and Keeper of Archbishop Robinson's Library there. To him, as much as to Sir James M Stronge, must be given credit for the survival of this wealth of ancient crosses: as Dr Leslie, remarks, "No doubt Bishop Reeves's connection with the parish contributed to their preservation". In August 1884, following luncheon (with speeches) in the dining hall with Sir James and Lady Stronge, "on the terrace, at the foot of the most interesting of the Tynan crosses, the Very Rev Dean Reeves read to the assembled members" of the Royal Society of Antiquaries of Ireland the paper reprinted in their Journal for that year: upon which it seemed impossible to improve, until the appearance of Peter Harbison's magisterial work, The High Crosses of Ireland.

Photographs: Village Cross, Michael O'Connell; Terrace Cross, MBR.

Situation: Village Cross; td Tynan; Grid ref. H 765 430; Well Cross and Terrace Cross, td Fairview or Mucklagh; Island Cross, td Corfehan, all three grid refs (as HMNI rather idly puts it) in the "area of H 758 428"; all in Parish of Tynan, District Council of Armagh.

References: Village Cross, monument in state care; others, scheduled monuments. Coote, 'Armagh', 1804, p 328; Lt Bailey, OSM, 1835, and E A Williamson, 1838, Armagh, I, pp 126, 132; Lewis, TD, II, 1837, p 664; Reeves, JRSAI, XVI, pt 2, 1883-4, pp 412-430; Leslie, 'Armagh clergy', 1911, pp 27, 77, 436; T G F Paterson, in PSAMNI, 1940, pp 64, 68; M Roe, in 'Seanchas Ardmhacha', I, No 2, 1955, pp 112-113; R Hayward, in 'Ulster illustrated', October 1959, p 24; HMNI, 1983, pp 83, 150; Harbison, 'High Crosses', 1992, I, pp 180-182, II, pls 629-640; A Hamlin, in 'From the isles of the North', 1995, pp 187-196; files in MBR.

Lisleitrim Rath and Crannog, Cullyhanna

8. T G F Paterson, in 1940, says: "Treble-ringed earthen fort with very deep entrenchments. About 130 yds in diam. Contains a souterrain. The lake below the fort has a large crannog, on which some finds were made". Unsigned notes of 1983 in the MBR say, of the rath, "In a dominant hill-top position at the south-east end of a ridge commanding an extensive view to south, east, and north-east. This massive multivallate rath is one of the most spectacular in the county ... There is inevitably some doubt whether the outer bank and ditch are part of the original monument - the bank now forms a steep-sided field boundary... It may be significant that in 1838 Donaldson recorded that the site was then enclosed by "three ramparts"; he also recalls a local tradition that "there was a cave constructed under the platform... which is now closed up" ". Now somewhat overgrown, muddy, and difficult of access; but if this remarkable site could be given a wash-and-brush-up, and made more easily accessible to visitors, it could constitute a very considerable tourist attraction.

And, the notes say of the crannog, "This artificial island is unusually large for a crannog, measuring about 161 feet north-south by about 144 feet east-west. The island is very overgrown and no ancient features can be recognised. In 1966 a small trial pit was excavated at the centre of the crannog ... finds included many sherds of souterrain ware" and several layers of ash and charcoal. Donaldson says that earlier discoveries included "a kind of spit for roasting meat and an iron pot of an antique form". It is certainly the largest, and most generously wooded, crannog that I have seen.

HMNI simply describes the group as "trivallate rath with crannog in nearby lake"; but, with a glint of humour rare in official publications, also remarks: "Crannogs are unfortunately somewhat hazardous to visit, whether in bogland or open water, and are best viewed from a distance, as their original builders intended"!

The relationship between the rath and the crannog is unclear, although it has been suggested that the juxtaposition of a large rath and a crannog may be an indication of a royal site.

Photograph: MBR.
Situation: The fort stands about a quarter of a mile north-east of the lough; td, Kiltybane or Lisleitrim; Parish, Creggan; District Council, Newry & Mourne; Grid refs, fort H 903 207; crannog H 898 204.
References: Scheduled monument. Donaldson, 'Upper Fews', 1838, p 51; T G F Paterson, in PSAMNI, 1940, p 75; 'Creggan: journal of the Creggan Local History Society', I, No 3, 1989, p 10; HMNI, 1983, pp 27, 150; unsigned notes in MBR.

Rathtrillick Rath, Middletown

9. "This fort is extraordinarily elaborate and large, possessing no fewer than four ramparts ... Between these are three deep and wide trenches. The diameter of the inner space appeared to be about 60 or 80 yards, and the diameter of the whole fort would probably be two or three times that. There have been trees on the top in the past but they have been cut down and their stumps are visible ... The entrance appears to pass through two ramparts in a straight line, then to go along one of the trenches before going through the last rampart ... The best view of the fort is to be had from Ashfort House on the opposite slope which looks right into the fort" (1935). (Alas, Ashfort House is now no more).

"Large treble-ringed earthen fort, extreme diam. about 140 yds, with trenches still from 16 to 20 ft deep" (1940). Part of Bishop Stearne's property, acquired by him in 1730, and said to have been most strictly preserved from encroachment and damage by his trustees. Overlooking the village of Middletown and the border with County Monaghan, now much overgrown with trees and brushwood, difficult to see and difficult of access. An attempt to tidy up the site failed at the height of the Troubles due to intimidation of the workmen. Might not the clearance and proper presentation of this important monument, perhaps as a collaborative cross-border project, be a worth while celebration of peace?

Photograph: QUB Department of Archaeology.
Situation: Td, Rathtrillick; Parish, Tynan; District Council, Armagh; Grid ref. H 757 379.
References: Scheduled monument. Report by 'D A C' (D A Chart), 11 April, 1935, in MBR; T G F Paterson, in PSAMNI, 1940, p 69; 'Historical sketches of Tynan and Middletown,' 1995, p 10.

Lisnamintry Rath, Portadown

10. On the summit of a low hill, interspersed with trees, an earthwork of much apparent intricacy. Classified as an Early Christian rath or farm settlement, but I wonder: not only are there remains of very substantial double banks and ditches, there are also projections and corners not usually found in a classic ring-fort.

Described in a paper in the MBR prepared by Michael Yates in 1981: "In the centre is a relatively level, roughly circular, platform, 105 feet in diameter, and raised about 5 feet above the surrounding ground. Around the perimeter of the platform there are remains of a bank, now spread, and measuring up to 11 feet 6 inches wide and 1 to 2 feet in height. The outer side of the bank on the west appears to have been revetted with stone. A partly water-filled ditch, 18 feet wide and 6 feet deep ... surrounds the site. On the north east the ditch is interrupted, perhaps providing a causeway for an entrance ... Beyond the ditch, on the east and north, there is a berm, 10 to 13 feet wide, followed by a second bank measuring 8 feet wide and 1 foot high ... To the north west and north east there is a second ditch up to 11 feet 6 inches wide and about 1 foot deep ... The site is very overgrown, but beneath the undergrowth there seems to be a reasonably well-preserved monument."

For once, none of the usual earlier authorities record this monument: it was missed by the Ordnance Surveyors, and even by the eagle-eyed Evans and Patterson of PSAMNI. Since 1981, the undergrowth has all been cleared away, leaving only the mature trees; it is attractively presented to the public, with even a notice-board-mounted drawing to stimulate the imagination, showing a pastoral family bringing home the cows for the night over the causeway.

Photograph: MBR.
Situation: Up a green lane off Ballygargan Road; td, Lisnamintry; Parish, Seagoe; District Council, Craigavon; Grid ref. J 046 544.
References: Monument in state care. Oram, 'Craigavon', UAHS, 1971, pt III, p 9; HMNI, 1983, p 83.

Corliss Fort, Crossmaglen

11. HMNI says only "Corliss Fort, bivallate rath". T G F Paterson was a little more forthcoming: "Very fine single-ringed fort with open souterrain. About 70 yds in diam. Ring ramparted, also trench. Very imposing structure. Two other forts in the same townland. On the road opposite the Black Rocks". In August 1939 this rath was excavated by Oliver Davies, who reported "Corliss Fort is one of the best preserved in county Armagh. The internal area is about 130 feet across... It is surrounded by two ramparts and a ditch ... the original height would have been over 20 feet, and the slope of the outer rampart very steep." Certainly, one of the most handsome raths in the county.

Dateable finds in the course of this dig included part of a medieval pot of the 14th century, and carved bones, like combs, apparently of the same period. "It is difficult to dissociate Corliss Fort from the dateable finds. Its excellent preservation suggests that it is fairly recent. It would therefore be unwise to consider it as part of the frontier works known as the Black Pig's Dyke, whatever the course of that earthwork was". Estyn Evans opines: "The rath itself may well be early medieval".

Also known as "Donaghy's Fort", and as "the Beech Fort", no doubt from the attractive ring of beech trees with which it is crowned: though perhaps somebody will need soon to look to their regeneration.

Photograph: MBR.
Situation: About 2 miles north-west of Crossmaglen; td, Corliss; Parish, Creggan; District Council, Newry & Mourne; Grid ref. H 893 168.
References: Scheduled monument. T G F Paterson, in PSAMNI, 1940, p 71; O Davies, in 'JCLAS', IX, 1940, pp 338 - 343; Evans,'Guide', 1966, p 58; HMNI, 1983, p 150; 'Creggan: journal of the Creggan Local History Society', I, No 3, 1989, p 12.

Killevy Old Churches, Meigh

12. "The two churches are aligned in a row east - west and are linked by later walling, giving the impression of a single very long building." In fact not internally connected, they are sited in a delightful walled enclosure on the hillside, with beech trees around the periphery, and a variety of conifers amongst the ancient gravestones. The west church is the older. "Its W wall with the massive lintelled door may date from the 10th or 11th century and the rest of the church from the 12th. The E church is medieval with a decorated 15th-century E window" (HMNI).

The nunnery here was founded in the 5th century by St Monenna (also called St Darerca, or St Bline), said (by some) to have been a sister of St Patrick: she seems to have been an exceptionally tough and characterful nun, who reminds me of my wife's friend, Sister Genevieve of St Louisa's College, Belfast. The saint was born in 409 and in 450 erected a wooden church here, said to have been replaced by one of stone in 518, although no modern authority would now accept these building dates. The convent was plundered in 790 and in 923 by Vikings either from Carlingford or Strangford Lough (the authorities differ) but survived the experience. It was suppressed in 1542, but remains a place of pilgrimage.

Estyn Evans says "the smaller of the two churches, both roofless, has a fine trabeate west doorway, with well-fitted masonry of large stones". An unsigned, undated, note in the MBR says "The west church is the earlier, perhaps 9th or 10th century, measuring 41 feet by 22 feet, with a massively lintolled west door, dressed in granite, and a small round-headed east window. The east church (originally about 30 feet by 22 feet) lacks original dateable features, but may be 13th century. With the exception of a plain north door, all the openings are insertions of the 15th or possibly early 16th century, at the time the building was extended to link with the west church".

No trace remains of the round tower, blown down in a gale in 1768. Leslie quotes Keane: "The ruin itself is very interesting and there are still to be seen a small ancient window and an ancient Cyclopean doorway ... The greater part of the building as it now stands, seems to be the work of early Christian times. The locality abounds with superstitious legends and heathen traditions, in all of which Finn McCuille, his dog Bran, Tuath de Danaan witches, and Finian heroes are prominent actors". Somewhat more historically, this was where, on 10 November 1477, Archbishop Edmund Connesburgh of Armagh held a significant meeting with his successor-to-be, the Papal Nuncio, Ottaviano Spinelli, otherwise de Palatio.

Photograph: Michael O'Connell (see also colour-plate IVa).
Situation: Td, Ballintemple; Parish, Killevy; District Council, Newry & Mourne; Grid ref. J 039 222.
References: Monument in state care. Keane, 'Towers and temples', 1867, p 358; JRSAI, XVI, 1883-4, p 432; Leslie, 'Armagh clergy', 1911, p 329; O Davies, in JCLAS, IX, 1938, pp 77-86: T G F Paterson, in PSAMNI, 1940, p 77; Evans, 'Guide', 1966, p 59; Gwynn and Hadcock, 'Medieval religious houses', 1970, p 321; HMNI, 1983, pp 81-82.

Franciscan Friary, Armagh

13. It is difficult to be sure how much of this ruin dates from the 13th century, how much from the 15th century, and how much from Archbishop Robinson's 18th-century wish for a fashionable eye-catcher. The UAHS listers lean to the last alternative: they say "founded in 1264, suppressed in 1542, and finally destroyed during fighting in 1595. What was left of the buildings became a quarry for building stone until used to create a fashionable romantic ruin for Archbishop Robinson as part of his overall planning of the demesne". Certainly, Paterson reports that "great quantities of stones were taken from it in 1765 for building purposes".

However, Chris Lynn, who reported on his excavation in 1975, is confident that the greater part of the ruin dates from the 13th century, when Archbishop Patrick O Scannail brought the friars minor to Armagh, a small part being of the 15th century. He adds: "The surviving fragments of

the building are unremarkable architecturally but sufficient remains to give an impression of the proportions and scale of the original friary with its long narrow church and south aisle". Indeed, HMNI says that, at 49.8 metres, this is the longest known friary church in Ireland. In the course of the archaeological dig, "over 1,000 articulated skeletons, comparatively recent in date, were removed from the interior" and carefully reburied.

Photograph: Michael O'Connell.

Situation: Near the entrance to the Palace Demesne;. td, Parkmore or Demesne; Parish, and District Council, Armagh; Grid ref. H 879 448.

References: Monument in state care; outside conservation area. T G F Paterson in PSAMNI, 1940, p 67; C J Lynn, in UJA, 3rd series, XXXVIII, 1975, pp 61-80; HMNI, 1983, p 85; 'Buildings of Armagh', UAHS, 1992, p 176.

Moyry Castle, Jonesborough

14. A small, square three-storey keep at one corner of a rectangular bawn, built in a great rush during the month of June 1601 in order to command the trackways and approaches leading to the Gap of the North. Fynes Moryson records "The eighth of June being Monday, the Lord Deputy drew his forces out of Dundalke, and marched two miles to the hill of Fagher, near the pace of the Moyry, where he encamped. And while he lay there, his lordship caused a fort to be built in the said pace, at the three mile water, not rising from thence until he had made this fort defensible, so as leaving some warders in it, the workmen might in his absence finish the building". And on 6th October, the Lord Deputy - Mountjoy - wrote from Cork to the Lord Chancellor in Dublin "Pray send here the Dutch engineer that was with me at the building of the fort at the Moyry, and as many with him as he shall name fit to assist him. Send them speedily. His name is said to be Leuni Rose or some such name". In fact, his name was usually written "Levan de Rose"; when he was naturalised in Dublin in 1618, after many years of service, he was shown as "Levander Rose, of Graunte, native of Upper

Germany". It is rare indeed, in Ireland, to be able to record with complete confidence both the exact date and the author of a building nearly 400 years old: but in this instance, the evidence is unambiguous.

This pass, carrying the main road northward into Ulster, had for long enjoyed a most unsavoury reputation. It was not a pass in the usual sense of the lowest point between two mountains; it was, rather, a glen or valley, with a causeway of wooden planks, running between extensive bogs and thick woodland through which the native Irish could "skip" with ease, but heavily-burdened troops could not. So long previously as in 1343, the Justiciary, Sir Ralph Ufford, suffered great loss in the pass - "having lost his clothes, his money, his vessels of silver, and some of his horses, he also lost some of his men; yet, by the help of the men of Uriel, he, at last, made his escape into Ulster". Things had not improved when, 250 years later, in May 1600, Mountjoy was sharply attacked in the pass by 1200 foot and 220 horse. A year later, on his next passage through the gap, he fortified it after cutting down the woods: ""the bawn and tower were completed within the month ... and garrisoned immediately" by a force of 12 men under the command of Captain Anthony Smith.

"The castle consists of a square tower with rounded corners and walls 1.22 metres thick set in the corner of a partially preserved walled enclosure or bawn which stands up to 2.75 metres high". The ground floor is remarkable for having a pistol-loop in each corner, as well as in the middle of each wall; very obvious once inside, they are almost invisible from a distance. Paterson observes that "there are no windows in the N face which carries the fireplaces, causing an external swelling on that side". The first floor has fireplace, window recesses and gun loops; the second floor is taken up by a single chamber with fireplace and windows; about this a wall-walk, and a small exposed latrine. "A gabled roof would originally have risen from wall-walk level but has been destroyed. Access between the floors must have been by ladder as there is no evidence for a stair. Both this and the exposed and windy latrine probably reflect the hurried construction of the castle and the fact that long-term occupation was not planned" (unsigned and unattributed notes in MBR).

Davies observes: "the principal living room was apparently on the first floor and was probably occupied by the Constable. The men may have camped in the bawn, as at Birt, or have lived in the upper storeys. The normal garrison was twelve, though in emergencies, to judge from the number of loop-holes, about 25 could be effectively accommodated. The castle was built entirely as a stronghold."

The discomforts of a person taken short in bad weather whilst under attack must have been not inconsiderable.

Photograph: MBR.
Situation: Off roadway uphill under Kilnasaggart railway bridge very close to the border with County Louth; td, Carrickbroad; Parish, Killevy; District Council, Newry & Mourne; Grid ref. J 057 146.
References: Monument in state care. CSPI, 1601-3, p 115; Moryson, 'Itinerary', 1617, pt 2, p 106; W Reeves, in UJA, 1st series, I, 1853, p 225; Rogers, 'Topographical sketches', 1874, p 77; UJA, 2nd series, XVI, 1910, p 62; T G F Paterson, in SARC outings journal, I, 1928, p 15, in Armagh County Museum; T G F Paterson, in PSAMNI, 1940, p 79; O Davies, in PBNHPS, 1940, pp 31-38; E M Jope, in UJA, 3rd series, XXIII, 1960, pp 101-103; Hayes-McCoy, 'Ulster and other Itrish maps', 1964, p 2; R Loeber, in 'Irish sword', XIII, 1978-9, p 233; Loeber, 'Biographical dictionary', 1981, p 58; HMNI, 1983, pp 85-6.

Gatehouse, Charlemont Fort

15. Although this is the only known building in the north attributable to Sir William Robinson (author of Charles Fort, Kinsale, in the 1670s; the Kilmainham Hospital and Marsh's Library, both in Dublin, in the 1680s and in 1704 respectively), its present lamentable state reflects no credit on the Department of the Environment. Yet their own listers call it "an important and rare surviving element of military architecture in the province". It has suffered many indignities over the years, including the deplorable refusal to accept the site into state care when it was offered in 1948, the building of an odiously inappropriate bungalow on the escarpment, and the prolonged failure to provide the surviving fragment with the protection it deserves. At the date of writing, slates, rafters and floors have been allowed to fall in, the little wooden cupola is derelict, one of the four wooden doors has been allowed to disappear altogether, and fallen stones litter the ground both within and outside the entrance archway.

The first fort, and the first (wooden) bridge over the river Blackwater, were built in June, 1602. "When the structure was completed, Lord Mountjoy (Charles Blount) named it Charlemont from his own Christian name, and placed in it a garrison of 150 men, under the command of Captain Toby Caulfield, whose descendants, the Earls of Charlemont, adopted the name of this place as their title" (Rogers). "The place was strong by nature, being bounded on the east and south by huge impassable bogs; and on the north and west by the river Blackwater, which is here 36 feet broad, and 16 feet deep ... the fortifications around it were palisadoed: a dry ditch and counter-scarp within which was a double rampart, and still more inward a thick stone wall, and regular flankers and bastions, a drawbridge well fortified, and within all, the magazines, a guard-house, and a large square tower" (Rogers, quoting Harris).

The original gatehouse and drawbridge seem to have been replaced, since a letter from Sir William Robinson of 26th April, 1673, says that "we are now ... preparing for a new drawbridge and entrance", the contractor being a Mr Johnson. "The gatehouse as it appears today is substantially Robinson's design of 1673 but probably refaced in sandstone ashlar upon its assuming a more decorative rather than a defensive role" (Dean). Sir William Robinson, about whose early years little is known, held many public offices in Ireland, and was Surveyor-General from 1671 until his retirement on grounds of infirmity (gout) in 1700. In his later years he was much embarrassed by litigation and allegations of fraud, the latter substantiated after his death. "Prior to 1712, the year of his death, he was visited frequently by Jonathan Swift" (Loeber). After the death of his wife in 1708, there had been rumours that he had married their mutual friend, the widow Esther Vanhomrigh; but Robinson proclaimed that he was "as indifferent to matrimony" as a castrato!

The gatehouse of an artillery fort seems an odd kind of gate-lodge, but the best description of this building known to me is in Dean's book, Gate Lodges of Ulster: "Situated in a position of strategic importance are star-fort earthworks with pointed bastions and a governor's residence. During its turbulent history it was occupied by a garrison and used as an ordnance depot for the north of Ireland ..." (Probably in 1858) "the large plaque bearing the Caulfield arms was incorporated above the semi-circular-headed entrance archway which springs from a stringcourse that continues through the flanking walls from the frontispiece. These screen walls each have three loopholes at rampart level. On either side of the arms a chamfered slit for observation from the watchroom, over which are pediments on back and front elevations. The tympana display fine clock faces. Pulleys and chains remain from the old drawbridge ... over the front archway a wrought iron lamp bracket and on a side elevation what is

perhaps a mason's monogram EW".

This is not the place to recount the part Charlemont Fort played in the events of 1641 or 1690; the reader is referred to J J Marshall's History of Charlemont, from which, however, it seems legitimate to quote his romantic description - "the grey old stronghold that had heard the tramp of the soldiers of Queen Elizabeth, had been seized by the daring bands of Sir Phelim O'Neill, had given shelter to King James, and echoed back to Legar Hill the thunder of Schomberg's cannon what time they bombarded its walls". In 1806, described by Sleater as "At Charlemont on the Blackwater, a fort in very good repair"; and, over the page, "Charlemont, called from a Mount built by Charles Blount, Lord Mountjoy. It is reckoned a garrison, and has a governor on the military establishment".

In 1835 the Governorship was abolished as a sinecure, but the fort continued to serve as a Royal Artillery barracks and depot, designed for 5 officers, 151 non-commissioned officers and men, and 79 horses (see Charlemont Cottage - 148). In 1858, the Government sold the entire establishment to Francis William Caulfeild, 2nd Earl of Charlemont, the local landowner whose family had long associations with the fort. At this point, all but the square central mansion and the gatehouse were demolished; for Lord Charlemont was more interested in Roxborough House, his exotic Frenchified mansion designed by W J Barre, just across the river in County Tyrone. The residence was occupied only by a caretaker, and a museum of Irish Volunteer material associated with the first Earl. However, in the early morning of 30th July 1920 "a body of some 40 men, part of whom were masked, but all with arms", threatened the caretaker and set fire to the house to prevent the army from taking occupation of it again. In 1921, the ruins were sold to a contractor who "in turn disposed of the brick and stone of the old fort to all and sundry who required cheap building material".

Photographs: W A Green, Ulster Folk Museum WAG 1771, 1772.
Situation: Portadown Road, Charlemont; td, Charlemont; Parish, Loughgall; District Council, Armagh; Grid ref. H 855 558.
References: Listed B1 (15/1/24). Sleater, 'Topography', 1806, pp 174,176; Rogers, 'Topographical sketches', 1874, p 93; Marshall, 'History of Charlemont', 1921, passim; 'Irish sword', III, 1958, p 186; E M Jope, in UJA, 3rd series, XXIII, 1960, pp 101-103; Loeber, 'Biographical dictionary', 1981, pp 88-96; Dean, 'Gate lodges,' UAHS, 1994, p 35.

The O'Connor's Stronghold, Derrywarragh Island, Maghery

16. A most curious and enigmatic pillar-like antiquity prominent on the tip of the peninsula dividing Maghery bay from the mouth of the river Blackwater. (Derrywarragh is an island only by virtue of the canal cut through the base of the peninsula). Marked on the Ordnance Survey map of 1834 only as "ruins", in more recent editions shown as "The O'Connor's Stronghold" for unexplained reasons. Thomas McIlroy's Ordnance Survey memoir of 1837, however, uses a more sensible name: "On Derrywarragh Island" he says "stands a ruin called "The Chimneys" which appears to be the remains of a large house". To me, this appears to be a group of chimney-stacks, containing at least four flues serving chimney-breasts on three storeys, the only part still standing of a sizeable Elizabethan or Jacobean house. Notes in the MBR say "Existing remains, which are about 18 feet by 14 feet, rising to a height of 25 - 30 feet, have an appearance which suggests erection in the 17th century". Possibly, an experienced chimney-sweep could provide as much information as an archaeologist.

There remain a few courses of narrow bricks at the very summit; below this is a mass of reddish and black rubble-stone bound together by a hard cohesive mortar, with a number of rectangular apertures evidently designed to accommodate beams or joists.

T G F Paterson, writing to Dr Chart in 1927, says: "Tradition calls the ruin "O'Neill's Castle", and it is so spoken of by the fishermen and inhabitants of the district who say it was used as a prison. Nobody in the district knows of it as "O'Connor's Stronghold", of that I am positive ... The stones of the castle are mostly rough field stones though there is a great deal of red sandstone in the upper part of the remaining wall ... I am sorry I can tell you so little. Rogers may be correct in his assumption that it was built by Mountjoy. It certainly resembles Moyry Castle in ways, but that of course is no proof of its having been built by the same man".

In fact, this theory seems to be disproved by "A Prospect of the Head Land of Derry Woragh" prepared by Sir Thomas Phillips in 1685-6, at which, later, date, some kind of modest building seems to be shown on the site, but certainly not a three-storey tower. At this time, Phillips prepared plans and estimates for a large artillery fort here at a cost of £44,990. The walls, of stone or brick, were to be 24 feet high and ten feet thick; there was to be an inner citadel "upon the Higher Ground"; £1500 was allowed "for mounting 125 gunns on New Plattforms and Carriages"; there was to be "a Dwelling House for the Governor and other Officers"; and provision was made for "all other Necessaries that are belonging to a Fortification as Bell, Clocke, and Chappel". This was one of the six sites in Ireland which he particularly recommended should be fortified at a total cost of £331,136 (the others were Dublin, Passage West, Kinsale, Limerick and Culmore Fort). This particular recommendation was not adopted, but the present structure may represent the surviving element from a much more modest scheme adopted instead. Alternatively, it may have been a light-house or "sea-mark" intended to indicate the mouth of the canal cut; for Livingston's map of Lord Charlemont's estate at Maghery in 1768 appears to indicate a kind of campanile-like tower, with a pyramidal (or possibly conical) top; and a rather similar tower is indicated, though with less clarity, on Williamson's map of Lough Neagh of 1785.

Lord Charlemont and Dr Chart, in 1939, say "Appearance of existing remains which are about 18ft by 14ft, rising to a height of 25-30ft, suggests erection in 17th century, possibly as a watch tower to protect mouth of Blackwater" (PSAMNI). Oram suggests that it was "a watch tower belonging to Derrywarragh Castle". Bassett says only that "Maghery is a favourite summer resort for excursionists and tourists. Derrywarragh Island has the necessary romantic features to attract sightseers and help to amplify the pleasures of a day's outing". The site, though at the end of a very long and muddy lane, is certainly most attractive; the views over the coastline of Lough Neagh spectacular; and it is evident that the romantic cottage on Coney Island nearby, built in 1895,

with its clearing through the woodland, was deliberately aligned on the pinnacle.

The Monuments and Buildings Record contains numerous dramatic photographs of this inscrutable monument, but no satisfactory account of its history.

Photograph: W A Green, Ulster Folk Museum WAG 1767. Map: R Livingston, 1765, D 291/2 in PRONI.

Situation: On shore of Lough Neagh; td, Maghery; Parish, Tartaraghan; District Council, Craigavon; Grid ref. H 929 642.

References: Scheduled monument. Phillips, 1685-6, T 1720/1/ pp 126-130, Livingston, 1765, D 291/2, Williamson, 1785, D 604/1, all in PRONI; OS map 1834; T McIlroy, OSM, 1837, Armagh, I, 1837, p 121; Bassett, Armagh, 1888, p 217; letter from T G F Paterson to D A Chart dated All Hallows Eve, 1927, in MBR; PSAMNI, 1940, p 61; Oram, 'Craigavon', UAHS, 1971, pt III, p 14; unsigned notes in MBR.

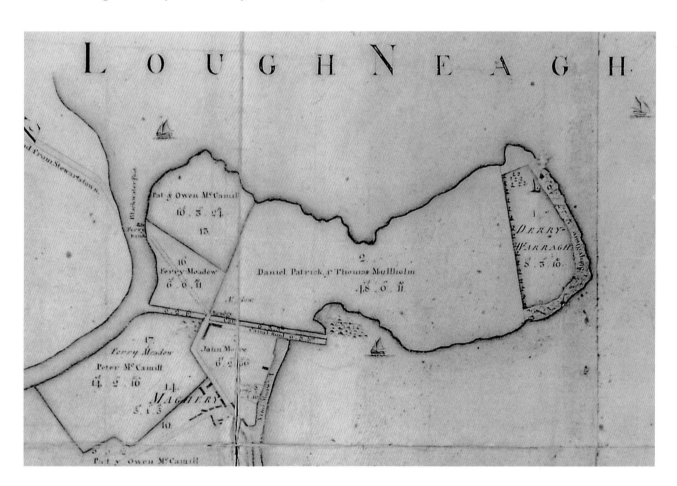

CHURCHES AND CHAPELS

Thomas Cooley's standard design for churches, No 9; compare Lisnadill (19). Drawing: Archbishop Robinson's Library

CHURCHES AND CHAPELS

As might be expected, the primatial county of Ireland is rich in ecclesiastical buildings. The two grandest by far are the two great cathedrals in the city of Armagh itself, one with its square tower, the other with its twin spires: as Bertie Rodgers wrote in 1952,

There is a through-otherness about Armagh
Of tower and steeple,
Up on the hill are the arguing graves of the kings,
And below are the people.

Both cathedrals (39 and 47) are discussed in some detail in the following pages. Each has its signal merits, each its demerits. But there can be no doubt that the most exquisite church in the county is neither of the cathedrals, but the private chapel, beside his palace, designed by Thomas Cooley but completed by Francis Johnston in 1781 for Primate Robinson (22). Indeed, that wealthy and bountiful (if reserved and chilly) prelate built many churches throughout his enormous arch-diocese (it takes in the whole of the county of Armagh and also a large number of parishes in the counties of Louth and Tyrone, and even a handful in the counties of Meath and Londonderry. Dr Beaufort,[1] writing in 1792, listed 17 parishes, with 23 churches, within the county; Canon Leslie,[2] in 1911, listed 43 parishes, each with its church, lying wholly or partly in the county). Sir Charles Coote, in 1804, justly remarked "The churches throughout this county, and indeed through this whole metropolitan diocese, are extremely well appointed, simple and chaste in their architecture, and display a lightness and elegance for which they are justly admired" ... and "The churches are in excellent, indeed, mostly, in elegant repair".[3]

Thomas Cooley prepared standard drawings, and specifications, for his patron's church-building programme, still preserved in Archbishop Robinson's Library in Armagh;[4] only one of these churches, Lisnadill (19) still stands almost unaltered. The specifications are sufficiently interesting to deserve extensive, if not complete, quotation:

Instructions for the Contractors for Building Churches.

Masons & Bricklayers. The Foundations of all Churches to be sunk untill a proper stratum be found to build on. & the Foundations to be brought in two Courses, up to one foot nine inches above the levell of the Church Yard, & 4 inches below the Flagging of the Isles of the Church ... all the Externall Walls are to be in Thickness as marked in the respective Plans, Observing to lett the externall face of the Walls batter back in the proportion of half an Inch in each

Ten feet in hight. All the Openings of Doors and Windows to be Arched. The front Arches of Stone Hamard, and dress'd quite fair, as well on their Beds as on their fronts. The Inside Arches to be Brick. All the Work to be carried on in Courses not exceeding fourteen inches, nor less then 12 Inches in hight, & each Course to be grouted except the first Course of Foundations - And the Work of the Church to be carried up as nearly on a levell, all round, as possible, or the Nature of the Work will Admitt..

Carpenter. All the Carpenters Work to be executed with the kind of Red Balk of the Growth of Riga, Memel or Onega. The Roof to be constructed exactly by the Section and the dimentions of the Timber by the Bill of Scantlings. The Rafters on back of Truss'd Roof to be laid Hollow two inches between the Ridge and Eaves Stones, and the Wall Plate to be continued the Whole Length and Breadth of the Building. No bay of Roofing to exceed Nine feet in length ... The Floor to be of Inch & quarter Red Plank, on Ground Joint five Inches by three, laid on dwarf walls of Brick or Stone in bearings not to exceed Six Feet Six Inches and the Earth between the Walls to be kept six inches clear of the Underside of the Joist. All outside Doors to be putt together with White Lead & all the Doors to be framed out of two inch Red Plank. Door Cases of best firr six inches by five inches & screwd into the Jaumbs by Nutts and Screws. The Window frames to be in form and Scantling agreeable to the Designs for that purpose. The Pues to be of one and a half inch framing and five-eighths pannill; the Seats of Bearers and the fram'd Backs, to be of one and a half inch Deals.... Plain Jaumb Linings & Plain Mouldings round the Doors. Neat Plain Hand Rail of Base Moulding with Turn'd Ballusters to the Communion Table, as pr design. Red Sheet Deal Kneeling Board and bearers of Red Whole Deale ... The Pulpit, Reading Desk and Clerks Desk to be framed in the best manner out of one and a half Inch Red Plank, well season'd...

Stone Cutter. The Eaves Course to be five Inches thick and five inches projection & to have a neat bed of at least ten Inches - & to be worked with a Sunk Throat on Under Edge. The Window Stools to be five inches thick in front & to be worked with an half inch Drip rebate, to project three Inches each way, & to have a sunk throat workd on the under edge, & if from the extraordinary Length it shall be necessary to sett them out in two Stones, the Joints to be secured from drawing water by a raised joint ... The Inside Edge next the Slates to be brought to a thickness to admit the Slating to go three inches at least down the

Inside Edge next the Slates to be brought to a thickness to admitt the Slating to go three Inches at least Under the Stone. All Stone Door fronts to be Broad Tooled; the Halfpaces and steps to be sett with a Drip of half an inch to a foot. And the joints of the Bonds and Parts in the Door Cases to be regularly broke.

Slater. The laths to be made strong of the best red firr, the Slating to have a Peg and Nail in each Slate, the Peg over the Lath & the Nail through the Lath, the Slates to be dressed square to the Shoulder, no Mortar to be used without, but to be carefully rendered within with well tempered Mortar.

Plaisterer's Work. All the Walls and Ceilings to be of strong common Plaister well sett and whited, the Outside of the Church to be Roughcast...with Wash'd and Guaged Sand and fresh Lime.

Painter. All the Deal Work wherever found to be painted the Inside work three times in Oile of Colour, & the Outside Work four times in Do, the Dressings of Doors and the Doors & Columns of Gallerys Light Stone Coulour, the Pues & Gallery-Fronts of a Light Oak Coulour, Scurting of a Chocolate Coulour, the Hand Rail of Communion Table Mohogany, the Ballusters flatt White.

Glazier. All the Frames to be glazed with the best Irish Crown Glass in large Quarrys sett in Lead and secured to the Stay Barr of every other Quarry by a Copper Band and the Rebate to be puttyed outside and inside.

There are a large number of, mostly quite small, Church of Ireland churches of the second half of the 18th and the first half of the 19th centuries; both Presbyterian and Roman Catholic congregations tended to build larger but fewer churches.

With the exception of Ballymoyer (41), there are not very many interesting episcopalian churches built after 1850, though of course many were enlarged or extended, and many spoiled in the process. Leading architects such as Sir Charles Lanyon, and for that matter Welland & Gillespie, seem to have received few commissions in the county. Unhappily, violence and population movements

have enforced the closure of a number of Protestant churches in South Armagh, and a number of Roman Catholic ones in North Armagh: some abandoned, some bricked up, at least one (at Forkhill: by W H Lynn, of 1866) rather well converted into a private dwelling-house. Most of the churches of the later Victorian and Edwardian period are either Roman Catholic, or non-conformist. Of the latter, only a handful were built in the classical style so popular just across the Bann in County Down: the Scotch Church in Armagh city (42); the First Presbyterian churches in Portadown and Lurgan (45 and 46); and the Methodist church in Portadown (44) are the best representatives of this tradition. The tall First Presbyterian church in the Mall, Armagh (51), by Robert Young of Young & Mackenzie, is probably the best example of that other, Gothic, strand in Presbyterian architecture.

Roman Catholic churches tended to be fairly unpretentious until the early years of the twentieth century, for in the years before and after the famine, the building of St Patrick's great cathedral in the city of Armagh took first priority, and first claim on the purses of the faithful, so potent was its symbolism. The other most distinguished Catholic churches in the county are of late date - George Ashlin's Saint Catherine's, Newry, of 1882 (49), and J J McDonnell's St Peter's, Lurgan (50), finished in 1901. I have seen no contemporary church, of any denomination, which I could whole-heartedly admire: and can only offer my apologies to the architectural profession.

Of course, there have always been, and still are, a multitude of smaller, modest, vernacular, churches, chapels, meeting-houses and gospel halls, sprinkled over the rolling Armagh countryside; many of them have considerable charm; and I have selected a few for description in the chapter which follows. But had I tried to discuss them all, there would have been no room whatever for secular buildings in this book!

References: 1. Beaufort, 'Memoir', 1792, p 107. 2. Leslie, 'Armagh clergy', 1911, passim. 3. Coote 'Armagh', 1804, pp 9, 131. 4. Bound volume of Cooley drawings, dated 1773-4, shelf number Z XXI 33.

Thomas Cooley's standard design for churches, No 9. Drawing: Archbishop Robinson's Library

Creggan (C of I) Church

17. A simple, modest, country church, of blackstone with granite dressings, in a very remote and much troubled district, with apparently only nine families of parishioners: yet, with the oil of prosperity oozing out of every aperture. Due to its position, close to the border, in debateable territory; and due to the vigorous efforts of its energetic rector, the Rev. Mervyn Kingston (a resident of County Louth); the parish has benefited from over £600,000 of grants from Community Relations, European, International Fund for Ireland, and such-like sources: so that the restoration of church, organ, subsidiary buildings, and 13 acres of parkland, to constitute (like Notre Dame) a tourist attraction as well as a place of worship, have all been successfully completed under the supervision of Leighton Johnston, architects. Donaldson notes the existence of a large rectory in its own small demesne, built before 1622, but greatly improved about 1785 when a new wing was added and the demesne laid out. The rectory has apparently gone, but the splendid trees, and the attractive river Creggan, remain. Several poets of local note are buried in the graveyard. There is a modest little visitors' centre, devoid however of any notice as to its hours of opening. The place is now in apple-pie order, and it looks as though Mr Kingston still has further aspirations for his tiny parish.

"There is one church in good order, with a tower to it, situated on the glebe, in the rector's demesne, and in the centre of the parish" (Shaw Mason). "The church is a spacious and handsome edifice in the centre of the parish, built in 1758, and to which a lofty square tower was added in 1799" (Lewis). The Parliamentary Gazetteer is notably more cautious: it says only "the church's date or cost of erection cannot be ascertained". Leslie thinks that Lewis's dates are "a mistake", because the vestry minutes of 1741 refer to a purchase of ladders: but I cannot see why the ladders might not have been wanted in order to mend the roof of the earlier church on the site? The accuracy of the date for the tower, however, is confirmed by a plaque announcing: "This Tower erected by the Parish of Creggan in the Year of Our Lord 1799; Cs Crawley, Jm Gilmore, Church Wardens". (For the possiblility of an Early Christian church in the graveyard, see the entry for Creggan Old Church - 5 above).

The listed group comprises: church, vault, gateposts, perimeter wall, charnel house, sexton's dwelling, and schoolhouse. The antiquity of these buildings is debatable: possibly some 16th-century work, probably some 17th-century work, may be incorporated in the 18th-century structures. Hugh Dixon notes that one of the side walls of the nave is much thicker than the other, which would support such a view. On the other hand, Rev. Simon Nelson, who died in 1847, says "the present church is built in a transverse line over the old building;" - and adds, "the local tradition says that the McMahons and the O'Neills buried their dead here, and that the last of the O'Neill dynasty" (ie, the O'Neills of the Fews) "lies in same place". The vault has within it the remains of 150 persons, the last having been placed there in 1920. The church itself is a simple three-bay hall church, having paired round-headed lattice windows with a roundel between each pair. The east window has three stained glass lights, one each for faith, hope, and charity. The tower has handsome Irish crenellations (as have the walls and square gate-pillars) and is clasped tightly by iron rods to hold it together. The interior has a modest gallery borne on

clustered columns, and is otherwise very plain and simple.

Photograph: Michael O'Connell (see also colour-plate IVb).
Situation: In the village of Creggan; td, Creggan Bane Glebe; Parish, Creggan; District Council, Newry & Mourne; Grid ref. H 923 159.
References: Listed B+ (16/16/1). Mason, 'Statistical account', I, 1814, p 206; S Nelson, Ms history of parish, c 1840, printed by T O Fiaich, in 'Seanchas Ardmhacha', VII, No 1, 1973, pp 1 -64; Lewis, TD, 1837, I, p 433; Donaldson, 'Upper Fews', 1838, p 83; PG, I, 1845, p 451; Leslie, 'Armagh clergy', 1911, p 207; L P Murray, in JCLAS, VIII, 1934, pp 117 -135; Hugh Dixon, notes and ground plan in MBR; 'The Times', 6/12/1997; BNL 10/12/1997.

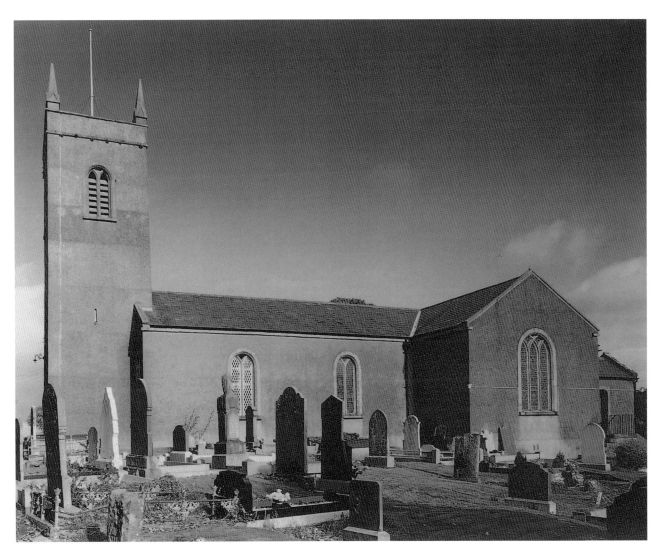

Mullavilly (C of I) Church, Laurelvale

18. There seeems to be considerable disagreement about the history of this building. "The church was built in 1736 at an unknown cost", says the Parliamentary Gazetteer. "There is ... a chapel of ease called Mullavilly church ... It was built in 1755 and is capable of containing 600 ... It has no spire" (Lt Bennett of the Ordnance Survey). But Samuel Lewis says "prior to 1755, this formed part of the parish of Kilmore, but in that year seventeen townlands were set apart to form the parish of Mullavilly, shortly after which the church was erected at the cost of Primate Robinson, but it was not consecrated until 1785". Robinson's involvement I doubt, for Mullavilly lacks the sophistication of his other churches.

Canon Leslie seems to agree on the date 1736; quoting

Lodge, he says "In 1775 the chapel was not yet consecrated, but had been in use for 40 years ... The church was built at the sole expense of Dean Brandreth, rector of Kilmore, on a piece of land ... which, never having been legally conveyed to the churchwardens, is not consecrated". This was set right in 1809 when Jerome, Count de Salis (of the Holy Roman Empire) executed the necessary conveyance; the consecration accordingly took place in the following year. Brandreth, a Cambridge graduate, came over to Ireland as chaplain to the Lord Lieutenant, the Duke of Dorset, and tutor to his son; he was appointed rector of Kilmore in 1736. According to his memorial in Kilmore church, he "was removed from this life to a better one, Wednesday the third day of October 1764, in

the 69th year of his age. He loved our Nation and hath built us a Synagogue." The church was enlarged in 1820, and again in the 1890s.

A rather plain church, whose principal distinction resides in the remarkable rectangular Gibbsian doorcase in the face of the tower, which has four modest corner pinnacles, louvred openings, and a clock (telling the right time). The older part of the church has paired lattice lancets; the newer parts (chancel and transepts) have round-headed arches with four-light, three-light, and two-light paired lancets within the stone frames. The exterior, including the tower, is otherwise covered in rather gloomy rough-cast. Inside, there is a pine gallery on quatrefoil wooden columns; a timber barrel roof, with a particularly interesting and congenial structure at the crossing; and two excellent marble memorials, with urns, to Thomas Kelly of Dawson's Grove, obit 1779, and to Mrs Elizabeth Kelly, obit 1807 - neither, so far as I can find, signed, but both of high quality.

Photographs: Michael O'Connell.
Situation: Off Mullavilly Road, Laurelvale; td, and Parish, Mullavilly; District Council, Armagh; Grid ref. J 013 483.
References: Not listed? G A Bennett, OSM, 1835, Armagh, I, p 62; Lewis, TD, 1837, II, p 410; PG, II, 1846, p 826; Leslie, 'Armagh clergy', 1911, pp 21, 389.

St John's (C of I) Church, Lisnadill

19. Designed for Archbishop Robinson by Thomas Cooley; erected 1772, consecrated ten years later on 2 November 1782. "The church is a spacious edifice in the later English style, with a square embattled tower, erected by Primate Robinson in 1772, and has the arms of the founder over the entrance" (1837). "An elegant structure ... Sittings 300; attendance 150" (1846). "Still in a good state of preservation" (1888), and indeed today.

"Lisnadill is unique in that it is the only church built to Cooley's designs that has escaped major alteration in the 19th century" (Erica Loane). "The church has been built almost exactly to Cooley's design no 9 ..." (See pages 23 and 25). "The measurements of the church fit exactly to the plan ... On the west face" (of the tower) "the oculus is flanked on either side by a coat of arms, a feature not shown on the drawing. They are the same as those on Grange, the one on the left belongs to Robinson as Primate and the one on the right belongs to Dean Hamilton ... The windows follow the drawings but they are attractively latticed like those in no 6." Internally, "the closeness with which the drawings have been followed is evident by the inclusion of the rather peculiar triangular buttresses which jut into the nave above the balcony." And: "A confusing aspect of Lisnadill is that it has 1772 carved on a string course and this has been taken as the date at which it was built. The plans on the other hand are dated 1773. There are two possible explanations, one is that the date refers to

the founding of the parish, while the other is that Cooley included the plans of Lisnadill in his twelve patterns after it was built." Personally, I lean to the latter explanation.

There is an excellent cutstone screen, with modern gates, at the entrance to the well-kept churchyard. The side walls, and the completely blank exterior of the east wall, have been roughcast; only the plinth, and the sills and surrounds of the unusually wide pointed windows, are of ashlar. The church seems to be so light and airy that vertical Venetian blinds are required. The interior is today rather startling: pale lemon walls, dark red ceiling, and bright blue (unpierced) east wall with paraclete, creed, Lord's prayer, and the whole of chapter XX of Exodus neatly painted on it. The scumbled pews in the nave and gallery are original, but the woodwork in the 'chancel' is modern, though quite congruous. Altogether, a remarkable unspoiled survival.

Photograph: Michael O'Connell.
Situation: 60, Newtownhamilton Road; td, Ballymoran; Parish, Lisnadill; District Council, Armagh; Grid ref. H 885 405.
References: Listed B: it should surely be A? (15/15/6). Original drawings by T Cooley in Archbishop Robinson's Library, Armagh; Stuart, 'City of Armagh', 1819, p 448; Lewis, TD, 1837, II, p 286; PG, II, 1846, p 659; Bassett, 'Armagh', 1888, p 181; Leslie, 'Armagh clergy', 1911, p 348; E Loane, Thomas Cooley, TCD thesis, 1983, pp 44-46, copy in MBR.

St Aidan's (C of I) Church, Salter's Grange

20. "The site of Grange church, within two miles of Armagh, on the Loughgall Road, was peculiarly well chosen by Primate Robinson. This church stands conspicuous on a commanding eminence, and being adorned with a beautiful spire and steeple, forms a striking and picturesque object from every part of the country" (Stuart). "Built by Robinson as much as an embellishment to his city as a necessity ... It was certainly noticed by contemporary travellers" (Loane), including Arthur Young: "The church is erected of white stone and having a tall spire makes a very agreeable object in a country where churches and spires do not abound, at least such as are worth looking at." Reciprocally, it enjoys a splendid view of Armagh city with its two hill-top cathedrals; or did, until injudicious new building was allowed on the opposite side of the road.

This was one of Thomas Cooley's churches, built as a slightly narrower version of his design No 10; authorities differ as to the date of its erection, some saying 1773, others 1779; since it was not consecrated until 1782, the later date seems the more likely. "There was a custom established from the first, for the male members of the congregation to sit on one side, the female members on the other" (Leslie).

The façade is nicely framed by school-house, teacher's house, gate pillars and stone boundary wall - noticeably similar to the pillars and wall at Lisnadill (19). It, the tower, spire and pinnacles, and the carved armorial bearings of Archbishop Robinson and his Dean, Hugh Hamilton, above the pointed doorway, are of well-cut ashlar; the sides and back, and also the crenellations of the front wall, are of more humble roughcast. The lattice windows in the side walls are said to be Victorian. The church was enlarged by the addition of transepts and apse in 1843, and again remodelled in 1905; so that much of its original character has been lost. Williams says "There is little evidence here of Philip Hardwick (commissioned to adapt this Regency Gothic church of the Molyneux family to the requirements of the Ecclesiologists) apart from the chancel and the pulpit. Interior now dominated by a good Arts and Crafts window by Beatrice Elvery above the altar (1910)". Otherwise, internally, it is now notable principally for two features: the elegance of the cornice: and the numerous and accomplished white marble monuments to successive Molyneux baronets of Castledillon, and a particularly elegant neo-classical monument to one Turner Macan, obit 1813, the odd man out. As Loane remarks "if the interior is disappointing, it is certainly compensated for by an exterior which embodies all the pretty, if unexciting, aspects of Cooley's gothic designs."

Photograph: Michael O'Connell.
Situation: Salter's Grange Road; td, Salter's Grange; Parish, Grange; District Council, Armagh; Grid ref. H 883 486.
References: Listed B+ (15/3/20); Original drawings by T Cooley in Archbishop Robinson's Library, Armagh; Young, 'Tour', 1778, p 104; Stuart, 'City of Armagh', 1819, p 448; Lewis, TD, 1837, I, p 670; PG, I, 1845, p 286; Leslie, 'Armagh clergy', 1911, p 306; E Loane, Thomas Cooley, TCD thesis, 1983, pp 38-41, copy in MBR; Williams, 'Architecture in Ireland', 1994, p 12.

St Vindic's (C of I) Church, Tynan

21. Built in 1784. The nave and the attractive tower with its vestigial angled buttresses and tall slim corner pinnacles are of nicely-dressed stone. The transepts and chancel were added in 1822 at a cost of £646. In 1835, Lt Bailey of the Ordnance Survey remarked that "The parish church is situated within the village. It is very neat and kept in excellent order". But three years later, his colleague, E A Williamson, wrote "Tynan church, built 1780, is a roughcast building rather out of repair, will contain 300 persons, average attendance 200".

There is a wealth of genealogical information to be gleaned from the very numerous memorial tablets, many of them to members of the Stronge family, on the walls of the interior. There is a pleasing gallery borne by two simple columns.

Photograph: Michael O'Connell.
Situation: Dartan Ree, Tynan; td, Tynan; Parish, Tynan; District Council, Armagh; Grid ref. H 766 430.
References: Listed B (15/11/15). Lt Bailey, OSM, 1835, and E A Williamson, 1838, Armagh, I, pp 127, 131; Lewis, TD, 1837, II, p 664; Leslie, 'Armagh clergy', 1911, p 435.

Archbishop Robinson's Chapel, Armagh

22. A most elegant little building, in the form of a Greek temple, of the highest quality: worthy to rank with Sir William Chambers's Casino Marino for Lord Charlemont near Dublin, Michael Shanahan's Temple of the Winds for the Earl-Bishop of Derry at Downhill, and Athenian Stewart's Temple of the Winds for Lord Castlereagh at Mount Stewart. Bence-Jones considers it "one of the most beautiful surviving eighteenth-century ecclesiastical interiors in Ireland"; Curl calls it "the exquisite Ionic prostyle tetrastyle Roman temple:"; and McParland speaks of its "brittle elegance". It was designed for Archbishop Robinson in 1781 by Thomas Cooley, and completed after Cooley's death by Francis Johnston. Described by Coote in 1804 as "a very grand chapel for the use of the primate's family, suitable to so princely a residence"; and by Stuart in 1819: "The front exhibits a handsome portico of the Ionick order, and the whole edifice is in the most chaste and correct style of architecture, and decorated in the most tasteful and elegant manner". Drawings of the interior both by Thomas Cooley, of 1781, and by Francis Johnston, of 1785, survive in the Irish Architectural Archive; Bernadette Goslin justly comments, "Johnston's early drawing style shows an amazing minuteness of detail".

The chapel stands a few paces to the west of the palace (80) by which it is somewhat overshadowed since the addition of the extra storey to the latter. It is built of the same ashlar limestone, with a pedimented portico borne on four Ionic columns. The windows have semi-circular heads. Internally, the vestibule has three doorways: one giving access to the chapel proper, one to the stairs leading to the charming curved-backed musicians' gallery, and one to the former vestry. There is a curious early 19th-century lavatory off the gallery. The Primate's pedimented, and beautifully detailed, throne stands against one side wall, an elegant fireplace immediately opposite. (The original chimney has mysteriously disappeared, to be replaced by a tin cowl, invisible from the ground, but distressing from the upper windows of the palace). "The internal bays are divided by Corinthian pilasters set on a podium of panelled waxed oak approximately one and a half metres high above the floor. The stalls and throne are also of waxed oak of superb design and quality. The floor is a chequer of stone quarries, alternately local limestone with smaller pieces of black Kilkenny marble. Above the entablature rises the shallow coffered barrel-vaulted ceiling, each coffer containing an undercut plaster rosette" (UAHS, 1992). The chapel was extensively restored in 1985-6, but the panelling is showing signs of distress, and further work may be needed soon. What a shame that this charming building no longer serves its original purpose: today, it is used for occasional meetings, concerts and exhibitions.

Photographs: Michael O'Connell (see also colour-plates IIIb, Vb).

Situation: To the west of the Palace; td, Parkmore; Parish, and District Council, Armagh; Grid ref. H 878 443.

References: Listed A (15/18/17). Drawings 2,3, in RIAI Murray Collection, IAA; Coote, 'Armagh', 1804, p 323; Stuart, 'City of Armagh', 1819, p 416; McParland, 'Francis Johnston', 1969, pp72,73; Bence-Jones, 'Burke's guide', 1978, p 12; Curl, 'Classical churches', UAHS, 1980, p 13; 'Ulster architect', February 1987; B Goslin, unpublished Catalogue of the Murray Collection in IAA, 1990, p 42; 'Buildings of Armagh', UAHS, 1992, p 173 (and see that bibliography).

Ardmore (C of I) Church

23. "Moyntaghs was formerly part of the parish of Seagoe, but in 1765 it was erected into a separate parish ... A small church was built in 1765, close to the shore of Lough Neagh, but it was blown down in a storm on Nov. 4th, 1783; after which accident the new one was built, in 1785, on a more eligible site; its elevated situation and tapering spire render it an interesting object when viewed from the lake or any of its neighbouring shores; the late Board" (of First Fruits) "gave £76.18.5½, British currency, towards its erection" (Lewis).

Thomas McIlroy of the Ordnance Survey, in the same year (1837) was less well informed: "Ardmore church ... is a plain stone building supposed to have been erected in 1797, not known what cost or how defrayed ... At the east end is a tower on which is a wooden spire. In the tower is a belfry containing one bell. The accommodation is for 200 persons and the general attendance is 200. The interior is very plain, the windows are rectangular". (They are not rectangular now). His colleague, Lt Bennett, thought the parish church had been built in 1799. Oram says it was dedicated in 1787, and remarks "The masonry of the battlemented tower is of a slightly different character and may be a later addition". The listers say "1787 spire and part tower rebuilt after the Big Wind". But it was in fact a different wind: the spire blew down on the night of 11

December 1883, and after some debate as to priorities, the offer by Mr Bright of Portadown to "erect new spire, raise bell, put in new loft, paint church, replace main and vestry room doors, put up new pulpit and altar, and replace communion rails", all for £190, was accepted. The pleasant Victorian pulpit came from St Mark's, Portadown.

A simple, rustic hall church, the nave of random rubble with three pairs of Gothic-arched pointed lattice windows on the south side only; the tower rendered in 1978 except for the voussoirs of the pointed door-case, topped, within its Irish crenellations, by an octagonal green-copper-covered spire. Very prominent on top of its hillock in the midst of the loughshore flatlands, with a (somewhat altered) old schoolhouse nearby. The interior plain and pleasing, with panel-fronted gallery on cast-iron columns: but these, like the cast-iron font, have been exotically painted to imitate streaky marble. Best of all, the original 18th-century box-pews survive, very little altered.

Photograph: Michael O'Connell.
Situation: Church Road, Ardmore; td, Derryadd; Parish, Ardmore or Montiaghs; District Council, Craigavon; Grid ref. J 022 621.
References: Listed B (14/3/5). G A Bennett, OSM, 1835, and T McIlroy, 1837, Armagh, I, pp 93, 89; Lewis, TD, 1837, II, p 405; Oram, 'Craigavon', UAHS, 1971, pt III, p 12; Collins, 'Ardmore Parish Church', 1995, passim; 'Clergy of Down and Dromore' 1996, p 169.

St Luke's (C of I) Church, Loughgall

24. An inscribed stone in the tower states: "This Church was built AD 1795 Revd William Bisset Rector Robert C Cope Esqre James Stothers Church Wardens." But, though begun in 1795, it seems that work had to be suspended for several years "owing to the turbulent state of the neighbourhood"; and the pews seem to have been incomplete so late as 1803. However, in 1804 Sir Charles Coote wrote "A fine new church has lately been built". The present gallery, with its pair of cast-iron columns, was inserted in 1822. By 1837, described as "a neat edifice in the early English style, with a square tower ... is of hewn marble" (a common description of the time for limestone) "and the interior elegantly arranged".

Erica Loane points out that, despite quite close similarities with nos 6 and 10 of Cooley's drawings in Archbishop Robinson's Library, Armagh, he "could not have built Loughgall since he died in 1784; it seems quite likely that, as was the case at Ballymakenny, the architect was Francis Johnston and he was building the church loosely to Cooley's designs". And: "Loughgall demonstrates what seems to be generally the case in Cooley's designs, that all the interest is in the facade at the expense of the very plain side view; here it is emphasised by the ashlar facing which is not continued round the corners". Certainly, the stonework of facade and tower is elegantly detailed; it is a pity that it has fairly recently been obtrusively over-pointed. There is a particularly pleasing fillet around the plinth; and what appears to be a mason's mark on the top step at the door. The lattice side-windows are probably not original. There are nice, probably Victorian, wrought-iron gates and overthrow.

Between 1863 and 1866, the church was enlarged from a simple hall-type to a T shape by the addition of two sizeable transepts. The designs may have been by Welland and Gillespie, but the supervision seems to have been provided by W J Barre, who was paid £35 for his work. Unfortunately, the result is creditable to neither party: whilst the exterior is inoffensive, the very long plain back wall, despite a Victorian window and some panelling of the 1920s, compromises the original character of the church.

Photograph: Michael O'Connell.

Situation: Main street, Loughgall; td, Levaleglish; Parish, Loughgall; District Council, Armagh; Grid ref. H 950 518.

References: Listed B (15/2/24); in conservation area. Coote, 'Armagh', 1804, p 347; J C Innes, OSM, nd, Armagh, I, p 76; Lewis, TD, 1837, II p 313; PG, II, 1846, p 693; Leslie, 'Armagh clergy', 1911, p 352; E Loane, Thomas Cooley, TCD thesis, 1983, pp 58-60, copy in MBR; Reilly, 'Loughgall', 1995, passim.

Presbyterian Church, Tartaraghan

25. The plaque inset in the wall, facing the road, is inscribed: "Tartaraghan Presbyterian Meeting house 1824". Thomas McIlroy of the Ordnance Survey, writing in 1837, says "There is a Presbyterian meeting house situated in the townland of Ballynarry. It is a rectangular stone building, whitewashed and slated, 55 feet long and 32 feet broad, expense of building or when erected not known. The interior is commodious. It is fitted up with pews. It is unceiled. The accommodation is for 500 persons and the general attendance is 200."

The stonework now rendered, no longer whitewashed. This remains nonetheless a very plain but attractive country meeting house, with four broad pointed windows in each side wall. The slated roof has two shiny ventilators on the ridge and a knop on the upstand of each gable. A lower session-room has been congruously added to the north, a near-symmetrical (but, of brick, so less congruous) porch has been added to the south.

Photograph: Michael O'Connell.
Situation: Cloncarrish Road; td, Ballynarry; Parish, Tartaraghan; District Council, Craigavon; Grid ref. H 943 594.
References: Not listed. T McIlroy, OSM, 1837, Armagh, I, p 118; inscription on front wall.

Cloveneden Presbyterian Church, Loughgall

26. "I see a stone church on a hill. Inside it are the old box pews, the eighteenth-century pulpit with its flutings and scallop-shells. And in the pulpit - yes - I see myself, lean and severe. These are my people facing me in their pews - George, John, Willie, Myra, Dorrie - all of them. My flock." So wrote (and spoke) their minister, W R Rodgers, in his 'Professional portrait of a country parson', produced in the Belfast studio by his friend Louis MacNeice, and broadcast in the home service of the BBC at 7 o'clock on the evening of Sunday 1st September 1946.

An inscribed plaque inset into the front wall, above the central window, says: "This house was re-built by the parishioner" (sic) "of Loughgall. AD 1791. Revd. Moses Hogg". On the gable-end, but painted only quite recently, "1704", the date of the establishment of the congregation. The (undated) Ordnance Survey fair sheets say "Loughgall Presbyterian meeting house, situated in the townland of Cloveneden, is a plain stone building, roughcast, white-washed and slated, 64 feet long and 38 feet broad. It was built in 1791, the cost not known. There is accommodation for 500 persons and the general attendance is 100. The interior is very plain, having pews, a mud floor and no ceiling." Described in 1835 as "now much out of repair".

Today neatly painted and in good trim, "renovated and extended" in 1971, though some of the detailing - especially the picture window at the back - is rather inappropriate. Unfortunately, at this date the interesting internal box-pews, and almost all the other interior woodwork, had to be removed due to an acute infestation of woodworm: and were not replaced. Only the pulpit balusters remain. The church stands perched on top of its drumlin, several miles from Loughgall village, roughcast colour-washed a creamy yellow, with quoins, window-surrounds and plinth painted grey. There are five pointed window-openings in the facade, two larger, three smaller, one of the latter with a blank wall behind it; the entrance is in the gable.

Although the Gothick glazing-pattern has been reproduced, the sliding sashes have not; and the new glazing-bars are of varnished hardwood. A square chimney-stack surmounts the gable-end of the slated roof.

That excellent poet Bertie Rodgers (whom I knew, though not well) was minister here from 1934 to 1946, when he went to London to join Louis MacNeice at the BBC. He had never really been cut out for the ministry: Dan Davin recalls Harden Rodgers reminding him, after her father's death, "of how the pulpit in Loughgall was so high that, on those Sundays when Saturday had been the night before, Bertie - as even that staid parish knew its pastor - could stoop in a pause of his preaching, some cautiously contrived colon, and retch gently, invisible to his devout and Sunday-sombre flock". So far as I know, although they were certainly of importance to him, he never referred to his church, to his manse, or even to Loughgall, in his published poems. In the graveyard at Cloveneden he is buried - "W R Rodgers / poet and preacher / 1909-1969"; also his second wife Marianne Gilliam, who died in 1976.

Photograph: Michael O'Connell.
Situation: Cloveneden Road, Loughgall; td, Cloveneden; Parish, Loughgall; District Council, Armagh; Grid ref. H 892 531.
References: Listed B (15/1/9). J C Innes, OSM, nd, and C Bailey, 1835, Armagh, I, p76, 80; radio script, 1946, D 2833/D/4/1 p 4, in PRONI; D Davin, 'Introductory memoir' to Rodgers, 'Collected poems', 1971; H Dixon, notes in MBR.

Vinecash Presbyterian Church, Portadown

27. A fine, largeish, classic, Presbyterian hall-church: the front stuccoed, with quoins, and carefully arranged round-headed windows and doorway, nicely painted in two shades of grey; the side walls pebble-dashed, each with three pairs of round-headed windows; ornamental cresting (now incomplete) on the ridge; gallery; and inscription in the gable, "Vinecash Presbyterian Church 1879". It is on the site of a much earlier church; the congregation's first minister was a Scotsman, Alexander Bruce, called to Vinecash in 1697.

The interior of the church is very plain but very attractive: distinctly old-fashioned for so late a date, but none the worse for that. There are scumbled box-pews; a nicely-pierced front to the gallery; and a blue-painted recess behind the pulpit, with door into the robing-room.

Photograph: Michael O'Connell.
Situation: Just off the Red Lion cross-roads; td, Farra; Parish, Drumcree; District Council, Armagh; Grid ref. H 974 529.
References: Not listed. Tercentenary booklet, 1997, passim.

St Malachi's (R C) Church, Camlough

28. G Scott of the Ordnance Survey wrote, about 1835, "In the townland of Corrackcroppan, originally very old, was rebuilt about the year 1816, expenses paid by subscription. There are 41 seats in the gallery, would accommodate 6 persons each; between 200 and 300 attend on Sundays. Dimensions 60 by 36 feet"

The listers say "an interesting T-plan church, with galleries in each of the three arms. The detail is simple Gothic". And: "The original tripartite windows with interlocking tracery in cut stone remain in the three gables of the two-storey portion". The side galleries are reached by twin, stone, external staircases. The walls are roughcast and painted cream, with smooth stucco quoins. There is a pleasant little belfry, with cross on top, in an idiom apparently peculiar to this district. In the gable of the porch is a (later) stone, inscribed with the date "1816". Although there are a number of these pleasantly old-fashioned T-shaped Catholic churches in South Armagh, not many of them antedate emancipation.

Photograph: Michael O'Connell.
Situation: Carrickcroppan Road, Camlough; td, Carrickcroppan; Parish, Killevy; District Council, Newry & Mourne; Grid ref. J 032 268.
References: Listed B+ (16/19/3). G Scott, OSM, nd (1835?), Armagh, I, p 54; notes in MBR.

St Patrick's (R C) Chapel, Ballyargan, Ballymore

29. "The Roman Catholic chapel of Ballyargan is ... a plain rectangular whitewashed building 66 feet long and 24 feet broad, rebuilt in the year 1807 and is now (1837 July) undergoing repairs. It has a gallery around 2 sides and is capable of accommodating 900 persons. Over the altar there is a large oil painting of St Peter in good preservation" (OSM). The painting and the side galleries have gone, but this is still that rarity in Ireland, a simple, pretty, rustic, pre-emancipation Roman Catholic church. On the side wall, a sun-dial inscribed "Made by Thomas McCreesh, Anno Domini 1826"; above the door, a pleasing statuette of St Patrick in a niche. Three pointed windows in each side wall; a cross at each gable; no bell-cote. Internally, plain and seemly - a welcome absence of bondieuserie - plain pews, modern gallery with harmonium, and classical marble altar.

Photograph: Michael O'Connell.
Situation: Mullaghglass Road; td Ballyargan; Parish, Ballymore; District Council, Armagh; Grid ref. J 042 428.
References: Not listed. J Hill Williams, OSM, 1838, Armagh I, p 6.

St John's (RC) Church, Middletown

30. One of the few Roman Catholic churches in the county ante-dating emancipation in 1829, Middletown chapel appears to have been "renovated" - implying some kind of earlier church on the site - in 1826, at a cost of £1,250, by one Father Lappin. Initially it had neither bell nor belfry. Two galleries were added in 1834, at a cost of £300. In 1838, described as "A large oblong building quarter of a mile east of the village, situated in a hollow, surrounded with planting, white-washed, in good repair, and 98 feet by 40 feet" (OSM). The bell-tower dates from 1857.

The tower bears the surprising inscription:

"How terrible is this Place
This is no other but the House of GOD
And the Gate of Heaven.
1826
Immortal be the Memory of
The Rev.   May 15 1845"

The missing name must surely be that of Father Bernard J Loughran: if so, would it not be an act of corporal charity to restore it to its place? Or was his name expunged because of some dreadful offence?

This is basically a simple barn-church, with the altar in the long wall, of random rubble with cutstone quoins and trim, excellent round-headed Georgian windows, and, half-way along the long wall, a square, quoined, three-storey bell-tower with Irish crenellations. It was rather drastically restored in 1994-5 by Dennis O'Neill, architect, of Portadown. "From the initial design stages, it was decided that as much of the original building form and fabric should be retained as possible, and indeed that

where possible any alteration previously undertaken should be corrected to reinstate the building to its original form. The existing window frames were unfortunately beyond salvaging, but the new window frames were designed as replicas of the intricate originals ... In our scheme for St John's church, it has been our intention to restore a very old, unique and much-loved building to its former splendour." Unfortunately, this admirable aspiration is slightly spoiled by over-obtrusive pointing of the stonework of the tower, and the heaviness of the glazing bars.

The old altar, originally brought from Italy, with its elaborate red marble colonettes, has been broken up and reconstituted so as to provide a new, smaller, free-standing altar; lectern; and sedilia. The Gothic detailing of the altar contrasts a little oddly with the arched reredos with its celtic details. There is much new woodwork, including a sheeted pine ceiling above the heavy original roof-timbers, and a completely new U-shaped gallery. In general, this must be considered a success. The tabernacle door incorporates a reproduction of the remarkable and very beautiful bronze 12th-century crucifixion plaque, found nearby in Marrassit or College Hall townland in 1844, belonging to the Bell collection in Edinburgh, now on loan to the Ulster Museum, Belfast (see page xiv).

Photograph: Michael O'Connell.
Situation: Off Monaghan Road, Middletown; td, Carandoogan; Parish, Tynan; District Council, Armagh; Grid ref. H 763 381.
References: Listed B (15/11/26); OS map, 1835; E A Williamson, OSM, 1838, Armagh, I, p 132; 'Historical sketches of Tynan and Middletown', 1995, pp 15, 92-3, 99, 294-297.

St Paul's (C of I) Church, Tartaraghan

31. "A neat country church, roughcast and whitewashed. It was built in 1816 and cost £1300, defrayed by the Board of First Fruits ... The interior is neat, the pews are large and commodious. There is a gallery at the east end. The accommodation is for 550 persons and the general attendance is 500. At the east end of the church is a belfry containing one bell with the date 1799 on it" (OSM). The Parliamentary Gazetteer is more informative: "The church was built in 1816, partly by means of a loan of £738.9.2³/4 from the late Board of First Fruits, and partly by a sum of unrecorded amount raised by subscription. Sittings, 450; attendance 430 ... In 1834, the parishioners consisted of 3,700 churchmen, 359 Presbyterians, 11 other Protestant dissenters, and 2,100 Roman Catholics". The original design is said to have been by John Bowden of Dublin. Consecrated 1819. The chancel was added in 1890.

The preponderance of episcopalians in this part of the county, and their comparative prosperity, have led to a number of alterations both inside and outside the church, and not all for the better. The rubble walls of nave and tower are no longer either roughcast or whitewashed, but look well enough. Sanctuary and vestry are later additions in cut blackstone; and there is a dreadfully insensitive boiler-house, prominently sited at the foot of the tower, of concrete scratched with crude joints in imitation of stonework. Narrow Victorian Gothic pitch-pine pews have replaced the original "large and commodious" box-pews. The roof timbers of the ceiling are oppressively dark and Victorian. The modern lych-gate is, in itself, quite pleasant, but its suburban red tiles are quite out of keeping with the materials proper to the site.

The square tower has Irish crenellations, and an inset plaque "The Foundation Stone of this Church was laid on Wednesday 7th September 1816 by James Verner of Church Hill in this County", with the names of incumbent and vergers. In their day, the Verners were great people, and

Church Hill a great house; today, they are all gone, and the house has crumbled into a Peatland Park. The best surviving feature of this church is the delightful curling cantilevered stone staircase fitted into the pine-panelled cylindrical space inside the stone cube of the tower.

Photographs: Michael O'Connell.
Situation: Off Clantilew Road; td, Breagh; Parish, Tartaraghan; District Council, Craigavon; Grid ref. H 943 585.
References: Not listed. T McIlroy, OSM, 1837, Armagh, I, p 118; PG, III, 1846, p 318; Oram, 'Craigavon', UAHS, 1971, pt III, p 11; 'Portadown Times', 13/9/1991.

Holy Trinity (C of I) Church, Drumsallan, Eglish

32. "A large handsome edifice, having a square tower with pinnacles; it was erected in 1821" (Lewis). Perched on its hill-top, this is a simple, classic example of a Board of First Fruits Church, with its Irish crenellations and spiky corner pinnacles. Three bays deep, it has three pairs of pointed windows in each side wall, all with plain glass in iron lattices, which, with the triple window over the altar, make this an unusually light and airy church. In the chancel, an elegant (though unsigned) memorial, with angelic figure, commemorating James Johnston of Knappagh (104), who had been largely instrumental in the building of the church, and who died on 27th December 1823, only three months after its consecration.

"It cost £1,790.16.2, made up of £923.1.5$^{1}/_{2}$ a loan from the Board of First Fruits; subscriptions £532.0.9 ... sale of materials of old church, £23.6.8$^{1}/_{2}$; and a handsome donation of £312.7.1$^{1}/_{2}$ from Primate J G Beresford" (Leslie). "Sittings, 350; attendance, 168 in winter" (PG).

Photograph: Michael O'Connell.
Situation: Maydown Road, Killylea; td, Drumsallan; Parish, Eglish; District Council, Armagh; Grid ref. H 810 480.
References: Listed B (15/12/16). Lewis, TD, 1837, I, p 597; PG, II, 1846, p 172; Leslie, 'Armagh clergy', 1911, p 296.

St Mark's (C of I) Church, Armagh

33. An uncommonly attractive church, with its buttresses and pinnacles, said by the UAHS listers to have been built in 1811 to designs by Francis Johnston, and enlarged and "rebuilt" only 20 years later by William Farrell. If so, the tower and front must be Johnston's work; the side walls are Farrell's; the chancel is of 1866, "in total contrast to the delicate Gentleman's Gothick style of Johnston and Farrell" (UAHS, 1992). There was a further refurbishment in 1896, when the hefty marble pulpit was inserted to designs by J J Phillips of Belfast.

"There is a chasteness and correctness in the design and a harmony in the parts of this edifice, highly agreeable to the spectator, and the effect is heightened by the very vivid colour of the hewn calcareous stone with which it is constructed" (Stuart, 1819). "A handsome edifice in the later English style: the interior is elegantly finished; the aisles are separated from the nave by a row of arches resting on clustered columns, from the capitals of which spring numerous ribs supporting a handsome groined roof. This church, which is indebted for much of its decorations to the munificence of the present primate, was built at an expense of £3,600, and contains about 1500 sittings, of which 800 are free" (Lewis, 1837). Built as a chapel of ease to the cathedral and consecrated in 1814, it thereafter became the parish church, serving also as a chapel for the Royal School and as the garrison church.

As the UAHS listers point out, "It is interesting to note that the detail of the finial, with its Chinese-like swag ornament, is similar to those on the tower, so either Farrell copied Johnston or else replaced Johnston's finials by his own". The church is approached from the Mall by a fine Church Walk with its avenue of lime trees, with good wrought iron gates and screen.

Photograph: Michael O'Connell.
Situation: Between the Mall East and Victoria Street, Armagh;. td, Corporation; Parish and District Council, Armagh, Grid ref. H 882 454.
References: Listed B+ (15/17/13); in conservation area. Stuart, 'City of Armagh', 1819, p 547; Lewis, TD, 1837, I, p 73; PG, I, 1845, p 80; Bassett, 'Armagh', 1888, p 93; 'Buildings of Armagh', UAHS, 1992, pp 134-136.

St John's (C of I) Church, Mullaghbrack, Kilcluney

34. Externally, not a particularly prepossessing church; internally, a mass of contradictions; but not without interest. Said to have been out of repair in 1657, but in good order at the Primate's visitation of 1693; "too small for its congregation" in 1777; the tower built in 1814; the church enlarged and rebuilt in 1830, "at an expense of £1,787, of which £1,035 was defrayed by the incumbent, £200 by the Earl of Gosford, £100 by the Lord-Primate, £32 by subscription, and £400 by parochial assessment" (Lewis).

It stands proudly on its hill-top supported by gates, pillars and knops of 1821, parish hall, school house, Orange hall and new rectory, surmounted (in the season) by a well-braced union flag flapping in the wind. The square tower has corner pinnacles, quoins and two prominent string-courses of cut-stone, otherwise roughcast. Symmetrically disposed are two pointed doorways, each surmounted by a square-headed window and label moulding.

Internally, an interesting early example of the use of cast iron. In essence, it is a double-aisle church which contains an almost square space divided lengthways into three cubes, separated by four tremendous iron clustered columns carrying a coffered ceiling on shallow segmental arches; and horizontally into two cubes separated by the gallery carried on five subsidiary cast iron columns. The whole floor of this wide hall is divided by a honeycomb of yellow-scumbled box-pews, with a semi-circular cut-out facing the entrance to accommodate the font. Perhaps regrettably, the comfortable family pew of the Achesons,

Earls of Gosford, has now been converted into a rather messy children's play-area, much out of keeping with the sonorous memorials on its walls.

Several of the monuments on the walls of the church are of interest. There is a fine, chimney-piece-like monument of 1638, inscribed IHSB, with tinted flowers and fruit. There is a splendid classical memorial to Dean Swift's friend, Arthur Acheson, died 1749, by John Van Nost the younger. There is also what Homan Potterton describes as "a simple, but beautiful, urn carved in relief against a pyramid" by John Bacon the elder, in memory of Rev. John Jones, Ll B, who died in 1794: "Bacon's piety is apparent, and a relief on the urn of the Good Shepherd reminds one of the earthly calling of the deceased". There is also a pleasing memorial by J Johnson, sculptor, of Belfast, to Martha, wife of Robert Boyd of Marlacoo, who died in 1843.

A church which may appeal more to those who like studied informality than to those who like the austere and the seemly.

Photograph: Michael O'Connell.

Situation: Church Road, Mullaghbrack; td, Mullaghbrack; Parish, Kilcluney; District Council, Armagh; Grid ref. H 958 423.

References: Listed B (15/13/50). Lewis, TD, 1837, II, p 410; Leslie, 'Armagh clergy', 1911, p 385; Kerr, 'Parish of Mullaghbrack', 1953, passim; Potterton, 'Irish church monuments', UAHS, 1975, pp 35, 86.

Clare (C of I) Church, Tandragee

35. "The parish was created as a Perpetual Curacy on 6th March 1840, 4 townlands being taken from Mullabrack, 5 from Loughgilly, and 12 from Ballymore parishes ... The church was consecrated on October 13th, 1842 ... At Disestablishment Clare ceased to be a Perpetual Curacy and became part of Ballymore Parish" (Leslie). The church itself is of no great interest, a slim, tall, early Victorian exercise in simplified Gothic, with bell-cote atop the gable, considerably spoiled however by pebble-dash on the front wall and the blocking-up of the two narrow pointed windows flanking the entrance. However, very unusually, the plans, specifications, and contract documents survive in the diocesan records: including elevations and sections, by William Farrell & Son, architects, dated June, 1840, "to accommodate 218 persons in pews and aisle sittings at the Eleven Lone Ends near Markethill county Armagh".

The interest resides principally in the remarkable pair of symmetrical "lodges" flanking the path to the church door, not incuded in the architect's drawings, presumably originally sexton's house (with chimney) and school-room (without chimney), now used only for storage. They have granite quoins and ventilator surrounds, otherwise they are built partly of mellow brick and partly of rubblestone, with pretty brick label mouldings, oversailing eaves, and paired lattice windows. Together, they and the little church make a charming group against the all-important backdrop of their surrounding trees.

Photograph: Michael O'Connell.
Situation: On the road from Tandragee to Newry; td, Clare; Parish, now part of Loughgilly; District Council, Armagh; Grid ref. J 012 429.
References: Not listed. DIO 4/32/C/8/4/1, 14, in PRONI; Leslie, 'Armagh clergy', 1911, p 177.

Charlemont (C of I) Church

36. J C Innes, of the Ordnance Survey, wrote in 1833 "Charlemont church, situated at the south end of Charlemont in the townland of Corr and Dunavally, is a neat stone building, roughcast and slated, corniced with whinstone, having 2 minarets on the porch and a small erection of masonry for a bell, but there is none in it at present ... Built in 1831", with which the datestone concurs. Samuel Lewis's informant did not entirely agree: he says "The church is a handsome structure, resembling in front one of the grand altars of York Minster; it was built and consecrated in 1833, by His Grace the Lord Primate, and contains a handsome monument to the late Mrs Jackson". The Parliamentary Gazetteer takes a third view: "The church was built in 1832, by means of £300 raised in various ways within the parish, and of £900 gifted by the late Board of First Fruits". Built at the instance of the Rev Silver Oliver of Loughgall to provide a suitable place of worship for the Protestant soldiery in Charlemont Fort close by. The judicious Canon Leslie simply says "Charlemont was constituted a Perpetual Curacy out of Loughgall parish on February 12, 1830. William Lord Charlemont

conveyed on Aug 13, 1830, 2 roods as a site for the church which was built soon after and consecrated on Mar 19, 1833, by the Primate ... It was altered and improved in 1862".

Certainly it has the look of a Board of First Fruits church, and so is very likely by William Farrell. It is interesting to compare it with Armaghbreague (37) to which it bears a considerable resemblance. But whereas Armaghbreague's bell-cote has just one pinnacle, like a unicorn, Charlemont has two set side by side; and in consequence, irresistibly reminds the viewer of a rabbit.

Unhappily, no longer in use: the church figures in the UAHS list of buildings at risk.

Photograph: Michael O'Connell.
Situation: In Charlemont village; td, Corr and Dunavally; Parish, Charlemont; District Council, Armagh; Grid ref. J 854 554.
References: Listed B (15/1/32). Datestone, 1831; J C Innes, OSM, 1833, Armagh, I, p 76; Lewis, TD, I, p 323; PG, 1845, I, p 388; Leslie, 'Armagh clergy', 1911, p 173; UAHS, 'Buildings at risk', VI, 1999, p 50.

Armaghbreague (C of I) Church

37 (left). A pretty little rustic church, consecrated in 1831, and attributed by the listers to William Farrell. Samuel Lewis says "The church, situated on the summit of one of the Fews mountains, is a small neat edifice, in the early English style; it was built in 1831, at an expense of £600, a gift from the late Board of First Fruits". Richard Oram's notes, in MBR, say "Standard design by William Farrell for Board of First Fruits. Many churches like this were built but few have survived in so pure a form".

The church stands in an attractive small graveyard with yew trees (and, alas, some more intrusive conifers). The entrance gates are flanked by a quadrant wall of weathered stone. It has a funny little pinnacle on top of its bell-cote,

instead of spire or steeple. The side wall facing the road is of random Armagh marble, the other walls are faced in a reddish Roman cement, except for the cutstone angled buttresses, quoins, and trim. Three pairs of pointed lattice windows face the road, two on the far side, and a colourful east window.

Photograph: Michael O'Connell.
Situation: Close to Armaghbreague cross-roads; td, and Parish, Armaghbreague; District Council, Armagh; Grid ref. H 894 305.
References: Listed B1 (15/8/30A; boundary wall, 15/8/30B). Datestone, 1829; Lewis, TD, 1837, I, p 75; Donaldson, 'Upper Fews, 1838', 1923, p 86; Leslie, 'Armagh clergy', 1911, p 120; R Oram, notes in MBR.

St Luke's (C of I) Church, Mullaghglass

38. A delightful little church of 1833, at some distance from the main road, set amidst trees in the rolling countryside north of Newry. Very unusual, too, in its layout and design; absolutely unspoiled; cruciform within a square; no tower, no spire, no belfry: just bell and wheel; prickly pinnacles, angled buttresses; and a charming curly overthrow at the gate. According to Lewis, the parish of Killevy had, prior to 1773, four churches, situated at Cloghinny, Camlough, Meigh and Drumbanagher. "The church at Drumbanagher was used as the parochial church till 1832, when one was built at Cloughinny, by a grant of £2,000 from the late Board of First Fruits: it is a spacious cruciform structure, in the later English style". Canon Leslie, however, says that "the church was ... consecrated on October 23rd 1833 as the parish church of Killevy, and dedicated to St Luke. It is known as the parish church of Mullaglass since 1870".

The Board was wound up in 1833, when its functions were transferred to the Ecclesiastical Commissioners. The Board's last architect for the province of Armagh was William Farrell, to whom the listers attribute this church: and they may well be right; but to me, it does not look much like his work: perhaps rather by Joseph Welland, whose son undertook so much church-building later in the century? However that may be, I entirely agree with the listers who describe it as "an excellent example of Gothic Revival, elaborately detailed, in a prominent rural setting".

Externally, it has the appearance of a treble-cube, with eight tall, slim, pinnacles, each adorned with a carved fleur-de-lys, at the corners. The walls are of rubble-stone, with dressed trim. There are five tall slim pointed windows in each side wall, the outer four latticed, the central window on each side with stained glass. The east window is original, a delightful geometrical lattice composition of diamonds of red, blue and clear glass. There are especially pretty geometrically-glazed circular windows at each side of the porch.

Internally, the roof is carried on very tall white-painted wooden clustered columns; the ceiling is pale blue, the carpet is red, the pews are grained, everything is simple, seemly, and almost exactly as it must have been 166 years ago. A real gem.

Photograph: Michael O'Connell (see also colour-plate VIa).

Situation: At Cloghinny, off the road from Markethill to Newry; td, and Parish, Mullaghglass; District Council, Newry & Mourne; Grid ref. J 054 317.

References: Listed B+ (16/21/12). Datestone, 1833; Lewis, TD, 1837, II, p 145; Leslie, 'Armagh clergy', 1911, p 387; Craig, 'Architecture of Ireland', 1982, p 288.

St Patrick's (C of I) Cathedral, Armagh

39. At the heart and apex of the little old city of Armagh, the Protestant cathedral stands on its splendidly prominent hill-top site, the hill of sally-trees. Here in 445 AD, a century before St Augustine came to Canterbury, St Patrick established, within the ramparts of an earlier hill-fort, the church which he decreed should be pre-eminent over all other churches in Ireland. Armagh was raided very many times by the Vikings (and others); it is said that 26 burnings and plunderings are recorded between 670 and 1642. Like many another Irish church, it was both fortified, and fired, in the course of the 17th century. The present building may incorporate some stones of the successive churches on the site: at least the crypt seems to date from the rebuilding of Archbishop O'Scannail of 1270; and the tracery in the aisle windows is probably that inserted by Archbishop Hampton in 1613. Part of the ceiling in the nave, though not that of the chancel, appears to be the work of Thomas Cooley in 1765.

Archbishop Simms, in his essay on the cathedral in the UAHS The Buildings of Armagh, quotes from a letter (whereabouts unspecified) written by Francis Johnston in 1823, looking back on the problems of his earlier years: "Having spent I may say some years in and out of the old Fabrick, I am almost acquainted with every stone of it, and am very sorry to add that it is a dangerous subject to attempt any considerable improvement upon. The Lord Primate Robinson fitted up the west aisle for the morning service about fifty years ago and made other repairs and improvements to the Church and no alteration, no, not

even a brush of paint has, I believe been used (at least in the west aisle) since that time ... A very superb steeple was designed by Mr Cooley from that of Magdalen College, Oxford, and was carried up under my superintendence about seventy feet above the roof of the Church, when the piers and arches supporting it were perceived to be giving way and the Primate immediately ordered it to be taken down" (in 1783). Nothing of Cooley's steeple appears to be now visible, except, possibly, the lowerworks of the present square tower upon which Johnston proceeded to superimpose a much more modest and less weighty bell chamber and spire (the latter since removed): "this eminent and ingenious architect erected a tower upon the cathedral arches, furnished with a light and graceful spire, the ball of which is 150 feet from the ground" (Wright), but "which, from a fear of overpowering the foundation, was necessarily curtailed in its proportion" (Lewis).

The cathedral today - whilst, as the UAHS listers say, "there is every reason to believe that the general format is still the work of O'Scannail, incorporating the earlier work of St Patrick" - is in fact almost entirely the creation of Lewis Cottingham, brought in from England in 1834 by Archbishop Beresford when the structure had fallen into a lamentable state of dilapidation.

Cottingham, in that year aged 47, was a specialist in church restoration. In the previous year, he had undertaken a major commission at St Alban's; and on that precedent he based many features of his work at Armagh - the choir screen; the choir windows; the altar and reredos, amongst others. Colvin considers that "Cottingham's careful restorations of buildings that were often in a serious state of decay were more respectful of the surviving medieval fabric than the more doctrinaire restorations of later Gothic Revivalists ... at Hereford, Armagh and the Norman gateway at Bury St Edmunds he showed considerable technical skill in dealing with formidable structural problems."

Samuel Lewis's contemporary account is interesting. "Primate Beresford, on his translation to the see, employed Mr Cottingham, architect, of London, and the restorer of the abbey of St Alban's, to survey the cathedral with a view to its perfect restoration, and the report being favourable, the undertaking, towards which his Grace subscribed £8,000, was commenced under that gentleman's superintendence in 1834." (In the end, the restoration was to cost £34,000, of which Archbishop Beresford

contributed £24,000 out of his own pocket). "The piers of the tower have been removed and replaced by others resting upon a more solid foundation, in the execution of which the whole weight of the tower was sustained without the slightest crack or settlement, till the new work was brought into contact with the old, by a skilful and ingenious contrivance of which a model has been preserved. The prevailing character of the architecture is the early English style, with portions of the later Norman, and many of the details are rich and elegant, though long obscured and concealed by injudicious management in repairing the building, and, when the present work now in progress is completed, will add much to the beauty of this venerable and interesting structure. The series of elegantly clustered columns separating the aisles from the nave, which had declined from the perpendicular and will be restored to their original position, was concealed by a rude encasement, with a view to strengthen them; and many of

the corbels, enriched with emblematical sculpture, were covered with thick coats of plaister ..."

That is the positive view. The negative view is rather different. In August, 1838, a somewhat bilious George Petrie wrote to Lt Larcom of the Ordnance Survey: "The cathedral here is nearly finished - I mean its re-edification. I had heard so much in praise of this work of Cottingham's - an English architect of high character - that I expected too much, and consequently suffered a disappointment. The restorer of the cathedral of Armagh should be an Irish historical architect and antiquary. This Mr Cottingham is not; and in consequence he has destroyed the associations which the antiquity of the building did, and should still, excite, by making it a regular English parish church of Tudor architecture, the only style it is probable with which he is acquainted. Even the material - English sandstone - has an English look ... The screen is indeed beautiful in its way, but it is a way we never had in Ireland". (The screen was subsequently taken down in 1888).

And a few years after Petrie, in 1843, Thackeray commented: "The cathedral is quite too complete. It is of the twelfth century, but not the least venerable. It is neat and trim as a lady's drawing room. It wants a hundred years at least to cool the raw colour of the stones, and to dull the brightness of the gilding". The judicious compilers of the Parliamentary Gazetteer, published in 1845, take a middle view: "The pile, though not for a moment to be compared with most of the stately and richly ornate cathedrals of England, is a passable specimen of the later pointed style of architecture. It is cruciform; and measures 119 feet in the clear from end to end of the transepts, and 183 feet from east to west, or along the choir and the nave. A square tower, whose battlement is 31 feet above the roof, and 110 above the ground, rises from the intersection of nave and transepts; and is surmounted by a spire of 40 feet in height".

In 1906, that excellent writer Stephen Gwynn wrote: "Climb the hill to the cathedral, which looms up square and solid over you as you pace the Mall between ranged and respectable elm trees. The cathedral is a little respectable too, and a little squat; but for all that, massive and dignified. The interior is, to my mind, exactly what a cathedral of the Irish Protestant church should be. Nothing is older than the Boyne; all severe, clear, cold, frugal almost to the point of stinginess in ornament, yet with a creditable attempt here and there in details to keep up the tradition of Irish art".

The most recent critic, Galloway, tends to agree with Thackeray: "the interior, certainly very fine, is perhaps at first a little disappointing. Something is lacking and it is probably a sense of antiquity as Thackeray suggests". But: "Cottingham's work may be alien to Armagh, but is antiquarian in inspiration. He bridges the gap between Strawberry Hill Gothick and the romantic revival ... His restoration represents an old-fashioned pre-Tractarian High Church tradition that has an integrity of its own".

In 1903 the chancel walls were heightened and faced in stone, and the arches of the crossing were raised; in 1913 the present altar and reredos were installed, though the reredos behind them in the Lady Chapel is attributed to Cottingham; in 1950 the Regimental Chapel of the Royal Irish Fusiliers was dedicated in the south transept.

The most impressive external aspect of the cathedral is the view of it from the outskirts of the city, where the fine square tower, with its Irish corner crenellations, dominates all around it. As the compilers of the Parliamentary Gazetteer correctly remark, "the proportion between the height

of the roof and that of the tower seems defective to a spectator at the base of the hill, but appears quite symmetrical when the edifice is seen from a remoter distance"; adding, a little gratuitously, "and the disproportionate elevation of the spire was occasioned by the obstinacy of the architect whom Archbishop Robinson employed to construct it". The various walled areas of greenery around the cathedral are somewhat wasted. It is disappointing that the cathedral clergy do not worthily maintain the excellent scheme prepared by that very great landscape architect, Sir Geoffrey Jellicoe, at the instance of the late John Lewis-Crosby.

The most attractive feature of the interior is its remarkable collection of monumental sculptures. These include an Iron Age pagan idol, fragments of the 11th-century High Cross which used to stand in Market Street, and a slab commemorating the burial here of King Brian Boru after his death at the battle of Clontarf. (Petrie, writing in 1832 in the Dublin Penny Journal, airily remarks "here were interred the heroes of Clontarf - the venerable Brian, and his son Murchard, and his nephew Conan, and his friend Methlin Prince of the Decies of Waterford - here their bodies, which had been conveyed thither by the Clergy, lay in funeral state for twelve successive nights, during which psalms, hymns, and prayers were chaunted for their souls; and well did they merit those pious honors".

There is also a splendid series of Caulfeild-Charlemont memorials, the earliest dating from 1698, in the chapter-room in the north transept, and many 18th- and 19th-century memorials. Of these last, the best are Roubiliac's statue of Sir Thomas Molyneux, which Potterton considers "the most exquisite piece of post-Renaissance carving to be found in Ireland" (see page 261); Rysbrack's recumbent figure of Dean Drelincourt, described by Stuart as "an exquisite piece of workmanship, perfected by the hand of taste"; and the bust of Archbishop Robinson. Potterton

says of this "Although the memorial is signed "Bacon Sculptor, London, 1802", for some reason it is reputed to be by Nollekens": the UAHS listers appear to prefer Nollekens; the display inside the cathedral tactfully suggests that the bust is by Nollekens, the rest of the monument by Bacon; a diplomatic compromise? Maybe the answer is to be found in Rogers: "the sculptor, Bacon, must have forgotten that the name of "Nollekens, 1776" is chiselled on the bust" - but I have been unable to verify this. The kneeling Archbishop Stuart, by Sir Francis Chantrey, was singled out for special praise by Thackeray; and the Sebastopol memorial to Lt Kidd RN, of HMS Albion, a member of the naval brigade, is by Thomas Farrell.

The way in which the clerestory windows are inset into the spandrels of the nave arches is highly disconcerting, (though, as Gordon Wheeler has pointed out to me, not unique: the original clerestory windows in the 13th-century shell of the present Down Cathedral were in the same position). Yet the interior of the cathedral does have a certain dignified consistency, as well as one of the best collections of sculpture in Ireland.

Photographs: Michael O'Connell; before removal of Cottingham's screen and raising of the crossing, Robert French, NLI, WL R287; Wood-engraving: DPJ, I, 1832-3, p186.

Situation: On Cathedral Hill; td, Corporation; Parish and District Council, Armagh; Grid ref. H 874 452.

References: Listed A (15/20/1); in conservation area. Drawings 75,76,76a in RIAI Murray Collection, IAA; G Petrie, in DPJ, 8 December 1832, p 186; Wright, 'Scenes in Ireland' 1834, p 232; Lewis, TD, 1837, I, p 73; PG, I, 1845, p 79; Stokes, 'Life of G Petrie', 1868, p 123; Rogers, 'Memoir', 1876, p 40; Gwynn, 'Fair hills of Ireland', 1906, p 123; Potterton, 'Irish church monuments', UAHS, 1975, pp 35, 40, 44, 75, 76; B Goslin, unpublished Catalogue of the Murray Collection in IAA, 1990, p 60; Guidebook, 1991, passim; 'Buildings of Armagh', UAHS, 1992, pp 1-4, 57-63, and see detailed bibliography on the latter page; Galloway, 'Cathedrals of Ireland', 1992, p 13.

St Saviour's (C of I) Church, Battlehill (or Bottlehill), Portadown

40. A pleasing, if rather ordinary, blackstone church of 1856 (datestone in the porch) with chiselled limestone trim; good ogee-headed windows, for the most part paired, with lattice panes. The octagonal limestone steeple and spire, with a carved cauliflower sprouting from each gablet, are charming, and provide a delightful eyecatcher for the passer-by on the road between Armagh and Portadown. "The builder was Mr. Richard Cherry of Loughgall. Local tradition states that the architect was a Mr. Fulton who came out frequently from Armagh whilst the work was in progress, presumably William Fulton of Palace Row, Armagh. Consecrated 8th April 1858" (Paterson). However, one wonders if the steeple and spire, in a different stone and looking as if by another hand, were not added later to the designs of a more sophisticated architect, conceivably even Charles Lanyon, with whose work it has something in common.

In 1838, J Heming Tait of the Ordnance Survey firmly wrote down "Bottlehill: so pronounced"; but Paterson says that "local people state that the proper name is Battlehill ... a portion of Cromwell's army escaped there for a period during which they completed the destruction of Mulladry Castle". Leslie says "St. Saviour's was originally a District Curacy in the parish of Kilmore. It was erected into an Incumbency in 1871, when 6 townlands of Kilmore and its offshoot parishes of Mullavilly and Richhill - viz, Clanroot, Derryhale, Battlehill, Mulladry, Ballinteggart and Drumnahuncheon - were constituted the parish".

Photograph: Michael O'Connell.
Situation: Vicarage Road, Battlehill; td, Mulladry; Parish, Kilmore; District Council, Armagh; Grid ref. H 975 508.
References: Not listed. J H Tait, OSM, 1838, Armagh, I, p 68; T G F Paterson, Armachiana, X, p 91, in Armagh County Museum; Leslie, 'Armagh clergy', 1911, p 406; SARC outings journal, II, 1929, p 104, in Armagh County Museum; 'St Saviour's centenary year book,' 1958, passim.

St Luke's (C of I) Church, Ballymoyer

41. Although it bears a datestone announcing "This church was erected Anno Domini 1821", and Canon Leslie reports its consecration in 1822, in outward appearance it is a striking and unusual example of exotic mid-Victorian architecture. Lewis describes it as "a large and handsome edifice with a lofty square tower, built in 1822 by aid of a gift of £900 from the late Board of First Fruits". The listers say that the nave is of 1821, the chancel of 1855, and the porch of 1877; and that W J Barre was the architect of the chancel. Canon Leslie merely says that the church was "enlarged" in 1865. But it seems that this was almost a complete rebuilding: on its reconsecration in 1865, the Irish Ecclesiastical Gazette reported - "we say the new church, although it stands on the old foundation. The original walls have been externally recased, and new windows introduced, with the addition of a chancel and vestry, the style being Middle Pointed. The roof is open-timbered, with coupled trusses, carved and braced, the pitch being equilateral. The nave is fitted with open seats, and paved with black and red tiles; the chancel, which is 19 feet deep, is divided by a wrought iron scrolled rail, and paved with encaustic tiles of a most beautiful and appropriate design. The reredos of Dungannon stone, supported by pillars of Connemara marble, with richly carved capitals, has medallions containing sacred emblems in bold relief. A double arch on the south side of the chancel gives entrance to the vestry ...The architect is W. J. Barre, Esq, of Belfast. And the whole expense (with the exceptions specified) has been borne by Marcus Synnott, Esq". It is satisfactory to note that, after the consecration, the

Archbishop and assembled clergy "adjourned to Ballymoyer House, where a splendid déjeuner had been prepared". The exotic guest-list included Mrs Guillemard; Lady Mary King; Baroness von Steiglitz and Miss Cavognari; and, last but one, W J Barre, Esq, Belfast (Ulster Gazette).

The Dublin Builder, in 1863, had already reported the intention to proceed with " a complete restoration of the building, ... to be carried out under the direction of Mr Barre". And the diocesan records contain a plan, unsigned and undated, and the specifications of 1863 for "erecting chancel, robing room, and fuel store, and fitting out church with pews, pulpit, desk, communion rails, etc, as per plan"; but not the tower or baptistry. My guess is that most of the interior is the work of Barre. This opinion appears to be shared by Colin Hatrick, who writes "The church is a good unaltered example of the work of W J Barre", and draws attention to the quality of Hardman's stained-glass windows (but fails to notice the, to my mind, even finer font).

However, the position is greatly complicated by contract drawings in Dublin, dated 1867, and signed by Welland & Gillespie, marked "Newtownhamilton" (but evidently in fact Ballymoyer, only a few miles away) showing the west elevation and a very strange tower with its gabled summit, pretty well as built but turned sideways: and with a "Note. The upper part of Tower referred to in last paragraph of specification is not included in the contract". According to the present rector, the upper part of the tower was built in its present form at the same time that the base of the tower was altered by Marcus Synnott's widow, and in his memory; so, certainly after Barre's death, after a two-year illness, in 1867.

And it is still further complicated by the fact that the ground floor of the tower is fitted up as a baptistry, the tremendous font being convincingly attributed both by the Dublin Builder and by the Irish Ecclesiastical Gazette in 1865 to William Butterfield, no less, and having been contributed by the Rev. Garrett Wall, rector from 1849 until September 1866, in memory of his son of the same name who died aged 11 in 1863. The baptistry walls are lined with reddish, patterned, encaustic tiles; the octagonal basin of the font is carried on eight marble columns and, typically of Butterfield's taste for polychromy, is composed of yellow, black, pink, blue-grey, white, and red marble, reading from the base upwards. Moreover, it is surmounted by an astonishing great iron cover, painted black with gilded knobs, like an ornate mini-dome, borne on self-balancing counter-weighted chains rising high into the tower above.

Finally, to complicate matters even further, a plaque in the side wall of the baptistry says that his widow dedicates the baptistry and porch in memory of Marcus Synnott "who built the chancel and beautified the nave" and died at Brighton in October 1874. The font appears not to have been known to Paul Thompson, despite the fact that in his magisterial book on Butterfield he devotes a lengthy section to his fonts - "Always of stone, free-standing, raised on a pedestal, it is in fact by definition a pure piece of architectural sculpture. Butterfield's fonts reveal in fascinating sequence his attitude to line and volume". This is an interesting discovery, for it had been generally believed that St Mark's, Dundela was Butterfield's only surviving work in Ulster - Hugh Dixon tells me that he had provided designs for Lambeg parish church, all now swept away. It is possibly significant that Butterfield had been on friendly terms with John Hardman, author of the glass in Ballymoyer, though it appears that by 1865 the two men had fallen out (over the style of the windows in Rugby school chapel, at which I stared for so many hours as a schoolboy). But it is

still surprising that the rector of a very remote Irish parish should order so elaborate a memorial to his son from the most distinguished English ecclesiologist of the day.

The furnishings of the church are pretty much in their original state, though there is a strange, later, rood-screen incorporating what appear to be Masonic symbols. Altogether, with the astounding concatenation of work by Barre, Welland & Gillespie, and Butterfield, this is the high peak of Victorian ecclesiastical architecture in the county.

According to Leslie, the parish is named for the Mac Moyer family, hereditary keepers of the Book of Armagh, of whom the last, Florence Mac Moyer, a Franciscan monk, is buried here: he "pawned the book for £5 to enable him to go to London to give evidence against the R. C. Archbishop Oliver Plunkett in 1680".

Also in the churchyard are the ivy-clad ruins of the earlier church, built in the reign of Charles the First. It has heavy round-headed windows, and is a rare relic of its period; interesting but unfortunately, close

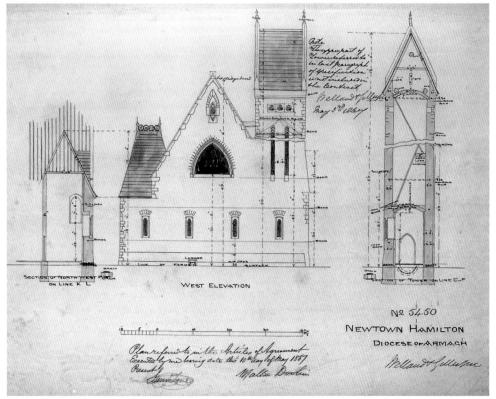

WEST ELEVATION

Nᵒ 5450
NEWTOWN HAMILTON
DIOCESE OF ARMAGH

inspection is not advisable, as it is of doubtful stability. In 1837, Lewis reported "The walls of the original church were erected in the reign of Charles I, but the clergyman appointed having been murdered, it remained unroofed until 1775, when Primate Robinson caused the work to be finished ... The remains of the former church, with the exception of the roof, are in good condition, and form a picturesque and interesting object".

Photographs: Michael O'Connell (see also colour-plate VIII). Drawings: RCB.
Situation: Ballymoyer Road, Glenanne; td, Whitecross; Parish, Bally-moyer; District Council, Newry & Mourne; Grid ref. H 964 307.
References: Listed B (16/20/4). Lewis, TD, 1837, I, p 154; drawings of 1845, 1864 and 1867, portfolio 2A in RCB; DB, V, 1863, p 197, and VII, 1865, p 144; 'Ulster Gazette', 17/6/1865; 'Irish Ecclesiastical Gazette', 17/6/1865; undated specifications and plan in DIO 4/32/8/9/5/5, in PRONI; Leslie, 'Armagh clergy', 1911, p 141; Thompson, 'William Butterfield', 1971, pp 290 , 464; H C Hatrick, notes in MBR; information from Rev. C F Moore, and from Hugh Dixon.

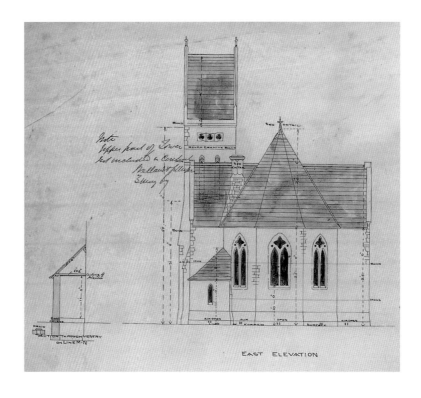

EAST ELEVATION

Scotch (Presbyterian) Church, Armagh

42. Despite bearing the date 1837 on its face, this church was opened for worship on 11 February 1840 by Dr Henry Cooke, no less, having cost £2500: the debt had been cleared by 1845. The gallery, with its intricately-patterned front, was inserted in 1849. This congregation sprang from a split in 1837 within the First Congregation: but the history of Presbyterianism in Armagh is exceptionally confused and confusing. Notwithstanding the proximity of the First Presbyterian church (51) just along the Mall, but formerly in Abbey Street, the Scotch Church has always been generally referred to as "the Mall Congregation."

"When the building was erected, it was a plain building without a gallery and devoid of much of the decoration it has today. Its façade has not changed much. It has a complex classical front with triangular pediment, full height pilasters and raking Greek window frames in the end bays of the first floor. Along with the date of the erection of the Congregation, MDCCCXXXVII, its front bears the words "Scotch Church" - an indication of the congregation's theological orthodoxy" (Lockington). "An excellent three-bay ashlar limestone building. Ionic pilasters support a full cornice and frieze, the centre bay breaking forward with paired pilasters and pediment over. In the frieze there is a very fine stone inscription "SCOTCH CHURCH MDCCCXXXVII". The ground floor has rusticated stonework around the segmental headed recessed windows and first floor windows have Egyptian lugged architraves. The doorway has double scroll brackets

supporting a shallow cornice and tall double doors each with twelve panels. Good steps and low panelled walls with original railings and lamp standards" (UAHS listers). "Simple Palladian façade of 1837 that does not quite live up to the monumentality of its gate piers" (Williams, in uncharitable mood). "A complex classical front with triangular pediment, full-height pilasters, and other careful details such as the raking Greek window frames in the end bays of the first floor" (Dixon).

The UAHS listers say "Architect possibly William Murray" but to my eye its rather shallow classicism looks more like the work of Thomas Duff (who was working on the Roman Catholic cathedral at just this time) or his partner, Thomas Jackson: (compare the illustrations on pages 55 and 56 of Hugh Dixon's excellent Introduction to Ulster Architecture). But I stand open to correction: I have been unable to discover any relevant records. The adjoining five-storey stone warehouse was acquired by the congregation and well restored, to provide church hall and offices, in 1992.

Photograph: Michael O'Connell.
Situation: The Mall West., Armagh; td, Parkmore; Parish, and District Council, Armagh; Grid ref. H 877 453.
References: Listed B+ (15/17/22); in conservation area. Bassett, 'Armagh', 1888, p 95; Lockington, 'Mall Presbyterian Church', 1987, p 10 and passim; Dixon, 'Introduction', UAHS, 1975, p 55; 'Buildings of Armagh', UAHS, 1992, p 150; Williams, 'Architecture in Ireland', 1994, p 12.

Former and present Methodist Churches, Portadown

43, 44. "Portadown is the great stronghold of Methodism in the County Armagh" (Bassett). Most unusually, the old church and manse are still standing, more or less unspoiled, at 26 and 28 Thomas Street, while the new church and manse of 1860 were built further down the same street, but on the opposite side. It seems most convenient to treat of both together.

In 1837, "The Wesleyan chapel ... is a neat whinstone building corniced with freestone. It is sixty and a half feet long and forty and a half feet broad, having two minarets in front and a portico projecting 18 inches. It was built in 1832 and cost 1,000 pounds, of which sum the late Mr John Johnson of Lurgan gave 150 pounds and the rest was raised by public subscription. There is accommodation for 700 persons and the general attendance is 400. The interior is neat, having instead of pews, benches with rails across the back. There is a gallery at the east end. On the wall at the right hand side is a monument with the following inscription: 'As a memorial of undying affection the trustees of this chapel have erected this tablet to perpetuate a grateful recollection of their late friend and brother Thomas Shillington who exchanges mortality for life, 15th April 1830, aged 63. he was the nursing father of methodism in this town and neighbourhood for nearly 40 years. An epistle of Christ known and read of all men.' " (OSM). "It was a plain but commodious structure. In the basement storey was a large school-room, and at one side a house in which the superintendent minister resided ... The old chapel and minister's residence are offered for sale by public auction on Monday 23rd January 1861 ... They are spacious and substantial and capable of being converted at a comparatively trifling expense into a manufacturing

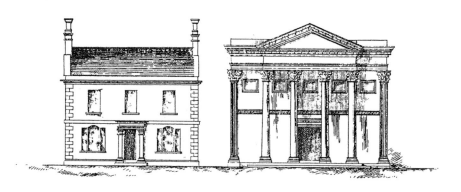

Front Elevations of Manse and Chapel towards Thomas Street

or commercial establishment" (Green). And so they were: now, and for many years past, occupied by A & D Thornton Ltd, Wholesale Merchants, and hardly at all spoiled by commercialisation, at least from outside. With its datestone, its little pinnacles, its copious quoins, and its Gothick-glazed upper windows, the church is a delightful building; its neighbour, the former manse, is a narrow two-bay three-storey house (unusually) of mellow red bricks, freestone quoins, a pretty fanlight, and Georgian glazing.

The replacement church "is in Thomas Street. It is a spacious edifice, and has a handsome portico, supported by four great pillars with Corinthian capitals. In the interior a gallery resting on thirteen ornamental pillars runs all round. The front is tastefully ornamented, the pulpit is mahogany, and the Communion rails of the same wood ... erected in 1860, and with the school-house attached, and minister's residence, cost about £5,000 ... In March, 1858, after the old building had been found defective in

several of the requirements, the next step was to appoint an architect and Mr. Boyd, Belfast, was chosen" (Bassett). Was this the same Mr Boyd who may have worked on First Lurgan Presbyterian Church (46) a year or so earlier? The first service in the new church was held on 1 October 1860.

An agreeable pleasant stucco classical facade, with a blackstone side elevation round the corner. The portico is a bit too tall for its width; there are four Corinthian columns, two pilasters responding to the outer columns, and two pilasters at the corners of the front wall. The stringcourse incorporates a Vitruvian scroll. All nicely painted and in good order; fine railings.

Photographs: Michael O'Connell. Drawings: from Green, between pp 36 and 37.
Situation: 26-28, and 33-37, Thomas Street, Portadown; td, Tavanagh; Parish, Drumcree; District Council, Craigavon; Grid ref. H 011 536.
References: Listed B (14/14/10), and B+ (14/14/13). McIlroy & Innes, OSM, Armagh, I, 1837, p 29; Bassett, 'Armagh', 1888, p 287; Green, 'Methodism in Portadown', 1960, p 47; Oram, 'Craigavon', UAHS, 1971, pt I, p 3.

Side Elevation of Chapel, and Front of School towards New Street

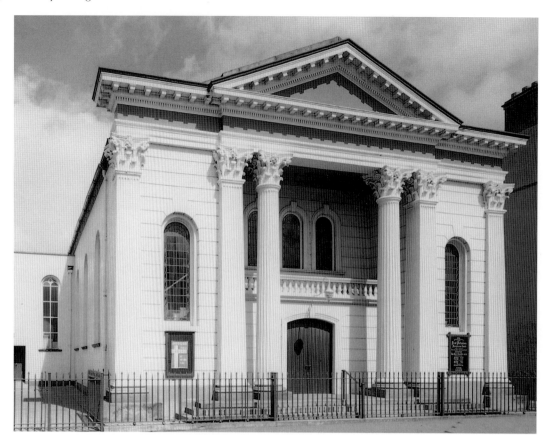

First Presbyterian Church, Portadown

45. Although the plaques outside this rather grand stucco classical church bear the dates 1822 and 1891, the façade in fact dates from 1858, in which year it was described as "a building extremely well planned, graceful and perfect in symmetry". The recessed portico comprises a pediment carried on two fluted columns and four fluted pilasters, in antis, with Corinthian capitals. The rusticated stucco is rather oddly painted in cream, white, and burnt Siena, but looks on the whole very well. As with many churches of this type, the classicism does not turn the corners. "Handsome interior; gallery faced with charming iron grille with shamrocks, on cast iron columns with crude floral capitals. Good deal box-pews; geometrical window astragals" (Oram).

It was in December 1856 that a resolution was passed "That this congregation put itself in a position to build a new House": the opening service took place on 29th August 1858. Gallery added 1875-81; rebuilt and enlarged, Young & Mackenzie, 1882. The extension of 1891 was onto the site of the old school-house at the rear. "The architect" (unfortunately unnamed) "took advantage of this encroachment to effect a complete renovation", including the addition of two large transepts, lecture hall, and vestry. It is extremely difficult to establish which parts of the present building are of which dates: but it does seem that the finest element, the façade, is of 1858.

Photograph: Michael O'Connell (see also colour-plate Vc).
Situation: Bridge Street, Portadown; td, Edenderry; Parish, Seagoe; District Council, Craigavon; Grid ref . H 014 542.
References: Listed B (14/12/12). Clow, 'Centenary book of First Presbyterian Church, Portadown', 1922; 'Century for Christ', 1958; Oram, 'Craigavon', UAHS, 1971, pt I, p 3.

First Presbyterian Church, Lurgan

46. "A structure of considerable dignity, with a handsome portico. The interior is spacious, and tastefully appointed" says Bassett. This is one of the, quite rare, examples of the late classical style in the county; it makes one of the most important statements of architectural significance in the town. Yet, the anonymous historian of the congregation, though conscious of its character, seems never to have cared enough to record the name either of architect or builder, and even the date remains uncertain.

The congregation, one of the earliest in Ulster, goes back to 1684. The first church on the present site, acquired in 1825, was certainly built in 1828: McIlroy, in 1837, says "It is a large stone building ... built in 1828 and cost £2,200, defrayed by subscriptions. The inside is handsomely fitted up. The gallery is large, in front of which there is a good clock. There is a handsome lustre suspended from the centre of the ceiling. The accommodation for 1,000 persons, the general attendance is 500 ... The congregation is 3,000. It has increased treble since the appointment of the present minister, the Rev. Hamilton Dobbin, in 1801." In 1829 the General Synod was held here when "Dr. Cooke and Dr. Montgomery of Dunmurry ... met in an unfortunate and acrimonious debate over the Arian controversy".

The galleted blackstone side walls of the hall, with their granite surrounds to the windows, look as if they date from 1828. The classical façade, and the eminently Victorian interior, "lavishly fitted out with pitch pine seating and panelling" can be dated to 1859-60. "During the ministry of Rev. Lowry Berkeley" (1858-78) "the congregation so greatly increased in numbersd that enlargement of the church building was necessary" ... "the front elevation, however, still retains some of the features of Regency style architecture ... a style which reflects the conservative character of the Lurgan Presbyterians of nearly a century and a half ago" (Outline history). The Ordnance Survey map of 1859 appears to show the building as enlarged.

It is clearly not the work of a fairly sophisticated designer: the classical trimmings are applied in an amateurish, if pleasing, manner. The four tall Doric columns are irregularly spaced. The pediment they carry is too tall for its width; it incorporates the burning bush of Presbyterianism in the tympanum. The central doorcase below is framed by console brackets carrying an even more ill-proportioned pediment, with only a flagpole-holder in its tympanum. The whole façade is of nicely-painted creamy stucco, with the ground floor rusticated. The front corners of the building are generously curved in a most unclassical way. In each storey there are five round-headed openings divided into circular window and twin narrow round-headed ones below. The church is set back from the street behind railings, and a modest but useful square of grass. Internally, the traditional porch contains twin curly staircases giving access to the galleries. These, spanning three sides of the hall, are carried on fluted columns painted white, but with their Ionic capitals very oddly painted brown.

Gordon Wheeler has pointed out to me the similarities between this church, and the Great Victoria Street Presbyterian Church in Belfast, which Larmour dates to 1860-1, illustrates, and tentatively attributes to John Boyd of Boyd and Batt.

Photograph: Michael O'Connell.
Situation: Between 60 and 62, High Street, Lurgan; td, Lurgan; Parish, Shankill; District Council, Craigavon; Grid ref. J 085 581.
References: Listed B (14/24/14). T McIlroy, OSM, 1837, Armagh, I, p 114, OS maps 1835, 1859; Bassett, 'Armagh', 1888, p 349; Outline history of First Lurgan congregation, 1966, passim; Oram, 'Craigavon', UAHS, 1971, pt II, p 8; Larmour, 'Belfast', 1987, p 23.

St Patrick's (R C) Cathedral, Armagh

47. This is a most curious example of a very important building which changes both architect, and architectural style, half way up the walls. The bottom half was designed in 1838, in the English Perpendicular Gothic style, by Thomas Duff of Newry; the top half designed in 1853, in the French Decorated Gothic style, by J J McCarthy of Dublin. And just to complicate matters, the interior décor, applied to the conflicting structures of these two architects, is in part to the 1904 designs of Ashlin & Coleman of Dublin, in part to the 1972 designs of McCormick, Tracey and Mullarkey of Londonderry. The result, unsurprisingly, is a disappointing muddle, quite lacking in the unity and integrity to be expected in a building of such importance (though Father Coleman, in 1900, surprisingly, thought that "the whole structure ... shows a striking unity of design"). Of course many other cathedrals have grown

THE CATHEDRAL AS ORIGINALLY DESIGNED BY MR. DUFF, ARCHITECT. NEWRY

and changed over long spans of years and changes of mastermind; but it makes an instructive contrast with its English counterpart, Westminster Cathedral, built to the designs of J F Bentley for Cardinal Vaughan between 1894 and 1903.

It is interesting that on 3 February, 1840, the Building Committee, "His Grace the Primate in the Chair, resolved unanimously that Mr. Duff be appointed our architect; and resolved, that Mr. Duff is to receive five per cent of the full amount expended on the building of the cathedral for his superintendence of the work, and that he will give the Committee one per cent as his subscription thereto". Galloway suggests that his success at the Roman Catholic cathedral of St Patrick and St Colman in Newry, dedicated in 1829, "probably led to the commission to design the cathedral at Armagh". Unlike his former partner, Thomas Jackson, Duff was himself a Roman Catholic. According to the 1905 Guide, in Duff's lifetime "34 feet of the walls were built for £26,000, Dr Crolly himself personally supervising the work with the assistance of several foremen".

The explanation for the original change of style is, that building was interrupted in 1844 by famine and cholera; Duff himself died in 1848; it was only in 1853 that a new Building Committee settled with his widow for £100 cash down, and the return of all drawings and papers relating to the commission. Work under the new architect did not actually begin until 1854. McCarthy had attacked Duff's work in the Irish Catholic Magazine in 1847, but he was

stuck with the ground-plan, as the walls had reached the tops of the aisle windows, but without tracery. "He completely changed the appearance of Duff's design by getting rid of the pinnacles on the buttresses, the battlemented parapets on nave and aisles, and by making the pitch of the roof steeper" (Sheehy); also by introducing flowing tracery and numerous carved details. Maurice Craig comments, dryly, "Characteristically, he altered the style from Perpendicular to Decorated, so that the spectator must support the absurdity of "fourteenth-century" works standing on top of "sixteenth-century" (except for the tracery which was harmonised); but in most ways it is a very successful building". It was dedicated in 1873.

The sacristy, synod hall, grand entrance, gates and sacristan's lodge were built later (Galloway says, sexton's lodge and gateway in 1887, sacristy and synod hall between 1894 and 1897), to the designs of William Hague, and he was "engaged on the designs for the great rood screen behind the high altar when he died in March, 1899. Mr. Hague's work was taken up by Mr. McNamara of Dublin who subsequently superintended the designing and building of the rood screen, the beautiful Celtic tracery of the mosaic passages and floors, and the complex heating and ventilating system". Further very extensive interior work was undertaken between 1900 and 1905 for Archbishop Logue to the designs of Ashlin & Coleman of Dublin. The cathedral was reconsecrated in 1903. A great deal of this excellent work has been removed.

St Patrick's cathedral, with its twin spires, stands tall on

THE CATHEDRAL AS FINISHED BY MR. J. J. M'CARTHY ARCHITECT, DUBLIN.

its hill-top, successfully out-soaring its squatter Protestant rival on the opposite hill. It looks its best from a distance, approached over the drumlin country to south and west, reminiscent, when the light is right, of the twin spires of Chartres dominating the rolling plain of the Ile de France. Stephen Gwynn wrote of it in 1906: "Today Ireland is full of churches, all of them built within a hundred years - and almost every church, let it be clearly understood, is crowded to the limit of its capacity with worshippers. But here at Armagh is the greatest monument of all - planted as if in defiance so as to dominate the country round and outface that older building on the lesser summit: the costliest church that has been erected within living memory in Ireland; and not that only. It is in good truth a monument not of generous wealth (like the two great cathedrals of Christ Church and St. Patrick's in Dublin) but of devoted poverty: the gift not of an individual but of a race, out of money won laboriously by the Catholic Irish at home and in the far ends of the world ... So viewed, I question whether modern Christianity can show anything more glorious: yet in other aspects the new St. Patrick's Cathedral must sadden the beholder. The stone of which it is hewn, as the money that paid for the hewing, is Irish: but the ideas which shaped the fabric are pure Italian..."

Externally, its best features are the twin broached spires, the great traceried seven-light west window, and the arcade with the eleven apostles above the central porch. Internally, its best feature is now the very high hammer-beam roof with a winged angel at each angle. Formerly, it was the marvellous lacy and frothy high altar,

screen pulpit and rails of white Caen stone, all the work of Ashlin & Coleman; but these were unhappily ripped out and simply discarded in the re-ordering after Vatican II: two of the beautifully-carved crockets stand on my window-ledge to this day, having been rescued from the dump by the late Kenneth Adams. This was justified at the time on the grounds that "the fine character of the interior was marred by the later introduction of screens, elaborate altar rails and pulpit": and what the architects set out to achieve was "a return to J J McCarthy's original concept ... They recommended a simplification of the interior, which would also add a greater formality to ceremony". If these were the objectives, few people think they have been successfully achieved. The new fittings already appear dated, and are utterly incongruous. "Neither the quality of the replacements nor the skill of the craftsmanship can disguise the total alienation of the new work from the spirit and meaning that was McCarthy's ecclesiological and architectural inspiration. In this setting, these modern intrusions appear dispassionate and irrelevant" (UAHS, 1992). Jeanne Sheehy acidly records "the replacement ... of a fine late Gothic revival chancel with chunks of granite and a tabernacle that looks like a microwave". It is hard to divine why the church in Ireland has proved to be so much more insensitive in such matters than in most other countries.

However, one must agree with Galloway's sympathetic summing up: "Ignoring the work at the crossing, which now has an empty feeling, this great cruciform cathedral has much beauty ... The great height, the exquisite perfection

of architectural detail, and the caring decoration of every surface of the walls ... uplifts the heart and mind ... although the building has a soaring loftiness, there is not a trace of gloom. This is Gothic Revival at its very best."

Photographs: Michael O'Connell (see also colour-plate VIb); the old high alter, IAA. Wood-engravings: from Gallogly.
Situation: Cathedral Road, Armagh; td, Corporation; Parish, and District Council, Armagh; Grid ref. H 873 457.
References: Listed A (15/20/20); in conservation area. Gallogly, 'History of St. Patrick's Cathedral', 1880, passim; Stuart, 'City of Armagh' (ed. Coleman), 1900, p 443; Guidebook, 1905, Appendix A; Gwynn, 'Fair hills of Ireland', 1906, p 118; Sheehy, 'J. J. McCarthy', UAHS, 1977, pp 39-42; Craig, 'Architecture of Ireland', 1982, p 294; O Fiaich, 'St Patrick's Cathedral', 1987, passim; 'Ulster architect', June/July 1990, p 58; 'Buildings of Armagh', UAHS, 1992, pp 70-76, and see the detailed bibliography on the latter page; Galloway, 'Cathedrals of Ireland', 1992, pp 17-20, 185.; J Sheehy, in 'Irish arts review', XIV, 1998, p 185; copy minutes of Building Committee, in MBR.

Gospel Hall, Glenanne

48. A pretty little wayside gospel hall of corrugated iron, beautifully painted, walls and roof blue-grey, wooden trim gleaming white: all spick and span. Three bays deep, plus porch at the front and store at the rear. Two conical ventilators on the roof-ridge. To the left of the porch, a placard announcing "The Wages of Sin Is Death", and to the right another, announcing "The Gift of God Is Eternal Life". Very neat and tidy little garden on one side, very neat and tidy little car-park on the other. It was built in 1923, by whom is not remembered.

Photograph: Michael O'Connell (see also colour-plate VIIb).
Situation: On the road from Markethill to Glenanne; td, Glenanne; parish, Loughgilly; District Council, Armagh; Grid ref. H 986 350.
References: Not listed. Information from Mr Walter McIlveen, Markethill.

49. As the listers say, "the church and priory form an important group": both by George Ashlin, of Ashlin & Coleman, architects, Dublin. The Dominicans came to Newry in 1870, started building soon after, and the work was completed and consecrated in 1882. Both buildings are set high on a steeply sloping site, above the road, and all the more impressive from their elevation, especially the very tall and soaring octagonal spire at the centre of the composition. To the right is the body of the church, of granite with yellowish sandstone trim. At the head of a high flight of steps, pointed doorways; above them the carved exhortation "Laudare, Benedicere, et Predicare", surmounted by a floppy-eared dog. It appears that Domini Canis - God's Dog - is the Latin rebus chosen by the Dominican order as its symbol or, so to speak, mascot.

In 1886, four years after its consecration, George Bassett wrote: "Of the Dominican Church, in Queen Street" (as it was then known) "justice requires it to be said that a more beautiful and symmetrical edifice is not to be found in Ireland. From its ornate and lofty tower to the least finished detail, it is a harmonious work. Three arched doorways opening from a broad platform, reached from the street by a flight of steps, are of Portland stone, the central one being particularly deep and richly ornamented. The nave is supported upon splendid pillars of polished granite, which rest upon white marble bases. The capitals, in Portland stone, are different in design, and support six arches at each side, over which are twelve clerestory windows ... The building of the church was begun in 1871; Mr. Ashland was the architect, and Mr. Peter Shane, clerk of works ... Since then the tower and spire have been erected by Mr. Jas McAdorey, builder, Dundalk, at a cost of £2,000. The Convent has also been added. The total amount expended on Church and convent thus far is about £16,000".

Internally, polished columns, with very strongly carved floral capitals, bear pointed arches: from the springers angels bear up colonettes on which stand statues of the saints. There is a very fine blue-and-white-patterned barrel-vault ceiling. Happily, the church has been much less altered than most, and retains its lacy white High Altar: there is also good carving in the pulpit and side altars. Altogether, a much more sympathetic composition than the later church by the same architect just up the road at Cloghogue (52).

St Catherine's (R C) Church and Priory, Newry

Photograph: Michael O'Connell.

Situation: Dominic Street, Newry; td, Ballynacraig; Parish, Newry; District Council, Newry & Mourne; Grid ref. J 081 260.

References: Listed B1 (16/29/1); Bassett, 'Down', 1886, p 98; centenary booklet, 1982.

St Peter's (R C) Church, Lurgan

Baron Lurgan, gave a site in North Street, upon which a handsome church was created and dedicated in 1833 ... and enlarged in 1885 so as to give accommodation for 2,500 worshippers". Oram says "1901, on site of earlier church of 1833, enlarged 1885". The Latin plaque inside the church suggests that the first stone of the new church was laid on 29 June 1867, chancel and transept built first, old church then demolished, nave and tower completed 1901, restored 1927. Which to believe? 1833? 1867? 1885? 1901? The plaque in the church gives the names of numerous ecclesiastics, but that of no architect and of no builder.

It seems that the original church on this site was indeed dedicated on 1 September 1833. By 1865, it had become too small for the increasing Catholic population, and the foundation stone for the present chancel and transepts, to designs by Ashlin & Coleman of Dublin, was laid on 29 June 1867; these "new additions" were dedicated on 27 June 1869. Sixteen years later the Very Rev. James O'Hare found another major extension necessary, and this time employed J J McDonnell, architect, of Belfast. Between them, they contrived an almost complete rebuilding, retaining only the transepts and sanctuary of 1869: "so skilfully, however, has this been embodied in the new building, and so harmoniously complete, as a whole, does the church appear, that few indeed would recognise in it a trace of the building of other days ... Space was found for only 1,200 people in the old church; in the new one as many as 1,900 can be conveniently accommodated ... Mr. McDonnell ... has exceeded all his previous efforts, which is saying a good deal for one who is responsible for so many beautiful churches throughout Ireland" (Lurgan Times, 1897). Work started almost immediately on the tower, which cost £10,000, and was dedicated in 1901. In 1922, the sanctuary was decorated in mosaic and a new High Altar was erected.

Internally, a very seemly, sober and traditional church, with no jarring modernisms, or incongruous bondieuserie either. The old High Altar has been kept; the new free-standing one is wholly in keeping; pews, confessional boxes and stations of the cross are all old-fashioned but pleasing. The high vaulted wooden ceiling, with clerestory below, is carried on grey polished marble columns interspersed with pointed arches. A refreshingly unspoiled church.

50. A large, tall, conventional late-Victorian church in the French Gothic style popular at that time, of squared black-stone with grey sandstone trim, and pink marble colonettes at the doorways. The very lofty slim octagonal spire, like the upper part of the tower, of pale stone, is the best exterior feature of this church, just as Welland & Gillespie's spire is the best feature of the Church of Ireland parish church: Lurgan is fortunate to have two such fine spires so close together.

The architectural history of the building is obscure and confusing. Bassett, in 1888, says "In 1829, Charles, 1st

Photograph: Michael O'Connell.
Situation: North Street, Lurgan; td, Derry; Parish, Shankill; District Council, Craigavon; Grid ref. J 081 588.
References: Listed B (14/20/1A). Bassett, 'Armagh', 1888, p 353; 'Lurgan Times', 30/6/1897; IB, XLIII, 1901, p 845; Oram, 'Craigavon', UAHS, 1971, pt I, p 8; Clendinning, 'Shankill', 1983, and in 'Lurgan Mail', 3/9/1987; H Dixon, notes in MBR.

First Presbyterian Church, Armagh

51. "The church was finished in April, 1879, and cost between £10,000 and £11,000" (Bassett). This fine High Gothic church was built by Young & Mackenzie, architects, of Belfast, then at the peak of their powers. It is to be compared with J J McDonnell's St Peter's church in Lurgan (50), rather than with either of Armagh's two cathedrals, for its style is later than that of either.

"It is built of roughcut local limestone with Dungannon sandstone dressings; the style is Decorated Gothic Revival ... It is rare to find such a fine and very substantial mid-nineteenth-century church surviving almost intact down to the last detail. Only the introduction of the modern light oak communion table and chairs in front of the pulpit disturbs the period completeness ... The square tower rises up in four levels with clasped buttresses and small lancet or round windows piercing the blank walls at the first two levels. At the third level there are tall paired pointed windows while at the top level only one tall pointed window, with louvres. Here the flat buttresses are slighty battered in silhouette as they change into five-sided banded buttresses topped by tall octagonl pinnacles that clasp the base of the soaring octagon spire...The interior of the church with its U-shaped and steeply-raked balcony gathered around the pulpit and, at ground level, the pews following the curve of the centre balcony has much of the dramatic atmosphere usually associated with an old-fashioned theatre auditorium. The balconies are carried on eight cast-iron columns, with Gothic capitals, on top of which is a second tier of columns rising up to flat arches supporting the concealed nave roof trusses above the pine-sheeted heavily coved ceiling ... The splendid three-seater pulpit with impressive Gothic back-rest to the central seat is reached by two symmetrically placed staircases one each side of the pulpit. This assemblage is set against a magnificent three-bay mahogany arcade of Decorated Gothic arches infilled with elegantly laid out organ pipes painted in the traditional manner" (UAHS listers).

"Architecturally, one of the finest features of First Presbyterian is its graceful spire of 185 feet in height which is seen to best advantage when silhouetted agains the setting sun" (Dr Temple Lundie: and an accurate observation). "A faded photograph in the vestry of a bearded patriarch commemorates the architect, Robert Young, who was responsible for the best churches of his firm ... Armagh is more conventional than his earliest Presbyterian church in University Street, Belfast (1874) but also relies for its impact on richly sculpted portals juxtaposed to a soaring spire, an external drama that an earlier generation of worshippers would have approached with deep foreboding" (Williams).

Sacred Heart (R C) Church, Cloghogue, Newry

52. Prominent on its hill-top outside Newry, isolated by an unexpected pitch-and-putt course, looking down on the road and railway line to Dublin, itself overlooked by the border check-point: with its curious square tower and fish-scale dome, it has always seemed very un-Irish to me, though ironically it was dedicated on Easter Day of 1916. Damaged by bombs and battles at the check-point on several occsions, but all made good. I have never been able to remember what building I have seen that this church reminds me of: Venice? Istanbul? Ravenna? France? Spain? Portugal?

Designed by Ashlin & Coleman of Dublin: G G Ashlin had been a pupil of A W Pugin, whose sister he married. According to an unusually helpful plaque inside the church, "Ecclesia, opera constructionis cura Ashlin et Coleman, architectorum insignium, confecto, in divinum cultum die 23 mensis Aprilis anno 1916 benedictione dedicata est." The foundation stone had been laid by Cardinal Logue in 1911.

Externally, rather a dour-seeming granite church, in a curious mixture of styles: apart from the tower and domelet, with the triple arcade at the top, there are a large plate-tracery rose window, a very Gothic niche for a statue of Christ, and many round-headed openings finished in a style somewhere half-way between the Byzantine and the Celtic Revival. Internally, the mixture of styles continues, with barrel vaulted ceiling, gallery, clustered columns, classical white marble, two pairs of charming carved angels in the manner of Canova, and particularly fine gold mosaic-work in the chancel, again combining the Byzantine style of Ravenna with Celtic interlace.

This is a building which repays closer examination. It is admirably detailed, and very coherent, despite the (at first) disconcerting mingling of styles. It is as Edwardian in its pomp and circumstance as Belfast City Hall; and, though out of fashion today, perhaps deserves as much respect.

Photograph: Michael O'Connell.
Situation: Dublin Road, Newry; td, Dromalane; Parish, Killevy; District Council, Newry & Mourne; Grid ref. J 081 239.
References: Listed B (16/13/34). IB, LIII, 1911, p 466, LVI, 1914, pp 384 supp., 388; commemorative booklet, 1991, passim.

◁

Photograph: Michael O'Connell.
Situation: The Mall West; td, Parkmore; Parish, and District Council, Armagh; Grid ref. H 877 453.
References: Listed B+ (15/17/20); in conservation area. IB, XX, 1878, p 19, XXI, 1879, pp 63, 169; Bassett, 'Armagh', 1888, p 95; Lundie, 'First Armagh', 1973, p 31; 'Buildings of Armagh', UAHS, 1992, p 147; Williams, 'Architecture in Ireland', 1994, p 11.

St Brigid's (R C) Church, Glasdrummond, Creggan

53. A very large and imposing church, whose appearance belies its date: on a basilica plan, of dressed granite, with portico and square campanile - all most surprising for 1928. The explanation is that the stones of an earlier building, of 1840, Ravensdale Park, County Louth, by Thomas Duff, which had been burned down in the Troubles of 1922, were re-used to build the church. In May, 1926, William H Byrne & Son, architects, of Dublin, advertised for tenders: "Intending contractors should visit the site of the proposed building and inspect the large quantity of materials thereon which will be available for the new building." "When the Land Commission acquired the estate, the late Peter Sheerin, P P, bought the ruins and had the stone and

bricks transported to Glassdrummond, where work began in 1928. The architects, realising the beauty of the Italian tower and portico of the old castle, decided to reconstruct them exactly as they had existed, and used all the beautiful granite Ionic columns and entablature in forming a portico to the main entrance of the church. This noble portico supports the saints of Ireland - Patrick, Brigid, Colmcille and Oliver Plunkett - and above them worked in rich mosaics is an image of Saint Brigid, under whose patronage the church is dedicated ... On Saturday September 24th 1932 His Excellency Cardinal McRory solemnly consecrated the altar; the dedication ceremony on Sunday 25th at a High Mass celebrated by Most Rev.

Dr Mulhern, Bishop of Dromore" (Kieran).

The contract was for £26,089; the value of the rescued materials brought in at £7,820. "The Architects realising the beauty of the Italian tower and portico which formed the most striking features of the old Mansion House decided to reconstruct the tower exactly as it existed in Ravensdale ... Having reached this decision it was an easy matter to work in all the Newry granite facing in the remainder of the exterior walls and all the old bricks in lining them so that when the church was finished hardly a stone or brick taken from the old buildings was wasted,

east wall with stained glass depicting the Virgin, and the central figure of Christ crucified above the fine altars is enclosed in a classical aedicule. "The nave ceiling is divided into three saucer domes, and the sanctuary barrel ceiled ... the plasterwork of the interior was executed by Mr John Ryan of Dublin"(O'Neill).

If stones could speak, what might not these stones say? It is a good cross-border joke that in 1988 it was described as one of the vanished country houses of Ireland; whilst all the time, just over the border, it had reappeared in the guise of a church.

and very few new stones were needed" (O'Neill).

(In 1806, Sleater described "Ravensdale-Park, Wm. Chichester Fortescue, Esq. On the side of Flurry river, and the side of Carlingford mountains. Demesnes laid out and cultivated by the late Right Hon. James Fortescue". The new Ravensdale House was one of the last major projects of Thomas Duff before his death in 1848 - and appears to have been rather uncharacteristic of his work: it looks like an attempt on his part to catch up with the styles of Lanyon and Barre. Bence-Jones describes it as "a large and somewhat severe early Victorian mansion of granite, of plain but irregular aspect, dominated by a tall Italianate campanile with an open belvedere at the top. Built for Thomas Fortescue, 1st Lord Clermont ... Partly two-storey and partly three, but mostly of the same height; eaved roof. Entrance front with a deep central recess enclosed by a screen of arches and Ionic pilasters and columns, the tower being at one side of the recess". Later the home of Lord Clermont's younger brother, Chichester Fortescue, subsequently Lord Carlingford. For some time it was one of the several lavish homes of Sir Daniel Dixon, timber merchant, property developer, M P, and Lord Mayor of Belfast, who apparently cut out all the timber on the estate, and then sold the place on to the Earl of Arran.)

Externally, very large, clear-cut and impressive; only the crosses atop pediment and campanile, and the rather unexpected mosaic in the tympanum of the pediment (by Messrs Oppenheim of Manchester) proclaim the building's, so to say, conversion. Internally, I concur with the listers' view that it is "a beautifully proportioned architectural space". Twelve brown Norwegian granite Doric columns carry arches which in turn carry the domes of the ceiling. The chancel contains white Corinthian columns and pilasters, a Diocletian window high up in the

Photographs: Michael O'Connell; Ravensdale House, IAA. Drawing: copy in Cardinal O'Fiaich Centre, Cullyhanna.

Situation: On road from Creggan to Ballsmill; td, Glasdrummond; Parish, Creggan; District Council, Newry & Mourne; Grid ref. H 962 147

References: Listed B+ (16/16/3). Sleater, 'Topography', 1806, p 173; 'Newry Commercial Telegraph', 5/3/1840; IB, LXVIII, 1926, p 355, LXIX, 1927, p 358, and LXX, 1928, p 282; Bence-Jones, 'Burke's guide', 1978, p 240; Glin, 'Vanishing country houses', 1988, pp 108-109; T Kieran, in 'Creggan: journal of the Creggan Local History Society', I, No 4, 1990, p 66; P O'Neill, in JCLAS, XXIV, 1997, p 8; documents in Cardinal O Fiaich Centre, Cullyhanna.

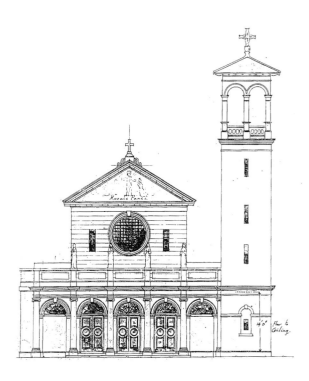

St Colman's College Chapel, Newry

54. Externally, of red brick, with a nicely detailed square tower and diminishing pinnacle, with very tall slit windows, providing a satisfying termination to the long range of college buildings of various dates from 1879 to 1960 (with more at the rear). Within, an astonishingly rich little interior in a very Roman kind of Romanesque style. Completed in 1938 to the designs of John J Robinson of Dublin (who had built the adjacent bishop's palace (80)

five years earlier).

In unusually chatty mood, the listers say: "There is lavish use of Italian marbles for side altars, reredoses, and nave columns. The columns are of unusual design, their shafts consisting of three drums of diminishing girth, marked by set-backs as they go up". (Could it be that the mason, having never heard of entasis, misinterpreted the architect's intentions?). "The impressive open oak truss roof is also of unusual design, incorporating large Celtic cross motifs in king posts. The interior is otherwise notable for the good oak joinery of the stalls against the west wall; the fine series of stained glass windows by the Clarke studio of Dublin; and the good set of opus sectile stations of the cross by Richard King of Dublin ... A very fine example of 20th century ecclesiastical architecture, unusually complete in its richness of interior finish and furnishings". I respectfully concur.

The re-ordering of altar and chancel in 1989, when the large marble baldacchino was removed, has been handled with tact. Since the school now has 850 pupils, and the chapel will hold a congregation of no more than 120, it has to be used in rotation. Its dedication is to Mary, Immaculate Mother of God.

Photograph: Michael O'Connell (see also colour-plate II).
Situation: Off Armagh Road, Newry; td, Lisdrumgullion; Parish, Newry; District Council, Newry & Mourne; Grid ref. J 083 280.
References: Listed B+ (16/25/21). IB, LXXIX, 1937, p 498.

Our Lady Queen of Peace (R C) Church, Mullaghbane, Forkhill

55. A remarkable monument to the taste of the 1950s, with a faintly Swiss or Austrian mountainy flavour, not inappropriate to its hilly setting; and with a tall, thin, free-standing campanile having very wide eaves to its pyramidal roof. It and the church itself are clad in a mixture of roughcast and smooth cement. Built in 1953 to the designs of Simon Leonard, architect, of Dublin; the builders were Ned and John Lynch. The campanile seems to have been a little later than the nave, possibly not part of the original design.

A panel beside the door is inscribed:

Hic lapis benedictus est

Ioanne Cardinale Dalton
Die xxix Maii MCMLV

The interior has patterned concrete panels, by no means unattractive, both in the angled ceiling and in the reredos. There are simple mahogany pews, and a very plain gallery. Today, very much out of fashion; but its day may well come.

Photograph: Michael O'Connell.
Situation: On road from Camlough to Crossmaglen; td, Aughanduff; Parish, Creggan; District Council, Newry & Mourne; Grid ref. H 971 209.
References: Not listed; datestone; local information.

Ready for the auction of contents: the dining room at Gosford Castle (65) in 1921. Photograph: MBR

CHAPTER THREE

GRAND HOUSES

County Armagh is not very rich in grand houses. There is nothing so sophisticated as Castlecoole, or Florencecourt, in County Fermanagh; there is no equivalent of Castle Dobbs, or Glenarm Castle, in County Antrim. Yet it still has some fine houses, discussed in this chapter. It has also suffered staggering losses. Unlike County Antrim, where five out of the eight grandest houses are still occupied and owned by descendants of the original builders, there is not a single such grand house in Armagh (though some middling and smaller houses have passed down through many generations).

County Antrim was largely settled in the 17th century by the canny Scots, mostly minor gentry from the lowlands. County Armagh, on the contrary, was almost entirely settled in the 17th century by English military men, and their tenants. Sir Charles Coote, in 1804, reiterates Pynnar's survey of names and acreages:[1] Brownlow, Obins, Cope, Sacheverell, Dillon, Acheson, Poyntz, Mandeville, the leading names. On the whole, it cannot be said that, in the long term, they managed their affairs and estates well. No doubt they suffered from unhappy relationships with the former, expropriated, owners of the land, and with rebarbative tenants. They may have exhibited some of the vices, as well as the virtues, of the British military mind. A few flourished for a while; some acquired titles, usually for services to Dublin Castle. But many squandered their estates through one or another form of dissipation. The fact remains that not one of the original builders' families still owns or inhabits a grand house in the county; only two retain some of the land, in each case without the house: Close, of Drumbanagher; and Stronge (originally, canny Scots Strang), of Tynan.

There are three houses in the county - two grandish, one modest - now in the care of the National Trust; their future therefore seems secure: Ardress (60), the Argory (66), and Derrymore (106). Five architecturally very important houses appear to be, at the time of writing, at considerable risk: Richhill House (56); Killevy Castle (70); Ballinahone House (59); Gosford Castle (65); and Brownlow House (69). The list of vanished houses is long and heart-breaking: Carrickblacker House; Churchill, home of the Verners; Clontilew, of the Obrees; Silverwood; Drumsill; Elm Park; Ballymoyer; Drumilly (a lovely house which I was privileged to see, with its Chinese wallpapers and tremendous conservatory, before it was demolished by that most philistine of agencies, the Northern Ireland Ministry of Agriculture); Drumbanagher (212), one of the most distinguished accomplishments of the Scottish architect William Playfair; the Pavilion, which seems to have been an enchanting Regency villa, with extensive gardens, in the heart of Armagh City, built for Captain Algeo between 1804 and 1808, vested and demolished in the brutal 1960s; and, most recently - indeed, since this book was started - the remains of Tynan Abbey (64).

It is accordingly important to value the more the survivors which remain. Of these, I judge the most important, from an architectural point of view, to be Richhill House, possibly the first dwelling-house in Ulster designed not for defence; Playfair's Brownlow House; Hopper's Gosford Castle; and Papworth's Killevy Castle. None of these is past rescue; each of these is presently in a more or less distressed physical condition; it is my most earnest hope that each can, by one means or another, be restored to hearty good health.

Reference: 1. Coote, 'Armagh', 1804, Appendix.

Richhill House (or Castle)

56. "It is said that Major Edward Richardson erected, circa 1665, a new house at Legacorry, which later became known as Richardson's Hill, subsequently shortened to Richhill. But does it incorporate parts of an earlier house built by his father in law Francis Sacheverell some time after 1610?" (J C Crozier). "It was built between 1655 and 1698 (in view of the stair arrangements probably in the early half of this period) and would seem to be the earliest surviving example in the province of a country house with no provision for defence" (Jope, 1952). It is peculiar that the house is often called Richhill "Castle", and that Lewis refers to its "castellated turrets", the Parliamentary Gazetteer refers to it as a "castellated pile", and Bassett calls it a "stately turreted mansion", all three descriptions being manifestly inaccurate. Writing in 1960, Jope says "There is no certain dating evidence for the building of Richhill. Edward Richardson paid poll tax on the property in 1660, and though no hearth tax was paid in 1664, a house must have been built there soon after. The most distinctive features of Richhill - shaped gables, panelled brick chimneys, symmetrical layout with centrally-placed stair projection at the back - were current in England throughout the 17th century ... The house has been little changed architecturally since it was built". But a somewhat different account is given in unsigned and undated notes in the MBR: "Richhill was formerly Legacorry: the original house here is said to have been built in 1664 by Francis Sacheverell of Reresby" (an ancestor of Sacheverell Sitwell). "In 1680 it passed to the Richardson family, who continued there until 1881, when, as the result of a family disagreement, Elizabeth Richardson, co-heiress of William Richardson MP, left her third share to her cousin Lord Gosford". However, according to the Valuation books, from 1864 until 1881 the house seems to have been

occupied by one Louisa Bacon; from 1891 until 1898 by Henry Tate; from 1898 until 1906 by Thomas Griffiths, MD; from 1906 to 1927 by Major Berry; then by a Mr Kingston from Cork. Thereafter, it was used for some time as an agricultural training school, until castle and land were acquired by Mr Samuel Hewitt.

R M Young, writing in 1909, was more explicit: "Richhill Castle, the residence of Major Robert Gordon John Johnstone Berry, is a noble turreted mansion ... It had its origin between the years 1610 and 1618. In the former year, a grant of Legacorry etc. was made to Francis Sacheverell Esq of Reresby, Notts, whose son Francis married a daughter and heiress of Sir John Blennerhasset, Baron of the Exchequer. Their only child, Anne, married Major Edward Richardson, MP for Armagh ... In 1794, William Richardson married the famous beauty, Dolly Munro, who had rejected the offer of marriage of the Marquis Townsend, the Viceroy of the time. After her marriage, Dolly Munro settled down quietly at Richhill, where she died in 1811."

Coote, in 1804, says that "The appearance of the town is interesting, which is considerably increased by the elegant demesne of Mr Richardson, whose residence is in full view from the street". Lieutenant Bennett of the Ordnance Survey, in 1835, calls it "a very old and substantial building but of no particular beauty". Bence-Jones describes Richhill as "an important c17 house ... 2 storey with gabled attic in high-pitched roof. "U"-plan entrance front with projecting wings to form a shallow 3 sided court, 5 bay centre range, 1 bay in the end of each wing; 1 bay on inner face of each wing. Pedimented curvilinear "Dutch" gables on ends of wings; also 2 similar but smaller gables in centre range, and one on the inner face of each wing. Tall brick chimneystacks with arched recessed

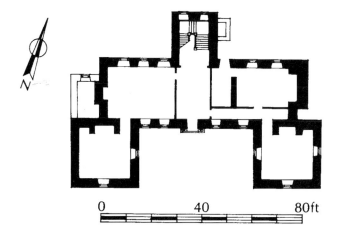

panels. c 18 century doorway with Doric columns, entablature and pediment. Magnificent wrought-iron gates, made 1745 ... now at Hillsborough Castle, co Down, where they were taken 1936" (see page 281). Hugh Dixon comments "Its plan with wings placed somewhat like flankers looks back to the medieval tradition, but the rigid symmetry of the façade and the tentative use of classical details on the doorway and Dutch gables give the house a new Renaissance aspect".

Professor Jope has a number of illuminating observations to make, both in his notes of 1952, and in his important article on 'Fortification to architecture' of 1960. "Richhill House has many features which raise interesting points of ancestry. The square projecting staircase tower at the back is an archaism, for such stair-towers were usual in England in the 16th century, and were already being superseded by staircases within the building in the more ambitious houses of the later 16th century; only rarely can they be found even early in the 17th century" (1952). "The ground-plan with wings set forward in echelon has its roots in the European or English 16th century house-designs with corner towers or partitions, a layout seen also on Scottish towers. Wings thus set are rarer, plain cross-wings being the usual in England"... "The basic layout of the main oblong block has its roots in the medieval hall-and-cross-passage house type, which was very persistent through the 17th century because it was convenient. At Richhill the entrance hall has been partitioned into a vestibule by light screen-walls, perhaps not original"... "The hall lay to the left of the entrance, the kitchen (by the size of its fireplace) being to the right. The wings must have contained private dining and withdrawing rooms. The upper floors would have contained sleeping chambers, with perhaps a further large public room over the ground floor hall, as indicated by the extra fireplace with corbelled-out chimney-stack at the back. The walls are of local rubble harled over, with brick chimney-stacks having recessed panels with semi-circular heads and imposts"... "The general appearance of Richhill, with shaped gables and scantily-windowed, can be seen in English smaller houses of the mid-17th century, as at Glinton Manor, Northants, and beyond this, in Holland and Denmark. The type is rare though not unknown in Scotland, but the English origin of the Richhill design is indicated by the panelled brick chimneys and the pedimented gables. The latter - a "Holborn gable" - though Flemish in ultimate origin, was brought to England about 1610 and soon became fully naturalised" ... "Chimneys with recessed semicircular-headed panels were mainly current in England during the middle decades of the 17th century, but the style had a long history ... Though it seems to have

a French origin, in Britain it is English and not Scottish, perhaps because French brick styles did not find much favour among the stone-building Scottish patrons and their masons ... The close comparison between Richhill and Brazeel" (near Dublin, probably 1650) "and the English mid-17th century group - Swakeleys, Scole, Moyles Court - are the strongest reason for considering Richhill a house of the later 17th century, and it is to this period that the datable examples in the New World belong" (1960). "At Richhill the small windows set in an expanse of blank wall are in contrast to the profusion of windows in the walls of most larger English houses from the mid-16th century onwards. The aspect is colonial (compare 17th century brick houses in New England: though such window proportions may be seen also in Scotland) ... and the small window area may be due to a late and tentative feeling for a domestic style here, and perhaps a reluctance to expose the occupants too much in a still unsettled countryside ... The interior joinery is of interest. The staircase is of good quality, itself more appropriate to the middle decades of the 17th century than its setting in a square projecting tower, and some of the window surrounds are remarkable efforts, perhaps of native craftsmen" (1952).

It is a very attractive house, liberally ornamented with creepers and ivy, perched on its hill-top and set back slightly from the square at the head of the village street. A stone eagle sits atop one of the massive chimney-stacks. The staircase in particular is very fine. The approaches have been altered, and the window-sashes were renewed in the mid 19th century; the house has now been divided into three, providing homes for three branches of the same family. Nevertheless, its character remains substantially intact: a close examination carried out in recent years by Richard Oram and Philip Robinson revealed that all the original, numbered, roof-timbers are still in place.

Photographs: Michael O'Connell; MBR; W A Green, Ulster Folk Museum WAG 2663. Plan: Hugh Dixon.
Situation: 1, 2, and 3, The Square, Richhill; td, Legacorry; Parish, Kilmore; District Council, Armagh; Grid ref. H 945 482.
References: Listed B1 (15/13/1); in conservation area. VAL/1B/229A, p 24, VAL/12B/10/37A-F, in PRONI; Coote, 'Armagh', 1804, p 385; G A Bennett, OSM, 1835, Armagh, I, p 63; Lewis, TD, 1837, II, pp 183, 513; PG, III, 1846, p 149; Bassett, 'Armagh', 1888, p 203; Young, 'Belfast and province of Ulster', 1909, p 249; E M Jope, notes in MBR, 1952; E M Jope, in UJA, 3rd series, XV, 1960, pp 118-120; H G Leask, in 'Studies in building history', 1961, p 248; J C Crozier, in 'Craigavon Historical Society review', II, No 2, 1973; Dixon, 'Introduction', UAHS, 1975, p 25; Bence-Jones, 'Burke's guide', 1978, p 241; Dean, 'Gate lodges', UAHS, 1994, p 42; unsigned and undated notes in MBR.

Raughlan House, Derryadd, Ardmore

57. An attractive long, low, two-storey house, roughcast and colour-washed in ochre, Georgian-glazed, whose best feature is the two-storey bowed projection containing the front door: a delightful recessed doorcase with a pair of slim fluted columns and above that, instead of a fanlight, a finely carved stone lunette, with two string-courses. The six-panelled door, and the detailing, both inside the entrance hall and outside, appear to be original. A canted bay window has been added to the double-width drawing-room at the south end of the range of buildings. Some of the upper windows are two-light, two of the principal ground-floor windows are three-light. The roofline is punctuated by seven chimney-stacks. There are extensive out-buildings. Sited amidst woodland at the head of a lawn sloping gently down to Lough Neagh and its reed-beds: still an exceptional site, it must have been even more charming before the successive lowerings of the water-level of Lough Neagh.

"Raughlin, the seat of J. Forde, Esq, is surrounded by plantations, gardens and pleasure-grounds of a luxuriant character, and commands splendid views of the lake and the counties of Tyrone, Derry, Antrim, Down and Armagh; in the lake is an island, beautifully planted with fruit-trees and evergreens, the whole forming a beautiful spot in the midst of a boggy and unproductive tract" (Lewis); the island now an integral part of the demesne. Oram says "A two-storey rambling house, the subject of many alterations and additions since its 17th century foundation. The point on the lough shore where the house

stands is heavily wooded, giving an air of mystery". But the listers say "Early 19th century with later additions".

The house, sometimes called Rockland, is reputed to have been first built, as fishing, boating, shooting, or hunting lodge, in the late 17th- or early 18th- century, by the Brownlows of Lurgan; in 1698, Anne Brownlow married Matthew Forde of Seaforde. Their younger son Arthur Fforde became rector of Lurgan; his son James married his cousin Elizabeth Forde in 1759; and their son, Captain James Fforde, leased Raughlan from his Brownlow cousins. (The Fordes of Seaforde use one "F", the Ffordes of Raughlan two). The house remained in Fforde ownership until 1971, when it was bought by Ralph Spence; from whom it was acquired by its present owner in 1993.

Lt Bennett of the Ordnance Survey, writing in 1835, says "Mr. Forde of Raughlin or Rathlin is the only resident gentleman in the parish. His house is situated on a point on the lake between Derryadd and Raughlin bays ... There is a windmill for grinding corn and a drying kiln in Derryadd townland near the lough shore, the property of Mr. Forde. This is the only mill in the parish nor is there any manufacture except linen, which is carried on in the

houses of the individual". The valuers of 1836 classified the house as 1B, measuring 107ft by 19ft by 14ft high with extensive offices; and noted, of James Forde Esq, "Did hold 200 acres, but now holds only 36 acres. Deduct for offices in farmyard not now required" £10.14.0, leaving the (not inconsiderable) valuation at £32. In 1862, the house was valued at £50. This Valuation book contains a ground plan and key which show that the original return in the centre of the house must have been demolished, and the new one added at the back of the south end of the house, after that date. Bassett, in 1888, says only "Derryadd is a rural post office, 4 miles north-west of Lurgan. Lord Lurgan and Mr J. Forde are the landlords of the district".

Photographs: Michael O'Connell (see also colour-plate XIa).
Situation: Raughlan Lane, Derryadd Road; td, Derrymacash; Parish, Montiaghs; District Council, Craigavon; Grid ref. J 038 612.
References: Listed B1 (14/3/10). Bennett, OSM, 1835, Armagh, I, p 92; VAL 1B/221, p 22, and VAL 2B/2/18, p 98, in PRONI; Lewis, TD, 1837, II, p 405; Bassett, 'Armagh', 1888, p 387; 'Burke's landed gentry of Ireland', 1912, p 222; Oram, 'Craigavon', UAHS, 1970, pt III, p 13; information from Patrick Forde of Seaforde.

Acton House, Poyntzpass

58. Acton House appears to have been built soon after 1775 by one Alexander Thomas Stewart (a relative of the Stewarts of Ballintoy, and so of Lord Castlereagh) whose mother had inherited the property from the Poyntz family of Poyntzpass. It is named after the village of Iron Acton in Gloucestershire from which the Poyntz family came into Ireland. In 1619, Lieutenant Poyntz built the bawn,

80 feet square, whose remains stand a little lower down the hill . According to Stewart, "At Curriator, Lieut. Sir T Pointz possessed a tract of land, with a bawn of 80 feet square, and a lime house. On this he erected another bawn, one hundred feet square, and a brick and lime house". The present house is believed to stand on the site of the earlier one; it is apparently referred to as "a fine

seat" in the Post-Chaise Companion, though I have been unable to track down the reference, but it certainly appears on Taylor and Skinner's road map, surveyed in 1777. It is mentioned in 1804 by Coote: "the neat town of Acton, which, with the adjoining mansion, demesne and manor of the same name was some years since purchased by Mr. Hanna, a very eminent merchant of Newry, fom the then proprietor, Mr. Stewart, a lineal descendant of the original family".

By 1835 it was "the residence of C. R. Dobbs Esquire. The ornamental ground is of trivial extent" , though according to the valuation of 1836, 94 acres of land went with the house, which was classified 1A and valued at £37.18.0 after an abatement "for being too large". (The Dobbs family was related by marriage to the Stewarts). In 1838 "the residence of Mr. Dobbs JP [is] a large square house of a plain and comfortable appearance". Conway Richard Dobbs, born in 1800, had been an officer in the

Royal Navy; on his retirement, he and his family lived at Acton until he inherited Castle Dobbs, outside Carrickfergus, from his father, when he is reported to have taken with him to Kilroot, as part of his entourage, the Acton poet, John Quin. In 1846 the place was occupied by one Peter Quinn, of Newry (presumably no relation of the poet). In 1865 the house was valued at £55, the occupier

being Robert Quin Alexander, followed in 1888 by Lt Col William J Alexander, succeeded in turn in 1923 by Captain H C Alexander. The father of the present owner acquired the property between the wars.

It is, from the front, a sophisticated square three-bay two-storey roughcast house with attic and basement, hipped roof and central chimney-stacks, and Georgian glazing pattern intact, the windows flanking the entrance set back in arched recesses. It has a particularly fine doorcase with radial fanlight, geometrical side-lights, Ionic columns, and lions' masks above the capitals. The garden front looks out from its hilltop across the railway line and Acton lake, and has a generous bow to accommodate the ellipse within, although the upper storeys are not quite symmetrical. Inside, the detailing is of high quality: the best feature is the charming elliptical dining-room, with the marble chimney-piece elegantly curved to match the wall above, tall windows running right down to the floor, chair-rail, and fan centre-piece to the ceiling. There is also a nice curving staircase supported by a slim central column, and the L-shaped hallway has Ionic pilasters. A house of considerable distinction.

Photographs: Michael O' Connell.
Situation: Acton Road, Poyntzpass; Td, Brannock, parish Acton (formerly Ballymore), District Council Armagh; Grid ref. J 059 407.
References: Listed B1 (15/6/11). Taylor and Skinner, 'Roads' 1778, p 22; Coote, 'Armagh', 1804, p 368; Stuart, 'City of Armagh', 1819, p 640; G A Bennett, OSM, 1835 and J H Williams, 1838, Armagh, I, pp 6,10; VAL 1B/214, p 40, VAL 12B/15/23A-E, in PRONI; Bassett, 'Armagh', 1888, p 247; U J A, 2nd series, VI, 1900, pp 159 - 160; 'Before I forget: journal of the Poyntzpass & District Local History Society', V, 1991, p 85; information from Sir Richard Dobbs.

Ballinahone House, Armagh

59. "To be let, an elegant new built House and Demesne, and several Farms in the Townland of Ballinahone, about half a mile distant from the City of Armagh, adjoining the Corporation: most of the Farms have been dropp'd and under Grazing these seven Years, and in great Condition; and are greatly advantaged by a new Road through them, now a very great Thoroughfare, where Limestone and Turf are easily conveyed to all the adjacent Farms ... Proposals to be made to Henry Cust, Esq; in Armagh" (BNL, 20 October 1779). Mr Cust was a considerable local entrepreneur: he had been appointed revenue collector for the Armagh District in 1738 and, by fair means or foul, amassed a fortune for himself. In 1769 he was High Sheriff; he was nine times Sovereign of Armagh; as a member of the Grand Jury, he was well placed to secure the construction, at ratepayers' expense, of the "very great Thoroughfare" which so much advantaged the farms which he rack-rented to tenants, himself paying a much lower rental to the Church of Ireland. It seems that in 1779 he retired to his town house in Armagh, where he died in 1781 aged 74.

Whether he found a tenant, or whether some relative of

the same name moved in, I do not know; but in 1806 Sleater shows Ballynahone, near Armagh, twice on the same page, as in the occupation of Mr Cust. The place was bought in 1819 by the Rev. William Lodge, rector of Killybegs, who had been educated at the Royal School, and had married a year earlier the daughter, Anne Storey, of a fellow parson. It looks as though he commuted between Armagh and Donegal while his wife, his children, and his sisters, all lived at Ballinahone, where his sister Mary died in 1835 and his sister Letitia in 1848. In 1836 the house was described in the Valuation book as occupied by Miss Lodge, valued at £32. 2. 0, with the note "good situation near Armagh - allow for contiguity balanced by over-valuation". In 1862, Lewis Anderson, County Inspector in the R I C, occupied it under lease from Anne Lodge; the valuation had increased to £45. Her husband died at Killybegs in 1862, and three years later she sold the Ballinahone property through the Landed Estates Court to one Denis Burke. In 1867, he, and in 1873, Captain Clarke, appear as occupiers.. Thereafter, most confusingly, Ellen B Maziere is shown as holding under the executors of Denis Burke; yet by 1896 one

M C C Burke is shown as holding under the executors of Ellen B Maziere. Between these dates the house seems to have been occupied by Burkes, Babingtons, a Mr Coote and a Mr Lonsdale. Perhaps Mrs Maziere had been a Miss Burke? Fitzgerald and Weatherup reproduce an Allison photograph of Ballinahone which they date around 1913, on the back of which is a note: "At the front steps a groom holds Mrs Burke's horse as she prepares to ride with the Tynan and Armagh Hunt." This is in Mr Paterson's handwriting: he came to the city in 1911.

Ballinahone House is situated on a hillside, looking out over the valley of the Folly glen, but hard to find, tucked away between a nursery garden and an extensive post-war housing estate. It is worth the détour, despite its present air of dereliction, for it is by no means beyond restoration. The house and demesne were acquired in the mid-fifties by the present owner's father, who divided the house in two, and let out the left-hand side of the front part to tenants. This section has lain empty for some time; proposals to restore the house as a whole were put forward in 1979 and again in 1982, but evidently not proceeded with; it seems new proposals are now under consideration, and deserve every available support, for it is a fine mid-Georgian mansion.

L-shaped, two-storey on basement, built by Henry Cust between 1770 and 1776; the sun-dial on the gable wall, dated 1685, seems to have come from another house. The round-headed doorcase and flanking windows stand at the head of nine broad cut-limestone steps; the front wall of the three central bays is of rusticated ashlar. The remaining walls are of rubble encased in roughcast, some of which has fallen off to reveal the stones behind. The ground floor is seven bays wide, the upper floor three. The central bays break forward, with quoins in the upper storey, topped by a pediment: "in the tympanum are armorial bearings, now very badly eroded but almost certainly of the Cust family". The gables are topped by massive chimney-stacks, eight chimney-pots to the left, seven to the right. It is a pity that the Georgian glazing-bars have at some date been replaced by Victorian plate-glass. Nevertheless, this is still a handsome and imposing house.

Photograph: Michael O'Connell.

Situation: Up an avenue past the Ballinahone primary school; technically, 42, Hamiltonsbawn Road, Armagh; td, Ballynahone More; Parish, and District Council, Armagh; Grid ref. H 893 440.

References: Listed B (15/18/23); outside conservation area.VAL 1B/21A, p 9, VAL 2B/2/32E, VAL 12B/10/21A, C, E and G, in PRONI; T G F Paterson Manuscript Collection, No 57, Vol 3, in Armagh County Museum; Taylor and Skinner, 'Roads', 1778, p 26; BNL, 20/10/1779; Clarkson and Crawford, 'Ways to wealth', 1985, pp 57, 64-66; 'Buildings of Armagh', UAHS, 1992, p 46; Allison, 'Way we were', 1993, p 25; information from owner, and from file in MBR.

Ardress, Loughgall

60. It is with a sense of unease that, hesitantly, I place Ardress amongst the "grand houses" of County Armagh: externally, it is a somewhat overgrown and lumpish collection of disparate buildings of different dates and in different styles. Its unexpected claim to grandeur resides in the drawing room - "the great surprise of the house: ... the most sophisticated room in the county" (Dixon, in MBR).

The house is not lacking in historical interest, however. It is built on the site of an earlier house, evidently destroyed in 1641, belonging to the Clarke family, of Summer Island (63). The present house appears to date from around 1675 (some suggest ten years earlier), and to have been built originally as a five-bay, two-storey house, one room deep, divided into three compartments by cross-walls supporting the roof-timbers. Richard Oram tells me that there is a complex herring-bone drainage system under the basement floor, running into an enormous elliptical brick culvert which emerges under the window to the left of the front door.

Of the original roof, Philip Robinson writes "The Ardress roof is one of only four such late 17th century "English" roof-timbering systems identified in Ulster (ie, with oak principal rafters, butt purlins, common rafters and windbraces, but without any ridge purlin). The others are at Springhill (c 1680?), New Row, Coleraine (c 1675) and Waringstown House (1667). Such single-skin roofs were intended for a tile, shingle or slate covering, and not for thatch."

Although that roof, slated, is still visible from a distance, the façade of the house is now very different. The pale-pink-washed roughcast walls are framed by stone quoins, topped by a most peculiar "undulating parapet" with urns (the central one of Coade stone, earlier and of better quality than the flanking pair) and punctuated by central doorcase, four three-light windows (two of them false), thirteen orthodox Georgian windows (four of them false) and a pair of sidelights flanking the projecting pedimented portico with its Tuscan columns. The side view of the garden front is even more peculiar: curving screen walls with niches completely fail to unite the disparate elements of three-bay two-storey return (of 1810), two-bay two-storey gable-end (of about 1780) and two-bay 17th-century gable with narrow windows. The view from the corner is oddest of all, with the sharp cutting edge of the angled screen wall lunging out into space, whilst containing only an unfinished void within the quadrant. Hugh Dixon, in 1975, took a tolerant view of all this, calling it "a great success for it allowed a second front with curving wings to be formed at right angles to the main facade, enjoying a different vista of country to the west".

Aesthetically, however, I find it something of a disaster, though historically it is fascinating. It seems the house was first extended by the addition of two single-storey returns to the rear at some date before 1722. On 11 October 1760, "the beautiful Miss Sara Clarke of Ardress" was married, in Clonfeacle Church, to George Ensor, an architect, originally from Coventry, who since 1744 had been clerk of works to the Surveyor-General of Ireland in Dublin Castle. An individual of some distinction, he designed the Rotunda and many grand private houses in Dublin; the County Infirmary and (perhaps) the Seven Sisters in Armagh; and the charter schools in Roscommon and Athlone. At some date between 1778 and 1783, he and his wife retired from Dublin and settled in Ardress. "If we assume that Ensor did not start renovating the house till after his father-in-law's death, then the extensions cannot have begun earlier than 1778, and were probably either under way or complete by 1783" (Loane).

It was he who added both the classical portico, and the drawing-room, with its magnificent plasterwork (colour-plate IIIa), so much admired by Hugh Dixon, an astonishing provincial work by that very cosmopolitan Dublin stuccodore, Michael Stapleton. There is external evidence that Ensor and Stapleton knew each other. The Stapleton drawings in the National Library of Ireland include two remarkably close to the executed work at Ardress: "the void ovals and roundel shapes of the design are filled with the typical medallions that recur in Stapleton decorated houses, i.e. 'Minerva and kneeling Greek hero' - wall opposite window; 'Cupid bound and pelted' - wall opposite fireplace; and over each door 'The Rustic Marriage'. On the chimneypiece wall over the mantelpiece, 'Herculaneum veiled figure holding a leafless branch and a suspended burning vessel', with 'Ceres holding a cornucopia' in the recess beside the mantelpiece" (Carr, who points out that similar figures can be found in the Examination Hall of TCD, Belvedere House, Dublin, and Lucan House). As Con Curran rather wryly remarks, "His work, like that of all his contemporaries, was derivative, and in his figure work he too often brings into play the moulds that lay, up to a few years ago, in the atelier of his home at No 1, Mountjoy Place". But: "his talent lay in selection, good ordering and accomplished execution, but what chiefly distinguishes him is the good taste and charm with which he married natural and more formal ornament".

The drawing room is indeed very splendid. There is a frieze of putti; the ceiling is geometrical; the walls are chastely ornamented with festoons, husks, reeding and urns, all in the taste of the Adam brothers. The present colours, though persuasive, are not original: at least one visitor from earlier days regretted "the old plain ceiling (much off-white) and the apple green walls". There survives an interesting photograph of the drawing room at this time in the Centenary Souvenir booklet of St Francis's Church, Annaghmore, with an, at first glance, surprising caption attributing the plasterwork to Angelica Kauffman; but Stapleton seems to have based at least one of his medallions on the Bartolozzi engraving of Kauffman's painting of 'Cupid bound' (Loane). This splendid drawing room, so unexpected in a very rural part of County Armagh, formed part of a second plain two-storey block set by George Ensor against the spine wall so as to turn the house into a double pile.

After his death in 1803, the property passed to his son, also George, a lawyer of liberal and enlightened views, who, probably around 1810, added the wing containing the dining-room; the curving screen walls; and the new block to the north of the house. Erica Loane, in her very thorough analysis of Ardress, concludes that these additions were the work of a much less competent architect than George Ensor senior: " ... there are aspects of his plan which are either carelessly handled or eccentric. Not only is it without a door between the drawing-room and the dining-room but there is no way of passing from one to the other without stepping outside ... one wonders whether, having been subjected to the rigours of an Irish winter, the soup was ever entirely hot". George Ensor junior must have spent much of his time in Dublin or elsewhere, and the house may have been let; the Ordnance Survey memoir, undated but of about 1838, shows it as "the residence of George Inver, Esq", though this is probably no more than a slip. However, the Valuation book of 1836 shows George Ensor as the occupier, neatly describes it as "an old double house, partly ornamental", and values it at £37.6.0. On George Ensor's death, a bachelor, in 1845, his nephew Charles Ensor inherited it; in the 1862 valuation it was described as "old house not in good order, only part occupied", but valued at £50. From his son Captain Charles Howard Ensor the National Trust, with the aid of the Ulster Land Fund, acquired Ardress in 1960. A number of 19th- and early 20th-century additions were demolished in 1961.

There is an extensive, and enjoyable, cobbled farmyard to the north of the house, very little altered from its 18th-century appearance, and containing a collection of agricultural equipment and machinery built up with the help of the Craigavon Historical Society; not to mention some rare breeds of animals, and several different breeds of bats.

Photographs: Michael O'Connell (see also colour-plates IIIa, XIb).

Situation: Ardress Road, Loughgall; td, Ardress East; Parish, Loughgall; District Council, Armagh; Grid ref. H 913 558.

References: Listed A, outbuildings B (15/2/48). Stapleton drawings, 2355 and 2362a, in NLI; E Carr, Catalogue of Stapleton drawings, UCD thesis, 1985, copy in IAA, pp100,117; VAL 1B/230, p 53; VAL 2B/2/28A, p 71, in PRONI; Lewis, TD, 1837, II, p 313; J C Innes, OSM, nd, Armagh, I, p 80; 'St. Francis Church, Annaghmore, centenary souvenir', [1956], p 9; R McKinstry, in IGS Bulletin, II, No 4, 1959, p 41; Curran, 'Dublin decorative plasterwork', 1967, Chapter 11, passim; Dixon, 'Introduction', UAHS, 1975, p 42; Paterson, 'Harvest home', 1975, p 141; Bence-Jones, 'Burke's guide', 1978, p 11; E Loane, in 'New perspectives', 1987, pp 119-122 ; NT guidebook, 1990, passim; Gallagher and Rogers, 'Castle, coast and cottage', 1992, p 1; notes by H Dixon, and of 1982 by P Robinson, in MBR; information from R Oram.

Dobbin's House, Scotch Street, Armagh

61. A very splendid stone town house built, perhaps to designs by Francis Johnston, in 1811 or 1812 for the wealthy Leonard Dobbin, sovereign of the city and agent for the Bank of Ireland, later to be Member of Parliament for Armagh. It is not quite clear whether the house was originally intended to be purely residential, or whether it was meant to serve also as the bank; but certainly, after Mr Dobbin's death, it remained in use as bank and bank manager's house until the 1970s, when the bank moved out, and the building, used in 1977 as a temporary post office, fell into some dereliction. Valued at the very large sum of £84 in 1835.

Hugh Dixon writes of it: "The assured dignity of the building marks it as the work of a designer of more than local consequence. It seems likely for once (in the city where so much is erroneously ascribed to him) that this is the work of Francis Johnston. As an example of the very best in town house design of the late Georgian period it is almost without rival in Ulster; indeed, it must rank with the best in Ireland".

I cannot improve on the description in the UAHS Buildings of Armagh, so will not try. "An extremely handsome three-bay, three-storey building and basement. Ashlar stonework with blocked chamfered quoins; fine cornice and blocking course. On either side are screen walls with doorways and oculus windows over. Sash

windows with glazing bars. Stone chimney stacks gabled. Splendid doorway with sidelights, four engaged Tuscan columns, cornice and segmental fanlight with integral lantern and approached by a flight of steps fanning out each side with railings to basement areas. The house is set back from the street to provide a front garden ... Good contemporary railings with stone retaining wall to the street; fine railing lanterns each side of the front entrance. The side walls of the adjoining houses form part of the composition; finely carved urns adorn the gables".

In 1980, the building was bomb-damaged, but sensitively repaired and restored as, and the extensive courtyard and outbuildings to the rear converted into, sheltered accommodation for the elderly, by the Fold Housing Association, under the sensitive supervision of the late Philip Bell, then chairman of the UAHS. The work was completed, and the buildings officially reopened, in November 1981. The front view is considerably marred by a central hand-rail, surely unnecessarily obtrusive; and by wires which surely, here, could and should have been laid for a short distance underground?

Photographs: Michael O'Connell; Michael Campbell.
Situation: 36, Scotch Street, Armagh; td, Corporation; Parish, and District Council, Armagh; Grid ref. H 874 452.
References: Listed A (15/18/3); in conservation area. Datestone at rear; drawings in IAA; VAL/1B/21B, p 31, in PRONI; TGF Paterson, Armachiana, IV, p 71, in Armagh County Museum; JIA, IV, 1987/88, pp 68-69; 'Buildings of Armagh', UAHS, 1992, pp 183, 184, 189, 190; H Dixon, undated notes in MBR.

Marlacoo House, Hamiltonsbawn

62. A fine, large, foursquare house, three-bay and two-storey, with hipped roof and modern red-brick chimney-stacks. Built of blackstone, roughcast, its walls are almost completely masked by ivy and creepers. It has an excellent classic doorcase, with fluted stone columns, and fanlight. There may well have been an earlier house here; the lake has been a place of importance for centuries; although it is now submerged, Hugh O'Neill, Earl of Tyrone, used a crannog in the lake in 1595 as a place of safety in which to store "his munitions, his money, his jewels, and whatsoever most precious things he had, including his wife" (Paterson).

The present house was built about 1815 by a Mr Robert Boyd. It appears that he bought the 100-acre demesne (including Marlacoo lake, its feeder streams, and a water-mill), in 1813, subject to a lease of part to a Mr Kells, the leasehold however being charged with a number of annuities. In 1837, the Valuation book shows Mr Boyd residing here, the house placed in category 1A, measuring 53 feet by 29 feet 6 inches by 21 feet, valued at £22.18.0, the flax mill and store valued at another £9.18.0.

After Robert Boyd's death, the house was let from year to year to the Rev. Alexander Irwin; but the Boyd family put the place up for sale by auction, through the Encumbered Estates Court in Dublin. This was probably a device to take advantage of the powers of the court to discharge or compound the annuities. The sale was advertised for 26 June 1856, and the "Descriptive Particulars" are flattering:

"The lands are adjacent to the great Public Road from Armagh to Tandragee ... and in a most respectable quiet neighbourhood. They are all of prime quality, well sheltered and watered. The late Mr Boyd built a capital and comfortable residence on the lands, suitable in every respect for the residence of a Gentleman, with excellent Offices, Orchard, Gardens, etc, situate in an extensive Lawn, ornamented tastefully by Plantations, which occupy about 5 acres, all terminated by a Lake of considerable extent and beauty. The House and Offices are in good order and fit for the immediate reception of a gentleman's family ..."

It seems the house was not sold, and Mr Irwin remained in occupation, under lease from Horner (or Homer?) Boyd. Major J S Boyd occupied it for a while about 1870; then (perhaps because his military duties took him abroad) it was let to Dr Francis Clarke, MD; then, about 1880, Boyd, a Colonel by now, moved back in and remained there until his death at the turn of the century.

Thereafter the house was occupied in turn by Henry Fulton, a Belfast architect; Colonel Mansergh; and a Presbyterian minister named George Kelly. In 1908 the freehold was bought by Dr Robert Quin MD, who installed the brass voice-pipe which still leads from the front door to the pillowside of the master bedroom. After his death, his widow lived on at Marlacoo until 1943, when it was acquired by John McDonagh, a Quaker furniture manufacturer, who sold to the present owners in 1975. It is today in excellent order, well-loved, and provides an appropriate seat for the Chair of the Historic Buildings Council of Northern Ireland.

Photograph: Michael O'Connell.
Location: 146, Marlacoo Road, Hamiltonsbawn; td, Marlacoo Beg; Parish, Mullaghbrack; District Council, Armagh; Grid ref. H 985 450.
References: Listed B (15/4/1). D 958/2, VAL 1B/231 p 28, VAL 2B/2/29, p 24, VAL 12B/11/3 A to E, all in PRONI; Lewis, TD, 1837, II, p 409; T G F Paterson, Armachiana, XXI, p 93-97, in Armagh County Museum; Pierce and Coey, 'Taken for granted', 1984, p 124.

Summer Island, Loughgall

63. An attractive Georgian house, very difficult to date with confidence from its appearance: but see below. Henry Clarke "of Anasamry" died in 1727. By 1769, his descendant Henry Clarke is described as "of Summer Island"; he had gone up in the world by marrying a Miss Cope of Drumilly. His son John occupied Summer Island in 1803; one John O'Donnell, probably husband of John Clarke's sister, is shown as the occupier in 1799 and 1807; and Walter O'Donnell, only son of the latter, had changed his name to Walter Clarke by 1805, and is shown as occupier under that name in 1816. According to one version, Harry "the unknown" Verner bought the place from Walter Clarke at some date before 1837, and leased it to the Atkinson family; but there is in existence, pasted into a Crowhill scrapbook (D 1382), a will of 1819 by which Walter Clarke left the "house demesne and lands of Summer Island at Anasamry, with the trees thereon", to his sister Elizabeth O'Donnell for life and, failing male issue, to Louisa Atkinson eldest daughter of Joseph Atkinson of Crow Hill. One way or another, a branch of the Atkinson family lived there until 1907 when the Cowdy family bought it from the Verners; though in the 1862 valuation, the occupier is shown as "Sir William Verner Bart", and a value of £57 placed upon the house and gate lodges .

However reliable this account of the succession to the property may or may not be, it does not tell us whether the house now standing is the original one, or a rebuilding. Dean describes it as an "elegant classical villa", and suggests a date of about 1820 for its pretty gate lodges (155). An unsigned note in the MBR suggests that the limestone of the gate pillars, which the author too dates to c 1820, is the same as that used in the quoins of the house; but then spoils his argument by suggesting 1780 as a possible date for the lodges. In fact, what looks like a crude representation of the present house, and both the gate lodges,

appears on a "Map of the Townland of Annasamery, part of the estate of William Clarke Esq., June 1794, by William Kigan" (T 2431); so a date around 1780 would have seemed possible: and Belinda Jupp dates the demesne to c1780. But a newspaper cutting of 12 November, 1833, garnered by the late T G F Paterson, indicates a substantially later date: for it reads: "SUMMER ISLAND / To be let, / and immediate possession given, / The HOUSE and DEMESNE of SUMMER ISLAND, in the County of ARMAGH. / The House has been lately built, contains every desirable accommodation, and has been occupied for some time by the Family who are now leaving it. The Offices are excellent, and in good repair. The Demesne contains 93 Acres of Prime Land." "Lately built" must surely mean built within the past ten years: so a date around 1825 seems most likely.

The house is five bays wide, two storeys on a projecting basement plinth, the upper parts of the walls having a slight batter, of cream-painted stucco contained within cutstone dressings. There is a very fine fanlight above the wide doorcase, which incorporates two engaged columns and two pilasters. The windows retain their Georgian glazing bars. The roof is hipped, with heavy dentils at the eaves, and a pair of fine big chimney-stacks on the ridge, one carrying seven pots, the other eight.

Photograph: Michael O'Connell.
Situation: 30, Summer Island Road, Loughgall; td, Anasamry; Parish, Loughgall; District Council, Armagh; Grid ref, H 880546.
References: Listed B+ (15/1/1); outside Loughgall conservation area. Taylor and Skinner, 'Roads', 1778, p 26; VAL 2B/2/28A, p 61, D1382 folder 2, D 2538/A/37, 78, 119, 125, and T 2431 all in PRONI; Wilson, 'Post-chaise companion', 1803, p 615; advertisement of 12 November 1833, in T G F Paterson Manuscript Collection, No 56, Vol 4, in Armagh County Museum; C Bailey, OSM, 1835, Armagh, I, p 80; Lewis, TD, 1837, II, p 313; Bassett, 'Armagh', 1888, p 186; unsigned notes in MBR; Jupp, 'Heritage gardens', 1992, A/043; Dean, 'Gate lodges', UAHS, 1994, p 42; information from Mrs Diane Cowdy.

Tynan Abbey

64. The Tynan Abbey demesne of the Stronge family in County Armagh; the Caledon demesne of the Alexander family in County Tyrone; and the Glaslough demesne of the Leslie family, just across the border in County Monaghan; together comprise a very considerable area of parkland, woodland, farmland, and lakes, through which twine the rivers Tynan, Cor and Blackwater. On the night of 21st January 1981 a body of armed men made its way across the border, forced entry to Tynan Abbey, shot dead its owner Sir Norman Stronge and his only son James, set fire to the house, and retired across the border. Understandably, the family has preferred not to return to the house or to restore it. At the time of writing, its walls still stand, a stark and melancholy ruin, like so many others in Ireland. In 1995, Historic Buildings branch of the Department of the Environment sent a memo to the planners recalling that listed building consent to partial demolition had been granted in 1983, but noting that the branch "is keen to have the listing status retained and has suggested leaving things as they are at the moment in the hope that the property be reinstated or stabilised as a ruin. It still holds a lot of historic and architectural interest in its present state". In this, the branch is undoubtedly correct.

The Stronges, or Strangs, were a family of Scottish origin who settled in Ireland in the 17th century. Dr John Stronge married Elinor Manson in 1714, and through her inherited property at Tynan, of which he was rector. Upon this land was a house called Fairview, built before 1703, for in that year Thomas Ashe recorded that "Captain Manson lives upon it and has built a very pritty house well timbered and regularly built. It is two storey high. There are good chambers and garrets above staires, a hansome Parlour, a common Hall, a Kitchen Sellars and their

Convenient Offices a Good Stable Barne and Cow house a Good Garden and Orchard." Parts of this house, in which James Stronge lived until his death, unmarried, in 1785, were incorporated into the later house, including the former library. There is said to have been a datestone in the fine stone north yard, but this is now not to be found. James Stronge's brother Matthew was a successful merchant in Liverpool. Matthew's son, Rev. James Stronge, born in 1750, married in 1785 Helen Tew, daughter of Margaret Maxwell of Fellows Hall, Killylea, niece of John, first Lord Farnham. So far as I can find, though he took holy orders, Rev. James Stronge never held any cure of souls in the diocese of Armagh. But he was a pushful person: on 13 May 1801 he wrote to Government applying for "a deanery in the North", and on the same day the prime minister, Lord Addington, applied on his behalf for a baronetcy, which he eventually secured in 1803, only to die in the following year. His son James Matthew, second baronet, then inherited the property and in 1810, aged 24, married Isabella Calvert of Furneaux Pelham Hall, for whose benefit he decided to enlarge, remodel and rename the house at Tynan in the romantic manner then fashionable. (It seems that there was never an "abbey" proper at Tynan, despite its wealth of Celtic crosses, and the existence of an early Christian monastery associated with St Vindic on or near the site of the parish church).

The date when Fairview House became Tynan Abbey is variously given as 1810, 1813, 1816 and 1820. By July, 1816, work seems to have well advanced: Mrs Calvert, Sir James's mother-in-law, herself born in Ireland, recorded in her journal: "Saturday 13th [July 1816, Tynan] ... the country abt. very ugly and so I think this place, but wd. not have them think I was of that opinion for the world ...

I don't think I shall ever like the house, but indeed there is no judging of it in the state it is in ... I have a comfortable enough room ... Fanny [Mrs Calvert's daughter] sleeps in the bed with me and Timewell [her maid] in the dressing room ... Edmond [her son] next room to us ... all the other rooms near us are unfinished even without windows ... the stair case without bannisters and all about unfinished ... unplastered and full of rubbish and workmen ... in short I never was in a much more disagreeable place ... the nights being short is a gt. comfort, for I shd. grow nervous were they long and every place open about ... August the 4th ... to say the truth I have had quite enough of Tynan ... I particularly dislike living in a house full of workmen, and were it not that the nights are short, I really shou'd be miserable for every part of the house is open and unprotected and in the long nights, I shd. die of the fright ..." And, in the course of a later visit in June 1822: "Tynan Abbey. This house is good and very pretty and the place very nice, but somewhat exposed. At all events, I would not be condemned to live in Ireland for anything ..."!

The house is very large and somewhat rambling, evidently of at least three different dates, but all in a Tudoresque style with crenellations, dormers, a turret, a spire, and many ornate chimney-stacks punctuating the skyline. "The entrance hall resolutely medieval" says Dixon. The entrance front is asymmetrical, with pointed windows and a prominent square tower incorporating porch with oriel window above: the gable-end facing the garden was completely occupied by an enormous traceried window, like that of a college chapel, but the tracery all perished in the fire. There are curious gargoyles, some portraying monks and nuns. This must be the last part of the house to be built, and appears just as it was before the fire in a drawing of 1853 reproduced by E M Richardson. W J Barre's biographer says that he was responsible for "extensive alterations and additions for Sir M Stronge, Tynan Abbey", so presumably this section must be his

work. W H Lynn prepared drawings in 1877. On 19 March 1877, John Ynyr Burges "went to Tynan Abbey, the seat of Sir James M Stronge, where I had passed many happy days. The interior of the house is much improved by a handsome new staircase and a boudoir. There is a great addition of pictures and china".

The other end of the garden front terminates in the octagonal stone spire of a small chapel, and a square turret containing the water-tanks. Behind these, a range of red-brick kitchen chimneys look as if they might be survivors from a much earlier house on the site. In between, a long row of gabled dormers surmounts a three-storey block of which the base breaks forward to form an arcade not unlike a cloister. All this is executed in a medley of materials - stone of more than one kind, brick, rendering and stucco.

Dean thinks it possible to make "a confident attribution" of the central part of Tynan Abbey to John Nash, and is followed by Mansbridge and, more cautiously, Colvin. In correspondence with Dixon, Peter Reid suggests a comparison with Nash's Aqualate Hall in Staffordshire of 1806-9, which certainly had a rather similar arcade. The Tynan attribution rests partly on a set of architectural drawings, not however corresponding with the house as built, which Dean says were by A C Pugin of the Nash office, but which were destroyed in the fire; and on the proximity of Caledon, where Nash undoubtedly worked between 1808 and 1810. For my part, I am doubtful; I wonder whether this might not more probably be the work of James Pain or his brother George Richard Pain, both pupils of John Nash, who, according to Colvin, "was instrumental in establishing them as architects and builders in Ireland, where they had an extensive practice as designers of churches and castellated houses".

Descriptions of the house vary in their degree of enthusiasm for its architecture. Lt Bailey of the Ordnance Survey, in 1835, thought it "a remarkable handsome

building". Three years later, George Petrie, in a letter of 1st August 1838 to Bailey's superior officer, Captain Larcom, described it as "Sir J Strong's fine specimen of bastard and vile Gothic architecture". However, it appears that he was suffering from an acute hangover that morning: "I dined with Bennett, and left him at near one o'clock when I thought it only ten. But I am not the better of the raking today, and can scarcely write to you for headache".

Sir Bernard Burke, in 1855, took a more kindly view of it: "a spacious house in the abbey style, and has a picturesque appearance, bearing a very happy semblance of an ancient edifice, a deception which is not a little heightened by the nature of the surrounding country". Richard Hayward, in 1955, hedged his bets: "the house today, still curious in style and dubious in architectural integrity, but mellowed by time, humanised by generations of affectionate occupancy, and standing amidst a lush landscape of typical Armagh parkland adorned with noble trees". Its valuation varied from £125 in 1839 (but "for being too large deduct 5%") to £126 in 1923, when it was marked "no revision necessary" by reason of "the RUC occupying part of the premises rent-free for protection purposes". During the second World War, part of the house was occupied successively by Scottish, US and Belgian troops, and the parkland was colonised by Nissen huts. Some years after the fire and murders of 1981, in 1988, a mysterious explosion took place in the cellars, and a workman was injured: it may have been a booby-trap bomb. Since then, the skeleton of the building has remained gaunt and tragic, increasingly invaded by vegetation.

Postscript

The ruins of Tynan Abbey were finally demolished in November 1998, for reasons of public liability. The stone carvings and certain other details were rescued. Because it was so interesting a house; and because this entry had been written in its entirety before demolition took place; I

have, exceptionally, allowed this now disappeared building to retain its place in these pages.

Lithograph: from Burke. Photographs: RJ Welch, Ulster Museum, W 02/22/1; PRONI; MBR.

Situation: Cortytynan Road, Tynan; td, Fairview or Mucklagh; Parish, Tynan; District Council, Armagh; Grid ref. H 759 423.

References: Listed A (15/11/1). VAL 1B/236 p 177, VAL 2B/2/43B, p 122, VAL 12B/10/39A-E, T Ashe, A view of the Archbishoprick of Armagh in 1703, T848/1, p 30, T 1282/4, p 44, all in PRONI; Colchester Mss, PRO 30/9, Application book, pp 4, 56; Taylor and Skinner, 'Roads', 1778, p 266; C Bailey, OSM, 1835, Armagh, I, p 127; Lewis, TD, 1837, II, p 664; PG, III, 1846, p 433; Burke, 'Visitations', 2nd series, II, 1855, p 19; Stokes, 'Life of G Petrie', 1868, p 123; Dunlop, 'W J Barre', 1868, pp 43, 71; Bassett, 'Armagh', 1888, p 209; Hughes, 'Tynan Parish', 1910, p 114; Calvert, 'Irish beauty', 1911, p 363; Richardson, 'Next door neighbours', [1926], pp 29, 76; Marshall, 'Parish of Tynan', 1932, passim; R Hayward, in 'Ulster illustrated', VII, 1959, p 24; Bence-Jones, 'Burke's guide', 1978, p 279; Deane, 'Ulster countryside', 1983, p 208; Hon Mrs Calvert's diaries, Vol. 18, in the Rare Books Collection, Firestone Library, Princeton University, as quoted by Jeanne C Fawtier Stone, in 'Princeton University Library chronicle', XLVII, 1986, pp 342-3, 345; Mansbridge, 'John Nash', 1991, p 208; Dean, 'Gate lodges', UAHS, 1994, p 43; Colvin, 'Dictionary', 1995, p 721; H Dixon and others, notes and photographs in MBR.

Gosford Castle, Markethill

65. An important work by one of the leading London architects of the first half of the 19th century, Thomas Hopper (1776-1856). Sir Howard Colvin says that Hopper was an eclectic designer who held the belief that "it is an architect's business to understand all styles, and to be prejudiced in favour of none"; and considers that "his most interesting and original works were the two Norman castles" (Gosford and Penrhyn) "in which he effectively combined picturesque massing with a remarkable repertoire of Romanesque detailing which owed something to his familiarity with the twelfth-century keeps of Rochester and Hedingham". Also, "In his best days his flow of spirits was exuberant; his powers of conversation remarkable; his memory most tenacious. He never drank anything stronger than water, and could bear a marvellous amount of fatigue". His pupils included the young Belfast architect, John Millar, who worked on this commission with him, and signed a drawing showing the proposed front elevation.

The design was commissioned by Archibald Acheson, second Earl of Gosford, after the previous house had burned down. Bence-Jones says that it was "largely paid for by his wife, the daughter and heiress of Robert Sparrow, of Worlingham Hall, Suffolk: so that it is possible that the choice of so strange a style as Norman was hers; she was a life-long friend of Lady Byron so may have absorbed some of Byron's exotic and somewhat sinister brand of romanticism".

Building work began in 1819, and did not finish until around 1850, if then; the Valuation book of 1838 gives an extremely detailed description, while that of 1863 lists "buildings erected during the last 24 years and in progress" in equal detail: total valuation, £350. J Binns, in 1837, reported "Lord Gosford is building a baronial residence, under the supervision of Mr Hopper, the architect. Though far from being finished it has already cost about £80,000. The battlements and corbels struck me as being too light, and the arrangement in some parts appeared rather cramped, but the situation is good, and the grounds are well wooded". Samuel Lewis's rather less sniffy description appeared in the same year: "Gosford Castle, the seat of the Earl of Gosford, is a sumptuous and stately structure in the Norman style, built of granite from the Mullaglass quarries: the castle has been 17 years in progress of erection and is not yet completed; it is situated in an ample and highly improved demesne, about a quarter-mile to the east of the former mansion, which was built on the site of the castle originally erected by Sir A Acheson in 1617".

Not all the stone came from Mullaglass: the owners of the sloop 'William' had great difficulties in recovering from Lord Gosford £78 for the freight on 62 tons of Portland stone from Weymouth to Newry in August, 1826. It is hard to tell when the building became habitable. Evidently it was not so in 1820, but it was taxable, at £24.13.5, made up of £3.0.0 for 14 hearths, £15.3.0¾ for 57 window

lights, £2.16.10 for a 2-wheeled carriage drawn by 1 horse, £1.2.9 each for one jaunting car, one male servant, and one horse: plus 4.4 for one dog. On 4 January 1834, Hopper writes to Lord Gosford "I shall be happy to congratulate you on your actual occupation of the Castle". And, rather sadly, six days later, "I am glad Major Close" (of Drumbanagher, 212) "agrees that he has got so perfect a house and sincerely congratulate Mr Playfair who is a very clever man although I suspect it has not cost him one hundredth part the thought, and but a small portion of the trouble, which I took to try to make Gosford Castle as convenient and as good as I wished it to be ... I have always felt a sorrow that I ever went to Ireland. I now consider it a misfortune ..." (Mowl). The Parliamentary Gazetteer of 1846 just says "The mansion is called Gosford-Castle, and is a quite new and spacious structure, in the early style of castellated baronial architecture". Between 1838 and 1845 Thomas Duff of Newry was still working on "additions, alterations and improvements" costing £5,400; and work continued under his successor as Hopper's assistant, G A Burn, until Hopper's death in August 1856: "For the 12 months previous to the decease of Mr Hopper ... I may fairly say that the superintendence of the works at Gosford was entirely in my hands".

In January 1862, John Ynyr Burges visited Gosford, and recorded in his diary: "We found the large round room completed, all but the fireplace...The castle appears an immense library, for my room is full of books and all of the choicest kinds, with the most perfect bindings. The new apartments consisting of long corridors and morning rooms belonging to this family, and sleeping ditto, are handsome and comfortable, and the beautiful and rare china does not fail to give a most picturesque effect. The ceilings in the more ancient part of the castle are well imagined. The Norman cornice is most happily introduced. The staircase is very appropriate. The dining hall brings you back to feudal days. The table, which is profusely

covered with every delicious viand and the choicest wines, rather beats the banquet hollow of our Norman ancestors. The sideboard or buffet takes a very sightly place amidst a recess of Norman-form columns with massive pendants dropping from its ceiling ... You eat, drink, talk and laugh immensely. There is something in the air and cheer around you that encourages you to do so".

The listers succinctly describe its style as "predominantly Norman Revival with Saxon and some 14th century details thrown in ... This is the earliest major composition in the Norman Revival style anywhere in the UK". It was followed very shortly after by Hopper's even more massive Penrhyn Castle near Caernarvon.

Gosford is remarkably large, remarkably elaborate, and exceptionally well built - indeed, it appears not just defensible but practically indestructible. It is dominated by its great square keep with corner turrets containing chimneys, with subsidiary round and square towers. Bence-Jones considers that "the garden front ... has a strange beauty; the stone seems pale, Norman becomes more like Southern Romanesque. The grouping is masterly; the walls are at different angles to each, so that there is a great sense of movement ... Although Norman was really unsuited to C19 living, the interior does not suffer from the heaviness one finds at Penrhyn".

The first critic to remark the importance of Gosford was Robin Fedden, "that unusual creature, a competent aesthete" (Jennifer Jenkins) who became Historic Buildings Secretary of the National Trust in 1951, the year in which the Trust acquired Penrhyn through the Land Fund; and who accordingly, in researching the history of Hopper and his work, seems to have visited Gosford about 1952, and to have carried out some interesting research into the account books in the estate office. He derives Gosford from Nash's Killymoon Castle of 1803, and Nash's unfinished work at Shane's Castle of 1816, via Hopper's employment by Lord O'Neill after some misunderstanding with Nash: but still points out of Gosford, that "It must be regarded as one of the most original buildings of the first half of the nineteenth century for it has no immediate antecedents. The immense granite castle, reputed to be the largest pile in Ireland, with over 150 rooms, sprang fully fledged in its elaborate neo-Norman detail from Hopper's imagination. A three-storey keep, such as Hopper was to repeat at Penrhyn, and a massive round tower containing a circular drawing room, are the salient features of the main elevation. Both are ponderously machicolated and achieve those effects of weight and gravity which are the hallmarks of Hopper's 'Norman style'". Fedden considers the entrance front, the work of "an architect less bold", inferior; in fact it seems to have been by Hopper's principal assistant, Burn, and to have departed only in minor respects from Hopper's original intentions.

Of the interior, Fedden writes that "the effect is cramped and oppressive ... only the dining room, with engaged pilasters of pink Armagh marble and white plaster decoration, is effective and pleasing. Some of the carving at Gosford was undertaken by John Smyth, Master of the Dublin Society's Modelling School, and like his father, Edward Smyth, a talented sculptor. Though the building has been for nearly a generation empty and unfurnished, Hopper's careful and solid building shows no sign of decay ... Possibly his masonry is thicker than any which had been built in the British Isles since medieval times. It is characteristic of the architect that the gigantic wall which encircles the park should be provided with a coping of cumbrous boulders, undressed and set side by side upon the walltop".

It appears that Fedden, like Bence-Jones, prefers Gosford Castle to Penrhyn. Not so Tim Mowl, who dismisses Gosford as "a clumsy experiment" ... "What Thomas Hopper evolved" at Penrhyn "was how to arrange Norman elements asymmetrically but with a satisfying and picturesque profile". But, says Mowl, these two great castellated buildings were to be the last of their kind. If the Norman Revival style "had been chosen as the style to reshape Windsor for George IV, its establishment would have been secure. Instead, Wyatville dressed Windsor in the Gothic of Edward III's reign and that, effectively, was the end of the neo-Norman road for domestic architecture".

The history of the castle has been chequered. It cost over £40,000 up to 1829, though Lord Gosford had deliberately incurred incumbrances of £67,000. "Lord Gosford, unfortunately for his successors, managed to combine land purchases, building, and personal extravagance to such an extent that his incumbrances more than doubled" - to £112,858 - "in two decades ... During the initial stages of building the Gosfords resided at Rostrevor ... Estate finances were at breaking point in these years of building ... With the death of the third earl in 1864 the Gosford seat became demoted to the status of a rather superior holiday residence; a tradition, continued for many years, came into being that Christmas should be spent at Markethill and that the demesne should be used for grouse shooting in August and September ... but the facade of opulence gave way to reality" (Gourley). The fourth earl was an extravagant friend of King Edward VII; he was forced to sell off the library in 1888 to pay a racing debt, long before the King's accession, and in 1921 was forced to sell off the remaining contents (see page 72). The castle stood vacant until 1940, when, like many another, it was commandeered, and used first by the British army, then by the US army, with a prisoner-of-war camp in the grounds. After the war, it was used at one time as winter quarters for a travelling circus, at another as a store for the Public Record Office. Then, in the 1970s, it was for a time once again occupied as a British army base in the Troubles. In 1978, the Department of Agriculture, which had acquired the demesne for a forest park, granted a 99 year lease of the castle to a consortium of businessmen hoping to restore and convert it into a luxury hotel. Work proceeded sporadically: at one time a restaurant was opened, but forced to close again; completion seems a long way off, but it is greatly to be hoped that it will come in the end, for this is a building of quite outstanding interest and significance.

Gosford is not without some diverting literary associations, apart from the tenuous association between the Lords Gosford and Byron. Jonathan Swift certainly stayed with the Achesons in the previous house on the site for several months in 1729, and went so far as to publish a poem evincing his intention of building nearby a house of his own, to be called "Drapier's Hill"; but changed his mind. More recently Gosford provided the model for Castlemallock in A Dance to the Music of Time. In the second volume of his memoirs, Anthony Powell writes: "The Divisional Tactical School was quartered in Gosford Castle, Co Armagh, an 1820 neogothic pile (said to have been the first mock-Norman castle built in the British Isles), surrounded by a fine park ... An air of inexorable gloom hung over Gosford, undissipated by the crew of

seedy bad-mannered middle-aged officers who made up the staff of the Divisional School. The place figures as Castlemallock in *The Valley of Bones*, one of the paperback covers of which was designed by Osbert Lancaster, who, though he had never seen the Castle, brought by instinct an extraordinary verisimilitude to Gosford's keep and turrets." Incidentally, Powell and his wife seem to have lived for a time during the war in 19, Wellington Park Terrace, Belfast, in which I lived subsequently, until I sold it to my friend the historian J C Beckett: for how many blue plaques does that house qualify?

Photographs: Michael O'Connell; postcard in SELB Local Studies Library, Armagh; MBR. Elevation drawing: John Millar (from photograph in MBR).

Situation: In Gosford Forest Park; td, Gosford Demesne; Parish, Mullaghbrack; District Council, Armagh; Grid ref. H 946 412.

References: Listed A (15/7/1A). Elevation drawing by John Millar (photograph in MBR); VAL 1B/213, pp 111-114, VAL 2B/2/12A, p 14, D1606/1/2/53, 68, 69, 117, 124; D1606/2/4/5; D1606/2/8/581; T1282/2, p 88, all in PRONI; Lewis, TD, 1837, II, p 409; Binns, 'Miseries and beauties of Ireland', 1837, I, p 195; Byrne, 'Carlingford Bay', 1846, p 267; PG, II, 1846, p 279; Young, 'Belfast and province of Ulster', 1909, p 218; R Fedden, in 'Studies in architectural history', II, 1956, p 58; R S Gourley, Gosford estates 1610-1876, university thesis, 1973, copy in PRONI; Bence-Jones, 'Burke's guide', 1978, p 143; Powell, 'Faces in my time' 1980, p 105; P Larmour, in 'Ulster architect', March 1985; T Mowl, Appendix, in NT, 'Penrhyn Castle, Gwynedd', 1991, p 89; Jenkins, 'From acorn to oak tree', 1994, p 166; McMinn, 'Jonathan's travels', 1994, p 126; Colvin, 'Dictionary', 1995, p 512; BNL, 2/1/1997.

The Argory, Derrycaw, Charlemont

66. Described by the late Gervase Jackson-Stops, no mean critic, as "a remarkably atmospheric Greek Revival house of the 1820s, designed by the Dublin architects John and Arthur Williamson" ... "Exotic and cosmopolitan". Strangely, accorded only a B+ rating by the listers, though Gervase would certainly have accorded it an A: and so would I.

The name is as exotic as the house. There is no such word as an argory in the English language; and the suggested derivation from the Irish "hill of the garden" is somewhat suspect. It is tempting to believe that, with its overtones of augury and argosy, it was a happy invention of the highly civilised (and travelled) young Dublin barrister, Walter McGeough, for whom the house was built. Jackson-Stops suggests the name Argory was not used before 1837 (when Samuel Lewis so refers to the house), but a conveyance of 4 March 1818 refers to "all that part of Derrycaw called the Argory" (D 288/A/5/21).

The circumstances of its building were as unusual as the name. Joshua McGeough, who died in 1817, provided in his will that his son Walter might not live in the family home, Drumsill, so long as any two of his sisters remained unmarried. The son therefore decided to use his share of his father's estate to build a house of his own on the family's Derrycaw estate; and employed as his architects the otherwise little-known Williamson brothers of Dublin, whose mother had come from Armagh, who had worked

for Francis Johnston, and whom he evidently recommended. They seem to have provided the designs; the work was supervised by the youthful Thomas Duff of Newry.

The researches of Anne Lavin have thrown some light on the careers of the Williamsons - a third brother, Matthew, the eldest, though also an architect, seems not to have been involved with the Argory. They appear in the Dublin street directories between 1815 and 1837 sometimes as architects, sometimes as measurers, sometimes as builders. Their only known architectural works remain the "part completion of James Gandon's designs" for Emo Court, Co Leix, in 1812; the Argory around 1820; and the two seaside houses they built for themselves around 1830. They seem to have prospered principally as property developers at Rathmines. Out of the proceeds, they built themselves at Monkstown two adjoining "simple classical country-style houses reflective of the period, with large gardens down to the sea, coach-houses, stables and outbuildings": still standing, and still with their hipped roofs and Elizabethan-revival chimney-stacks. Lavin remarks that "an interesting stylistic link can be made between 53 Mountjoy Street" (their Dublin house), "Albany House" (Arthur's house at Monkstown), "Berlin Cottage" (at Rathmines) "and the Argory ... They all have similar diamond and lozenge-shaped subdivisions to the glass sidelights of the windows - in the Argory these appear on the west front door".

Work on the main block started in 1819, and was more or less complete by 1824, when Walter McGeough assumed the additional name of Bond, "out of affectionate regard to the family of his deceased grandmother". In 1837, house, gate house, gardener's house and offices were all in category A and together valued at the remarkably high figure of £124.2.10, by 1863 increased to £170. The house is of Caledon ashlar with Navan limestone trim; of two storeys, and seven bays. Some (but not others) of its Georgian-glazed windows were lengthened about 1880, without detriment to the appearance of the house. The north wing, with its octagonal upstairs library, was an early addition of 1826, though damaged by a fire in 1898. There is some good plasterwork, attributed to a Mr

Anesfree, said by Thomas Duff in 1822 to have been "the principal stucco plasterer in Belfast".

As to the central block looking out over the curve of the river Blackwater, "The strength of the baseless Doric columns and entablature, the bold use of different types of rustication, and the detail of the pediment with its acroteria and central "jelly-mould", make the centrepiece a highly accomplished composition. The elliptical arch over the doorcase may be derived from Bélanger, and the massive label-mouldings above the first-floor windows each side are also reminiscent of the world of Boullée and Ledoux. One can find parallels for the door, with its squashed fanlight and glazed side-panels, in Dublin townhouses of the period, while the carved stone lion spewing

a great acanthus leaf down on the unsuspecting visitor adds a peculiarly Irish note of comedy" (Jackson-Stops). (And: letter, in MBR, from Hugh Dixon to Peter Marlow: June 1979: "You were right to look at the lion's mouthful: it occurs at Townley Hall, and the Bank of Ireland ...") And: (from the same letter): "The frieze of mutules and guttae, or "blocks and corks", on the stairs and in the dining room, occur inside and outside Armagh court house, emphasising as they do at the Argory the choice of the Doric order ... conservative in its plan, with a liberal application of Johnston's idiosyncratic decorative detail". And, finally, from a letter from Hugh Dixon to Robert McKinstry of July 1979, "The Johnston-Williamson authorship seems clear - ie, the Williamsons working in a disjointed Johnstonian manner".

All this flurry of commentary is attributable to the handsome gift of the Argory (supported by an endowment from the Ulster Land Fund) made by the late W A N McGeough Bond, great-grandson of its builder, to the National Trust, on the last day of the fiscal year, 31 March 1979, as a result of delicate and long-drawn out negotiations in which I myself played a peripheral part. I particularly remember the magic of that drawing-room, stuffed to the ceiling with furniture in dust-sheets, paintings on the floor, and packing-cases, waiting to re-emerge from hibernation.

For my part, I find the most attractive feature of the house to be the hall and stair-well (colour-plate I): "near-horizontal sunshine floods in, reflected from the dazzling curve of the river Blackwater, striking sparks indoors from iron, steel, bronze, brass. Too easily we think of metal as the substance proper to the High Victorian age - the age of the iron horse and the iron ship. But here is a marvellous room, full of polished and chiselled metal, every bit of it pre-Victorian. The great cast-iron stove in the centre of the room, topped by a copy of the Warwick vase ... the double-curved marble staircase, its handrail (of mahogany inlaid with a central spine of ebony) borne on fine brass columns for balusters. There are three to a step; an extra fat one to help to carry the whorl at the foot of the stairs; eighty-six around the railing of the gallery; a total of 162 to be polished by the Trust's housekeeper!" (Brett).

The stable yard, 1820 coach house (with its cupola and

florid wind-vane), outbuildings, acetylene gas lighting system, gardens, riverside walks, south lodge, the Derrycaw lodge, and the Sunday school, are all charming ancillary delights. So is the former land steward's house dated, by an inscribed stone in the lintel of its front door, to 1698, and with a bog oak staircase, separately listed B1 (15/1/5). To me, the Argory comprises one of the most endearing groups of buildings in the county.

Photographs: Michael O'Connell (see also colour plate Xa); late 19th-century overdoor, MBR.

Situation: 144, Derrycaw Road, Charlemont; td, Derrycaw; Parish, Clonfeacle; District Council, Armagh; Grid ref, H 871 582.

References: Listed B+ (15/1/2). D 288/A/5/21, D 288/E, VAL 1B/225A, and VAL 2B/2/23, all in PRONI; papers and plans in the house; Lewis, TD, 1837, I, p 362; J R Ward, OSM, 1838, Armagh, I, p 21; Bence-Jones, 'Burke's guide', 1978, p 12; G Jackson-Stops, in 'Country life', 30 June and 7 July, 1983; Pierce and Coey, 'Taken for granted', 1984, p 164; Mills, 'Noble dwellings of Ireland', 1987, p 23; Gallagher and Rogers, 'Castle, coast and cottage', 1992, p 5; P O Marlow, NT guidebook, 1992, passim; C E B Brett, in 'Apollo', May 1995, p 18; A Lavin, Leinster Square, Rathmines, UCD thesis, 1995, passim; files in MBR.

1 - 5, Charlemont Place, The Mall, Armagh

67. A terrace of five very grand cut-stone houses looking out over the greenery of the Mall, built between 1827 and 1830 as a speculative venture by Lord Charlemont. His architect was William Murray, his builder John Barnes. The layout is classical late-Georgian: each house three-bay, and three-storey on basement. The end pavilions are later, but seemly, additions. For some reason, No 5 was valued at £65 (a very high figure for a town house) and £5 more than its neighbours.

"Superbly regal in scale", say the UAHS listers. "Ashlar stonework, blocked parapet, overhanging cornice with dentils and modillions, stepped quoins. First-floor balconies are contemporary. Cut-stone Doric doorcases, cornices decorated with paterae. The doors of Nos 4 and 5 are original. The interiors of these two units remain practically intact ... The whole group is fronted by fine railings casing swept stone stairways leading to each entrance". They go so far in their enthusiasm as to comment "There is really very little in all Ireland that could match the style and quality of this exceptional terrace". Not every

Dubliner might agree with that, but certainly they are very fine.

The houses seem originally to have been occupied by professional, clerical and military men, changing hands with great frequency. By 1973, Nos 1 to 3 were occupied by the County Council, No 4 by the Freemasons, and No 5 by the Armagh City Club. Since 1990, the whole terrace (and the extensive buildings constructed on its backlands) have belonged to the Southern Education and Library Board, which is much to be commended for its conscientious restoration after the devastation caused by the explosion of a large bomb in the roadway in April 1989.

Photograph: Michael O'Connell.
Situation: The Mall East, Armagh; td, Corporation; Parish, and District Council, Armagh; Grid ref. H 877 453.
References: Listed A (15/17/10); in conservation area. VAL 1B/21B, p 127, VAL 12B/10/4A-E, in PRONI; Stewart, 'RHA index of exhibitors', I, 1985, p 224; T G F Paterson, Armachiana, V, pp36-48; 'Buildings of Armagh', UAHS, 1992, pp 131-133.

Plate I *(overleaf)*:   Hall and stair-well, The Argory, Derrycaw (66). Photograph: Andreas von Einsiedel, NT Picture Library
Plate II: St Colman's College chapel, Newry (54)
Plate III *(opposite)*:   a. Drawing-room, Ardress, Loughgall (60); b. Archbishop Robinson's chapel, Armagh (22)

Plate IV (*opposite*): a. Killevy old churches, Meigh (12); b. Creggan Church (17)
Plate V: a. Former Masonic Hall, Armagh (181); b. Archbishop Robinson's chapel, Armagh (22); c. First Presbyterian Church, Portadown (45)

Plate VI (opposite): a. St Luke's Church,
       Mullaghglass (38)
      b. St Patrick's (RC) Cathedral,
       Armagh (47)

Plate VII: a. Cardinal O Fiaich
      Memorial Library,
      Armagh (177)
      b. Gospel Hall, Glenanne (48)

Plate VIII (overleaf): Font, St Luke's Church,
      Ballymoyer (41)

Bengal Place, 49-51 High Street, Lurgan

68. A grotesque example of the ill-effects of Ulster's Troubles.

On 11 October, 1837, Thomas McIlroy, compiling the fair sheets for his Ordnance Survey memoir, wrote: "There are 2 very fine houses at present building at the south-east end" of Lurgan. "They are of brick, stuccoed in imitation of Portland stone". They subsequently became known for some reason as Bengal Place. Later, the two houses were thrown into one to serve as the Orchard County Hotel. They were classified A by Oram and his UAHS colleagues in 1971; they could then still be described as "A fine pair of large three-storey stucco houses of c 1830, porches with coupled Ionic columns, Greek key pattern mouldings and good ironwork".

In 1974, a large bomb nearby caused extensive damage to No 49, which was left roofless and internally gutted; though No 51 was apparently quite undamaged when both were officially listed in 1976. They were classified B, and, presumably on the optimistic assumption that rebuilding was impending, described as "a double-house hotel of three storeys with Ionic porches and other classical details. The basement is enclosed with decorative iron railings." In 1979, the remaining walls of No 49 collapsed, and No 51 was by then reckoned to have become dangerous; demolition was recommended. In the event, however, the walls of both houses were, with the exception of a single red-brick chimney-stack, cut down to first-floor level. In February 1980, an official letter, surprisingly, confirmed that "this building can no longer be regarded as a listed building" - despite the fact that it has, even now, never been either delisted, or the subject of any listed building consent for alteration. Nonetheless, planning permission was granted in November 1980 for a change of use from 'hotel function hall and kitchen' to 'gospel hall'. At this point, it seems, a flat roof or lid was fitted on the surviving carcase; the front window-openings were blocked up, and the placards painted with pious texts and platitudes; consorting strangely with the mutilated dignity of the twin porticos and their supporting railings.

This, now the stunted stump of a once-impressive building, standing as it does just at the security gates giving (or denying) access to the town centre, constitutes a melancholy symbol of the effects of bombs on Ulster's townscape.

Photographs: Before, MBR; after, Michael O'Connell.
Situation: 49/51, High Street, Lurgan; td, Lurgan; Parish, Shankill; District Council, Craigavon; Grid ref. J 085 581.
References: (Still) Listed B (14/23/1). T McIlroy, OSM, 1837, Armagh, I, p 111; Oram, 'Craigavon', UAHS, 1971, pt II, p 9; file in MBR.

Brownlow House, Lurgan

69. In my judgement, the grandest architectural set-piece in the county, by the distinguished Edinburgh architect William Henry Playfair: "its astonishing silhouette ... rears suddenly into view, like a stage set for a fairy tale, on the main Belfast-Dublin railway line" (Gow). "A remarkable structure of soft golden sandstone in the Elizabethan-revival style pioneered by Nash and Repton and popularised by Sir Walter Scott, with numerous tall spiralled chimney-pots, great oriel windows surmounted by pierced, pinnacled and curlicued balustrades, and a delightful romantic tower with lantern and dome ... The design has some kinship to Donaldson's Hospital in Edinburgh, by the same architect (begun 1842)" (Oram). "Of honey-coloured stone, with a romantic silhouette; many gables with tall ·finials; many tall chimney-pots; oriels crowned with strapwork and a tower with lantern and dome. The walls of its principal reception-rooms are decorated with panels painted to resemble verd-antique; while the ceilings are grained to represent various woods" (Bence-Jones). "The present mansion is one of the finest Elizabethan edifices in Ireland" (Parliamentary Gazetteer). "The informal Tudor of Brownlow, though much emulated, was rarely equalled" (Dixon).

Charles Brownlow, MP, created Baron Lurgan in 1839 for services to the Whig party, was as a student a fellow-lodger with the young architect in the Edinburgh home of the latter's uncle; and Brownlow's sister was married to Maxwell Close, who in 1829 employed Playfair to design his great Italianate house at Drumbanagher (now demolished but for its porte-cochère - 212) . As Gow remarks, "It is perhaps surprising that two of the finest houses by William Henry Playfair, the least travelled of architects, lay across the Irish Sea ... The success of Drumbanagher brought out a degree of brotherly rivalry in Charles Brownlow who, in 1833, commissioned from Playfair a new house for Lurgan. The first designs were for a classical

house "with a noble Corinthian portico" and "in the style of a Roman villa". But "Charles Brownlow proved a maddeningly indecisive client. A number of designs were tried and found wanting until Playfair, after careful inspection of what he considered to be an exceptionally beautiful site, devised the dramatic design with its diagonal plan where the public rooms radiate like the spokes of a wheel to take advantage of the views, but also recalls the Elizabethan's fascination with geometry".

There is a degree of uncertainty about the building dates. Gow suggests that building took place from 1838 to 1842, probably "in two stages in order to control costs". Of the nearly 300 meticulously signed and dated drawings by Playfair which survive in the Public Record Office of Northern Ireland, the earliest is a ground plan of 25 November 1833, which shows that the conception had already been fully worked out; elevations (but excluding the tower), and the elaborate detailing of the innumerable chimney-pots (all different) were ready by August 1834; the drawings for the tower date from 27 December 1836; detailed drawings for the ceilings, plasterwork and chimneypieces of the drawing-room, dining-room, library and great staircase, follow from January to October 1838; and the last drawing, numbered 286, for "the niche on the north side of the Ante-room" is dated 29 May 1839. So early as 29 July 1836, "Charles Brownlow Esq, New House" was already valued, with the offices, at the tremendous total of £307.17.11, despite the deduction of one half in respect of want of finish to the main body of the dwelling. The parts apparently already completed, and presumably occupied, include Family Wing at £44. 15.0 and Children's Apartments £27.6.4. The unfinished state of the house is confirmed by Thomas McIlroy of the Ordnance Survey, writing on 11 October 1837: "The seat of the Honourable Charles Brownlow, situated on the north side of Lurgan. The house is at present building. It is in the Elizabethan style and will be very beautiful when finished ... The grounds are well laid out. The garden is small and has a bad aspect. There are 2 artificial lakes in the demesne, the banks of which are wooded. They are the resort of immense numbers of wildfowl, mostly ducks. The family library was sold by auction some years since". Samuel Lewis, writing in the same year, says: "Near the town is Lurgan House, the residence of the Rt. Hon. Charles Brownlow, now being rebuilt on an extensive scale and in the Elizabethan style, with freestone brought from Scotland". Indeed, all the materials and all the workmen were brought over from Scotland, and Playfair, the most meticulous and exacting of bachelor architects, spared his unfortunate client no expense, demurring at every suggestion of economy. Gow records that between 1838 and 1842 the builder, Charles McGibbon, was paid £30,450; the plasterer, £1,245; plumber, £2,218; interior decorator, £2,236; furnisher and upholsterer, £3,289.

The result appears to have given satisfaction. In 1841, Playfair wrote to a close friend: "I came over last Wednesday at the pressing request of Lord Lurgan which I was more inclined to obey, as I had not been here since the house was entirely finished and I was desirous of beholding my Elizabethan Child. Brownlow has had the Ground dressed up in the most admirable manner and my oriel windows stand out charmingly in the midst of smooth velvet turf, skilfully sprinkled with flowers and shrubs and surrounded by magnificent trees. In the hope that you will not think me conceited I may say that I think the House more comfortable and more like an old manor house than any modern attempt I have yet seen. In a few years when I expect to be dropping into the grave, I anticipate that it will possess the character of old age by weather stains and vegetable incrustations. Lord and Lady Lurgan are delighted with it and overwhelm me with kindness."

The family lived there in great style for some years: "As

the Brownlows owned vast tracts of bog land in the Montiaghs, most of the fires were fuelled with turf, the stoking being carried our by a small army of servants whose sole task was keeping the fires burning in all the rooms" (Cordner). But in 1893, the third baron sold off his

Lurgan property, and in 1903 the house was, surprisingly, bought by Lurgan District Orange Lodge. The demesne has been a public park since 1911. During the first and second World Wars it was requisitioned for occupation by various units of the British, Belgian, and US armies, in 1943 providing a headquarters for General Patton. It has not been used as a private house for nearly a century, and over this period has acquired quite a few regrettably institutional characteristics. It has also on several occasions attracted the attentions of those not well disposed to the various organisations, mostly Orange or Black in hue, which share its occupancy; most recently, it was extensively damaged by fire in August 1996. The ball-room, and the grand staircase with its coloured glass, have unfortunately been completely destroyed. The trustees in whom ownership is vested are valiantly (and creditably) endeavouring, at heavy cost, to restore those parts of the building most at risk. At the date of writing, a visit to this exceptionally fine building is a rather distressing experience. But a number of rooms retain something of their original character. The entrance stairway, a bit like that at Clandeboye, is hopeless for a handicapped individual, but very splendid. The octagon room, from which all the other reception rooms radiate, retains its original marbled panels, as specified by Playfair and executed by Hay & Company of Edinburgh, and the dining-room and saloon also retain traces of the original "sumptuousness" of the house. And, even if large parts of the interior have, sadly, now lost irretrievably their authentic baronial flavour, the exterior - when fully repaired - will continue to provide the citizens of Lurgan with the most striking sky-line, and one of the finest buildings, in the County Armagh.

Photographs: R J Welch, Ulster Museum, W02/26/1; central diagonal enfilade of reception rooms, MBR. Drawings: W H Playfair, PRONI.
Situation: Off Windsor Avenue, Lurgan; td, Demesne; Parish, Shankill; District Council, Craigavon; Grid ref. J 084 587.
References: Listed A (14/24/18). Drawings in D 1928/P/8/A1-286 and D 1928/W/5, VAL 1B/223B, p 62, all in PRONI; drawings, letter-books and letters in Special Collections Department of Edinburgh University Library; T McIlroy, OSM, 1837, Armagh, I, p 113; Lewis, TD, 1837, II, p 323; P G, II, 1846, p 709; Bassett, 'Armagh', p 343; Oram, 'Craigavon', UAHS, 1971, pt I, p 9; Dixon, 'Ulster architecture', UAHS, 1972, p 10; Bence-Jones, 'Burke's guide', 1978, p 49; I Gow, in 'Architectural heritage', II, 1991, pp 79-83; Jupp, 'Heritage gardens', 1992, A/008; Cordner, 'Brownlow House', 1993, passim; Dean, 'Gate lodges', UAHS, 1994, p 34; Colvin, 'Dictionary', 1995, p 764; I Gow, in 'Irish arts review', XIV, 1998, pp 57-61.

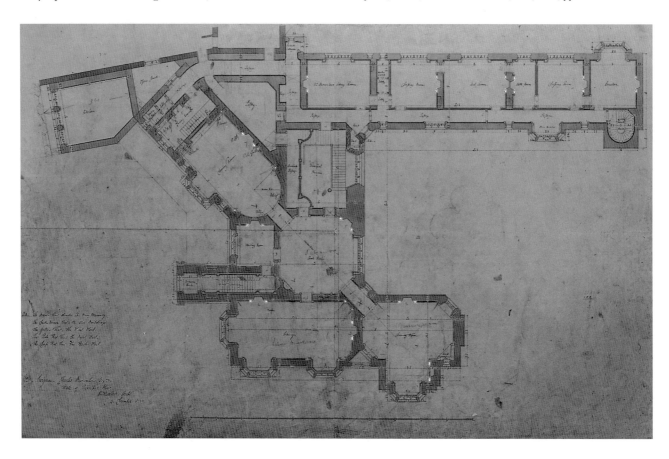

Killevy Castle, Meigh

70. An exceedingly fine, deceptively modest, pre-Victorian castle, designed in 1836 by George Papworth of Dublin, architect, for Mr Powell Foxall: a sort of scaled-down version of Gosford Castle (65). Formerly a modest farmhouse, Killevy Lodge, with two rooms on each side of the front door, and (apparently) an oval room with Georgian-glazed windows at the back; transformed by Papworth by the addition of four stone towers (three square, the tallest round) at the corners, machicolations, dripstones, three-light Tudoresque windows, along with outbuildings, belvedere, plantings, lake, and corn-mill fed from the lake; also, in polychrome, in the wall above the front door, the Foxall coat of arms and the discreet, if punning, Foxall family motto, "faire sans dire". Two-storey on basement, mostly of finely-dressed granite but with some areas of grey-painted stucco. The crenellations are marvellously convincing, as are the splendid mock-medieval studded front door (painted green), and the astonishingly tall and narrow slit windows. Gordon Wheeler has drawn my attention to the crafty way in which the crenellations of the entrance bay are carried back over the roof to enclose the original chimney-stacks. There is a fine terrace, with subsidiary turrets, and tunnels underneath to permit the servants to come and go unseen. Williams, with unusual eloquence, sums it all up nicely: "Sugar-plum Gothick castle ... All this deception would be believable were it not for the irrepressible

fantasy of the architect."

George Papworth (1781 - 1855) was the younger brother, and pupil, of the better-known English architect John Buonarotti Papworth, son of a notable stuccodore. He established a successful practice in Ireland, and designed Sir Patrick Dun's Hospital, and the King's Bridge over the Liffey, in Dublin. His drawings for Killevy were exhibited in the Royal Hibernian Academy in 1836, with the comment "now erecting".

Meredith Foxall of Killevy was one of the founders of Moore, McCann and Foxall's Bank, of Newry, which unfortunately crashed in 1816. But the shareholders seem to have salvaged more than the depositors; for in 1836 Poole Foxall, shown in the Valuation book as proprietor of Killevy, could afford extensive improvements to the former farmhouse: "The dwelling is undergoing repairs and additions, not yet all roofed, nor all built. Valued by estimation" at £12. 18. 10 for the dwelling, and £12. 4. 0 for the outbuildings. In the following year, John Heather of the Ordnance Survey remarked "Killevy Lodge, the residence of John Foxall Esq., is situated in the townland of Clonlum. It stands on the eastern base of Slieve Gullion and is built with considerable taste in a castellated style. It was completed during the present year. The patches of fir plantation that rise about it take away in some measure from the wild and barren appearance of the mountain". By 1888, these plantings had matured: "Killeavy Castle,

residence of Mr. Joseph Bell, is charmingly situated at the foot of Slieve Gullion. Mr. Joseph Foxall, over 60 years ago, planted a considerable portion of the mountain, and his successor, Mr. Powell Foxall, continued the example until a large tract has been covered" (Bassett). Byrne in 1846 considered "the delightful residence of Powell Foxall Esq., JP," to be "of the Elizabethan era, and certainly one of the most beautiful of the rural paradises which adorn the rich plains of Down and Armagh".

In 1852, the place was offered for sale by auction in Dublin through the Encumbered Estates Court, and the

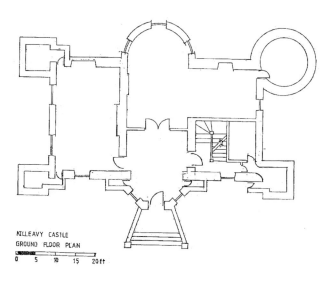

KILLEAVY CASTLE
GROUND FLOOR PLAN
0   5   10   15   20ft

sale particulars are illuminating: "The Demesne of Killevey Castle contains about 210 statute acres of Mountain Pasture, 90 acres of Plantation, and 156 of Arable Land, all in a ring fence, in the centre of which stands the Castle. It is a beautiful structure, in the baronial style, possessing every comfort and convenience. The accommodation on the basement storey comprises Kitchen, Scullery, Larder, Servants' Hall, Store-house, Pantry, Dairy, etc. Above there is the Parlour, with a Wine Cellar and Store-room, adjoining a Drawing-room, with Library and Conservatory attached. Over these are six Bed-rooms and four Dressing-rooms, Bath-room, etc, all and each of which, as well as the entire basement storey, are supplied with hot and cold water. The Castle stands on the side of a Mountain, and is surrounded with Plantations. The Pleasure Grounds are most tastefully laid out. There is an excellent Garden, of one acre, walled in, and an ornamental piece of water below the Castle ... The out-offices are on a corresponding scale of real utility and convenience".

However, the castle failed to find a buyer, and was "withdrawn from auction. Some of its outlying demesne was sold, and this presumably eased financial pressure on Foxall". Ten years later, John Foxall was still in occupation. In 1868 the occupier was William Gillespie; since 1881 it has belonged to the Bell family, and is locally referred to as "Bell's Castle". Its valuation has fluctuated surprisingly over the years. Between 1862 and 1889 it was valued at £22, £60, £30, £40, £60 again, £10, and £7. Was it damaged by fire? Was it perhaps divided up, and only partly occupied? By 1921, part of it was empty, another part rented by John A Bell from Reps Joseph Bell, the valuation a mere £22.

It is now, alas, empty, and in poor order, the victim both of vandalism and of burglary, though many interior features appear to survive - including even some of the original wallpaper. Although a condition report of 1992 refers both to dry rot and to woodworm, it concludes "it is not considered that the house is realistically beyond saving. This is a unique property with great potential and could once more be made into a comfortable home". It richly deserves its classification as one of only a handful of buildings in category A in the county. It is not helpful that this part of South Armagh has traditionally shown itself suspicious and unwelcoming towards outsiders. Dare one hope that happier days may come, and that this delightful building might, in some shape, become a showpiece of the Ring of Gullion?

Photographs and plan: MBR. Water-colour: Armagh County Museum.
Situation: 10, Ballintemple Road, Meigh; td, Clonlum; Parish, Killevy; District Council, Newry & Mourne; Grid ref. J 042 205.
References: Listed A (16/13/1). Stewart, 'RHA index of exhibitors', I, 1985, 1836:229; No 229 of 1836; VAL 1B/244B, p 121, VAL 2B/2/37F, p 12, VAL 12B/15/17 A-D, T 2677/1, all in PRONI; water-colour in Armagh County Museum; J Heather, OSM, 1837, Armagh, I, p 53; Lewis, TD, 1837, II, p 144; Byrne, 'Carlingford Bay', 1846, p 136; Bassett, 'Armagh', 1888, p 245; O'Kane, 'Lower Killevy', [1955], p 19; Craig and Knight of Glin, 'Ireland observed', 1970, p 70; Lyons, 'Incumbered estates', 1993, p 33; Dean, 'Gate lodges', UAHS, 1994, p 39; Williams, 'Architecture in Ireland', 1994, p 13; Colvin, 'Dictionary', 1995, p 732; notes and condition report in MBR.

Tandragee Castle

71. A remarkable building, on a remarkable site, amidst a medley of strange surroundings. The present is at least the third stronghold perched on this precipitate cliff: described in 1854 as "The baronial mansion of the Duke of Manchester, lately enlarged and beautified under the judicious direction of Isaac Farrell, Esq., Architect, is immediately adjacent to the town, which, with the noble plantations, gives it a very beautiful and picturesque appearance" (Richard Doyle). There is a datestone of 1852 in the approach wall flanking the gateway, with portcullis-like gates, at the top of Market Street; it seems probable that this, too, was the work of Isaac Farrell, "the leading Irish Methodist architect of his time", responsible for late classical Methodist churches in Dublin, Belfast and Coleraine. But surprising as it is in its contrast with his other built work, so far as it is known, this is borne out by a testimonial of 9 October 1833 from the estate's agent -

"Mr Farrell of Abbey Street is highly recommended as a most respectable and competent person" (Agent's letter-book, in D 1248/LB/1)

"The erection of the castle was commenced in 1830 and it was not anticipated that it would be completed before 1838, but was ready for occupation in 1837". According to Lewis, the stone employed came from the local quarry at Tullyhue. There seem to be three separate, and rather disparate, elements in the design. The entrance is through an archway, like that of an Oxbridge college, in a two-storey block with Tudoresque detailing, and turret. This gives access to a quadrangular courtyard: Williams describes this as "neo-Elizabethan ... treated with such austerity as to verge on neo-Classicism". Next, a very tall gabled range, containing the main living rooms, with very tall chimney-stacks, mullioned windows to the front, and an extraordinary angled oriel with splendid views across the ravine below: these appear on a water-colour of 1838 and in Doyle's little engraving of 1854. But the third element does not appear in either; it is the very prominent tall square keep, with crow-stepped gables, tall chimney-stacks, and corbelled-out square bartizans, of a harsher blackstone than the earlier work, but with an extraordinarily extravagant series of coronets and armorial bearings incorporated into the external chimney-breast. Unfortunately I have been able to find no evidence as to the date of this tower; it seems to me clearly by another hand; and one much under the influence of William Burn or David Bryce: after all, Burn designed Bangor Castle, Castlewellan, and Helen's Tower, and David Bryce designed Ormiston House, Belfast, all at around this period.

The builder of the present castle was Lord Mandeville, eldest son of the impecunious 5th Duke of Manchester, "whose fortune bore no proportion to his dignity". The old castle had come to him, with £20,000, with his first wife, Millicent Sparrow, whose family had acquired it from the St Johns, who had obtained it in succession to the outlawed Sir Oghie O'Hanlon. Lord Mandeville was a Commander in the Royal Navy at the time of his marriage in 1822, MP for Huntingdon for 11 years, and a most zealous Protestant. He succeeded as 6th Duke in 1843. A lady visitor in 1837 thought Tandragee very picturesque. "The town consists of one very long street ... At the top stands the castle, a large, dark, ponderous-looking gate facing you, with rather a frowning aspect, overhung by trees of immense growth ... The gates passed, you proceed by a short drive into a quadrangle, the four sides of which are formed by the castellated building, which is singularly antique in appearance, though, in fact, rebuilt within the past few years. The inner gates are fortified, after the old fashion of defensive warfare, the material is grey stone, and the 'tout ensemble' very feudal" (Tonna). In 1838, J Hill Williams of the Ordnance Survey writes "a fine large stone building of the Elizabethan style of architecture, enclosing a good court. It was commenced in 1830 and will probably be finished in 1838. It contains a large handsome chapel, wainscoted with richly carved oak, and it will also have an organ and gallery. The house contains large and commodious apartments, also a very valuable collection of theological works ..." And two years earlier, in 1836, a valuation of £280 had been placed on the castle; but this is annotated "I think £280 too much. The castle is too near the town - there should be some deduction made on that account and of the entrance to it which is confined by Craig's houses: £225". By 1864, the valuation had increased to £250, at which figure it remained until the end of the century.

The 7th Duke was described by Disraeli as "silly, but not dull". The 8th, 9th and 10th Dukes were all born at Tandragee; the first two had each the good sense to marry American heiresses; in 1932 the 9th Duke published his Candid Recollections of his happy memories of running barefoot round the immense demesne. Indeed, with its ravine, woods, lakes, bamboo island, parkland, and even bear-pit, some 400 acres within a stout stone wall, it must have been very splendid. Most of the contents were sold at auction in 1925. Describing the castle's declining years, the Duke wrote: "It is some time since I visited Tandragee, as owing to increased expenses and higher taxation it is impossible to keep several estates and country houses open. The principal rooms are closed at Tandragee Castle and the corridors no longer echo to gay parties. Sometimes my eldest son pays it a fleeting visit to see how everything is getting on, but it would sadden me too much to see the old place on only a passing call". Thereafter the house stood empty until the outbreak of the second World War, when it was commandeered by the British army. In October 1943 the Sixth US Cavalry regiment arrived: they remained in training, with their tanks and armoured vehicles, until May 1944; during this period, the bear-pit apparently came in handy for the confinement of drunken soldiers. After the war, the castle lay vacant until 1955, when it was bought by Mr Tom Hutchinson who roofed over part of the courtyard and used it for the manufacture of potato crisps.

Unhappily, over the years the castle itself has suffered much from vandalism, and from two major fires. The interior is inaccessible and, except for a few ground-floor rooms used as offices, uninhabitable; but it is not yet beyond restoration. ("Apart from the fire damage, the remaining masonry structure is in remarkably good condition" - March 1996, report in MBR.) Its surroundings are bizarre: the hill-top site is sandwiched between the fortified police station, and the churchyard; within its stone-walled perimeter are a series of very large modern industrial buildings housing the potato-crisp factory; several modern dwellings, one of them extensive; stabling and exercise paddocks for over 40 polo ponies; and below, in the valley and on the opposite hillside, woods, streams and ponds full of wildlife, pheasants, a polo pitch, a landing strip for a light aircraft, and an extensive golf course. Looking back across the valley, the view of the castle is still as dramatic and romantic as any in the county.

Photographs: Michael O'Connell. Wood-engraving: from Doyle.
Situation: Armagh Road, Tandragee; td, and Parish, Ballymore; District Council, Armagh; Grid ref. J 030 463.
References: Listed B (15/5/7). VAL 1B/214, p 280, VAL 12B/11/5A, p 67, D 1248/LB/1, D 1248/O/15, all in PRONI; G A Bennett, OSM, 1835, and J H Williams, 1838, Armagh, I, pp 9,3; water-colour by W Greenlees, 1838, in IAA; Lewis, TD, 1837, I, p 151, II, p 594; Tonna, 'Letters from Ireland', 1838, p 29; Doyle, 'Tours in Ulster', 1854, p 167; Bassett, 'Armagh', 1888, p 226; Manchester, 'My candid recollections', 1932, p 69; 'Complete peerage', VIII, 1932, p 376; Bence-Jones, 'Burke's guide', 1978, p 270; Williams, 'Architecture in Ireland', 1994, p 14; Dean, 'Gate lodges', UAHS, 1994, p 43; H Dixon, notes in MBR.

Castle Dillon, Kilmore

72. The present large, austere - indeed rather gaunt - house was finished in 1845 (basement datestone, 1844) for Sir George Molyneux, sixth baronet, to designs by William Murray, "to replace a rather low and plain mid-18th century winged house" (Bence-Jones). Samuel Molyneux, chief engineer of Ireland and "a most ingenious writer on the subject of gunnery", inherited the estate from the last of the Dillons of Castle Dillon in the mid 17th century; the baronetcy was accorded in 1730 to a successor who was Surgeon-in-chief to the army in Ireland. The third baronet built the Obelisk (208) and, in 1760, "the most costly park gates and offices of hewn stone in the three kingdoms", just possibly to designs by Sir William Chambers though there is no proof of this, now mutilated, blocked up and ruined. "In fine, the park gates and offices are in the best style of architecture and elegance and a suitable mansion house in the place of the present old one would render this seat one of the most agreeable in the Kingdom" (1786).

In 1804, Coote says that "the house is situated low and very old-fashioned, but the offices are modern and well-built". The offices he refers to are the stable block, designed in 1782 by Thomas Cooley, now alas very derelict and lacking half its slates: over 150 feet long, two storeys to the front but three-storey to the rear, thirteen bays long: the three central bays breaking forward and surmounted by pediment and cupola; each of the bays having a recessed archway framing either doorway or window-opening.

The later house has a nine-bay two-storey-on-basement central block, very plain, with a hipped roof surmounted by a pair of central chimney-stacks, and two three-bay single storey wings, all of ashlar: the only ornament a rather fine porch with pairs of angled Tuscan columns, perhaps modelled on Francis Johnston's porch at the Archbishop's palace, Armagh. Thiry-nine drawings for the house survive in the Murray Collection in Dublin. As Goslin remarks in her catalogue, "The early designs for Castledillon display features usual in Murray's Italianate formula

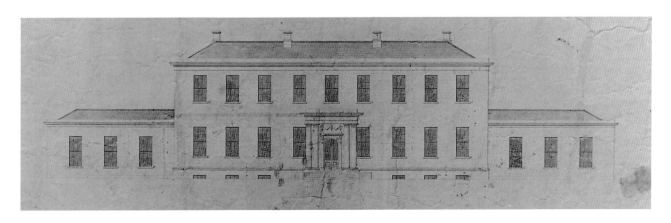

of house design. However, the final design, drawn up almost a year and a half later" (than that of 1842) "has an austerity which must be a reflection of the client's taste. In July 1844 contract drawings and specifications were signed by Charles and John McGibbon ... an Edinburgh builder who had built Brownlow House" (69) "for Playfair and Crom Castle for Blore". Sir George Molyneux, having inherited in 1842, lived to enjoy his new house only until 1848. Consistently valued at the very high figure of £250. It remained in the ownership of the Molyneux family until 1926, though it seems to have been let, for in 1888 it was "the residence of Captain George De la Poer Beresford, DL". For many years it was used as a sanatorium by St Luke's Hospital; parts of it were used by the army; it is today a nursing home.

Photographs: Michael O'Connell. Elevation drawing: William Murray, IAA.
Situation: Castledillon Road; td, Turcarra; Parish, Grange; District Council, Armagh; Grid ref. H 905 483.
References: House, listed B+ (15/3/1), stable block listed B (15/3/10). Drawings in RIAI Murray Collection, in IAA; B Goslin, unpublished Catalogue of Murray Collection, 1990, p 88; VAL 12B/10/25, in PRONI; Wilson, 'Post-chaise companion,', 1786, p 64; Coote, 'Armagh', 1804, p 346; Lewis, TD, 1837, II, pp 313, 514; PG, I, 1845, p 360; Bassett, 'Armagh', 1888, p 213; Molyneux, 'Molyneux families',1904, pp 133, 134; C Munro, notes in MBR, 1970; Bence -Jones, 'Burke's guide', 1978, p 66; Dean, 'Gate lodges', UAHS, 1994, p 35; J Kerr, in 'Craigavon Historical Society review', 1996/97, pp 7-15.

Dartan Hall, Tynan

73. An impressive, if austere, foursquare early Victorian mansion but somewhat in the late-Georgian taste; accordingly, something of a hybrid, yet a mongrel of strong character. Each front five-bay, two-storey on basement. The front door stands at the head of a flight of eight stone steps. The mixture of materials is intriguing: rubblestone walls with brick dressings but cutstone quoins, the central bays in the principal front stuccoed, with round-headed windows in the central bays only. The hipped roof, with heavy cornice and modillions, carries four enormous chimney-stacks with semi-circular chimney-pots or louvres. Some of the windows have been blocked up, but it is in contemplation to re-open them; most have horizontal glazing-bars in the Regency style. A puzzling house; perhaps there is here some association with Fellows Hall (74), especially in view of the Maxwell family connection.

This property was for many years the seat of the Cross family, 17th-century settlers from Lancashire, presumably relations of the Crosses at Portnelligan (100). There is a datestone punningly inscribed "W+C 1809" on the coach-house, but the main house does not look so early; there is another stone in the path at the back of the house inscribed with the date "1859", which seems much more plausible. It may have replaced, or may well incorporate parts of, an older house.

John and William Cross were concerned in the defence of Derry. John's son, Richard, who died in 1776, held Dartan as tenant of the Maxwells. In 1837 Maxwell Cross Esq inhabited a house here in category C+, measuring 58 feet, by 24 feet 6 inches, by only 14 feet 6 inches high, valued at £21.14.4. In 1862 here was a three-storey house, measuring 16 yards by 16 yards, in category 1A, house, gate-lodge, offices and land being together valued at £50. So it seems clear that by then Dartan Hall had either been built, or rebuilt.

Tradition has it that it had been built somewhat earlier than this by Colonel John Cross (1787-1850), a distinguished military man, "An Officer in the Army, who saw much service in the 52nd Light Infantry during the Peninsular War. He accompanied the expedition to Sweden in 1807" (aged twenty) "and proceeded thence to Portugal, 1808. He took part in the battle of Corunna, the actions preceding it, and all the subsequent campaigns with the 52nd Regt.; battle of Waterloo, and occupation of Paris; three times wounded; received the war medal with ten clasps; also the Waterloo medal; subsequently commanded the 68th Light Infantry, from which regt. he retired in 1843. Col. Cross was a member of the Royal Hanoverian Guelphic Order, Lieut-Governor commanding the Forces in the island of Jamaica; commission dated 28 July, 1838" (Burke). This must have been an exacting appointment, for in 1832 "the negroes had revolted, believing that emancipation had been granted"; which it was two years later; but "emancipation left the planters in a pitiable condition financially ... They were left with overworked estates, a poor market and a scarcity of labour

... Many estates, already heavily mortgaged, were abandoned, and the trade of the island was at a standstill". Nevertheless, Colonel Cross appears to have prospered: he is reputed to have brought back, and planted here, the seeds or seedlings which grew into the many fine specimen trees in the demesne.

According to his rather verbose memorial in Killylea church, heavily quoted by Burke, he first entered the service as a volunteeer from the Armagh militia. On his death, he was succeeded by his brother Maxwell Cross, then by Lieutenant-Colonel William Pennell Cross, described as "of Dartan" in 1886. Unfortunately, both the Lieutenant-Colonel's sons died without issue; and in 1906 the house was let to Jemmett Shaw Hamilton, son of the then Dean of Armagh. Thereafter, it seems to have been let to various tenants, its valuation declining to £48, then £30, and eventually £15 in 1924 with a note "house burnt, now offices only". At some date thereafter, the property passed to one Irwin Knox, who never lived there, but either let it, or allowed it to lie vacant: it had been vacant for many years when acquired by its present owner in 1987, since when it has been extensively restored.

Photograph: Michael O'Connell.
Situation: Kennedy's Road, Killylea; td, and Parish, Killylea; District Council, Armagh; Grid ref. H 791 444.
References: Surprisingly, not listed. VAL 1B/29B, p43, VAL/ 2B/ 2/8B, VAL 12B/10/39A-E, all in PRONI; Lewis, TD, 1837, II, p 159; PG, II, 1846, p 493; memorial in Killylea church; 'Burke's landed gentry', 1886, I, p 442; Bassett, 'Armagh', 1888, p 176; Young, 'Belfast and province of Ulster', 1909, p 367; Henderson, 'St Mark's, Killylea', 1982, p 62.

Fellows Hall, Killylea

74. A most peculiar house divided horizontally like a layer cake, and vertically by the front wall of the original dwelling: with a central staircase with exits at different levels on the first floor, as a result of the greater height of the principal rooms on the east or entrance front. In essence, the present orderly structure seems to date from 1802, plus a later upper storey: but the round-headed Victorian windows in this upper floor on the west front sit strangely above the triple Georgian-glazed (or Regency-pattern) windows below, and appear to date from between 1856 and 1862.

The estate had been granted by the crown in 1610 to "the Provost, Fellows and Scholars of Trinity College, Dublin", by way of endowment. "The result of a complicated web of sub-leasing was to establish the family of Bishop Maxwell of Kilmore (a former Fellow) as lessees of the greater part of the Armagh estate of 23,000 acres" (McCarthy). The senior branch of this Maxwell family inherited land around Keady, acquired the title of Barons Farnham, and still lives in Co Cavan.

The building history is hard to unravel, but is to some extent illuminated by the unusual series of datestones. The first builder of the house was James Maxwell, third son of the Rev. Robert Maxwell who had built Elm Park in 1626. There is a plaque with the Maxwell arms and the date 1664 over the door in the west wall; and another, in the south wall but inside an outbuilding, with the motto "NE CAMBIO NEC RECUSO" and the legend "STRUX-ERUNT JACOBUS MAXWELL ET ELIZABETHA UXOR EIUS ANNO DOM 1664". The next datestone,

this time in the back part of the north wall, reads: "The House that was Built on this Ground by James Maxwell in the year 1664 being Burned in the year 1752 was Rebuilt by Robert Maxwell and Grace his Wife in the year 1762 under the Inspection of their son John Maxwell". Finally, a stone in the front part of the north wall declares "Built by John Maxwell in 1802".

This John Maxwell died, unmarried, in 1820, tenant or lessee of a large estate. His niece, Helen Tew, had married in 1785 the Rev. Sir James Stronge, first baronet; and another niece, Margaret Tew, had married in 1784 the Rev. William Jones Armstrong. Ultimately, the Stronges ended up with some 2300 acres and two major houses, Fellows Hall and Tynan Abbey (64), and the Armstrongs with some 1900 acres, but no house; the division is perpetuated by a marker stone inscribed "WJA" on one side and "JS" on the other. Since the Stronges had their principal seat at Tynan, the house at Fellows Hall was leased to Thomas Knox Armstrong, whose grandmother had been a Maxwell, and who died in 1840. The next occupier seems to have been Lt Col George McClintock "of the Sligo Rifles", who married in 1850 Catherine Stronge, and acted as the family's land agent. In 1851, her father, the second baronet, took a new 21-year lease of Fellows Hall from the College; and in 1856 paid a lump sum to convert this into a lease in perpetuity. This presumably gave him sufficient security of tenure to embark upon the final enlargements and alterations to the house, hauntingly reminiscent as it is of Deane and Woodward's Museum in Trinity College, Dublin, completed in 1857.

The architect of the 1850s rebuilding is unknown. It seems clear that it cannot have been Benjamin Woodward, despite the resemblance to his style. It has been conjectured that it might have been Catherine McClintock's brother, Edmond Stronge (1822-1911) who was a civil engineer, and worked in the offices of Robert Stephenson, the great bridge builder; the two professions had not, in the 1850s, widely diverged. Another possible candidate is Frederick Butler, architect, of Dublin, who carried out other work at Loughgall, and, in later years, for the Armstrongs, at Killylea Church and Dean's Hill (81); but he seems an insufficiently talented performer, judging by the mediocrity of Loughgall Manor House.

The McClintocks lived on here for a century as tenants or lessees of the Stronges. "Sir James Stronge had begun the sale of the adjoining estates of Fellows Hall (1258 acres) and College Hall (1052 acres) before the passage of the Wyndham Act" (in 1903) "but he kept the mansion house of Fellows Hall and the adjoining 300 acres in his own hands ... It is a fine house on prime agricultural land" (McCarthy). The Colonel's widow is shown, in the Tenancies Schedule of 1907, as having been a yearly tenant at £80 a year since before 1901. However, notwithstanding their earlier reluctance, the Stronges agreed to sell in 1907 or soon thereafter, for the Land Commission papers note "an agreement in form H has been entered into for the sale of these lands as a parcel at £3725 to the Misses McClintock". The younger daughter, Miss Isa, who was master of the Tynan Hunt, continued hunting until she was well over the age of 70, and died in 1954; when the last remaining interest of Trinity College was got in, and the place was bought back by J R B Armstrong, great-grandson of the Rev. W J Armstrong, in whose family it remains.

The house is built on a slope, so that it appears two-storey on basement from the front, three-storey from the rear. The three bays are evenly spaced at the rear, but in the five-bay front there are three close-set round-headed windows above the porch, and on this front the upper window-sills are linked by a continuous string-course. The roof is hipped, with wide eaves, and prominent chimney-stacks in the outer walls. The house was succinctly described by Hugh Dixon in 1984: "The present entrance front facing east dates from the mid 19th century having the grouping of round-headed windows which characterises Italianate and some Ruskinian buildings of the period ... This part of the house, however, is built onto the Georgian house which faces west. Originally of just two storeys, easily identified by the Wyatt windows, a top storey was added as part of the Victorian extensions.

Many of the internal Georgian fittings, most notably the staircase, remain intact and in good order." It must be added that the staircase looks as if it might easily date from the 17th century. The thickness of the spine wall dividing the old house from the new is over six feet in places.

In 1838, the house was valued at £86.6.6, the measurements given as 66 feet 6 iches, by 24 feet, by a surprising 15 feet 6 inches high, which may be related to the flashings visible in the attic chimney-stacks; the occupier being T K Armstrong. In 1862, the valuation had, surprisingly, fallen to £76.10.0, measurements 66 feet by 24 feet by 3 storeys, occupier Colonel George (Arthur John) McClintock holding under Sir Jas M Stronge Bt. Although in fact he had died in 1873, Arthur John McClintock is still shown as occupier in 1875; the valuation remained around the £75 mark until 1929. The façade was at some date encased in Roman cement, with Ionic pilasters at the doorcase and console brackets over the ground floor windows. (This was unwisely hacked away in fairly recent years, laying bare the fact that the basement is constructed of semi-coursed rubble, the ground floor of coursed limestone ashlar, and the first floor of semi-coursed rubble blocks, now all aggressively over-pointed).

However, the composition and proportions of Fellows Hall - roof, eaves, chimney-stacks and round-headed windows - and its interior detailing make it still one of the most imposing and intriguing houses in the county.

Photographs: Michael O'Connell; from Young.
Situation: 67, Fellows Hall Road, Killylea; td, Fellows Hall or Crearun; Parish, Tynan; District Council, Armagh; Grid ref. H 790 429.
References: Listed B (15/11/10). Datestones; LR169/1/B (Grant in perpetuity of 30 April 1856), and Schedule of tenancies, 1907, VAL 1B/29B p 23, VAL 2B/2/8B p 6, VAL 12B/10/39A to E, D 3727/D/9, E/40, all in PRONI; Young, 'Belfast and province of Ulster', 1909, p 229; 'Burke's landed gentry of Ireland', 1958, p 31; Bence-Jones, 'Burke's guide', 1978, p 124; McCarthy, 'Trinity College estates', 1992, pp 90, 220; Dean, 'Gate lodges', UAHS, 1994, p 37; O'Dwyer, 'Deane and Woodward', 1997, passim; notes and letter of 8 August 1984 from H Dixon to R Oram in MBR; information from owners.

Ballyards Castle, Milford

75. It seems that the Simpson family acquired land in and around Ballyards about 1713. The family used the water-power of the Callan River to good effect, and prospered. Taylor and Skinner show "Sympson Esq" here in 1777 at an earlier Ballyards House, now gone. Around 1820, they built Beech Hill (122), but by the 1860s Colonel Thomas Simpson decided that he wanted something grander and more up-to-date. Accordingly, in June, 1868, specifications and estimates were prepared for a new house, to cost "General Works £3,124, Conservatory £87, Verandah £145, and Turret £264" - a total of £3,620. The actual contract, dated 5 August 1868 and made between "Thomas Simpson of Ballyards, Colonel in the Army", and "Thomas Ross of Armagh, Builder and Contractor", was indeed for £3,620. The house does not seem to have been completed until 1872, when a bill of extras was submitted.

I cannot improve upon Hugh Dixon's description in the MBR: "The present house was built from 1868 by Colonel Thomas Simpson to designs by Charles Sherry and Robert Hughes whose short-lived Belfast partnership was responsible for completing the Albert Memorial Clock after the death of W J Barre in 1867, and for the design of the Belfast Theatre Royal. The house is a fine example of High Victorian mixing of styles. The plan is irregular with an entrance porch set in a re-entrant angle beneath a lean-to roof ... The ground-floor windows are pairs of severe rectangular openings with two sashes of single-sheet plate-glass in each (very expensive in 1868 but very much the fashion for best rooms). The single upper windows have vertically divided sashes. Above this, the house becomes typically eventful with shouldered gables (Tudor), heavily-bracketed balconies (Venetian), files of linked chimney-stacks (Tudor again), of which one on a low wing is supported on sets of corbels flanking an arch (Scottish). At one corner a circular tower rises to a conical-capped belvedere with a complete vantage gallery again supported

on heavy Italian brackets. The stonework, regularly coursed but with rustic facings, is reminiscent of the work of W H Lynn (Culloden Hotel) and of Young & Mackenzie (Q U B Vice-Chancellor's Lodge, Victoria College, etc.)" Dean calls the whole thing "vaguely Scots Baronial".

Colonel Simpson died in 1892, and his widow lived on here for some years. By 1908 the house had been acquired by Maynard Sinton, who must have carried out considerable enlargements and improvements, for the valuation rose from £95 in 1908 to £145 in 1916. It was at this period that the name was changed from Ballyards House to

Ballyards Castle. The house has been in institutional use for a number of years, with consequential additions and alterations which have not improved its appearance.

Photographs: Michael O'Connell; from Young.
Situation: Ballyards Road, Milford; td, Ballyards; Parish, Lisnadill; District Council, Armagh; Grid ref. H 862 417.
References: Not listed. D 1522/3/2, D 1522/4/1/2, VAL 1B/27, pp 44-46, VAL 12B/10/9/A - E, all in PRONI; Taylor and Skinner, 'Roads', 1778, p 26; Lewis, TD, 1837, II, p 286; PG, II, 1846, p 659; Young, 'Belfast and province of Ulster', 1909, p 276; Dean, 'Gate lodges', UAHS, 1994, p 34; undated notes by H Dixon in MBR.

Killycomain House, Portadown

76. In its present form, a very strange late 19th-century house (or rather, pair of houses, for the left-hand part, known as "Westlawn", is in the occupation of a different branch of the same family). Originally, a long, low, five-bay farm-house with dormers, still incorporating 18th-century window casements, said to have belonged to a Mr Fyffe, though shown in the Valuation book as occupied in the 1870s by Anthony Cowdy under lease from Francis Greer. The place was acquired in 1880 by a timber merchant named John Collen, who added a massive extension, including an extraordinary tower with oriel windows and mushroom minaret; raised the walls and roof of the old house; and encased the whole in a rather disagreeable, but very ornate, pseudo-Jacobean, grey rendering. The valuation shot up from £30 to £68, with the note "old house raised & new addition".

The listers tentatively suggest that this might have been the work of Thomas Jackson. That is possible, for he did not die until 1890; but it does not look like his work to me: perhaps that of his son Anthony Jackson?

The houses are oddly divided: the two right-hand bays of the older house, with their low ceilings, form part of the new house, with its very high ceilings, florid plasterwork, and very pretty floral stained glass in coupled round-headed windows in the porch and on the stairs. There are extensive brick and stone stables at the rear, well restored, surrounding a central courtyard. The house stands in a large garden with many mature trees. There are extraordinary rocaille walls and archways at the sides of the house: their provenance does not seem to be remembered, but they are most unusual, and very striking.

The place was bought by the father of the present owner in 1936 with 26 acres of land, now largely built up, for £3000. During the war, it was requisitioned by the RAF who established a 'radio-location unit' on the roof of the tower.

Photograph: Michael O'Connell.
Situation: Killycomain Road, Portadown; td, Killycomain; Parish, Portadown; District Council, Craigavon; Grid ref.. J 027 543.
References: Listed, Killycomain House B1 (14/13/2A); West Lawn, B (14/13/2B). VAL 12B/14/4A - F, in PRONI; OS maps 1835 and 1905; Oram, 'Craigavon', UAHS, 1971, pt I, p 6.

Umgola House, Armagh

77. A very large late Victorian red-and-yellow brick mill-owner's mansion, set in an extensive and well-cared-for garden with many fine trees. It was evidently built about 1890 by John Compton JP, who in 1882 bought the Umgola damask weaving factory from its founder Thomas Wynne. Bassett says that "Umgola takes a front rank with the many charming places in the immediate vicinity of Armagh", but, surprisingly he seems to have been referring to the mill, not the house, for in 1888 Mr Compton's address is given as Richmond Terrace. The Valuation book shows this as the home of John Compton for the first time in 1891, at the surprisingly low value of £20: perhaps it had not then been completed. A substantial extension was added in 1905 to the plans, which survive, of J J Phillips, architect, of Belfast; it seems plausible that the earlier building should be attributed to him also, since he set up practice in Belfast (at first, as a specialist in Methodist churches) in 1890; but Hugh Dixon suggests that the architect was the local man, J H Fullerton. John Compton

was succeeded by his son George Compton before 1905; on the death of George Compton, the place passed to his married daughter and her husband, Captain Noel Smith. Thereafter, it passed through several hands before the present owners acquired it in 1979.

The house is very elaborate as well as very large, with fine fretwork-like barge-boards to its many gables: it is mainly of a rather hard bright-red brick, with yellow-brick ornamentation. Beside and below it on the hillside stand remarkable 'wire-tension' hot-house and greenhouse, in which vines, peaches, and exotic flowers continue to flourish; and a brick potting-shed.

Photograph: Michael O'Connell.
Situation: 29, Monaghan Road, Armagh; td, Umgola; Parish, and District Council, Armagh; Grid ref. H 865 442.
References: Listed B1 (15/19/14); outside conservation area. VAL 12B/10/ 4E, p 64, in PRONI; Bassett, 'Armagh', 1888, pp 125, 144; H Dixon, in 'Buildings of Armagh', UAHS, 1992, p 12; plans of 1905 in house; B Jupp, notes in MBR.

Torre Blanca, Mullavilly

78. An exotic and unexpected mansion: despite its Spanish name, really more in the American manner; very much of the 1960s; set down amidst rolling countryside (now invaded by development) between Portadown and Tandragee, in the middle of what used to be Sam McGredy's extensive rose nursery.

Bassett reports that the Castle Gardens of Portadown were converted to nursery purposes about 1873 by a Mr Grant; and that Messers Samuel McGredy & Son bought them 9 years later. "Mr. Samuel McGredy has had a life-long experience in nursery work and landscape gardening" (1888). The firm, removed from Woodside to Mullavilly, continued to prosper greatly, specialising in the breeding of roses; the family home, a modest five-bay farmhouse (now an old peoples's home), was sited amidst acres and acres of them. In 1965, at the height of the firm's prosperity, the incumbent Sam McGredy decided to build a modern house at the north of the site, and to incorporate in it luxurious accommodation for his numerous customers from all over the world.

He employed as architect Adair Roche of Munce & Kennedy, Belfast. Expenditure was lavish; materials and gadgets were all of the best. The three-storey, round-front-ed, white tower, with its picture windows, dominates the otherwise single-storey composition, looking out south-ward towards the Mourne mountains over what used to be a vast expanse of flowering roses: a highly dramatic con-cept. Curved glass, and specially-manufactured curved radiators, were installed, as well as many other modern delights: a swimming pool; a sauna; a cocktail bar; piped musak. The bedrooms (and their numerous associated bathrooms) are situated in a subsidiary flat-roofed wing to one side; the utilities are incorporated in the base of the tower; the garages and stores are in another separate block; the numerous living rooms, somewhat eccentrical-ly carved up into interlocking spaces, for the most part (except for two dining rooms and two kitchens) face south, and formerly looked over a swimming-pool and rosebeds.

An article in Homes and Gardens, written soon after the completion of the house, casts an interesting light on the relationship between architect and client: "Mr. and Mrs. McGredy's last house, which had 22 rooms, required a cook and maid to help run it. Their new house is designed so Mrs. McGredy can manage it herself, with only occasional help. They entertain constantly, and often on a large scale, and the architect was instructed to keep this very much in mind ... All interior fittings and colours of the house were chosen by Mr. and Mrs. McGredy one Thursday morning, in two hours. They both drew plans of what they required, and the architect worked from that point ... Swing doors of the Western movie type are a reminder of the days Mr. McGredy spent as a student in the United States of America ... The obvious efficiency of the house in no way distracts from its splendid comfort. If anything, it disguises its size, for though the number of rooms is not great, they are large areas, and accommodate a great many visitors. The high standard of all finishes and details sets off the atmosphere of rich hospitality, and everywhere one sits or turns, great bowls are loaded high with 40 or 50 magnificent roses."

Sam McGredy rewarded his architect, Adair Roche, by naming a rose after him; I have not been able to track down a description of its tint, scent, and other characteristics.

Very much of its time, very much not of its place, this ostentatious home is well suited to the needs of a large extended family with numerous belongings. When Sam McGredy decided in 1975, for personal reasons, to close down the business and emigrate to New Zealand, he gave away a vast number of rose-bushes (I was one of the for-tunate recipients). The purchaser of the house was Mr Albert Prentice, who made a number of interior alter-ations, and subsequently built himself, in the grounds, a new house of very different design; and from whom the present owner acquired Torre Blanca in late 1998. It is still an interesting house, but much the poorer for the loss of its swimming-pool, and above all for the disappearance of the "rectangular beds full of roses ... placed like colours on an abstract painting".

Photograph: Michael O'Connell.
Situation: Richmond Manor, Mullavilly, Tandragee.; td, and Parish, Mullavilly; District Council, Armagh; Grid ref. J 013 482.
References: Not listed (though perhaps it should be). Bassett, 'Armagh', 1888, p 297; H Rogers, in 'Homes and gardens', June, 1970.

CLERGY HOUSES

Edenderry House (82) doorcase. Photograph: Michael O'Connell

CLERGY HOUSES

Not surprisingly, Armagh is rich in clergy houses. Archbishop Robinson was particularly thoughtful for the comfort of his clergy. Thomas Cooley drew a plan[1] for a typical glebe-house, but there is no accompanying elevation, and there is no surviving evidence of his authorship of any of the existing rectories, though it is tempting to attribute Eglish glebe-house - now Edenderry House (82) - to him. Succeeding archbishops, and the Board of First Fruits, also contributed their quota. In a few instances - as at Dean's Hill (81), and Mullaghbrack (87) - wealthy clergymen built their own parsonages. This partly accounts for the considerable disparities in size and cost: Eglish is said to have cost a mere £184.12.3 in 1778, whereas Mullaghbrack cost £4,561.8.0 in 1829, a far larger difference than can be accounted for by changing money values. Dr Beaufort, in 1792, records that there are 23 glebe houses and 23 churches in the county, but adds a footnote: "Four of these glebe-houses are on the perpetual cures into which the parish of Armagh is divided, and there are five more appropriated to the choir".[2]

Dr Craig[3] and I are both on record as considering these houses "for the most part very simple, very appropriate, and very well built". This view was not shared by the Rev. Joseph Ferguson, curate at Ballymoyer, who wrote in 1816: "The glebe of this district contains 33 acres of arable ground, four or five of which are good ground, the rest indifferent. The glebe-house was erected, like most other buildings of the same description, in a manner reflecting little credit either on the skill of the architect, or the attention of the superintendant. These houses are generally built by contractors, who contrive to make them appear fair to the eye, but care not if they should tumble to the ground after they have received the money".[4]

There are good Presbyterian manses (86, 89, and 90) in and near the city of Armagh, and there is an unusual (former) parochial house at Middletown (91), but, generally speaking, the clergy houses of the other denominations are later and of less interest than those of the Church of Ireland.

It remains to note that, today, neither archbishop is worthily housed. Ara Coeli (92) - which to my eye stands no comparison with the fields of heaven, or even the Champs Elysées - is a large, rather dreary, rendered late-Victorian building which even Stephen Gwynn thought alien and inappropriate. Might it not be a good idea to commission a really first-class architect to build a really first-class piece of contemporary architecture, comparable with the excellent new O Fiaich Library (177)? Think of the symbolism! The Church of Ireland archbishop, although a member of the House of Lords in his own right, is equally unworthily, indeed somewhat ignominiously, lodged in what the UAHS listers[5] describe as "no more than a two-storey modern villa" (94), built in 1975 when the Representative Church Body so unwisely sold off Archbishop Robinson's princely palace. He has room to entertain fittingly neither his peers, nor his diocesan clergy (except, perhaps, at garden parties). Shame!

References: 1. Plan in Archbishop Robinson's Library, Armagh. 2. Beaufort, 'Memoir', 1792. 3. Craig, 'Classic Irish houses', 1976, p 39. 4. Mason, 'Statistical account', II, 1816, p 84. 5. 'Buildings of Armagh', UAHS, 1992, p 64.

Edenderry House (82) door-lock.
Photograph: Michael O'Connell

1 - 11 Vicars' Hill, Armagh

79. A charming curved terrace of Georgian houses whose dates vary from 1724 to 1794, framing the Church of Ireland cathedral's extensive hill-top churchyard. Numbered from the right, the first houses, Numbers 1 to 4, were built in 1724. "Four houses for the reception of clergymen's widows, were built by Primate Boulter on Vicar's Hill (formerly called Pound Hill) ... These were endowed with £50 per annum, and have formed a useful and comfortable residence for many respectable matrons, with their families". And: Archbishop Robinson "built two of the vicar's houses ... the other five were erected by him about the year 1780, and to these he then attached a spacious music-hall, in which the boys of the choir are initiated by the organist, into the elementary principles of harmony, and habituated to sing in concert. He built also, on Vicar's-Hill, a repository for wills and for records belonging to the archdiocese" (Stuart). These houses, built over the years, have been variously occupied, by persons more or less closely connected with the cathedral, and have now been transferred from the Trustees of the Cathedral Choir Fund to the Church of Ireland Housing Association. The enclave bears some resemblance to an English cathedral close, but because of the conformation of the site, many of the ground-floor windows look out on the high stone retaining wall of the churchyard, leaving only the upper windows to enjoy the view of cathedral, grass, and trees. There are gardens of varying size at the rear of the houses.

The first four houses in the street are three-bay, two-storey, roughcast, with very small Georgian-glazed windows upstairs, "whose single sash slides upwards into a wall cavity above the window", Gibbsian doorcases of dressed stone, with steps up to the front doors. Numbers 5, 6 and 7 were built in 1776, the first as Diocesan Registry: doorways with Tuscan pilasters; Number 7 has a radial fanlight. Numbers 8 to 10 were built in 1780: Number 9 contains the choir-practice room, with three tall two-storey windows, and a doorcase with thumping great Tuscan columns. Number 11, last and latest house, is a tall suave three-storey three-bay house of 1794, burned out in 1975, but well restored in 1996 under the supervision of Stephen Leighton: a plaque records that it was the birthplace of the composer, Charles Wood . The steps and railings at the foot of the street have, regrettably but perhaps understandably, been blocked up.

Despite the usage preferred by Stuart, Rogers, and the UAHS listers, a letter in the MBR of August 1975 from Canon Love lays it down that the correct usage is "Vicars' Hill", and not "Vicar's Hill".

Photographs: Michael O'Connell.
Situation: Cathedral Close, Armagh; td, Corporation; Parish, and District Council, Armagh; Grid ref. H 874 452.
References: All listed A (15/20/5); in conservation area. VAL 1B/21B, p 88, in PRONI; Stuart, 'City of Armagh', 1819, pp 427, 448; Rogers, 'Record', 1861, p 22; 'Buildings of Armagh', UAHS, 1992, pp 63,64; T G F Paterson, Armachiana, IV, p 15, in Armagh County Museum; unsigned notes in MBR.

Former Archbishop's Palace (now Council Offices), Armagh

80. "The palace is the most personal of the legacies from Archbishop Richard Robinson. The style is the restrained classicism characteristic of all his building works" (UAHS). "At Armagh the palace of white hewn stone 90 feet by 60, and 40 high. The town improved by the late Lord Rokeby when archbishop. With ideas truly episcopal, lateritia invenit, marmorea reliquit, the boast of the emperor Augustus" (Sleater, 1806).

"After his promotion to the primacy, Archbishop Robinson spent some time ... in maturing plans for the improvement of Armagh, where he intended to establish his chief residence. He lived during two years at Richhill, in the ancient family seat of the Richardsons," (56) "and in the interim caused the archbishop's house, in English-street, which was then in a most ruinous state, to be completely repaired. It was, however, manifest that such a house was an unfit habitation for the metropolitan of Ireland - His Grace therefore determined to erect in the vicinity of the city, an episcopal palace more worthy of himself, and of the elevated station which he adorned ... In the demesne lands, contiguous to the town itself, he erected, about the year 1770, a very elegant mansion, in a pure and pleasing style of architecture. This edifice, which is situated on a very gentle eminence, is 90 feet in length, 60 in breadth, and 40 in height. It is unincumbered with wings, and by its simply-elegant uniformity, arrests the attention of the spectator. The species of marble, or calcareous stone, with which it is built, produces a most striking effect, by the splendor of its colour" (Stuart, 1819). Inglis, in 1834, was less complimentary: "a building simple and chaste in design, but in no way remarkable for architectural beauty".

All this was designed, as a two-storey-on-basement mansion, by Robinson's usual architect, Thomas Cooley.

However, in 1825 Robinson's successor, Lord John George Beresford, employed Francis Johnston to add an extra storey, and a porch. The intention was, to provide additional accommodation for curates and visiting clergy, above the private quarters of the archbishop and his family on the first floor, the formal reception rooms on the ground floor, and the offices in the basement. Evidently the new stonework starts above the central Rokeby coat of arms, just below the window-sills of the top floor. Although Johnston made a very good job of it - his porch is delightful, and the join between old and new in the front wall is almost invisible - the outcome was rather cumbersome and over-large.

Unfortunately, this led the Representative Church Body, in 1975, to abandon the palace and demesne to their fate; rehousing the primate in a new 'see-house' (94) close to the cathedral, leaving behind almost all the paintings and furnishings, and taking with them only the splendid gate-pillars, designed by Thomas Cooley in 1771 (210). This was a lamentable decision; it would surely have cost no more to remove the top storey and restore the building to its original manageable proportions. So, the saintly Archbishop Simms and his successors, their visitors, and their guests, have had to endure invidiously cramped quarters in a "manifestly unfit habitation for the metropolitan of Ireland": all the more unsuitable since the present archbishop, like his great predecessor Primate Robinson, is the holder of a seat in the House of Lords. Happily, both palace and demesne were bought by the enlightened local council to provide it with municipal offices and a park; all credit is due to Armagh District Council for its management of this considerable public asset.

The compilers of the Parliamentary Gazetteer of 1845

viewed the palace, notwithstanding its enlargement, with approval: "an elegant and unostentatious structure ... a light and pleasing appearance ... the whole demesne, tastefully laid out, well kept, and chastely luxurious, is liberally thrown open for the recreation of the citizens". Amongst the ornaments of the demesne, admired by Arthur Young in 1776, are the primate's chapel (22), his obelisk (209), the stableyard, ice-house, conservatory, and the palace farm (103); as well as the ruins of the Franciscan friary founded in 1264 (13); and St Brigid's well. Of this last, Inglis remarks: "The Protestant archbishop's park is an awkward locality for a holy well, and since it has been comprehended within his Grace's domain, a rival holy well has been set up in a more convenient place"!

The palace is nine bays long and five deep: very plain and austere apart from the rustication of the basement, architraves to the windows, and hoods above those on the principal floor; and a carving of the archiepiscopal arms, surrounded by a wreath and suspended from his crook, above the porch. This is at the head of five stone steps, leading up to paired Ionic columns, with responding pilasters, set at an angle at either side of the doorway. The floor of the porch, made of radiating circles of dressed limestone, is exceptionally fine. Unfortunately, the original stone flags in the floor of the hall have been replaced by a

modern wooden floor. The reception rooms on the ground floor have fine chimney-pieces, plasterwork and joinery, though the library and its ante-room have been stripped and thrown into one to provide a council-chamber. The main staircase to the first floor does not rise directly from the hall, but is contained in its own separate space to the right, with an exceptionally beautiful feathery whorl of plasterwork, exploding like a Catherine wheel, in its ceiling; now somewhat spoiled by an obtrusive fitting to carry the weight of a (quite acceptable) lantern. The very carefully-planned setting of the palace is not enhanced by the large car park, nor by the security fence and gates; nor by the frequent parking of reproduction Edwardian tour-buses immediately in front of the façade.

Photographs: Michael O'Connell; MBR. Wood-engraving: Stuart frontis-piece.
Situation: Palace demesne, Armagh; td, Parkmount; Parish, and District Council, Armagh; Grid ref. H 878 443.
References: Listed A (15/18/16); outside conservation area. Young, 'Tour', 1780, p 103; Coote, 'Armagh', 1804, p 323; Sleater, 'Topography', 1806, p 174; Stuart, 'City of Armagh', 1819, p 446; Inglis, 'Ireland', II, 1834, p 274; PG, I, 1845, p 79; Bence-Jones, 'Burke's guide', 1978, p 12; Pierce and Coey, 'Taken for granted', 1984, p 8; 'Buildings of Armagh', UAHS, 1992, pp 171-7, and see bibliography there; Dean. 'Gate lodges', UAHS, 1994, p 33.

Dean's Hill, Armagh

81. Originally the Deanery: now a private house. Built in 1772 by the well-off and learned Dean Hugh Hamilton, "an eminent theologian, natural philosopher, and mathematician", one of the founders of the Royal Irish Academy, and author of works on vapour, conic sections, barometers, alkali, the permission of evil, and the existence and attributes of the deity. "Finding neither a Deanery House nor Glebe House in Armagh, he at once set to work and built the House in the Glebe lands, used as a Deanery and Rectory until the disestablishment. It was afterwards sold, and now" (1911) "belongs to H B Armstrong, DL"(Leslie), in whose family it still remains. According to family tradition, the house lay empty, but for pigs in the basement, until bought by Mr Armstrong in 1880. In consequence, he had to carry out considerable work to the house in 1887 under the supervision of J H Fullerton: and in 1896 added a two-storey-on-basement wing to designs by H C Parkinson, in order to accommodate his eight children. It is still remembered that Senator H B Armstrong, as he was to become, used to walk every day, for exercise, to the Court House; and then walk back, backwards, up the hill and up the long avenue to his own front door, in order to exercise those muscles not exercised on the outward trip.

The older part of the house is a tall, rather austere, double pile; three-storey on basement, four bays wide, with a fine cutstone pedimented doorcase framed by Doric pilasters at the head of a fan-shaped sweep of seven stone steps, with handrail, rising to the very solid front door. The walls are rendered, and without quoins, save in the basement; all the large windows are Georgian-glazed except those in the basement. At the rear, an attractive iron bridge leads from the central drawing-room window to the lawn across the basement area. Internally, the rooms are tall and well-proportioned but without much ornament. The best features of the interior are the square front hall, with six doorways, reminiscent of the near-contemporary rooms at Ballylough and Leslie Hill, both in County Antrim; the lugged doorcases; and the curving fans at the window reveals in drawing room and dining room.

Photograph: Michael O'Connell.
Situation: 34, College Hill, Armagh; td, Corporation; Parish, and District Council, Armagh; Grid ref. H 883 459.
References: Listed B1 (15/17/39); outside conservation area. Stuart, 'City of Armagh', 1819, p 528; Leslie, 'Armagh clergy ', 1911, p 23; Bence-Jones, 'Burke's guide', 1978 , p 100; 'Buildings of Armagh', UAHS, 1992, p 89; information from the owners, and from the County Museum.

Photograph: Michael O'Connell (see also colour-plates XIIb - c).
Situation: 114, Maydown Road, Benburb, Eglish; td, Edenderry; Parish, Eglish; District Council, Armagh; Grid ref. H 818 504.

References: Listed B+ (15/12/9). VAL 2B/2/4, p 88, in PRONI; Lewis, TD, 1837, I, p 596; Leslie, 'Armagh clergy', 1911, p 296; Mankowitz, 'Wedgwood', 1953, p 214; information from owners.

Edenderry House and Cottage, Benburb, Eglish

82. An extremely handsome former glebe-house, with detailing of great elegance and delicacy. "The glebe-house is commodious, and is situated on a glebe of 64 acres, given for that use by the late Joseph Johnston, Esq, of Knappagh, to Primate Robinson, who built the house" (Lewis). Canon Leslie says "Eglish Glebe House was built in 1778 at the exceedingly small cost of £184.12.3¹/₂". It is hard to reconcile this modest price with the high quality of the house, and of its details, particularly the doorcase (page 119), mantelpieces, carved newel-post, and door-furniture with appliqué blue-and-white Wedgwood plaques in brass circlets (colour-plate XIIb). It is possible that the more sophisticated decorative features were added by the Rev. John Young, perpetual curate of Eglish from 1777 until 1803, who had been a scholar of TCD in 1763, or perhaps by his wife. The Wedgwood & Bentley catalogue of 1779, reproduced by Mankowitz, remarks of "Bas-reliefs, medallions, cameo-medallions, tablets, etc, ... Chiefly classical subjects ... The Cameos are fit for ... inlaying in fine Cabinets, Writing-Tables, Bookcases, &c, of which they form the most beautiful Enrichment, at a moderate Expence ... The Ladies may display their Taste a thousand Ways, in the Application of these Cameos ..."

Standing well back from the road amidst fine mature trees, its facade is of five bays and three storeys, with cellar (not basement). The walls were until 1998 of red-painted roughcast, with quoins and Georgian glazing-bars. The original stonework has now been stripped, repointed, and laid bare in the course of a very extensive and careful restoration. The outstanding feature of the house is the beautifully carved stone doorcase (page 119), with broken pediment, elegant ewers carved in bas-relief on the imposts, and delicate lead fanlight. Over the back door,

a surprising stone panel carved with coronet and interlaced "C"s: Caulfeild and Charlemont, perhaps? If so, clearly a later import. There are several other pieces of finely-carved stonework in and about the buildings, including one which appears to represent a mask of Hypnos.

At right angles to Edenderry House itself, with separate drive and garden to its front but backing onto the yard of the main house, is Edenderry Cottage, an attractive lower two-storey range of mellow brick with lattice windows, probably originally added in the 19th century as a service wing for the main house: this, too, has some attractive stone-carvings incorporated into its outbuildings and garden walls. It would be pleasing to discover where all these came from: they are quite different in style from the classical clarity of the front doorcase.

The main house was occupied in 1803 by Rev. Silver Oliver; in 1807 by Rev. William Barker; in 1808 by Rev. James Tisdall; from 1826 to 1837 by Rev. W Barlow; from 1837 until disestablishment by Rev. Charles Waring; in 1864 it was valued at £28. "The glebe house was purchased for the parish at Disestablishment. The living was then worth £212.0.11" (Leslie). Sold by the Church of Ireland in 1936 to a Mr Shiells; bought from him by Major Maurice Johnston; since 1963, the home, successively, of Tim Herdman, Ted Montgomery, Anthony Oliver, and the present owners, who have recently completed a major restoration scheme prepared by Paul McCreanor, architect - overdue, for previous owners had neglected it, and one, reprehensibly, removed and sold a mantelpiece without action on the part of the authorities: the more the shame, since I think this is my most favourite building in the county.

Acton Glebe House, Poyntzpass

83. In 1789, the parish of Acton was established as a perpetual curacy out of the former parish of Ballymore. "In 1788 the Board of First Fruits granted £390 for building the church, and £150 for a glebe house, which was built in 1799" (Leslie). The listers describe it as an L-shaped house with later front addition and 19th-century parapet; several false windows; square south-east wing c 1820-30 with stair hall. In 1836, it was placed in category 1B, and valued at the modest sum of £7.17.0; but by 1863 the valuation had risen sharply to £21: so perhaps the later wing was added between these dates. For some reason, the valuation fell again , to £17, in 1923.

The older part of the house is two-storey, though it appears to be three-storey because of the ornamental false windows in the attic. The newer part has the front door with fanlight, and two more false windows. The house was sold by the Church of Ireland between the wars to a Mr McClean; it then passed to the Scanlon family; and was bought by the present family in 1939.

Photograph: Michael O'Connell.
Situation: 16, Acton Road, Poyntzpass; td, Brannock; Parish, Acton; District Council, Armagh; Grid ref. J 054 402.
References: Listed B1 (15/6/12). VAL 1B/ 214, p 139, VAL 2B/2/32C p 45, VAL 12B /15/23 A-E, all in PRONI; Leslie, 'Armagh clergy', 1911, p 84.

126

The Grange, Salter's Grange

84. A pleasant, simple, roomy, foursquare late Georgian parsonage: "The glebe house was built in 1781 at a cost of £487 odd" (Leslie). "The curate has a stipend of £100, paid by the Dean, with the glebe-house, a large and commodious building surrounded by a fine plantation, and a glebe comprising 37 acres, the two latter valued at £100 per annum" (Lewis). Two-storey, three-bay, roughcast, hipped roof; in contrast to the elegant stone doorcase at Edenderry House (82) not far away, the doorcase is a simple rectangle. But the ground floor windows are very spacious, with eight (unevenly sized) panes in each sash: whereas the upstairs windows are unusually small, with only three panes in each sash. (A drawing in PRONI of "Grange Glebe House - Robt Shepherd delint 1786" seems to be a red herring: it bears no relationship to the building on the ground, and may relate to another parish with the same name), although the only other Grange parish noted by Lewis to have a glebe house did not acquire it until 1832.

Internally, the feeling of spaciousness derives largely from the fine square central inner hall with the staircase climbing around three of its sides. A particularly pleasing detail is the garden window to the rector's study, where (to allow access and egress without going through the house) both sashes rise in a slot in the wall until they meet the underside of the window-sill of the bedroom above.

Nicely sited in a park-like hollow, reached by a long dog-legged lane ("the Bloody Lane", by oral tradition going back to the Battle of the Yellow Ford in 1597) starting just below Thomas Cooley's church (20). Sold off by the Church of Ireland around 1945, when the parish was amalgamated with Loughgall; bought by its present owners in 1968.

Photograph: Michael O'Connell.
Situation: 20, Salter's Grange, Armagh; td, Cabragh; Parish, Grange; District Council, Armagh; Grid ref. H 878 486.
References: Listed B (15/3/21). DIO/4/22/77/5, in PRONI; Lewis, TD, 1837, II, p 670; Leslie, 'Armagh'clergy',1911, p 307.

Ardmore Rectory, Derryadd

85. One of the more pleasing Georgian rectories still in use as such. Lewis says "the glebe-house, the residence of the Rev. D. W. MacMullan ... was erected by aid of a gift of £415 7 8½, and a loan of £55 7 8¼, British currency, from the late Board of First Fruits, in 1820; the glebe comprises 13 acres, valued at £16 5 0 per annum". The Parliamentary Gazetteer adds to this information "sittings 200; attendance 250. In 1834, the parishioners consisted of 995 Churchmen, 104 Presbyterians, 5 other Protestant dissenters, and 1,895 Roman Catholics".

In 1836, the valuers classified the rectory as 1B+, and attributed to it a value of £10.7.0, £3 more than the value they placed on the church. Thomas McIlroy of the Ordnance Survey says "The Glebe House ... is an old plain stone building, roughcast and whitewashed. It is 2-storeys high and is about 3 perches from the shore of Lough Neagh". The rector used to have a pier at which to moor his boat; though according to the parish history, Rev. Thomas Redcliffe, the rector at the time of building, desired to build the house with its back to the lough, but the bishop intervened to prevent "this undesirable architectural achievement". In 1862-3, the rector, Rev. John

Evans Lewis, seems to have been non-resident, for the house was vacant.

Set in its own private wood overlooking the Lough, this is a classic Board of First Fruits rectory, two-storey, four-square, hipped roof topped by a pair of chimney-stacks; roughcast; splendid central doorcase with elaborate fan-light and sidelights, with prominent stucco long-and-short surround; five fine triple windows in the front façade, all Georgian-glazed (not, however, Venetian, as Pierce and Coey seem to think). The woodwork, plasterwork and detailing, inside and outside, seem for once to be almost all authentic and original, apart from the introduction of the usual mod cons, and some inconspicuous additions to yard and outbuildings.

Photograph: Michael O'Connell.
Situation: Rectory Avenue, Ardmore; td, Derryadd; Parish, Montiaghs; District Council, Craigavon; Grid ref. J 022 621.
References: Listed B (14/3/6). VAL 1B/221, p 23, and VAL 2B/2/18, p 96, in PRONI; Lewis, TD, 1837, II, p 405; T McIlroy, OSM, 1837, Armagh, I, p 90; PG, II, 1846, p 820; Oram, 'Craigavon', UAHS, 1971, pt III, p 13; Pierce and Coey, 'Taken for granted', 1984, p 123; Collins, 'Ardmore Parish Church', 1995, passim.

Rosebrook House, Armagh

86. A most attractive house, one-storey from the front but with a substantial two-storey return, set on a hillside amidst magnificent trees, just across the road from Navan fort. "John Maxwell" (Minister of First Armagh Presbyterian church from 1732 to 1764) "after his settlement at Armagh, purchased the fee simple of a tract of land, named Eanach-Buidhe, and two townlands ... Mr. Maxwell gave to Eanach-Buidhe the new denomination of Rosebrook. Here he erected a neat and convenient dwelling-house, and planted orchards and forest trees, on an eminence encompassed with a flat plain, which, when he commenced his improvements, had been almost completely covered with water. His contemporary Dr. Barton informs us, that his mansion was, in a great measure, built with petrifactions found in the drained lands ... Rosebrook is now a delightfully rural retreat, and is still enjoyed by Mr. Maxwell's posterity ... He manured his grounds with marl, of which he found an abundant supply on the spot, and as he was a perfect master of the best system of practical agriculture then in use, his plan of farming was generally adopted by the neighbouring landholders". And, a delightful footnote: "Multitudes of cowslips are interspersed through the grasslands of Rosebrook. Mr. Maxwell had scattered a great quantity of cowslip seed over his farm about 73 years ago, and different kinds of that plant have continued to flourish there ever since" (Stuart, 1819).

"In 1764 the Rev Mr Campbell was installed and during his ministry a manse was erected in Abbey Street in 1769 in front of the church. The Ministers of the congregation had now left the country and the occupation of farming and have come to live in the city" (Lundie).

If this is indeed the original house built, it is supposed, about 1733, then it has been much altered later in the century, or perhaps in the Regency: the back part may well be the original house, the front part a later addition. The three-light windows of the entrance front outlined in black and surmounted by drip mouldings; the smooth stucco of the front wall, and the porch, look like work of around 1820. The listers describe it as an "early 19th century single storey farmhouse". The side walls are roughcast and whitewashed, with triple and single windows irregularly disposed, and a roof half-hipped to the rear. The house has two tall triple chimney-stacks. In 1835, it was classified 1B, valued at £21.17.2, and occupied by William Cross. Bought by John Leemon, the grandfather of the present owner, at a date unknown to the latter, but certainly before 1864; in which year it was valued at £18.10.0.

Photograph: Michael O'Connell.
Situation: 78, Killylea Road, Armagh; td, Rosebrook; Parish, and District Council, Armagh; Grid ref. H 847 447.
References: Listed B1 (15/14/17). VAL 1B/21A, p 56, VAL 12B/10/4 A-E, in PRONI; Stuart, 'City of Armagh', 1819, p 491; OS map, 1833; Bassett, 'Armagh', 1888, p 146; First Armagh Church diary, 1960; Lundie, 'First Armagh', 1973, p 22 (and illustration); information from owner.

Mullaghbrack House, Markethill

87. A very large and grand former rectory: "A gracious and beautifully situated residence, virtually unaltered since it was first built" (McHugh). Recently most sensitively and lovingly restored: the facade recoated with lime plaster, contrasting in texture with the limestone of quoins and detailing. Three-storey-on-basement, three-bay, the broad central bay breaking forward to embrace a wide segmental-headed recess, containing central front door, four side-windows with circular leads (but no over-door

fanlight) divided by simplified console brackets, each with three drip-like guttae. A larger three-light window above the doorcase; a smaller one above that; the remaining window-openings at the front of orthodox Georgian proportions, with glazing-bars (original or replacements) complete, though at least two windows are blank behind the bars, and there are wide three-light windows in the ground floor of the garden front.

The basement is paved over at the front of the house; runs through a narrow open area to the right; likewise at the rear, but over-arched by a pretty iron bridge leading from the morning-room window to the garden; and on the fourth side, the basement door, flanked by offices, reached by way of a gravelled incline running through the stone outbuildings surrounding the yard. The roof has wide over-sailing eaves carried on paired brackets, the outer sections set to a shallow slope, the central part flat; with prominent stone chimney-stacks. Altogether, a most imposing composition externally. Internally, a little disappointing: a curious reversed staircase dividing the front hall into two: the rooms tall and dignified, but - apart from some fan-mouldings in the shutters - detailed with less elegance than the exterior might have led one to expect: but no doubt the house will look better once it is fully occupied again.

Lewis says "The glebe-house, a handsome residence, beautifully situated, was erected in 1829, by the Rev. S. Blacker, LL. D, the present incumbent, at an expense of £4,561.8.0; the glebe, which consists of five townlands, comprises 1,146 statute acres, valued at £1,416 per annum." Dr Samuel Blacker was "a man of considerable wealth", brother of Lord Gosford's agent and one of the Blackers of Carrickblacker, who gave £1,035 towards enlarging and rebuilding the parish church, as well as presenting a silver flagon and communion plate. In 1838, the house was classified 1A+ - "Note: the above concerns are all new except the gate-house" - and valued at the formidable figure of £94.13.1, reduced however first to £78.1.3, then to £52. Rev. Dr Blacker lived here for 23 years until his death in 1849, when he was luckily succeeded by another rich rector, Lord John Beresford, nephew of the primate. "His wife, Christina or Lady John, is said to have been as plain as her husband was handsome, but what she lacked in looks she made up for in style" (McHugh).

In 1859 Lord John, to his surprise, succeeded his elder brother (who had fatally fallen from his horse at Carrick-on-Suir) as Marquis of Waterford, and was himself succeeded as rector by Dr J F Flavell. In 1863, the house was valued at £70. In 1869, rather surprisingly at the time of the disestablishment of the Church of Ireland, the Representative Church Body seems to have bought the glebe-house, and then on the death of Dr Flavell's widow, to have sold it to Lord Gosford, who in turn sold it to Mr Hugh Williamson in 1911. It was bought from him in 1924 by Mr James Morgan, grandfather of the present owner.

Photographs: Michael O'Connell (see also colour-plate XIIIb).
Situation: 20, Mullurg Road, Cornacrew, Markethill; td, Cornacrew; Parish, Mullaghbrack; District Council, Armagh; Grid ref. H 967 429.
References: Listed B+ (15/4/4). VAL 1B/213, p 101, VAL 2B/2/212A, p 41, in PRONI; Lewis, TD, 1837, II, p 410; Leslie, 'Armagh clergy', 1911, p 385; Kerr, 'Parish of Mullabrack', [1953], passim; M McHugh, 'Guide to St John's, Mullaghbrack', 1985; McHugh, 'Houses upon the glebe', [c. 1985], passim.

Keady Rectory

88. "The glebe-house was built in 1779, by aid of a gift of £100 from the Board [of first Fruits]" (Lewis). An interesting house of two different dates. The older house, now the back part, is believed to have been built by the direction of Primate Robinson. The front part, which stands some feet lower down the hillside, was added probably around 1818, the year when the Rev. E R Roberts, who had been curate here for 29 years, was promoted by Archbishop Stuart to be rector. Coote says that in 1804 the yearly value of the rectory (the office rather than the building) was £200, "Rev. Mr Close incumbent: the curate resides in a small parsonage, to which there is a glebe attached".

Externally, from the front a plain two-storey three-bay house, with walls of yellow-painted roughcast, some Georgian glazing bars (but some inappropriate ones), and a (probably slightly later) porch. From the rear, apparently four-storey, with dormers on top and barred basement windows opening into an area. The farmyard, stables, coach-house and servants' quarters of the original house remain practically unaltered.

Internally, the difference in levels results in a flight of steps from the front hall up to the former front doorway of the older house. The window-openings in the former front wall have been, ingeniously, converted into cupboards. The rooms in the front part of the house have very high ceilings, with the consequence that a single agreeable landing runs the full depth of both houses at first-floor level. But the best feature of the rectory is the staircase, making its way round a square stair-well, with shouldered bannisters at each corner, to the very top of the house.

The rectory is set well back from the road in an extensive woodland garden. Happily, it is still used for its original purpose; and its present occupier is good to it.

Photograph: Michael O'Connell.
Situation: 31, Crossmore Road, Keady; td, Crossmore; Parish, Keady; District Council, Armagh; Grid ref. H 843 350.
References: Listed B2 (15/10/4). Coote, 'Armagh', 1804, p 12; OS map 1834; Lewis, TD, 1837, II, p 34; Leslie, 'Armagh clergy', 1911, p 316.

Willowbank, Keady

89. In appearance an unusually grand late-Georgian rectory, this house was in fact built for himself (not by his congregation) by a Presbyterian minister, the Rev. Joseph Jenkins. Son of a Castleblayney farmer, he was called to Keady in 1816, retired in 1854, and died in 1862. Perhaps this house, which dates from about 1834, was paid for out of the proceeds of the family farm? There is a tradition that it was only lately built in the year of the Big Wind of Sunday 6 January 1839, and that Mr Jenkins stood at an upstairs window wondering whether his roof would hold fast: which, fortunately, it did. It was placed in category 1A, and valued at £24.18.2, in 1836.

It is a three-bay, two-storey house, with (invisible) attic, almost covered in creepers and climbers, with a well-detailed Ionic-columnar doorcase, fanlight, Georgian glazing-bars, hipped roof with corbelled eaves, and paired chimney-stacks (one of them a dummy). Some of the interior plasterwork is exceptionally vigorous: there are multiply-channelled covings around several of the ceilings, and a flamboyant ceiling rose in the hall. The house is reported to be very snug and dry, despite the fact that it has no foundations; when a drawing-room floor-board is lifted, there are the roots of the creeper outside the window!

The history of the house is remarkable, in that it seems never to have been either bought or sold: Mr Jenkins left it to his nephew Colonel Dobbin. He left it to his daughter Anna Dobbin; who left it, in 1935, to Dr Henry Dorman, grandfather of the present owner. However, its occupants have not always been its owners. The Valuation books show that Miss Dobbin was followed by James, then John, Robinson; by Dr Savage in 1880; and by Dr John G Allen in 1882. According to the rector of Keady, Mr Hogg, "Miss Leeper resided at Willowbank, with her sister, Mrs Allen, wife of the resident local doctor"; "Between 1890 and 1900 the Allens left Willowbank"; "Miss A. Gordon, resident at Willowbank", (the practice nurse) in 1928. For most of its life, the house has been home to a leading local doctor: originally, the surgery was inside the house; today it is housed in a modern extension to the rear.

Photograph: Michael O'Connell.
Situation: Armagh Road, Keady; td, Dunlarg; Parish, Keady; District Council, Armagh; Grid ref. H 531 248.
References: Listed B (15/9/1). VAL 1B/26A, p 28, VAL 1B/10/17A - D, in PRONI; Ms Presbyterian Fasti, II, 1503, in Linen Hall Library; Hogg, 'Keady', 1928, pp 11, 19, 39; Pierce and Coey, 'Taken for granted', 1984, p 125; information from owners.

Greenfield Manse, Armagh

90. A fine foursquare three-bay two-storey-and-attic red-brick house with handsome stucco architraves around all the windows, and a very good if austere tall portico of square columns and pilasters. A shield-shaped datestone high up in the back wall of the house is impressively inscribed "Built by the Second Presbyterian Congregation Armagh for the use of their Minister, William Henderson Minister, 1852". "This fine house, built in 1852, was originally the property of the Second Congregation but passed to the Mall Church on the demise of that body in 1915" (Allison). The UAHS listers find it "an attractive and well-maintained building in a landscape setting," and suggest that the architect was possibly W J Barre, a notion which would not have occurred to me: there seems to be no surviving documentation - so they may be right. However, though the rooms are lofty, well-proportioned, and well-detailed, there appears to be nothing particularly characteristic of Barre. An odd quirk is that the side window of the dining-room is segmental-headed, the back window, though of similar dimensions, square headed. All the windows have Georgian glazing. For many years the residence of the Rev. Dr David Graham, predecessor of the present minister.

Photographs: Michael O'Connell; PRONI.

Situation: 72, Newry Road, Armagh; td, Demesne; Parish, and District Council, Armagh; Grid ref. H 888 445.

References: Listed B1 (15/18/22); outside conservation area. Datestone; Lockington, 'Mall Presbyterian Church', 1987, p 32; 'Buildings of Armagh', UAHS, 1992, p 164; Allison, 'Way we were,' 1993, p 28.

Former Parochial House, Middletown

91. A most unusual house, one gable partly of stone, partly of brick above the paired round-headed windows; the front elevation and the rear partly rendered, but the front has a strange loggia of red brick, with some yellow brick relief; two two-storey canted bays, and between them this extraordinary Italianate loggia atop the porch. The roof is hipped, and incorporates fish-tail slates. There is a remarkable little upstairs oratory projecting from the rear of the house, topped by highly ornamental metal cresting. It appears to be, and always to have been, a pair of semi-detached houses.

According to the parish history, "Fr Charles McEvoy (1884-94) was renowned for his devotion to the poor. His curates were Fr Bernard O'Connor till 1889. Followed by the Rev. John Doctor Loughran who designed and built" (largely with his own hands) what was to become "the old parochial house in Middle-town. This priest was the composer of a celebrated poem, "Memorabilia", which he wrote in 1904, on the occasion of the consecration of St. Patrick's Cathedral, Armagh ... Fr McEvoy died on 13th February, 1894, and his successor was Father Patrick Mac Rory (1894-1921). At first he lived in a house opposite the new parochial house, which was the private residence of the curate, Dr. Loughran. When the latter was appointed curate of Dromintee, the parishioners prevailed upon Fr Mac Rory to take up residence in it". Father Mac Rory was hesitant about doing so as he was not particularly attracted to the building. In the end, however, he took up residence in the house. "A sum of money had to be raised to pay Dr. Loughran. The parish at last had a parochial house". As it was an extensive house, it long served as residence both for parish priest and curate.

It would seem that Father Loughran was both a man of means, and a man who had travelled in Italy. The last parish priest to live here was Father Carraher, who left in December 1994. The house still belongs to the parish, and the oratory is in occasional use, though a new, post-war, rather suburban, parochial house now houses the parish priest of Tynan and Middletown; and the old parochial house seems to house only the local ACE office.

Photographs: Michael O'Connell.
Situation: 10-12, The Diamond, Middletown; td, Middletown; Parish, Tynan; District Council, Armagh; Grid ref. H 753 388.
References: Not listed. 'Historical sketches of Tynan and Middletown', 1995, pp 105, 107; information from Fr Sweeney and Gabriel Mallon.

Ara Coeli, Armagh

92. "The palace of the Primate - modest, but in good taste - occupies a partly-secluded spot at the back of the Cathedral" (Bassett). "The first section was built in 1877 for Archbishop McGettigan, four years after the completion of the cathedral. It was altered and extended for Cardinal McRory in 1928 and it is his arms that appear carved above the entrance ... The porch is the most architectural element of the building, constructed of dressed limestone with granite Corinthian pilasters flanking the doorway ... Of two storeys, rendered, with a dressed stone eaves course supported by modillions. The sills and quoins are of dressed limestone" (UAHS). Somewhat surprisingly, the design for the original, very dull, building was by J J McCarthy, architect of St Patrick's Cathedral (47) next door, who sent off plans and specifications for the house just before Christmas 1875. The extension, completed in 1931, was by Ashlin & Coleman of Dublin, and cost £6,150.

A rather forbidding, grim, grey building externally, though it springs to a degree of life and warmth when the sun strikes its canted bays. Internally, a disconcerting mixture. The formal Victorian state reception and dining-rooms are impressive, if somewhat charmless; the numerous offices are a jumble of ancient and modern juxtaposed; the furnishings and pictures are likewise a mixture of Victorian and contemporary styles. Perhaps the most unexpected feature is the pseudo-circular oratory, with artwork by Ray Carroll, installed in an upstairs bedroom by Cardinal Daly in 1992.

Photograph: Michael O'Connell.
Situation: Cathedral Road, Armagh; td, Corporation; Parish, and District Council, Armagh; Grid ref. H 872 457.
References: Not listed; outside conservation area. Letter from J J McCarthy to Fr Byrne, 14 December 1875, and correspondence of 1931 in Box 7, Cardinal MacRory Archive, in O Fiaich Memorial Library, Armagh; Bassett, 'Armagh', 1888, p 101; 'Buildings of Armagh', UAHS, 1992, p 75.

Bishop of Dromore's Palace, Newry

93. A fine new palace for the Roman Catholic bishop of Dromore, Dr Edward Mulhern, was built in 1932 to the designs of John J Robinson, architect, of Dublin. Its site was in the extensive and attractive grounds of St Colman's College, on the outskirts of Newry, for which Robinson was to build a new chapel (54) five years later. The listers say, very properly, "An attractive asymmetrical two-storey house in a free Tudor-Gothic style built of Newry granite, with steep hipped slated roofs, large stone mullioned and transomed windows ... and a pointed Gothic doorway with chamfered reveals", surmounted, rather mysteriously, by what looks like a carved cardinal's hat. With its variety of gables, canted bays, and three-, four-, and five-light windows, this is an extremely effective composition .

There is an oratory above the front hall with very good stained glass by Harry Clarke; the staircase has fine oak bannisters. The listers note "this is probably the last sizeable building to be erected in Newry granite".

Photograph: Michael O'Connell.
Situation: In former grounds of St Colman's College, Violet Hill, Armagh Road, Newry; td, Lisdrumgullion; Parish, Newry; District Council, Newry & Mourne; Grid ref. J 082 278.
References: Listed B1 (16/25/20); notes in MBR.

The See House, Armagh

94. By Edwin Leighton, diocesan architect: 1975. "Tucked into the north side of cathedral hill, behind a high stone wall, and on the site of a former rectory garden, is the official residence of the Primate of All Ireland. Built in 1975 after the Palace" (80) "was sold to Armagh District Council, the house is no more than a two-storey modern villa ... It is only the handsome entrance gates that evoke any kind of primatial grandeur" (UAHS).

This is perhaps a bit unkind. Whilst it is very much to be regretted that the Representative Church Body, in far-off Dublin, was so idiotic as to sell - instead of modifying - the old Palace, yet the so-called See House is not, for its period, half bad; and does considerable credit to its architect.

Admittedly, it is not large enough to permit of entertaining on a primatial scale: the garden is perhaps big enough (DV, WP) for garden parties. But for a private house of this date, it has an exceptionally spacious feeling: large rooms opening into each other; exceptionally generous drawing-room, dining-room and kitchen; picture windows looking out over the city towards the observatory; open staircase with gallery, and a broad stained-glass panel, with primatial coats of arms, brought from the Palace (along with Cooley's gate-piers, 210); and a great amount of panelling. The exterior, with projecting porch, is of a pleasantly faded pink brick, glass, and varnished timber. Altogether, the house is very much of its time, but, I think, unfairly under-rated: though certainly a great come-down from its predecessor.

Photograph: Michael O'Connell.
Situation: Cathedral Close, Armagh; td, Corporation; Parish, and District Council, Armagh; Grid ref. H 873 453.
References: Not listed; in conservation area. 'Buildings of Armagh', UAHS, 1992, p 64; information from occupiers.

MIDDLING SIZED HOUSES

63 and 65 Canal Street, Newry (119). Photograph: Michael O'Connell

MIDDLING SIZED HOUSES

The county of Armagh is rich in fine houses of the middle size: perhaps because it was one of the first counties in Ireland to give birth to a rising middle class. So early as 1804, Sir Charles Coote was able to remark that "as the pursuits of husbandry, exclusively occupying the attention of the people, are scarcely to be found anywhere in this county, it is difficult to point out the farmer unconnected with manufacture":[1] and this despite the observation, under the heading 'Farm Houses and Offices', that "there is so material a difference in this respect, between the centre and the boundaries of the county, that no average report can be strictly given. In the former the houses are remarkably comfortable, surrounded with orchards and neat enclosures; in the latter the reverse is the case, though still improving".[2]

He is particularly complimentary about the Camlough district "which is worthy of particular notice, on account of the rapid stream, that flows from this small sheet of water, and performs more actual work in a line not quite two miles, than can perhaps be equalled in any part of Ireland; and the numerous works on its banks furnish an eminent instance of the superior spirit and industry of the people in this province, who so eagerly seize every natural advantage for furthering and encreasing their trade". He goes on to list Mr Duff's "very capital bleaching concerns"; Mr William Pollock's works; "the most capital boulting-mills in the county ... equal to manufacture 10,000 barrels of wheat, of Messrs Jackson & Co"; "on the next fall a good flax-mill is erected; and, at a short distance from it, another corn-mill"; then Mr Joseph Campbell's bleach-mill; then the flour-mills of Messrs Christopher Reed & Co; then "another fall, which is intended for some extensive manufactory, I understand in the pottery or foundery process; below this are two other falls, the property of Messrs. Atkinson and Co., on one of which they have erected a bleach-mill, and are about occupying the other in the same process".[3] Alas, every one of these concerns has long since closed, and the river that conferred so much power is no more than a thin trickle through a pipe.

A similar catalogue for the river Callan was not provided, but "on this water are numerous bleach-greens and mills, from Keady to Armagh; this appearance of wealth and commerce is very engaging, and the busy scenes on these banks are enlivened with many ornamental improvements".[4] All these busy entrepreneurs required suitable housing, even if not all of them prospered, and even if there were bad years as well as good ones. Now, all

this activity has quite ceased; see the frontispiece to this book.

Thirty years later, Samuel Lewis wrote "The general diffusion of the population is neither the result of a predetermined plan, nor of mere accident: it arises from the nature of the linen manufacture, which does not require those employed in it to be collected into overgrown cities, or congregated in crowded factories. Engaged alternately at their loom and in their farm, they derive both health and recreation from the alternation. Green lawns, clear streams, pure springs, and the open atmosphere, are necessary for bleaching: hence it is that so many eminent bleachers reside in the country, and hence also the towns are small, and every hill and valley abounds with rural and comfortable habitations".[5] The Parliamentary Gazetteer of 1845 says "At once the staple trade, a general and prime means of support, and a pursuit associated to a large extent with that of agriculture is, and long has been, the manufacture of linen ... The fabrics produced are cambrics, lawns, diapers, damasks, chequers, and a great variety of plain linens...The returns of the collectors of customs indicate a large increase in the quantity of linen exported from Ulster, between 1825 and 1835; and, with the exception of Antrim, no county is likely to have contributed more to the increase than Armagh".[6] It is noticeable that many fine houses of the middling size were built at just this period of expansion in the industry. It is perhaps surprising that so few date from the second half of the century, particularly the highly prosperous period of the American Civil War.

My friend and neighbour Denis Ireland could still, in 1939, write of handloom weavers working on the shores of Lough Neagh;[7] I myself remember the days when the weightiest linen merchants of Ulster, wearing stiff collars and bowler hats, would still assemble for lunch on Thursdays in the Ulster Club in Castle Place, Belfast. (In my day they took their hats off to eat, but my father remembered the custom to be otherwise, when an entire table was occupied by my Richardson great-uncles, all wearing their bowlers as they supped their soup.) Those days are long gone; and at the time of writing, the once-prosperous linen industry of County Armagh is all but extinct.

References: 1. Coote, 'Armagh', 1804, p 139. 2. Ibid, p 232. 3. Ibid, pp 360, 361. 4. Ibid, p 306. 5. Lewis, TD, 1837, I, p 65. 6. PG, I, 1845, p 75. 7. Ireland, 'Statues round the city hall', 1939, pp 46-57.

Ballyrath House, Armagh

95. "139 acres 1 roode at Ballyrath...This is very good land near Armagh ... There is on it a very good stone farm house, part of it lofted over and floored, with a barn, stable, maulte house and kilne, a turfe house, a tan yard, a garden and a young orchard. The improvements are all made by Scott the under-tenant" (Ashe, 1703). Whether the present house is the same must be uncertain. Very possibly that referred to by Ashe was a snug single-storey thatched house : the back stair tower bears the date 1710, so perhaps the house was raised by a storey in that year. A Miss Scott seems to have married a Hutchinson: by 1835 the place was occupied by one Matthew Skeaf, under lease from Captain Hutchinson, with a valuation of £10.15.0, which had risen to £13 by 1862. By 1873, the unfortunate Mr Skeaf had gone bankrupt, and the house and farm, still valued at the same high figure, seem to have been occupied by Mr Meyrick Copeland Jones under lease from Michael Garvey, who would appear to have acquired the interest of Captain Hutchison around the same date. The house remains in the ownership of the same family, but is now not in good order, and is at risk of demolition to make way for a modern bungalow on almost the same site.

The maps and records show that this unususal seven-bay two-storey roughcast and whitewashed house, with Regency glazing-pattern and green-painted trim, originally had two returns, and two barns. Of these, only the central stair-tower at the rear survives. There have been a number of alterations over the years, notably a new roof early in the present century, but this house is a remarkable survival, the more so as it altogether escaped the notice of the listers. It was drawn to my attention by Dr Noel Marshall; I brought it to the notice of Harriet Devlin of the UAHS for possible inclusion in its Buildings at Risk series; she carried out all the research, and I am indebted to her for the information contained in this entry.

Photograph: Michael O'Connell.
Situation: Ballyrath Road, Armagh; td, Ballyrath; Parish, and District Council,Armagh; Grid ref. H 854 445.
References: Not listed. T 848/1, A view of the Archbishoprick of Armagh 1703 taken by Thomas Ashe, VAL 1B/21A, VAL 2B/2/22, p 30, VAL 12B/10/4C and E, all in PRONI; OS map 1835.

Fathom House (formerly Park), Newry

96. The owner's title-deeds suggest a date of 1732 for this house built apparently by the Needhams, Earls of Kilmorey, perhaps as dower house, or agent's house on their Newry estate, at some distance from their principal property at Kilkeel, County Down. Rankin explains that the possessions of the Cistercian Abbey of Newry had been granted in 1552 to Sir Nicholas Bagenal. "The head of the Bagenal family, and their successors, the Kilmorey family, is in fact, the Hereditary Lay Abbot of Newry... in practice, the Bishop" (of Dromore) "was not able to exercise jurisdiction within these areas of his own see, and the lay impropriator exercised the right of patronage to the parishes" until disestablishment.

In 1813, the Kilmorey estate made a number of leases of lands in Fathom, including several to members of the Hollywood family. Let in 1837 to a Mr Benson, after whom the adjacent Benson's Glen seems to have been named. In 1880, the house was occupied by Mr Thompson Cooke under the Kilmorey estate; the valuation had been reduced from £30 to £18, with the note "This house is now occupied by a farmer and the valuation is much too high, the house being too large for the farm". In 1885 it was occupied by Margaret and Janet (or Jennett) Benson; then by Peter Cronin; by 1894 it was once again occupied by the Benson ladies, but the valuation had fallen still further to £14. 15. 0. In 1904 the house was let at £10 per annum, in 1905 it was vacant. Thereafter, it was occupied by the Hollywood family until at least 1922. (The fulsome Latin inscription in St Mary's

(C of I) church, Newry, to Gulielmus Ogle, armiger, de Fatham, appears to relate not to this property, but to the house some way to the north, now unfortunately much altered.)

The house has important plasterwork in the drawing room, unfortunately not in good order, with squirrels, foxes, cranes, and other creatures illustrating Aesop's fables. The squirrels at the corners of the cornice above the fireplace appear to be cousins of the squirrel in the ceiling of Montalto, County Down; the foxes and cranes in the mid-sections of the cornice appear to be country cousins of those in the Aesop room at Áras an Uachtaráin, in Phoenix Park, Dublin, attributed by McDonnell to Barthelemij Cramillion. (I am informed by Mr Irwin Major that there are similar fabulous creatures in the cornices of the old Collector's House, now belonging to the Convent of Mercy, at Warrenpoint Road, Newry, a house believed to date from the late 18th century). Fathom House has several shouldered door-cases in the early Georgian manner; and its original staircase. Originally, a double-pile house, rendered, two-storey-on-basement, three bays wide and four bays deep, apparently re-roofed in the 19th century when most of the Georgian glazing-bars (except in the four tall ground-floor side windows) were taken out. The console-bracketed doorcase, with rectangular fanlight, seems to be 19th-century; but the best external feature of the house, its magnificent flight of curved granite front steps, is certainly original.

The present owner, Peter Hollywoods's niece, was born

here; it had been sold in 1944 to a Mr Reginald McGivern; bought next by a Mr Armstrong; bought back in 1972. At present, it appears to be in rather poor order: a pity, for it stands on a magnicent site on the hillside overlooking the Newry River and canal, with a tumbling stream in the glen beside it, and a salmon and trout hatchery for good measure. Originally called "Fathom Park", but when the local council allocated the same name to a new housing estate, so much confusion was caused that the owners reluctantly renamed it "Fathom House".

Photographs: Michael O'Connell; Irwin Major.
Situation: 45, Fathom Line, Omeath Road, Newry; td, Fathom (Lower); Parish, Newry; District Council, Newry & Mourne; Grid ref. J 097 231.
References: Listed B (16/13/5). D 2638/8/94/3 and 10, D 2638/B/ 05/3, VAL 12B/15/1A-K, all in PRONI; Taylor and Skinner, 'Roads', 1778, p 11; Wilson, 'Post-chaise companion', 1803, p 19; Lewis, TD, 1837, II, p 433; Bassett, 'Armagh', 1888, p 235; McDonnell, 'Irish eighteenth-century stuccowork', 1991, pp 25, 27, and pls 110, 111, 145; F Rankin, in 'Clergy of Down and Dromore', 1996,.p 202; 'Old families of Newry', 1998, p 108.

Prospect House, Tandragee

97. A three-bay two-storey farmhouse: in the upper part of the front wall, a fire insurance token; and a datestone fairly persuasively inscribed "SWE 1724" (said by the owners to be the signature of S W Emerson: though, of course, it could have been removed from an earlier house on the site, or uplifted when an upper storey was added). However, the fanlight is framed in the kind of fluting sometimes seen in early Georgian mantelpieces, so probably this rather charming little house should be given the benefit of the doubt. Moreover, the internal doorcases have wooden reeding; and the staircase looks to be original. The roof is half-hipped; there is a single-storey canted bay, perhaps of Regency date, at each gable. Unfortunately, at some fairly recent date the walls have been encased in an inappropriate striated patent render, which detracts from the appearance of the house at close quarters; but it looks very handsome from the road.

In 1863, this house was occupied by Arabella Saunderson under lease from the Duke of Manchester; by 1875, it had passed to Robert Davison, at a valuation of £11; it remained in his family until bought by the father of the present owner in 1927, still valued at £11, but the freehold having been bought out under the Land Acts.

Photograph: Michael O'Connell.
Situation: 136, Ballymore Road, Mullahead, Tandragee; td, Mullahead; Parish, Ballymore; District Council, Armagh; Grid ref. J 038 489.
References: Listed B (15/5/2). Datestone; VAL 2B/2/33, VAL 12B/11/4 A-F, in PRONI; OS map 1836; notes by C Munro in MBR.

Dundrum House, Tassagh, Keady

98. The outstanding feature of this unlisted house is the very fine granite Gibbsian doorcase with fanlight. From a distance, the house and its outbuildings, with a great yew tree in its parkland, look most impressive: an early 18th-century dwelling for gentleman farmer or prosperous mill-owner. Two-storey and attic; five-bay; but all is not as it seems. Because of a severe outbreak of dry rot, all the original timbers have been stripped out and replaced. Whilst the original staircase and bannisters are said to have been meticulously reproduced, the Georgian sash windows have, unhappily, been replaced by plastic ones.

The extensive farmyards and stabling are well kept and nicely painted. At the foot of the avenue, magnificent cast-iron gates and pillars, white-painted; concealed and so saved from the British war effort of 1940. Possibly of much the same date as the house, almost certainly no later than the 1820s.

The place was advertised in the Newry Telegraph on 5 July 1826: "Bleach green and farm, as occupied by the late Adam McBride, Dundrum. The dwelling house and offices are fit for the immediate reception of a respectable family". In 1836 occupied by Samuel Kidd, and valued at £20.13.0, in category 1B, with the comment "small house, large farm". By 1864, the valuation had increased to £40, and the place was rented out by Mr Kidd's heirs, in quick succesion, to William McCaldin; William Calvert; Richard Browne; Samuel Jackson; James Morrison; and eventually, in 1876, to William Greer Barcroft; then Thomas M Barcroft. The local parson, Mr Hogg, records that "Dundrum House was tenanted in my early days by Mr. T M Barcroft, J P. In 1895 the family removed to Dublin and was succeeded by Mr. William Moffatt". Subsequently, it was occupied by the Armstrong and Coulter families, and was bought by the present owner's grandfather in 1943.

Jonesboro House, Jonesborough

99. "Colonel Jones built a fine house at the top of Jonesboro hill. It was originally a three-storeyed building, but the top storey has since been removed. The servants' quarters extended on the left hand side of the house, and the kitchen area on the right-hand side. There were also large cellars underneath the house which have now been closed up. The walls of the house were made by layers of mortar and wood with turf in the middle, and the ceilings contain many fine oak beams which run the length of the house. Many items of fine workmanship, including a magnificent staircase, were removed and sold by one of the subsequent owners" (McAleenan and Crilly).

Colonel Morris Jones was a Welshman, who is said to have obtained a grant of land here around 1750, to have built the village, and to have endowed it with his own name. In 1837 "the residence of Hamilton Skelton, Esq". The valuation, in December 1836, confirms this, places the house in category 1A, measuring 41 feet by 24 feet 6 inches by 18 feet, "value finally settled at £12 12 0", after adding fourpence in the £ for good situation. One of the "five two-storey houses, all slated", in the "hamlet", in the following year, according to Mr Scott of the Ordnance Survey. Mr

Skelton appears to have sold to William McFadden in 1891; three years later Thomas McFadden had taken over, and the valuation had dropped to a mere £9, presumably because of the deteriorating condition of the place. Since then, it has changed hands a number of times.

The main body of the house is of five bays and two storeys, with an uncommonly fine doorcase - radial fanlight and broken pediment carried on Tuscan columns. Some, but not all, of the Georgian glazing-bars survive. There is a single-storey two-bay extension at each side. The house is white-washed, with green reveals and, surprisingly, green window-sills. As the listers remark, "a little the worse for the ravages of time, but still of significant architectural and historical interest".

Photograph: Michael O'Connell.
Situation: 2, Main Street, Jonesborough; td, Edenappa; Parish, Jones-borough; District Council, Newry & Mourne; Grid ref. J 070 174.
References: Listed B+ (16/15/29). VAL 1B/243, VAL 12B/15/15 A-D, in PRONI; G Scott, OSM, (1837?), Armagh, I, p 46; Lewis, TD, 1837, II, p 33; McAleenan and Crilly, 'In the shadow of Slieve Gullion', 1990, p 42.

◁

Photographs: Michael O'Connell; Anthony Cranney.
Situation: 116, Dundrum Road, Tassagh; td, Dundrum; Parish, Keady; District Council, Armagh; Grid ref. H 872 358.
References: Not listed. VAL 1B/26A, p 35, VAL 12B/1/26A-E in PRONI;

'Newry Telegraph', 5/7/1826; Lewis, TD, 1837, II, p 34; Hogg, 'Keady', 1928, p 39; T G F Paterson Manuscript Collection, No 56, Vol 4, in Armagh County Museum; information from owner.

Portnelligan House, Middletown

100. At the end of a long (and well-kept) drive, with a gatelodge, on a hilltop, rather surprisingly turning its back on Doogary Lough, a charming if modest gentleman's seat. A seven-bay two-storey house, roughcast and white-painted, with tall gables and four very prominent brick chimney-stacks. The four bays to the left are evidently the oldest, incorporating a badly damaged datestone, above what was probably originally the front door but now a window: "HAEC DOMUS CONSTRUCT ... CROSS AD 17-5" (possibly 1765?). The house was built on land leased in 1731 for 999 years by Richard Cross "of Clontcarty gentleman" from Robert Maxwell of Fellows Hall (74 - see also the entry on the Cross Pillar, 206), and certainly this section of the house seems to date from the mid 18th century. It appears as "Portnalegan" on Taylor and Skinner's map surveyed in 1777.

The house and land remained in the Cross family for over 150 years. In 1767, Richard transferred them to his son John in exchange for an annuity; he made a will in 1774 dividing the property between his sons Alexander, John and Richard, and died in 1775. Alexander lived on, and prospered: a deed of 1829 recites that on his death each of his three sons and two daughters "will become entitled to Government stock and other property to a considerable amount", and by his will made in 1835 he remarks that his "legal debts will be very few". He died in 1842, but alas his sons John and Richard had died before him, each "of age, intestate, unmarried, and without issue"; and his third son was by then of unsound mind, and so remained until his death in 1872. The property passed to his daughters Margaret Tenison and Ann

MacDonagh, each of whom had married Dublin barristers; it is believed that it was Mrs Tenison who added to the house after the death of her father. (In 1864, the house was classified 1B, valued at £25, and occupied by Thomas J Tennison.) On her death, the place passed to her only son, Major William Cross O'Brien Tenison of the Armagh Militia. Finally, on his death, the property was sold by his widow Letitia in 1897 to one, William Couser; and passed through several hands before being bought by the father of its present owner in 1917.

At some date, probably soon after 1842, the house was extended to the northward by the addition of three bays containing a new front door and entrance hall, and a drawing room. At this time the older windows seem to have been enlarged to conform with the new ones, and new windows may have been inserted in the older part of the house; and the return may have been added. All the windows are divided by horizontal glazing-bars, those downstairs into four panes each, those upstairs three panes. There is a small porch, evidently early 19th-century, of slim reeded cast-iron columns carrying a minimal lid. The outbuildings bear a datestone of 1857. Dean says that gatelodges were built here before 1835 and around 1840 for Mr Alexander Cross.

Photograph: Michael O'Connell.
Situation: 236, Monaghan Road, Middletown; td, Portnelligan; Parish, Tynan; District Council, Armagh; Grid ref. H 784 383.
References: Listed B1 (15/11/5). Datestones; VAL 2B/2/43B, p 105, in PRONI; Taylor and Skinner, 'Roads', 1778, p 266; Dean, 'Gate lodges', UAHS, 1994, p 42; extensive notes by Hugh Dixon in MBR; information from deeds and documents in the custody of the owners.

Annahugh House, Kilmore

101. An attractive long, low, whitewashed, part ivy-clad, ten-bay, two-storey farmhouse, set well back from the road. It has great charm, but on closer examination this is slightly deceptive: for example, most of the 'glazing-bars' in the downstairs windows are painted (very neatly) onto the plate glass! The openings in the front wall are unevenly disposed. The front door, with a modest segmental fanlight and simple geometrical sidelights, is in the fourth bay from the right-hand end. Probably this was originally a straightforward five-bay farmhouse with the front door in the middle, but successive extensions have been added to the leftward. It has low ceilings, and is for the most part only one room deep. There is a narrow staircase behind the front door, and a stone outside staircase at the rear.

The house is alleged, on no particular evidence, to date from the 1650s; but the oldest part of it does not look any earlier than the 1770s, if so early as that. (One of the farm outbuildings has a datestone "Rebuilt 1865".) This seems to be the "House, warehouses, offices, land, quarry and lime kiln" occupied by David McClelland as tenant of the Rev. Richard Robinson in 1864, and valued at £8.10.0, far the highest valuation in the townland. It remained in the ownership of the McClelland family until acquired by the present owner around 1985.

Photograph: Michael O'Connell.
Situation:148, Red Lion Road; td, Annahue; Parish, Kilmore; District Council, Armagh; Grid ref. H 937 522.
References: Listed B (15/2/49). VAL 12B/10/31 A-E in PRONI; information from owner.

Darkley House, Keady

102. The architecture of this interesting mill-owners house is considerably out of the ordinary run. It seems to have been built in three stages. The oldest part seems to be the four-bay two-storey range at the rear, judging from appearances, perhaps early or mid-18th century; then the T was crossed by the two-storey range, incorporating the recessed porch, facing the gate lodge and public road, perhaps early 19th-century; then a further range, with gables facing the road, was added to one side, possibly at more than one date in the mid 19th century. These disparate elements are satisfactorily united by the white painted stucco, black trim, and Georgian glazing-bars throughout. However, MacNeice reports that when the Darkley Mill was advertised for sale in 1845, the mill house was described as "modern, having been built within the last twelve years, and fit for the immediate reception of a large family".

The most unexpected feature of the façade is the way in which a very modest front door is tucked away in the right-hand corner of a wide portico-recess, the projection above being carried on three black-painted iron columns, with a round-headed niche at each end of the recess and a three-light ground floor window in between.

This was in 1836 the home of Henry McKean Esq: the house, in category 1A, and farmyard were together valued at £28. 9. 6, his spinning factory nearby (with 150 spindles and large wheel) at £30. 12. 5. By 1864, William Kirk and William M Kirk (see 215) had taken a lease of Darkley from Henry McKean's widow; the house was still valued at £30, but the value of the spinnng mill (190) was now put at £460! In 1881 the house seems to have been let to a Mr Chambers, though William M Kirk was back in residence the following year. The occupier in 1885 was William Carter. According to the rector, Mr Hogg, "between 1890 and 1900 the Carters (who had resided at Darkley for 15 years) left it". After them, a Mr Purcell, a Mr Hunter, Jack Maginness M P, then a Mrs Evans, from whom it was bought by the oddly named Christian charity the Crossfire Trust - which owns it now.

Photograph: Michael O'Connell.

Situation: 95, Darkley Road; td, Darkley; Parish, Keady; District Council, Armagh; Grid ref. H 862 314 .

References: Listed B1 (15/8/10). VAL 1B/26C, p 28, VAL 12B/10/26A, B, C, in PRONI; OS map, 1834; Hogg, 'Keady', 1928, p 19; D A MacNeice, Factory workers' housing, QUB thesis, 1981, p 90.

Palace Farm, Armagh

103. A pair of linked symmetrical Georgian houses, at the head of a long drive, providing an imposing façade for Primate Robinson's extensive farmyard. The listers, surprisingly, suggest a date of 1820, possibly because the farm buildings do not rate a mention, amongst the Archbishop's other buildings, from Arthur Young who visited in 1780: though he did say "Amongst such great works of a different nature, it is not to be expected that his Grace should have given much attention to agriculture, yet he has not neglected it". It seems clear, however, that this complex was laid out by Thomas Cooley, probably around 1770, as part of the overall plan for the Palace Demesne. Sir Charles Coote wrote, in 1804 "his Grace's farmyard, implements of husbandry, and mode of culture, afford a bright example to the gentry, of what their valuable demesnes could yield under judicious management".

The UAHS listers say: "A pair of matching three-bay, two-storey stone-built dwellings of symmetrical design flank the main gate. The roofs are hipped and two stone chimneys rise off the central cross walls. The windows are small pane sashes, nine panes at first floor and twelve at ground floor level. The panelled entrance doors have shallow segmental fanlights and classical encasements. These features and the ground floor flanking windows are set into recesses, each with a segmental arched head. All the front windows have moulded stone encasements and the entrance is protected by a shallow hood supported on stone brackets. Both houses have been restored and sympathetically modernised in recent years". The pediment of the farm buildings in the yard behind the houses contains an attractive dovecote.

There is a remarkable square pond, with bridges to an island, in the garden of the right-hand house: appropriately enough for an ecclesiastical setting, it is teeming with carp.

Photograph: Michael O'Connell.

Situation: 50 and 52, Keady Road, Armagh; td, Parkmore or Demesne; Parish, and District Council, Armagh; Grid ref. H 882 429.

References: Listed B (15/19/13); outside conservation area. Young, 'Tour', 1780, p 104; Coote, 'Armagh', 1804, p 323; 'Buildings of Armagh', UAHS, 1992, p 176; Allison, 'Way we were', 1993, p 24.

Knappagh House, Killylea

104. This is one of the most interesting houses in the county, both architecturally and for its social history. One of my aunts, who spent several years in Tynan, recalls an extraordinary French-speaking enclave in the depths of rural Armagh: and this is it.

The date 1775, found recently on a piece of roofing lead in the course of repairs, seems earlier than one might have guessed; but it is corroborated by the appearance of "Knapage, - Johnston Esq" in Taylor and Skinner's Road Book of 1778. From the front, this is a three-bay house of two storeys, on basement, having a central pediment with half-oculus, parapet, string-course, and a very fine round-headed stone doorcase with Tuscan columns: the walls rendered save for dressed stone long-and-short work around each of the Georgian-glazed windows. The attic has windows only in the gables. The appearance from the rear is quite different from the front façade: here no less than six windows are crammed into the same length of wall in each storey, giving a remarkably high ratio of void to solid. Each of the dining room and 'salon' (not, here, drawing room) has three big windows looking out over the back lawn, and a fourth in the gable wall: the result is that this is one of the lightest and airiest Georgian houses known to me. There is a square stone-flagged hall; the main staircase through a door off it to the left; a round-headed window lighting the half-landing; and an elegant

extra fanlight at the top of the stairs. Much of the interior detailing is of high quality.

Mr Joseph Johnston of Knappagh, grandson of the Rev. James Johnston of Tremont, Co Down, "was the first member of the family to settle in County Armagh"; he died in 1778, having married in 1756 Anne McGeogh Bond of Drumsill. His son James married Martha Burgess of Parkanaur by whom he had six sons and nine daughters. He was High Sheriff of the county in 1790, and used some of the uncommonly extensive outbuildings at Knappagh to house the Knappagh Corps of Yeomanry, of which he was commanding officer. He was largely responsible for the building of Drumsallan church (32) in 1821, died in 1823, and was succeeded by James Johnston II. (James's brother Mr Joseph Johnston, also of Knappagh, provided the site for Edenderry House (82) in 1788 as a glebe house for Eglish parish, and died in the same year. His son Joseph Johnston II built and endowed a schoolhouse, and about 1830 built for himself Mullyloughan House - 121.) There is no evidence that I know of, either that Francis Johnston, the distinguished Armagh architect, was a near relation, or that he was concerned in any of these building ventures, though Dean seems convinced that he was of the same family, and Dixon has suggested (unconvincingly to my mind) his authorship for Mullyloughan. In 1775 Francis Johnston was aged only 15. It is not impossible that his father William Johnston, "a builder occasionally acting as an architect", might have been employed, but that is mere conjecture.

How the Knappagh Johnstons came by their money I have been unable to discover: but clearly they spent large sums - probably more than they could well afford - on their building ventures. "James Johnston went abroad about 1834 owing to embarrassed circumstances and finding it cheaper to live in France settled down in Paris, leaving his affairs in the hands of his cousin and brother-in-law George Robinson", barrister-at-law, of Armagh. On the way to Paris, he fell in with Augustine Barraux, a young French lady who ran a private millinery establishment in Harrogate. They set up house together at Passy, where at least one son was born before they were secretly married; not long thereafter, in 1838, James Johnston died, aged 48, of consumption; five months after his death a daughter, Anna Maria Amelia, was born. Her elder brother (or brothers) having died in infancy, Knappagh passed to her under her father's will.

This was naturally unwelcome to the family, especially to the two aunts still living in the house. In June 1839, the executors sold off all its contents in a week-long auction which realised £1903. 5. 5. Augustine came to Dublin and instituted proceedings in her daughter's name in the Chancery court there. The litigation dragged on until at least 1847, the aunts staying on in the house despite the sale of the furniture: or perhaps it was they who bought it in? A receiver was appointed by the court to collect the farm rents, which in 1846 totalled £1,370, but there were arrears of nearly £500. At length a settlement was negotiated with the help of a young Dublin curate, Richard Keene, who acted as protector and supporter of the widowed Augustine: and, at some date, married her (the Church of Ireland recorded her name as "Augusta Johnston alias Burrowes"). There were two children of this marriage, Richard Keene II and Augustine Keene II. Unfortunately, Richard Keene I, still a mere curate at St Andrew's church, died at Kingstown in July 1860, aged only 44. The twice-widowed Augustine and her children paid occasional visits to their aunts at Knappagh, where Anna Maria Johnston was shown as owner in 1863. But then another misfortune struck: Anna Maria died of consumption before attaining her majority: from 1864 until 1888 Augustine I was shown as owner and occupier.

Thereafter, the name of Augustine II, by then Mrs Terris, appears in the Valuation books; for she had married one Paul Terris, a Provençal whom she had met through her French relations. Unlike Augustine I, who had converted to the Protestant faith before her marriage, Paul was an extremely devout Roman Catholic, and Augustine II followed suit. Local tradition recalls that, on the first Sunday morning after the couple took up residence at Knappagh, the tenantry assembled to greet them outside Drumsallan church; when, to the consternation of one and all, the carriage clattered up the hill and, without stopping, down the other side, on its way to the Catholic church at Artasooly.

Of the three sons of that marriage, Paul was killed in the first World War; Edmund practised for many years as a surgeon in Paris; and Patrick, the eldest, having survived a war spent in the trenches as a French cavalry officer - being generally referred to as "the Major" - returned to Knappagh at the armistice. His devout father, with the help of some friendly priests at Chalons-sur Saone, provided an arranged marriage for him with a suitably devout French lady of good birth, Marguerite Cautin de Blaizey. Of the eight children of that marriage, four chose to make their lives in France, four in Ireland or England. Patrick Terris was twice President of the Ulster Farmers Union, and contributed from the Knappagh demesne the oak for the roof of the new Roman Catholic church built at Tullysaran in 1924. He lived on, a romantic lover of Ireland and a civilised patron of the arts, until 1976; his widow Marguerite died at Lourdes in 1987.

Amongst the Major's protégés was the artist John Luke who, with his mother, took refuge from the air raids on Belfast in the steward's house at Knappagh, and lived on there until 1950. His work was then little valued, though it has now, of course, come to be greatly valued. An eccentric man, he grew at Knappagh the vegetables which, eaten raw, constituted his entire diet, and received much kindness from the Terris family and another French family who likewise were refugees at Knappagh. John Luke was able to eke out a living by teaching art at the Manor House girls' school, at Milford nearby, at which my sister was then a pupil.

The house has recently undergone extensive restoration; it is still occupied by members of the Terris family and still provides a welcome for the countless French cousins. The present owner is engaged in putting together a book on the house and its associations: and I look forward eagerly to reading it.

Photographs; Michael O'Connell

Situation: 51, Knappagh Road, Killylea; td, Knappagh; Parish, Eglish; District Council, Armagh; Grid ref. H 807 473.

References: Listed B1 (15/12/1). Taylor and Skinner, 'Roads', 1778, p 226; D 2671, VAL 1B/236, p 75, VAL 2B/2/41, p 3, VAL 12B/10/22A to E, all in PRONI; T G F Paterson, Armachiana, IX, pp 83 - 95, and T G F Paterson Manuscript Collection, No 57, Vol 4, in Armagh County Museum; records in RCB, Dublin; memorials in Drumsallan C of I church and Tullysaran graveyard; Lewis, TD, 1837, I, p 596; PG, II, 1846, p 173; McParland, 'Francis Johnston', 1969, p 62; Hewitt, 'John Luke', 1978, pp 47, 80; Dean, 'Gate lodges', UAHS, 1994, p 39; notes in MBR; information from owner.

Silverbridge House, Crossmaglen

105. An attractive modest country house, in the middle of a pleasant demesne with fine old trees, three miles or so north of Crossmaglen. Very hard to date: the title-deeds go back to a marriage settlement of 1766 when a Miss Magill was betrothed to a younger son of the McGeough (later McGeough Bond) family of Drumsill (demolished) and The Argory (66), so presumably there must then have been some kind of a dwelling here. Walter McGeough "of Drumsill" was born in 1790, admitted a barrister in the King's Inns, Dublin, in 1810, assumed the additional name "Bond" in 1825, and was described as "of Drumsill, Silver Bridge and the Argory". His fourth son, Robert John McGeough JP, who did not adopt the additional name

"Bond", lived on at Silverbridge until his death in 1903.

Although parts of it may well be older, the present house looks to date from the early years of the 19th century. The walls are of rubble, roughcast, with label mouldings over the Georgian-glazed casement windows. Unexpectedly, the front door and narrow hall are at one side of the house; there is a good fan-light, and the door is flanked by fluted wooden Ionic columns, themselves contained in (imported) stone uprights. Above the door is a kind of wooden oriel. The front is gabled, and has canted bay windows on the ground floor. There are extensive out-buildings, including a wing for the agent's office, his living-rooms, and above him the servants.

In 1864, the house was valued at £33. By 1885, the valuation had fallen to £22. On the death of Robert John McGeough in 1903, the house was let for a time, then sold by his sister in Dublin to Andrew Coulter, a Liverpool merchant and one of the founders of the well-known firm of Lovell & Christmas. His son Gordon lived on here; and on his death in 1968 left it to the present owner, who first came to stay at Silverbridge as a boy in 1929. House and owner have to date gallantly withstood the pressures of the Troubles in South Armagh with the aid and support of a pack of dogs and a flock of goats.

Photographs: MBR; Michael O'Connell.
Situation: 3, Drumalt Road, Silverbridge; td, Ummeracam South; Parish, Creggan; District Council, Newry & Mourne; Grid ref. H 960 184.
References: Listed B1 (16/16/8). VAL 12B/12/5A-E, in PRONI; 'King's Inns admission papers', 1982; 'Burke's Irish family records", 1976; documents in owner's possession.

Derrymore House, Bessbrook

106. Evidently built between 1776 and 1787, by Isaac Corry. Writing in 1803, Sir Charles Coote says: "The very fine improvements of Derrymore show the correct and elegant taste of Mr Southerland, who planned them, and superintended their execution ... The young plantations already display a fine appearance of wood; the approaches are extremely well planned, and the cottage, which is as yet the only residence, is without exception, the most elegant summer lodge I have ever seen". From this, Lyn Gallagher infers that John Sutherland, a gardener and landscape architect, designed the house also: but this I rather doubt.

Certainly, a modest house of great charm, U-shaped, single-storey on "a rabbit-warren of a basement", thatched, roughcast and white-washed, with Gothic details such as quatrefoil windows and label mouldings; a fine large airy drawing-room linking the two wings. T G F Paterson called it a "small thatched mansion in the cottage-style then in vogue amongst the minor Irish gentry but of which practically no examples survive". Maurice Craig, whom I follow in classifying it as a "classic Irish house of the middle size", says that it "displays Gothic features such as may be seen at Luggala, Co Wicklow, Lisanoure, Co Antrim and Jenkinstown, Co Kilkenny; here crowned with a most attractive roof of thatch": and adds, unkindly, "There was a good early 19th century entrance-hall, demolished by the present owners". Hugh Dixon considers that "the individual parts retain the modest scale of Ulster vernacular building yet the central conception is rather grand".

Isaac Corry, its builder, inherited the site from his father, a merchant in Newry and MP for that town, but a comparatively landless member of the Corry family of Rockcorry, County Monaghan. Although he was to become Chancellor of the Irish Exchequer, he lacked the means, throughout his life, to support himself in great style. He was, however, literate and cultivated. He studied law at the Middle Temple; "bred to the law, and was actually called to the" Irish "bar in the year 1779 ... Soon disgusted, ... he threw away his bag, which had never been over-charged with briefs, and became an adventurer in the field of politics". The fact is, however, that he was elected MP for Newry in 1776, at the very early age of 21, three years before his call to the bar. In his earlier years he was an active patriot and Irish Volunteer, Captain-Commandant of the First Newry Company. But as time passed, his views became more sympathetic to those of the English government and in the end he earned much obloquy from patriots for accepting various paid offices, and eventually for supporting the Act of Union in alliance with his old schoolmate (at the Armagh Royal School), Lord Castlereagh. His motives can be questioned, but he was a man of real abilities, and all his life in want of funds. It appears that he had six illegitimate children to support; "those scenes of gaiety and dissipation in which part of his juvenile days was spent, and which contributed to give to his manners that polish which we admire, have also impressed on his face some of the indications of the bon vivant. He is still unmarried, having hitherto scorned the trammels of wedlock, and enjoyed the delights of love in the less moral way of a man of fashion". But he had the merit of allowing his offspring to bear his own name, rather than that of their mother, Jane Symms, and doing his utmost to assist them with influential god-parents. His support for the Act of Union led to his own downfall. A major figure in the Irish Parliament, he was unable to make good his standing in the new Parliament of the United Kingdom; he was found a sinecure, but by 1807 was in "a very bad state of health ... his legs greatly swelled

... he goes immediately to Cheltenham. He has advertised his place near Newry to be sold". But he did not succeed in selling Derrymore until 1810; he died at his home in Merrion Square,Dublin, in 1813, aged 58, leaving an estate of only £3,500.

The purchaser was a Lieutenant-Colonel Young, who added the hall to whose removal by the National Trust Maurice Craig took exception. Only five years later, in 1815, Colonel Young advertised the place "to be sold or let ... The house is built in the cottage style, and consists of a spacious drawing room and dinner parlour, with eight bedrooms; the basement storey is equal in accommodation to the first floor ... The Demesne is judiciously planted with about 140,000 trees of various ages. The house is built by the late Right Hon. Isaac Corry, who expended a great sum on it and the grounds. The recent possessor, Colonel Young, besides walling in a large garden, has spared no expense in rendering the house and offices commodious, and the lands productive".

It was advertised again on 6 August 1825, "To be sold or let ... the seat of Sir William Young, Bart., situated one mile from Newry. The house is spacious and fit for the reception of a large genteel family. The offices are numerous and convenient. The Plantations are extensive, and contain Timber valued at £2,500. The Garden is surrounded with a lofty wall covered with the choicest Fruit Trees". It did not prove easy to dispose of, despite its charms, but in 1828 the Youngs sold the place to Edward Smyth of Newry; in 1838 Isaac Smyth is recorded as the occupier; in 1859, John and Henry Smyth advertised the place for sale yet again - "There is a basement storey comprising a complete suite of servants' apartments and a large and well proportioned entrance hall, opening into a greenhouse and vinery - the reception rooms are numerous and very capacious". This time, it was bought by the

Richardsons, the Quaker builders of the model village at Bessbrook; some members of the Bessbrook branch of the family lived in Mount Caulfield House (139), others in a new house, of not very much architectural distinction, but with notable gardens and grounds, which they called 'The Wood House' in the demesne; but apparently "no member of the Richardson family ever lived at Derrymore". It was, presumably, let to tenants from time to time. In 1952, largely thanks to the good offices of Mr T G F Paterson, the house and demesne were acquired by the National Trust from Mr J S W Richardson. Rightly or wrongly, the decision was taken to rid the house of its later accretions and restore it to that state in which Isaac Corry and his bastards had known and loved it. That was a notable furnishing; I well remember standing back while Lord Antrim, Chairman of the Regional Committee of the National Trust, from the top of a ladder, adjusted the busts in their drawing-room recesses, while Lady Antrim told him he was doing it all wrong, and Commander White and I danced attendance down below.

Since then, the house has been attacked more than once, but fortunately has been successfully defended by its faithful custodians.

Photographs: Michael O'Connell (see also colour-plate Xb); W A Green, Ulster Folk Museum WAG 2728.
Situation: Derrymore Road, Bessbrook; td, Derrymore; Parish, Killevy; District Council, Newry and Mourne; Grid ref. J 054 279 .
References: Listed A (16/23/10). 'Public characters', I (1798-9), 3rd ed, 1801; Coote, 'Armagh', 1804, p 361; 'Dublin Evening Post,' 12/1/1815, 'Newry Telegraph', 6/8/1825, in T G F Paterson Manuscript Collection, No 56, Vol 4, in Armagh County Museum; G Scott, OSM, nd, Armagh, I, p 54; T G F Paterson, Guidebook, NT, 1963, passim; Dixon, 'Introduction' UAHS, 1975, pp 43-44; Malcomson, 'Isaac Corry', 1974, passim; Craig, 'Classic Irish houses', 1976, p 152; Bence-Jones, 'Burke's guide', 1978, p 102; Gallagher and Rogers, 'Castle, coast and cottage', NT, 1992, p 44.

Whaley's Buildings, 48 - 58 Castle Street, Armagh

107. The base of the stone urn topping the cornice at the corner of Castle Street and Upper Irish Street, Armagh, bears the inscription 'Whaley's Buildings / Castle Street / 1773'. (This denomination may or may not have been intended to extend to the adjacent houses in Upper Irish Street and Chapel Lane.) The Whaley family owned considerable property around Armagh; they were presumably related in some degree to the well-known Dublin family: Richard Whaley MP, who had in 1765 built No 86, St Stephen's Green in Dublin; and his better-known son Thomas ("Buck") Whaley, gambler, rake and patriot, who travelled to Jerusalem and back for a bet, and, having fled

from his gambling creditors to the Isle of Man, built there (but on Irish soil, specially imported) a large house known as "Whaley's Folly"; and died in 1800 aged 34. There is, however, nothing to indicate that any Whaley ever actually lived in this terrace.

The buildings had deteriorated greatly even before being extensively bomb-damaged, but were taken in hand by the HEARTH Revolving Fund for a very thorough programme of restoration in 1992-3, Dawson Stelfox being the project architect. The scheme also embraced the provision of two replacements for bomb-damaged houses in Upper Irish Street, and three new houses on the site of the former hall in Chapel Lane. It received financial assistance, by grant or loan, from the Northern Ireland Housing Executive, Historic Buildings Branch, the Architectural Heritage Fund, the International Fund for Ireland, and Ulster Garden Villages. The complex was formally declared open by Dame Jennifer Jenkins on 25 June 1992; and in 1995 received a Diploma of Merit under the Europa Nostra awards scheme.

The grandest, and probably the earliest, houses in the group are Nos 48 and 50. Because of the slope of the hillside, rising up to the Church of Ireland cathedral on its summit, these houses appear from the front to be two-storey-on-basement; but from the courtyard at the rear it can be seen that they are really four-storey. The rooms are handsome and well-proportioned,. with lugged doorcases. The ugly 19th-century red-brick hall at the rear of No 48 was demolished, to reveal "an extraordinary bow rising the full height of the back", with elegantly-curving window-sashes, which had to be largely rebuilt because of its structural condition. "A most handsome pair of robust and stylish three-bay, three-storey houses of coursed random conglomerate. Ashlar stone blocked architraves to windows and semi-circular Gibbsian doorways; four steps enclosed by solid ashlar stone parapets; cut-stone eaves parapet" (UAHS listers).

Nos 52 and 54 are two-storey houses, with basements, the first five-bay with coach-arch to the front, the second three-bay. The back yard wall incorporates a somewhat mysterious group of three ashlar arches found under the rubble on the site, purpose unknown; they have been re-erected here to provide a focus for the courtyard. Nos 56 and 58 share five bays to Castle Street and two to Upper Irish Street, two-storey, and constitute a pair of

ingeniously-integrated houses fitted into the two façades of the corner building, the one with the urn at the corner of the eaves cornice. All these are of similar rubble conglomerate with ashlar dressings. Parts only survive of the clever and sophisticated pattern of back-yard walls which ensured that, even on the very corner, each house had its own private back yard. On completion of the restoration scheme, all the fourteen houses comprised in it were sold on, subject to protective covenants.

Photographs: Michael O'Connell.
Situation: 48 - 58, Castle Street, Armagh; td, Corporation; Parish, and District Council, Armagh; Grid ref. H 873 452.
References: Listed B (15/19/4, and 15/19/5); in conservation area .Craig, 'Dublin', 1952, pp 221, 222; 'Buildings of Armagh', UAHS, 1992, p 57; 'Ulster Architect', April/May 1992, p 17; 'Ulster Gazette', 2/7/1992; 'HEARTH review', 1994, pp 33-35.

1 - 33 Barrack Hill, and 6 George's Street, Armagh

108. Dates unknown, but the military barracks at the top of the hill was established in 1773; some or all of these houses may date from the same decade; though the compilers of the (undated) Conservation Area Report in the MBR say "Built about 1820, most likely they were intended as officer's lodgings".

An interesting, long, terrace of random limestone houses, with brick trim, marching like grenadiers up the hillside opposite Gough Barracks. Numbers 1 to 5 are reproductions, three-bay three-storey houses; the gable-end of the corner house in George's Street, with its inset arch, pediment, and keystone, exceptionally well handled on a particularly sensitive site. Numbers 7 to 13 are two-bay three-storey houses; the rest are two-bay two-storey. After years and years of frustrating negotiation, all very well restored, to designs by Ian Donaldson, architect, by

Gosford Housing Association (Armagh) Limited, to provide 25 new dwelling units plus housing manager's office. The terrace had been allowed to fall into grave disrepair; the scheme eventually agreed upon involved the making good of all front walls, using stone and brick taken from the rear, the restoration of all wooden door and window details: the back parts are now modern, but the front is a fine specimen of exemplary restoration work, completed in 1990.

Photograph: Michael O'Connell.
Situation: 1-33, Barrack Hill, Armagh; td, Parkmore; Parish, and District Council, Armagh; Grid ref. H 882 453.
References: Listed B (15/17/40); in conservation area. OS map, 1834; 'Buildings of Armagh', UAHS, 1992, p 48; 'Ulster architect', June 1992; notes in MBR.

Course Lodge, Richhill

109. "Course Lodge was originally the private residence of Mr James Orr; that was 80 years ago" in 1888, when George Bassett wrote. It is said to have been named from the proximity of an 18th-century race-course; it still retains horsey associations, for it has in recent years served as an Equestrian Centre with 24 loose-boxes and a manège - not, as recently advertised, a ménage! Although a date of 1808 seems not implausible for the front part of the house, it seems to incorporate elements from an earlier building - in particular, a shouldered door-case of mid 18th-century character in the front hall. According to the title deeds, it belonged to William Richardson and John Morrison in 1812.

In 1837, it was valued, in category 1A, at £21.14.1; by 1864, at £28. From 1861 until 1903 it was a "Private Institution for Mental and Nervous Invalids, exclusively for the Reception of Ladies", but these only "of the higher class", of whom "the institution is licensed to accommodate fifteen"... "It is situated in a beautiful district of country, sufficiently elevated to ensure good sanitary conditions, with the necessary seclusion to maintain perfect serenity. To these advantages are added well-shaded walks, bowered resting-places, and a cozy tea-house"... "The dietary adopted during preliminary treatment consists for the greater part of vegetables, milk, eggs and poultry. In the advances towards convalescence a building-up process is begun, in which beef, mutton and fish are freely used" ... "Numerous testimonials from medical men, including Dr. G W Hatchell, Commissioner of Lunacy,

bear testimony to the fitness of Course Lodge for the object to which it is devoted, and to the kindly and judicious methods practiced by the proprietors", Messrs James and William Orr, and for supervisional management, the Misses Orr. In 1903, the property was acquired by the grandfather of the present owner as a private residence once again, when the valuation dropped to £18. Extensive refurbishment was carried out in 1978. At the time of writing the property is on the market.

It is a rather curiously-proportioned house, roughcast over rubblestone, with two oddly flat-faced bows flanking the doorcase, and with heavy quoins and long-and-short work around the windows and doors; fanlight over the front door, and Georgian glazing throughout; three-bay and two-storey at the front, with a long extension backward, and further extensions at right angles beyond that. There is a rather endearing boot-scraper built into the curve of the wall to the right of the front door. The house has been at some periods divided up to provide separate homes for two or three families.

Photograph: Michael O'Connell.
Situation: 38, Annareagh Road, Richhill; td, Annareagh; Parish, Richhill; District Council, Armagh; Grid ref. H 946 469.
References: Listed B (15/13/2). VAL/1B/229A, p 2, VAL/12B/10/37A-F, in PRONI; G A Bennett, OSM, 1835, Armagh, I, p 65; Lewis, TD, 1837, II, p 183; PG, II, 1845, p 517; and III, 1846, p 149; Bassett, 'Armagh', 1888, p 202; Pierce and Coey, 'Taken for granted', 1984, p 125; Allison, 'Way we were', 1993, p 29; 'Ulster Gazette', 15/5/1997.

Woodville House, Lurgan

110. A most attractive tall pink-washed house of three storeys on basement, with bosomy projecting bays, each with two tall windows on each floor instead of the expected three; severely damaged by bombs and fire in January 1972, but rebuilt; unfortunately flat roofs were substituted for the old conical ones on top of the bows. Doorcase with radial fanlight and Gibbsian surround; sills, and quoins (back and front), are of cut stone; there is a single window on each floor above the entrance; all the windows retain their original glazing-pattern though, perforce, many of the sashes are replacements. There is a very tall chimney-stack at each gable-end, with window openings irregularly disposed in the gable walls. A much lower but very long two-storey return was added between 1812 and 1815 to accommodate the numerous family of the owner, and there are tremendous ranges of outbuildings, some pink-washed, some stone, some of mellow brick; these contained

a substantial dairy run commercially. The house stands amidst fine trees, hidden away behind a screen of housing development in the former demesne.

The main part of the house was built at an unknown date by a member of the related Waite and Greer families, who had lived here, in this or a previous house, at least since 1757; their wealth derived at least in part from the distillery they operated in North Street. In 1816 John Waite was "of Woodvill", and he is shown as the occupant in Pigot's Directory of 1824; though by 1826 George Greer was "of Woodville". The Valuation books are unusually informative: that of 1836 says that the "dwelling is too high", valuing it and its offices at £42; but the distillery of Messrs Greer and Boyd, also in Dougher townland, was valued at £68, including engine house, corn mill, mash house, still house, feeding shed, pig sheds, copper house, forge, corn kilns Nos 1 and 2, spirit store, and numerous subsidiary sheds and offices. No wonder that, when he made his will in 1848, George Greer could afford to leave legacies totalling £30,000 amongst his younger children, while leaving the place (and distillery) to his eldest son John Waite Greer. Unhappily, the latter squandered the family fortune with nothing to show for it, and left only £3,000. The Griffith Valuation of 1862 calls Woodville "a very good well-finished 3-storey house", and provides a very clear layout sketch of the whole complex. Occupied

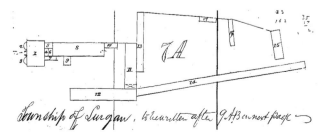

by George Greer BL JP in 1888; still occupied by his family, though after the bomb the top floors were converted to flats.

To my eye, the house would seem to date from the 1780s. Oram says "Late Georgian, three-storey, double-bow front, Byzantine styled porch" - this last I do not understand, unless it was removed by the bomb. Dixon says "some original shuttering and window-finishing/ reveals appear to date from about 1800 with the fan-finish associated with Francis Johnston's office". The ground floor contains a particularly fine dining room, with, answering the window-bow, a curved recess containing a specially-constructed sideboard, dated 1815, made (with other furniture) by the carpenters who had been working on the extension at the rear; and an almost equally fine drawing room. These rooms exchanged functions, and a

number of other changes were made in the rebuilding after the bomb. Dean says that there used to be three gate-lodges, "one lodge pre-1834 to Annesborough as the house was once known ... Everything, including the house, swept away". But the Greers were "of Woodville" certainly as early as 1826; there were in fact four lodges; the house certainly still stands.

Photograph: Michael O'Connell (see also colour-plate IX). Plan: PRONI.
Situation: At the end of Woodville Avenue off Lough Road, Lurgan; td, Dougher; Parish, Shankill; District Council, Craigavon; Grid ref. J 077 597.
References: Listed B1 (14/20/2). Pigot, 'Directory', 1824; title deeds in house; VAL 1B/223A, 1836, pp 55, 119, 127, VAL 2B/2/20A, p 50, T 2321/26, all in PRONI; Bassett, 'Armagh', 1888, p 385; Oram, 'Craigavon', UAHS, 1971, pt II, p 12; Dean, 'Gate lodges', UAHS, 1994, p 44; H Dixon, notes in MBR.

Fairview House, Tannaghmore, Lurgan

111. A pleasing seven-bay two-storey farmhouse, probably of about 1790, roughcast and white-painted, with black quoins, pilastered arch at porch, and trim; good radial fanlight; Georgian glazing-pattern complete. In 1835, "the residence of Mr Thomas Uprichard"; in the 1836 valuation, shown as Thomas Pritchard, and valued at £15.17.0; by 1862, probably because of the addition of the two-bay extension to the right, the value had risen to £30, though the house was then vacant; shown as "the property of George Ruddell", "formerly occupied by a farmer and manufacturer". Acquired, with extensive grounds, by the Craigavon Development Commission as a public amenity, the attractively landscaped gardens and outbuildings opened to the public in June 1969. Thoroughly

refurbished by Craigavon Council, and now occupied by a private tenant, having previously been subjected to much vandalism; its present appearance is respectable, apart from an exceptionally ill-placed satellite dish in the middle of the façade.

Photograph: Michael O'Connell.
Situation: In the middle of Tannaghmore Garden; td, Tannaghmore West; Parish, Seagoe; District Council, Craigavon; Grid ref. J 047 585.
References: Listed B1 (14/3/1). G A Bennett, OSM, 1835; Armagh, I, p 109; VAL 1B/222, VAL 2B/2/19A, p 46, in PRONI; Oram, 'Craigavon', UAHS, 1971, pt III, p 7; Pierce and Coey, 'Taken for granted', 1984, p 8; Jupp, 'Heritage gardens', 1992, A/007.

111, Bessbrook Road, Mountnorris

112. A traditional farm-house, close to the road, with out-buildings rising up the hillside behind. Recently, the main house has been very sensitively restored: the front wall is of white-washed roughcast, pierced by three three-light Georgian-glazed windows above, two below, flanking the asymmetrically-placed sheeted door, all prettily picked out in red; the gable-end slated. Inside, many original features survive.

Mountnorris was in Elizabethan times a place of military significance: Jope has wriiten of the plans in the British Museum of "Forte Mounte Norris on Owen Duffe Fluvius". Bassett says "The place owes its origin to the erection of a fortress by Lord Mountjoy during the rebellion of the Earl of Tyrone 1594-1603. At that time a morass, often containing a considerable amount of water extended north to Poyntzpass, a distance of about 5 miles. It was called Loughgilly. The Lough was removed by drainage. Mountnorris was named to compliment the commander, General Norris. The fortress was one of the strongest in Ulster". Family tradition has it that the out-buildings at the rear of this house, certainly older than the house itself, formed part of the military forage or ammunition stores associated with the fort. The main house was built by brothers James and John Magowan; and since the same family has lived and farmed here for seven generations, their evidence is not to be dismissed lightly as mere hearsay. The somewhat smaller and later so-called "Low House" next door belongs to the same family, and has also been sensitively restored in recent years, the whitewashed walls and blue trim contrasting nicely with the red trim next door.

Photograph: Michael O'Connell.

Situation: 111, Bessbrook Road, Mountnorris; td, Tullyherron; Parish, Loughgilly; District Council, Newry & Mourne; Grid ref. 997 343.

References: Listed (16/20/2). OS map, 1834; Bassett, 'Armagh', 1888, p 200; E M Jope, in UJA, 3rd series, XXIII, 1960, p 123.

Peacefield, Ballynacor, Portadown

113. According to the present owner, "a local farmer tells me that he has always understood, as recounted by his father and grandfather, that there were three brothers, commissioned officers of French origin, by the name of Ruddell, who came to Ireland with William's army in 1690, and that as a reward for services rendered, each of them was granted a property in this area. These were Peacefield in the townland of Ballinacorr, Fairfield in the townland of Aghacommon, and a third in the townland of Turmoyra, today a public golf course".

The long, low farmhouse to the rear bears a slate slab inscribed "D Ruddell 1788"; the fine upstanding three-bay two-storey block to the front was evidently added between 1836 and 1843, when David Ruddell (senior) died aged 85. The two, not quite at right angles, are now unified by white-painted roughcast and Georgian glazing. The newer block has a round-headed doorcase with fan-light and geometrical sidelights, a hipped roof, and two central chimney-stacks. This was a working farm house, so frills such as external quoins and internal window-ledges were omitted. It has been altered from time to time: some of the glazing-bars are replacements. The outbuildings are pleasant if modest: there is a stone outside staircase. The house can be glimpsed from the motorway, but is otherwise well screened by mature trees.

Oram considers this "One of the best examples of a Georgian farmhouse within the Craigavon designated area" and accords it an A. The valuation carried out on 20th May 1836 shows David Ruddell, occupier; category 1B; valuation £6.15.0; measurements, 45 feet long by 20 feet broad by 13 feet 6 inches high. By 1862, the front block had been added; category 1B+; valuation £20; measurements 12 yards long by 7 yards broad by 2¹/₂ storeys; with the comment "very respectable well built house and neatly kept".

The last surviving son of the builder, another David Ruddell, died in 1896, aged 83. For some years thereafter the land was rented out and the farmhouse allowed to fall into disrepair. In the 1920s, it was bought and put into reasonable order by Thomas Dunlop Gibson, DL, who was followed in turn by his sons Thomas and Archie. From this family it was acquired by the Craigavon Development Commission in 1966 to accommodate the building of the M12 motorway. It was finally bought, after the dissolution of the Commission, by the present owner, who had been a sitting tenant since 1967.

The Ruddell family connection was prolonged by the Rev. David Ruddell Wilson, Dean of St Patrick's, Dublin, who was born in the house in 1871 to a mother née Ruddell. He was a hymnographer as well as an authority on his predecessor, Dean Swift, and restored to the hymnal the so-called 'Peacefield Hymn', "A charming arrangement of an old Irish lullaby, named after the composer's family homestead."

Photograph: Michael O'Connell.

Situation: 22, Carbet Road, Portadown; td, Ballinacor; Parish, Seago; District Council, Craigavon; Grid ref. J 029 583.

References: Listed B (14/4/2). Headstones in Seago graveyard; OS map, 1835; VAL 1B/22, p 61, VAL 2B/2/19A, p 35, in PRONI; Oram, 'Craigavon', UAHS, 1971, pt III, p 6; illustrations in Shaffrey, 'Irish countryside buildings', 1985, p 64; information from owners.

Roughan House, Armagh

114. A straightforward three-bay two-storey late Georgian house, overlooking the Paper Mill Bridge over the river Callan. Roughcast, white-painted but not for a long time, Georgian glazing bars still intact; at present in a considerably distressed state, with a hay-field in the guttering, and the shutters shut: the family lives mainly in the back part of the house, but hopes to restore it to good order. "In the 1840s there were about 18 mills. The paper mill on the river Callan is shown on the Ordnance Survey maps of 1834 and 1860 but it was probably working from the late 18th century. The mill succumbed, like most of the others, to competition from cross-channel mills and was no longer marked on the 1904 map. Roughan House was built around 1810 on the proceeds of the paper mill" (H Devlin).

James Robinson of Roughan made his will in 1818 and died on 13 August 1819. In 1875, the house, offices, paper mill, flax mill and land were together valued at £121, occupied by James Girvin under lease from the estate of John Kirk. In 1883, house and offices were vacant, and remained so until 1905 when the house was occupied by Dr John Acheson and separately valued at £12. It has belonged to his family ever since.

Photograph: Michael O'Connell.
Situation: 161, Keady Road, Armagh; td, Lislea; Parish, Derrynoose; District Council, Armagh; Grid ref. H 856 393.
References: Listed B2 (15/14/5). OS map, 1834; VAL 12B/10/17B-D, in PRONI; T G F Paterson Manuscript Collection, No 56, Vol 4, in Armagh County Museum; McCutcheon, 'Industrial archaeology', 1980, pp 253-255, 278; H Devlin, in 'Buildings at risk', UAHS, VI, 1999, p 45.

Forkhill House

115. "At Forkhill, is a very fine seat of R. Jackson Esq" (Post-chaise Companion, 1786). The older part of the house, in the Gothick style, perhaps of the 1780s, still stands; the three-by-four-bay two-storey front part, perhaps of around 1800, is said to have been burned down in the Troubles of the 1920s, and subsequently demolished, though McAleenan and Crilly report that "one owner knocked down the house for the valuable lead and oak beams that were in the roof. He left the attached servants' quarters". The back section has been somewhat perilously patched up.

As it now stands, it is a three-bay and three-storey house with Gothick glazing in the upstairs windows (those on the ground floor having been altered when the old front door and its flanking niches were turned into windows), and a new and rather ramshackle porch added at the right-hand side, on the site of the later main house. The walls are roughcast over a mixture of cut-stone, brick and rubble. There are three splendid cut-stone or brick archways, one at the entrance to the drive, one to the left of the house giving access to the stable-yard, and one (more mysterious) at the rear of the house; these do not harmonise with the surviving house, but are presumably either survivors of the main house, or of the "improvements" made when the estate passed from Jacksons to Alexanders in the 1840s; or else in the 1880s. The yard, whitewashed and traditional, until recently part of an "open farm", is extremely attractive. There are considerable remains of an interesting garden.

Sir Charles Coote, writing in 1803, transcribes at length the eccentric will made by Richard Jackson, who died in 1787 aged 65. In consequence, says Lewis, "it was determined by act of Parliament that a portion of the rents of the estate of Forkhill should be applied to the use of the poor children of his tenants ... one-half the residue was appropriated to the propagation of the Christian religion in the East, and the other half to his sister and her heirs". It is not easy to be sure which references refer to Forkhill House, and which to Forkhill Lodge. In 1837, the place was let to John Foxhall, and valued at £42, reduced however to £28.8.0. "for too large amount by the tables". The extensive Jackson interests in Forkhill were bought out in 1840 by Henry Alexander, brother in law of the last

Jackson, whose son Granville had married the Jackson daughter. According to Bassett in 1888, Captain Granville Alexander, "an extensive property owner here, has lately spent from £6,000 to £7,000 improving his fine residence, Forkhill House. The demesne is open to the public, and is much frequented by excursion and pic-nic parties". The place seems to have been often let, to Major Close in 1886, and to a Dr Maloney in 1906, amongst others; but until his death in 1913 G H L Alexander Esq occupied it intermittently. In 1923 the occupier is shown as George McAleery; in 1924, after the main house had been destroyed (by whatever means), the Valuation book laconically remarks "revision postponed - value moderate". The surviving part was occupied by the De la Salle Brothers during the second World War, and is now in private ownership.

Photographs: Michael O'Connell; in possession of owner.
Situation: 22, Captain's Road, Forkhill; td, Tievecrom; Parish, Forkhill; Distrct Council, Newry & Mourne; Grid ref. J 028 145.
References: Listed B1 (16/15/31). VAL 1B/247, p 53, VAL 12B/15/13A-D, in PRONI; Wilson, 'Post-chaise companion', 1786, p 45; Coote, 'Armagh', 1804, p 362; Lewis, TD, 1837, I, p 633; Bassett, 'Armagh', 1888, p 221; Young, 'Belfast and province of Ulster', 1910, p 254; McAleenan and Crilly, 'In the shadow of Slieve Gullion', 1990, pp 20-25; Dean, 'Gate lodges', UAHS, 1994, p 37; B Jupp, notes in MBR.

Little Castle Dillon, Armagh

116. A congenial L-shaped house standing discreetly set back from the Portadown Road, Armagh, formerly in the countryside on the outskirts of the city but fast being surrounded by villas and bungalows: though it still retains a large garden and fine trees.

Said to have been built by the Molyneux family of Castle Dillon (72) as their dower-house. The listers just say "parts early 19th century", but the staircase and chimney-pieces look older than that to me. In 1862, it was classified 1A, valued at £6.3. 0, and measured 40 feet 6 inches by 20 feet by 11 feet: evidently at that date single-storey. For many years it belonged to a Frenchman who taught at the Royal School; it would be nice to think that this was M. le Parr "of the college" who published a Dictionnaire Idiomatique in Newry in 1827; but it seems more likely to have been M. S Deschamps, who was occupier from 1869 until 1903. In his time the house was valued at a mere £14. The lane at the rear was known as Frenchman's Lane.

In 1903, the house must have been greatly enlarged for Julia E M Molyneux, since the valuation almost doubled to £23. 10. 0. On her death in 1913, it was briefly occupied by a Mr Talbot; and in 1918 it was bought by Mr Thomas E Reid, whose family lived there until 1947; then it became the home of Field Marshall Sir Gerald Templer's mother, from whom the present owners bought it in 1969. His biographer records that after Loughgall Manor House was sold, "They found a pleasant small, but not too

small, house on the edge of the city of Armagh. It was called Little Castle Dillon, which sounded quite grand; but in fact it had been a school until, at the end of the 19th century, it had been extensively rebuilt as a dower house for the Castle Dillon estate ... Old Mrs Templer settled down there quite happily".

Externally, the central block comprises a gabled two-storey house with prominent square chimney-stacks, roughcast with creepers and ramblers; five two-light windows upstairs, and two triple windows downstairs flanking a simple rectangular doorcase; and a mildly Gothick front door. To each gable is attached a three-bay one-and-a-half-storey range, that to the left containing the dining-room. Behind that, in another two-storey range, its gable facing forward, a large drawing-room which looks out sideways up the garden.

At first glance, a rather unimpressive house, which nearly got left out of this book; but on closer acquaintance, it only narrowly misses being classified as a Grand House.

Photograph: Michael O'Connell.
Situation: 55, Portadown Road, Armagh; td, Killuney; Parish, and District Council, Armagh; Grid ref. H 893 463.
References: Listed B (15/17/63); outside conservation area. VAL 1B 224, p 32, VAL 12B/10/25A-E, in PRONI; OS map, 1835; T G F Paterson Manuscript Collection, No 56, Vol 4, in Armagh County Museum; Cloake, 'Templer, tiger of Malaya', 1985, p 170.

3 Dartan Ree, Tynan

117. A two-storey four-bay house of considerable character, roughcast and white-painted, at the top of a high bank and stone wall, with clipped yews, facing the church. The road was cut through between them in the mid 19th century: the curious name should by rights be "Dartan Rí", the highway of the king. Except for a square two-storey bay at the left, there are triple windows throughout, those upstairs lighting an attractive landing. The house is larger than it seems, and has an extensive yard and outbuildings at the rear.

Amongst these is the old dispensary "established 1820, has been of the greatest use and is well supported. Fever very prevalent this year, December 1837. Mr W Huston, surgeon" (OSM). It seems likely that the house antedated the dispensary, so a date around 1810 would be plausible. The house seems to have been used for many years as the residence of the doctor and his family or that of the curate. Dr Robert Huston lived next door from 1876 until 1927.

In 1865 No 3 was occupied by Charles T Huston, and valued at £17.10.0; then, until 1895, by his daughter or widow Catherine Jane. It then lay vacant for a year or so, and was next occupied by the Rev. George Tessier la Nauzé, curate, who lived here from 1897 until 1901, when he died unmarried. His mother lived on in the house until the freehold was bought from the Stronge estate by the father of the present owner. For many years, but no longer, surgery as well as home of the leading local doctor. There is a note in the Valuation book for 1912 "part used as dispensary".

Photograph: Michael O'Connell.
Situation: 3, Dartan Ree, Tynan; td, and Parish, Tynan; District Council, Armagh; Grid ref. H 765 430.
References: Listed B1 (15/11/16). VAL 12B/10/39A to E, in PRONI; E A Williamson, OSM, 1838, Armagh, I, p 131; Leslie, 'Armagh clergy', 1911, p 435; Marshall, 'Tynan Parish', 1932, p 77.

Sovereign's House, The Mall, Armagh

118. This was the first house to be built on the east side of the Mall, in 1810, for Arthur Kelly, contractor for the court house (169) nearby, who was Sovereign (i.e. Mayor) of Armagh almost continuously from 1805 until 1837. "Local tradition states that the materials used were surplus to the court house contract ... John Claudius Beresford, uncle of the primate, made a public comment on the coincidence of Mr Kelly's good fortune after which the court house and Mr Kelly's house were known as 'The Cat and Kitten'" (UAHS listers).

Very important to the streetscape on its corner site, a two-storey-on-basement three-bay building of squared limestone with an extensive railed basement area, and with an excellent, somewhat later, porch at the side with pilasters, regimental keystone, and segmental fanlight. Now the Museum of the Royal Irish Fusiliers, and an interesting and enjoyable little museum. The front, but not the side, punctiliously restored after severe bomb damage, the side wall part slate-hung, part cement-rendered, part roughcast, with two lamentable plastic windows; and unfortunately, the museum's appearance is distinctly unwelcoming as a result of occluded windows - blinds, shutters, and display cases placed right across the window openings in a way highly unsympathetic to the architectural merits of the building, not to mention the strip lighting. It would at least improve matters if the backs of the blinds and shutters were painted black.

Photograph: Michael O'Connell.
Situation: 1, Beresford Row, The Mall East, Armagh; td, Corporation; Parish, and District Council, Armagh; Grid ref. H 877 456.
References: Listed B+ (15/17/5); in conservation area. 'Armagh Guardian', 24/1/1936 and 31/1/1936; 'Buildings of Armagh', UAHS, 1992, p 129.

63 and 65 Canal Street, Newry

119. A very fine pair of stone houses in a very parlous state. The UAHS Buildings at Risk list calls them "This pair of wonderful merchants' dwellings of coursed rubble with fine ashlar dressings around the double door-cases and central coach-arch". Described in the Archaeological Survey of County Down (though in fact they are in County Armagh) as follows: "A pair of houses, each of three storeys, of coarse rough-dressed granite with plain eaves-cornice and slated roofs; the ground-floor entrances are dressed in V-jointed granite, the windows in brick with flat-arched heads. Each house is three windows wide, having separate cart-entrances which are semi-elliptical arched, with plain imposts and key-block. The house entrances are recessed within similar openings and flanked by unfluted Doric columns which support an entablature, with fanlight above. The cart entrance of No 63 is set between the house entrances, to form a uniform feature three bays wide; the cart entrance of No 65 is isolated at the north end of the frontage". However, since then it seems to have been appropriated, and masked, by the printing firm which carried on business next door in No 67.

Fred Hamond's researches, in the course of the re-listing process under way at the time of writing for the Department of the Environment, suggest that in 1836, No 63 was owned by Francis Ogle, and No 65 by Samuel Ledlie. He may well be right, but street numbers change so often that property values are perhaps a more reliable indicator: my own researches had led me to the tentative conclusion that this seemed to be the block occupied by Samuel Reid, and valued at £42, in 1835; and from 1866 until at least 1894 occupied by James F Erskine, under lease from the Kilmorey estate, and valued throughout at £40. Derelict, neglected, empty, but not beyond saving, and well worth the saving: one of the best late-Georgian buildings left in bomb-torn Newry.

Photograph: Michael O'Connell.
Situation: 63 and 65, Canal Street, Newry; td, Lisdrumgullion; Parish, Newry; District Council, Newry & Mourne; Grid ref. J 085 270.
References: Listed B1 (16/26/8A & B). VAL 1B/246A, p 30, C pp 35 and 47, VAL 12B/15/1A - G, all in PRONI; 'Archaeological survey of County Down', 1966, p 427 and pl 202; 'Buildings at risk', UAHS, I, 1993, p 71, II, 1995, p 49, V, 1998, p 54; information kindly supplied by Dawson Stelfox and Harriet Devlin.

Crow Hill, Annaghmore, Tartaraghan

120. A large and dignified house, if slightly gaunt, very prominent on top of its drumlin. Its origins are touchingly recorded in the front pages of a Hoope family household account book: "April 10th 1824 the old house at Crow hill was commenced to be taken down and on May 10 the first stone was laid May the God of all the earth take care of that old house" ... "Brownlees Arctiteck Christy Nugent Clark of Works". The house is crudely depicted on a "Map of Crow Hill Demesne The Sate of Joseph Atkinson Esquire" of 1829 by William Brawley (in PRONI).

A two-storey-on-basement, five-bay, house, white-painted roughcast, with pedimented breakfront, half-oculus in tympanum; good columnar doorcase, with wide segmental-headed fanlight opening and geometrical sidelights, at the head of stone steps and railings; Georgian glazing bars; grey-painted stone quoins; a subsidiary pediment on the three-bay side elevation; hipped roof. A surprisingly elegant and sophisticated house for this date. The rooms are airy, tall, and well-proportioned, all the detailing of high quality: mantelpieces, staircase, fluting, reeding, arched recesses, covings, and ceiling plasterwork. It is a great pity that the original delicate fanlight has gone, and that a really rather crude replacement has been substituted at some unknown date in the past; it would be worth a considerable effort to put matters to rights; for this is a really rewarding house, and in generally very good order.

"The seat of Joseph Atkinson, JP, DL" in 1909; "the mansion a plain substantial house without any architectural features ... the seat of the family since the latter part of the 18th century, when Joseph Atkinson married Sarah, daughter and heiress of Thomas Hoope of Crowhill". Thomas McIlroy, in his Ordnance Survey memoir of 1837, gives the house only a bare mention; but under "Habits and Occupations of the People" remarks that "they are very fond of following on foot the hounds which

are kept by Thomas Atkinson of Crowehill, and which meet 3 days in every week during the season". The valuation in the same year was £42.9.0, rising to £65 in 1862.

There is an agreeable but undated description of the house in a letter, in PRONI, probably mid-19th century, from some member of the Atkinson family: "the stately house ... is built upon a hill and surrounded by noble trees ... The house is of the modern style, its large windows and lofty rooms shows that it is the mansion of a gentleman. Its hall which in times long ago rang with the merriment of the chase, has died away". Bence-Jones says, I think incorrectly, that it was sold 1951/2 to the Ministry of Agriculture;

in fact, I am given to understand that the place was sold by the last of the Atkinsons to the father of the present owner in 1952; and that a number of documents relating to its history remain in the house.

Photographs: MBR; Michael O'Connell; from Young.
Situation: Drumannan Road, Annaghmore; td, Magarity; Parish, Tartaraghan; District Council, Craigavon; Grid ref. H 932 558.
References: Listed B (15/2/47). Account book, 1824, in Armagh County Museum; VAL 1B/233A, p 36, VAL 2B/2/21A, p 70, D 712/79 and D 1382/2, all in PRONI; T McIlroy, OSM, 1837, Armagh, I, p 118; Young, 'Belfast & province of Ulster', 1909, p 293; Bence-Jones, 'Burke's guide', 1978, p 96; H Dixon, notes in MBR.

Mullyloughan (or Glenaul) House, Benburb, Eglish

121. A substantial L-shaped mansion, with extensive stone yards and outbuildings. "Joseph Johnston Esq has commenced the building of a mansion at Mullyloughan and has laid the first stone himself on 25th March" (1825: Belfast News Letter). The datestone of 1830 in the yard no doubt records final completion. Hugh Dixon tentatively attributes it to Francis Johnston or William Murray, no doubt because of the doorcase, but I personally have my doubts, for the internal detailing is a bit disappointing. Perhaps, like Crow Hill (120), the work of 'Brownlees Arctiteck'?

The house is two-storey on basement, the walls clad in a kind of tinted Roman cement, with cutstone quoins and trim. The main front, looking out over the countryside, is of five bays, with central breakfront, pediment, and half-oculus: its centrepiece is a very fine doorcase with pairs of Tuscan engaged columns and sidelights all embraced below a wide and shallow segmental fanlight; at the head of a flight of seven broad stone steps with their original curly railings. The subsidiary front to the left is three-bay, but repeats the breakfront, pediment and half-oculus. The

basement is contained in an ashlar plinth; stout stone chimney-stacks with six pots on each; Georgian glazing-bars complete.

Although this is a comfortable and handsome family home, the detailing of its interior does not live up to the hopes raised by the elegance and sophistication of the doorcase. One wonders if this is one of the instances where a pattern-book doorcase could be bought, like a made-up chimney-piece, off the peg, and glued on as required?

The house was bought from the Johnstons, before 1900, as an investment, by W R Todd, who bought also Elm Park (now derelict) and the Priory at Benburb. He and his family only moved in around 1920; it is now occupied by his grandson, who farms the (attractive) parkland.

Photograph: Michael O'Connell.
Situation: 73, Maydown Road, Benburb, Eglish; td, Mullyloughan; Parish, Eglish; District Council, Armagh; Grid ref. H 823 495.
References: Listed B1 (15/12/12). Datestone, 1830; BNL, 6/5/1825; H Dixon, notes in MBR; memorials in Drumsallan church.

Beech Hill House, Milford

122. According to Samuel Lewis in 1837, "the principal seats" in the parish of Lisnadill are "Beech Hill, the residence of T. Simpson, Esq, and Ballyards, of J Simpson Esq". However, the Valuation book of 1836 shows the name of Mrs Simpson struck out, and that of John Kirk substituted: the house being in category 1A, and valued at £27. 17. 0. A fine, substantial, stone-built L-shaped house, three-bay front, two-storey on basement: one side one bay deep, the other three bays; Georgian glazing-bars complete. The walls are of coursed random squared stone, with channelled quoins. There is a very fine cutstone portico, its two Ionic columns flanked by responding pilasters at the head of four steps, with fanlight. The hipped roof has wide over-sailing eaves and a pair of symmetrically-placed chimney-stacks. The interior has some interesting plasterwork, cheerfully painted. Dean has suggested that the gate-lodge, built for Thomas Simpson Esq about 1825, may have been the work of J B Keane: it seems more than likely that house and gate-lodge were built at the same time, and by the same architect.

Although the townland of Ballyards (see Ballyards Castle, 75) was in the ownership of the Simpson family from the early 18th century onwards, the place seems to have changed hands more often than most. John Kirk was succeeded by Joseph Wilson in 1867; by John Davidson in 1870; by Major Thomas Simpson in 1881; by the Rev. George Robinson in 1883; by John Barcroft in 1898. By 1909, it was vacant and "out of repair", the valuation reduced from £46 to £38. It was to fall still further, to a mere £25 in 1915, when the occupier was Joseph Leemon. After him Acheson, Hamilton-Stubber, Acheson, and Gray, from whom the present owners acquired it in 1988. It is now in excellent order.

Photograph: Michael O'Connell.
Situation: 125, Keady Road, Armagh; td, Ballyards; Parish, Lisnadill; District Council, Armagh; Grid ref. H 861 410.
References: Listed B1 (15/14/2). VAL/ 1B/227, VAL 12B/10/9 A-E, in PRONI; Lewis, TD, 1837, II, p 286; Pierce and Coey, 'Taken for granted', 1984, p 125; Dean, 'Gate lodges', UAHS, 1994, p 34.

Derryallen House, Tandragee

123. A dignified three-bay two-storey-on-basement house, with hipped roof and oversailing eaves, of yellow-painted stucco, with stone quoins; fanlight and side-lights; slim glazing-bars complete. The date 1812 used to be inscribed on a window-pane, unfortunately broken by quarrying nearby, and the owners very reasonably think that is probably the date when the house was built.

This seems to have been the dwelling-house, in category B, measuring 18 feet 6 inches by 27 feet by 26 feet 6 inches high, with "drying-loft, car-house, etc", occupied by Walter Craig in 1836, and valued at £7. 5. 0. By 1863, both the house (now valued at £22) and "corn mill, kiln and warping mill" (together valued at £25) were in the occupation of Frederick Hardy. He sold the house in 1871 to William McCreight, who ultimately bought in the freehold from the Manchester estate in 1910.

It was bought between the first and second World Wars by a Major Hill who returned from the East with two Burmese batmen; these were lodged in the basement, and executed for him some admirable hardwood floors and panelling. He made considerable, and very sympathetic, additions at the rear, but the results included a most peculiar sort of hollow dome above the turn of the staircase. The present owners acquired the place about 1940, and keep it in excellent order.

Probably about 1900, the old mill building and chimney in the valley were demolished and the mellow bricks used to lay broad paths in the charming compartmented garden at the side of the house.

Photograph: Michael O'Connell.

Situation: 51, Markethill Road, Tandragee; td, Derryallen; Parish, Ballymore; District Council, Armagh; Grid ref. J 024 451.

References: Listed B (15/5/21). VAL 1B/214, p 161, VAL 12B/11/5A-E, in PRONI; Bassett, 'Armagh', 1888, p 233; information from owners.

Hockley Lodge, Kilmore

124. An unexpected Regency stucco cottage of the grander kind, perhaps of 1817-20, a bit out of place in the lush countryside of County Armagh, though perhaps with affiliations to the lamented Pavilion in the city. Bence-Jones describes it as "a Regency house of 1 storey over a high basement built ... onto an older two-storey structure." There is little, if anything, left of the latter, which, according to Sleater, was occupied by a Mr Shields in 1806. The entrance front (to the left in the photograph) has a flight of stone steps up to an imposing porch with Tuscan columns. The seven-bay south-facing façade terminates at each end in a pedimented pavilion, the pair linked by a remarkable two-storey cast-iron veranda. The three principal rooms, constituting an enfilade, are on the first floor, and now serve as nursing-home common-rooms, while the bed-rooms are mainly below. Some of the extensive out-buildings have been converted, reasonably sensitively, to provide additional accommodation. Other interesting out-buildings, unfortunately, remain unrescued: in particular, the charming octagonal dairy (now in very poor order), piggeries, and kennels.

The Regency house was built by the Hon. Henry Caulfeild, MP, younger son of the Volunteer Earl of Charlemont. Lt Bailey of the Ordnance Survey, in 1835, says that "Hockley Lodge, the residence of the Honourable H. Caulfield, is a modern house built in the cottage style, standing in a small demesne with a good walled garden and pleasure grounds close to the house"; and Lewis remarks that "Adjoining Castle Dillon is Hockley Lodge, the seat of the Honourable Henry Caulfield, brother of Lord Charlemont, an elegant modern residence, containing some stately apartments and an extensive and valuable library". In 1837, it was valued at £103. 8. 10, in category 1A, with a very detailed description of all its parts; in 1864, it was valued at £110, less than half the valuation placed on Castle Dillon. Caulfeild's widow occupied the house until 1881, when it was let to James H Stronge JP; then to Captain George D Beresford; then, in 1908, to James Wilson. In 1932, it was bought by Thomas H M Leader, who moved north from County Cork; sold in 1983 for a nursing home, and now the property of the Elim Trust Corporation.

Photograph: Michael O'Connell.

Situation: 11, Drumilly Road, Kilmore; td, Drumnasoo; Parish, Loughgall; District Council, Armagh; Grid ref. H 918 487.

References: Listed B+ (15/3/9). VAL 1B/ 230, p 44, VAL 12B/10/25A to E, and D 3653/15/1-10, all in PRONI; Sleater, 'Topography', 1806, p 176; C Bailey, OSM, 1835, Armagh, I, p 80; Lewis, TD, 1837, II, p 514; Bassett, 'Armagh', 1888, p 213; Bence-Jones, 'Burke's guide', 1988, p 298; Dean, 'Gate lodges', UAHS, 1994, p 39.

Dunlarg House, Keady

125. "A two-storey L-shaped farmhouse, three-bay front with projecting canted central bay", with the fan-lighted entrance tucked into the far side of the projection. "A ... formal symmetrical design at so small a scale, and apparently dating from the early 19th century, is very unusual" (Oram).

A handsome little house, the walls clad in white-painted roughcast, glazing-bars complete, with hipped roof; apparently closed up, though perhaps not, and at any rate, in good order. It is a pity that the new red-brick chimney-stacks were not roughcast and lime-washed to match the walls. In 1836 it belonged to James Kidd, and was valued at £10. 8. 1, but with the note "house unoccupied except by caretaker". In 1864, the value had increased to £20: occupied first by Rev Henry Carson, then by Joseph Gibson. In 1888 it was occupied by James Gibson.

Photograph: Michael O'Connell (see also colour-plate XIVa).
Situation: 217, Keady Road, Armagh; td, Dunlarg; Parish, Keady; District Council, Armagh; Grid ref. H 849 357.
References: Listed B2 (15/8/15A). VAL 1B/26A, p 33, VAL 12B/10/17A-D, in PRONI; Bassett, 'Armagh', 1888, p 171; R Oram, notes in MBR.

Ballintaggart House, Portadown

126. "Ballintaggart House, in the townland of that name, is a plain building commanding an extensive view over the surrounding counties. The ground and plantings are laid out with much taste, but it is uninhabited, the owner - Todd Esq being resident in England" (OSM, 1835). The house appears to date from a few years earlier, perhaps around 1825: this is supported by the Regency character of door-panels, reeding, fanlight, and other building details; and decisively confirmed by a newspaper cutting, dated 1 November 1833, "TO BE LET ... BALLIN-TAGART HOUSE AND DEMESNE ... The House is recently built, in a perfect state of Repair, and a Sum of

£3000 and upwards has been expended upon its erection and improvement. The Demesne contains about 105 acres of Land, and either the whole, or such part thereof as may be agreed on, will be let with the House. This place is in a peaceable and quiet Neighbourhood, as much as any part of the Empire. The House commands an extensive and delightful view of the adjacent Country, the most improved part of Ireland; the Demesne is well planted with Timber, and the whole would form a most delightful Family Residence."

It has been suggested that Ballintaggart can be identi-fied with Blamont, "one of the retreats of the celebrated Dean Swift". (The evidence for the association with Swift is scanty; perhaps the Dean lunched with Mr Bolton at the earlier house on or near this site after preaching in Kilmore church; I know of no evidence that he ever actu-ally stayed there). This seems to be based upon an over-enthusiastic interpretation of the writings of I W Ward in 1902, and, more recently, of the late T G F Paterson.

The older house seems to have been built by John Bolton before 1749, when he leased the property to John Black, senior, wine merchant, of Bordeaux, Belfast and Armagh. However, it seems that Bolton had lacked the funds to complete it; "Bolton's Folly - Black Esq" appears, in roughly the right place, in Taylor and Skinner's Road Book of 1778. (In 1795, my great-great-great-grandfather, Charles Brett, wine merchant, of Belfast, married Matilda Black (of Armagh) in Dublin: Mrs McTier wrote cattily

"Chas Britt goes up to be married to a fair Black with fifteen hundred"). "The Blacks seem to have been succeeded at Ballinteggart by the Todds. James Ruddell inherited the place from his uncle, Charles Todd, in 1814. Ruddell was born in 1738, was an indigo-planter, and afterwards made a second fortune as a wine-merchant in London. He died in 1852" (Paterson). The 1837 Valuation book shows Mrs Todd living there: it was classified 1A, and valued at £22, but "having part of the demesne let there are quite too many offices". From Todds it passed to the Bredon family, until in 1898 it was bought by Thomas Troughton, in whose family it remains.

A three-bay, two-storey-on-basement-and-attic house, the walls of cream-washed roughcast, with Georgian glazing-bars complete. The half-hipped roof carries twin chimney-stacks which have been rebuilt using cement bricks, unfortunately unplastered; there is a Victorian or Edwardian porch; there have been considerable alterations at the rear, and the basement windows have been boarded up: but the house still retains much strength of character. Internally, it has an unusual central staircase at the rear which runs from basement to attic in a succession of hair-pin bends. Now headquarters of a stud farm.

Photographs: Michael O'Connell; MBR.
Situation: 78, Drumnasoo Road; td, Ballintaggart; Parish, Kilmore; District Council, Armagh; Grid ref. H 977 520.
References: Listed B1 (15/3/4). D 1401/4,5,9, D 2271, VAL 1B/224A, p 9, all in PRONI; Taylor and Skinner, 'Roads', 1778, p 265; advertisement of 1st November, 1833, and notes, in T G F Paterson Manuscript Collection, No 56, Vol 4, in Armagh County Museum; G A Bennett, OSM, Armagh, 1835, I, p 51; I W Ward, in U J A, 2nd series, VIII, 1902, pp 176-188; Martha McTier, in 'Drennan letters', 1931, p 591; 'St Saviour's Church, Portadown, centenary year book', [1958], passim; notes by H Dixon (incorporating notes by DM Waterman), 1983, in MBR.

Harrybrook House, Clare, Tandragee

127. "Harrybrooke, the residence of Richard James Harden, JP, DL, Ballymena, near the village of Tanderagee, County Armagh, occupies an eminence in well-timbered grounds looking on to a picturesque sheet of ornamental water. It came into the posession of the family about the year 1800, through Robert Harden, grandson of Henry Harden, a Deputy Lieutenant of the county, the first of the family of whom we can trace any record in Ulster. He was born in 1710." (Young). The five-bay two-storey house is somewhat clumsily proportioned, with triple windows and an unimpressive little pediment incorporating, however, the family coat of arms and motto, and appears to Have been built at some time between 1805 and 1835, when it is noticed in the Ordnance Survey memoir. It is of white-painted stucco, with black trim. The columns at the front door appear to be Georgian Ionic, those (and the pilasters) at the porch appear to be Victorian Ionic. Bence-Jones rather curtly describes it as "A 2 storey house of early to mid-19th century aspect. Long low front with Wyatt windows, small central pediment-gable, and pillared porch. Irregular side." - and does not illustrate it. There are substantial outbuildings, listed as being of importance for industrial archaeology. In the 1836 valuation, the house is shown in category 1A, measuring 66 feet 6 inches by 24 feet by 18 feet high, with the fairly modest value of £20.14.0, excluding the annexed "old bleach mill and offices". The present slightly uncomfortable appearance is due to "alterations and additions" carried out in 1890 to the designs of the Belfast architect J J Phillips, when a new drawing room with bay window

and study were added to the left of the façade, with two bedrooms and a "pressing room" above.

Dick Harden, the last member of the family to live in the house, left it to go to England in the early 1970s. He was a great friend of my late father: my very earliest memory is of being dressed up in mustard-coloured velvet, aged around four, in order to attend as a page-boy at his wedding: but of the house as it then was I have, unsurprisingly, no recollection. The place was bought first by a Mr Carroll, who let it out as flats; then bought by the present owner in 1994, and by degrees modernised and restored as a comfortable country house.

Photograph: Michael O'Connell. Elevation drawing: J J Phillips, PRONI.
Situation: 49, Cloghoge Road, Clare, Tandragee; td, Ballyshiel Beg; Parish, Ballymore; District Council, Armagh; Grid ref. J 014 432.
References: Listed B1/IA (15/6/3). VAL 1B/214, p 146, and D1007/108/2, in PRONI; G A Bennett, OSM, 1835, Armagh, I, pp 10,13; Young, 'Belfast and province of Ulster', 1909, p 220; Bence-Jones, 'Burke's guide', 1978, p 149; sale notices, 1989.

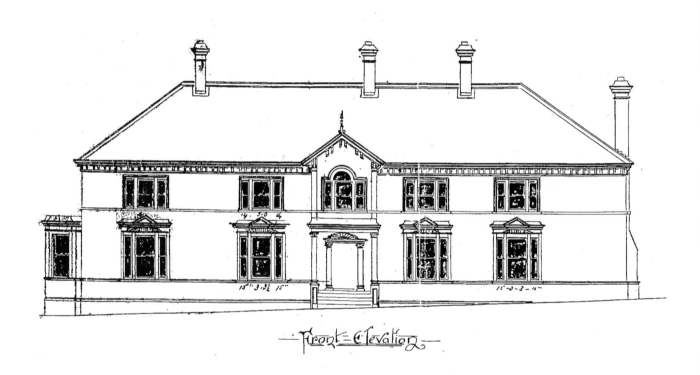

- Front Elevation -

Ennislare House, Milford

128. A plain but attractive three-bay, two-storey, cut-stone house, evidently of around 1830, with canted bay windows on the ground floor and fancy barge-boards at the gables, but otherwise rather austere. The interior contains plasterwork, mantelpieces and detailing of the period. The entrance is unfortunately masked by an inappropriate porch, perhaps Edwardian. The house stands at the head of a winding, thickly-wooded avenue, at the foot of which is a recently-restored gate lodge described by Dean as "A once perky little building for the Barcroft family ... a very pleasing Italianate composition".

In 1866, the house, gate lodge and steward's house, held by Henry Prentice from the Archbishop, were together valued at £40. It was next occupied by Albert and Rebecca Coote; and in 1888 by John Barcroft, JP, a member of a prominent Quaker linen family. He seems to have passed the place before 1908 to one Richard Garland, who bought in the freehold under the Land Purchase Acts; thereafter it was occupied, as owners or tenants, by members of the Mossan, Westhurst and Leemon families. It seems not to have been kept in very good order, for by 1929 the valuation had fallen to £24. It was bought in the early 1920s from the Garlands by the present owner's great-uncle, Robert Leemon.

Photograph: Michael O'Connell.
Situation: 130, Keady Road, Armagh; td, Ennislare; Parish, Lisnadill; District Council, Armagh; Grid ref. H 867 408.
References: Not listed. VAL12B/10/9A-D, in PRONI; Bassett, 'Armagh', 1888, p 143; Dean, 'Gate lodges', UAHS, 1994, p 37.

Kilnaharvey House, Richhill

129. A classic five-bay two-storey farm-house of about 1825, still Georgian-glazed, but pebble-dashed, and with somewhat unusual smooth-plaster ornamental strips around the reeded doorcase and window surrounds. The fanlight is segmental. The front wall is, in part, pleasantly masked in climbers. The place has fine trees and good outbuildings. The house is said to have been built for letting by Lord Gosford. In 1835, Lt Bennett of the Ordnance Survey wrote "on the west side ... there is a plain neat house called Killynaharvagh House". In the Valuation book of 1837 it was likewise named, category

1A, valued at £13.18.0, occupier, Major Atkin, then Mr George Langtree. Subsequently, occupied by Joshua Stevenson Hewitt, grandfather of the present owner, who bought in the freehold under the Land Acts in 1914.

Photograph: Michael O'Connell.
Situation: 21, Aghory Road, Richhill; td, Mullalelish; Parish, Kilmore; District Council, Armagh; Grid ref. H 963 473.
References: Listed B (15/13/27). VAL 1B/229B, p 124, in PRONI; G A Bennett, OSM, 1835, Armagh, I, p 72; land certificate; information from owner.

Bond's Mill, Salter's Grange

130. Just where the Salter's Grange road bends to cross the river Callan on a hump-backed stone bridge, an attractive six-bay two-storey house, of rubble stone with brick dressings, Georgian glazing-bars, rectangular doorcase and fanlight, and three chimney-stacks. The listers think it late 19th-century, since it first appears in its present form on the Ordnance Survey map of 1905-6; but, unless it is a freak, it certainly looks older - my guess would be, no later than the 1830s. The original house was probably three or four bay: just inside the front door, the ceiling is ornamented with a delightful roundel containing shamrocks, in the style popular in the years between Catholic Emancipation in 1829 and the Famine of the 1840s.

Many of the interior doorcases are reeded. Evidently a mill-owner's house; the mill seems to have been in the lower four-bay range of buildings to the right of the house, rather than in the fine ranges of stone outbuildings, with ventilation portholes, at the rear. In 1864, described as "old but substantially built, house too large", valued at £8; in that year John Anderson succeeded Alexander Pringle as tenant from Lord Charlemont. James Anderson bought out the freehold under the Land Acts in 1912, and the place still belongs to his descendants.

Photograph: Michael O'Connell.
Situation: 100, Salter's Grange Road, Salter's Grange; td, Aughnacloy; Parish, Grange; District Council, Armagh; Grid ref. H 879 506.
References: Listed (15/3/18). VAL 2B/2/5, p 14, and VAL 12B/10/23A-E, in PRONI.

Cloveneden (formerly Eden) Lodge, Loughgall

131. Formerly known as Eden Lodge or Villa, evidently built around 1830 by a Mr Marks (see Eden Hall, 132); and for many years a manse. A pleasant, roomy, foursquare house, roughcast and yellow-washed, with good doorcase and fanlight flanked by long windows down to the ground, and a distinctive half-hipped roof. In the 1863 Valuation book, "neat cottage, bad approach", value £24, category 1B, occupied by Henrietta Atkinson; then by Robert Templar; then by W J Griffith. In 1884, the elders of Cloveneden Presbyterian Church (26) bought it as their manse; thenceforward, it was occupied by a succession of ministers until a new (and much less attractive) manse was built in the 1950s, when it was sold to a Mr Carson, from whom the present owner bought it in 1992.

From 1934 to 1946, the minister was the poet W R Rodgers (universally known as "Bertie"). "There was always sun or moonlight on apple blossom, endless talk of life and death in the small big house full of books and the small hours that never grew smaller, and a gay drift of laughing girls flitting innocently carnal through the orchard" (Davin). "The minister's house was one of those Georgian farmhouses, spacious and stately, with its own apple orchard and field. But the minister's stipend being about £250 per year, the field was let out for another £10 a year. To this

was added Marie's small earnings as doctor to the hundred Loughgall families ... The idea of seeing the doctor in the minister's own house must have appealed to the sick and pious" (O'Brien). It was as well that the house was spacious: the poet's daughter Harden was born in 1939, Nini in 1941, and after the bombing of Belfast in the latter year they were joined first by Bertie's father and mother, and then by three "aunts" - in reality, first cousins of Marie's father - whose home in Hillsborough had been requisitioned by the army. This, too, was "the spacious book-scattered manse" where John Hewitt stayed for a

night in August, 1943, on his way to visit John Luke the painter at Knappagh (104), having walked from Portadown station "with some assistance from a ride on a hay-float". Well restored after a period of dereliction, and now in good order, except for the extensive stone outbuildings; although the lavishly oversailing eaves at the gable ends seem, from the Edwardian photograph, to have been clipped back at some time; and note the absence of downspouts.

Nini Rodgers still has a charming, simple, papier-maché model of the house made for her by her mother as a toy.

Photographs: Michael O'Connell; D 2886/A/2/2/7/1 in PRONI.
Location: 74, Cloveneden Road, Loughgall; td, Cloveneden; Parish, Loughgall; District Council, Armagh; Grid ref. H 892 531.
References: Listed B2 (15/1/18). OS map, 1834; VAL 2B/2/28B, p 19, VAL 12B/10/38A-D, in PRONI; O'Brien, 'W. R. Rodgers', 1970, p 26; Davin, 'Closing times', 1975, p 26; Hewitt, 'John Luke', 1978, p 41; information from Nini Rodgers.

Eden Hall, Loughgall

132. Tucked away behind tall trees (including a splendid old ivy-clad monkey-puzzler), a three-bay, two-storey roughcast gentleman farmer's house, the roof topped by four prominent chimney-stacks. There are brown-painted Georgian glazing-bars in all the (unusually wide) front windows, and in the Victorian porch. Well cared-for, in an attractive front garden; the back is that of a working farm.

This is one of four substantial houses in the townland, all built around 1830 by a Mr Marks, of which two have entirely disappeared. The interest of Mr Marks appears to have passed, whether by descent or by purchase, to Thomas Hall. It appears on the Ordnance Survey map of 1834, and seems to be the one, valued at £20 in 1864, occupied (as tenant from Thomas Hall) by James Anderson, then Matthew Burnside, then by the Rev. Richard McDonald, and a succession of the curates assisting the parish priest at Eagralougher nearby, ending with Fr McPeake. Acquired by the present family from a Mr McCartney in 1934.

The house is as attractive inside as outside: an unusual fanlight, concealed by the later porch; a large room upstairs described, by tradition, as "the ballroom"; original bannisters and handrail, lower than usual, to the curving staircase and landing; and shutters with fan-shaped inserts at the corners.

Photograph: Michael O'Connell.
Situation: 67, Cloveneden Road, Loughgall; td, Cloveneden; Parish, Loughgall; District Council, Armagh; Grid ref. H 892 534.
References: Not listed (surely it should be?). OS map, 1834; VAL 12B/10/38A-D, in PRONI.

Millmount, Keady

133. A foursquare mill-owner's house, for many years occupied by one of the Kirk family which owned the Annvale factory, as well as the mills at Darkley; or by one of their mill managers. In appearance, it is a house of around 1840 to 1850. But perhaps an earlier house was up-dated or enlarged. Since William Kirk only came to Keady in 1840, and since this house appears on the Ordnance Survey map of 1834, the Kirks cannot have been its first builders. Indeed, an advertisement in the Armagh Guardian of 14 August, 1827, offers "To be let the Bleach-Green and Farm of Millmount, near Keady, with the Dwelling-house, offices and mills, in thorough repair - applications to James Kidd on the premises".

John Kirk was shown as occupier in the Valuation book of 1864; his name was struck out in 1871, and that of William McKean (presumably the mill manager) substituted. It is very much a linen merchant's house, perched on the hillside overlooking the Keady glen whose river powered the mills, and close to the bleach-greens on which the linen was laid out.

The house is two-storey, three bays to the front and four to the side with a rather large ratio of wall to window; roughcast with smooth rendered quoins and trim; Georgian glazing in the windows, but plate glass in the segmental fanlight. The hipped roof, with its oversailing eaves, is topped by rather unfortunate spindly modern brick chimney-stacks. The attractive garden contains a baby monkey-puzzle tree.

The house was bought by its present owners when the Annvale factory changed hands in 1949.

Photograph: Michael O'Connell.
Situation: Glen Road, Keady; td, Racarbry; Parish, Keady; District Council, Armagh; Grid ref. H 850 343.
References: Listed B1 (15/9/22). OS map, 1834; VAL 12B/10/26A, p 69, in PRONI; T G F Paterson Manuscript Collection, No 56, Vol 4, in Armagh County Museum; Bassett, 'Armagh', 1888, p 168.

"Loughgall House", Loughgall

134. Confusingly so named; in fact, until 1975 the house occupied by the land steward, agent or farm manager for the home farm of Loughgall Manor House, of the Cope family, their successors the Templers, and then by the Ministry of Agriculture. In 1838, when the house was valued at £36.14.7, this was John Hardy; Lt Bailey of the Ordnance Survey remarks in 1835 that Mr Hardy, "agent to the Loughgall estate", has lately built a few comfortable cottages adjoining his own house. He lived on here until 1878, when the valuation had increased to £52; at this point the property appears to have been divided, and the part actually occupied by the steward valued in 1890, and from then on until 1929, at £32. Duncan McKea was the steward in 1890; he had three successors, Thomas Bogue, John Laing and James Moore, between 1903 and 1908; only James Moore stuck the pace, and he was still in residence in 1929. More recently, a Mr Rosborough acted as manager for the Ministry of Agriculture and occupied the house.

A very substantial two-storey-on-basement three-bay house, of stone roughcast, but with dressed stone trim. The railings and the fine doorcase are painted dark green. The latter, at the top of five stone steps, has a segmental fanlight, pretty geometrical sidelights, and a pair of fluted Ionic engaged columns; and could easily point to a late 18th-century date. However, the label mouldings over the windows; the unusual subdivision of the upper panes of the double ground-floor windows flanking the entrance; the oversailing eaves of the hipped roof; and the rather florid detailing of the interior plasterwork, would all point to a considerably later date. Since the house appears on the Ordnance Survey map of 1833, it seems best to date it to around 1830. At the rear right-hand corner, there is a most unusual veranda, with a room over it supported on a single iron pole; and a surprisingly extensive return.

The farm buildings for the estate lie just over the garden hedge, and in the past milk used to be served to the villagers out of one of the basement windows. The Ministry of Agriculture bought Manor House, demesne, and village complete, including this house, from the Templers for a total of £45,000 in 1947; and the present owner acquired the house from the Ministry in 1975.

Photograph: Michael O'Connell.
Situation: 19, Main Street, Loughgall; td, Levalleglish; Parish, Loughgall; District Council, Armagh; Grid ref. H 909 521.
References: Listed B (15/2/1); in conservation area. OS map, 1833; VAL 1B/230, p 54, VAL 2B/2/28C, p 31, and VAL 12B/10/33A,B,C,D,E, in PRONI; C Bailey, OSM, 1835, Armagh, I, 1835, p 79; conservation area booklet, 1993; Reilly, 'Loughgall', 1995, p 33; information from owner.

The Deerpark, Drumbanagher, Poyntzpass

135. Amidst very fine old trees (including a pair of monkey-puzzlers), on a hill-top site, a fine large farmhouse of uncertain date. The three-bay two-storey front and the gable walls are of finely-cut squared bluestone, with surprising granite dressings, recently disclosed when the plaster skim was stripped off. The central bay is recessed; mouth-organ fanlight, original door; Georgian glazing pattern. At first glance, it is reminiscent of work by John Hargrave or William Farrell, dating perhaps somewhere between 1825 and 1840. But the back wall, of rubble bluestone with brick dressings, half-concealed under a skin of plaster, looks earlier, as do many of the interior details such as shutters, the lock on the front door, other door furniture, and the impressive granite flagstones in several rooms. It looks as though a house of, perhaps, the 1780s might have been refronted at a later date.

However, it is not shown on John Greig's map of the Drumbanagher demesne and deerpark of 1818, but does appear on the Ordnance Survey map of 1835. It probably took its present shape soon after the lease of 10 August 1832 from Maxwell Close to "Alexander Kinmonth of the Deer Park, Drumbanagher, Gentleman" which was recited

in his daughter's marriage settlement of 1854. Close was shown in the Valuation books as the owner of the fine category 1A house valued at £17.4.0 inhabited by Alex Kinmonth in 1836. Successive members of the Agnew family lived in the same house at least until 1904. It was for many years occupied by the learned Dr Agnew, a medical man much respected in the district for his erudition; then passed to a Mr Elliott; and was acquired by the present owners about 1993. Now in excellent order.

The outbuildings are very extensive, and of considerable interest: in particular, a four-horse covered horsewalk, originally driving a millstone, uncommonly complete, and looking as if it could quite easily be restored to working order.

Photograph: Michael O'Connell.
Situation: 177, Tandragee Road, Poyntzpass; td, Killybodagh; Parish, formerly Killevy, now Drumbanagher; District Council, Newry & Mourne; Grid ref. J 063 361.
References: Listed B1 (16/21/21); horsewalk, B1/IA (16/21/22). D 1105/3, T 743/18, VAL 1B/217, VAL 12B/15/23A-E, all in PRONI; OS map, 1835.

Woodview House, Mullanasillagh, Armagh

136. On a hillside above the main road linking Armagh and Portadown, a fine three-bay two-storey-and-attic late Georgian farmhouse, roughcast, with vermiculated quoins and keystones to the ground-floor windows, and rather curiously shaped shouldered architraves, very nicely painted in brown and white. All the broad three-light windows have their glazing-bars intact, with a central segmental-headed doorcase (but no fanlight). Built by a member of the Running family about 1830 so as to face downhill onto the newly-opened main road; the older two-storey return may well be 17th-century. The Running family first settled here in 1615. William Running of Woodview was one of John Wesley's converts. In 1837, the house was classified 1A, measuring 48 feet by 23 feet by 20 feet, and valued at £21.5.7, less "deduction for want of

finish £1 0 0; deduction for close neighbours, £1 4 7". (One of William Running's "close neighbours" was John Running). In 1926, George Running, with his ten children, emigrated to New Zealand, and the place was bought by one Robert Albin; from whose son in 1976 it passed to the present owner. The house is surrounded by orchards and fruit gardens, whose produce is sold to passers-by in the season: and very good it is.

Photograph: Michael O'Connell (see also colour-plate XIIa).
Location: 137, Portadown Road, Armagh; td, Mullanasillagh; Parish, Loughgall; District Council, Armagh; Grid ref. H 918 476.
References: Listed B1 (15/3/15). OS map, 1835; VAL 1B/230, p 42, and VAL 12B/10/25A-E, in PRONI; information from owner.

Bann View (or the Pottery), Derrybrughas, Portadown

137. In 1694, the Robb family took a lease of this property from the Brownlows; there being a clay-pit of tolerable quality near the river, they established at some date a kiln in which they produced fairly crude crocks, tiles and bricks. In 1835 Lt Bennett of the Ordnance Survey took note of "Robb's pottery in this townland". The Valuation book of the same year is uncommonly informative: "unfinished new house not ceiled or plastered. Staircase not up. Cost about £150", (William Robb) "made brick himself. Would take £50 more to finish. Has no objection that it be now valued as finished as he intends that it will be so immediately. Intends old house as offices". It was classified 1A; valued at £15.11.3, less a deduction for "bad situation". The 1862 valuation shows Mary Robb as holder of a lease for lives, made in 1830, under Lord Lurgan, the value being increased to £18. Oram calls it "Bann View House", and says "probably built about 1840 with bricks made in a kiln on the site ... It is a striking and attractive house approached by an avenue of fine trees. The outbuildings lead to a riverside quay, and were probably part of the original pottery". The listers just say "Early 19th century ... late Georgian detail."

The house is built of a nice mellow mulberry brick, with window surrounds and relieving arches picked out in a lighter-coloured brick, and with sandstone quoins and window-sills. The wooden-pilastered doorcase has a shallow segmental fanlight. The roof is half-hipped, topped by twin chimney-stacks. The east-facing gable has two single windows above, a pair below; the west-facing gable five, an extra one in the attic; the front wall has three above, two flanking the door below; all Georgian-glazed. The house has a splendid south-facing view over a bend in the river Bann, centred on the tower of Portadown parish church three miles away. It is surrounded by mature trees with rooks' nests; their cawing happily drowns the hum of the not-far-off motorway. There are fine curly Victorian gates, railings and pillars of cast iron at the entrance to the driveway.

The pottery continued to trade until about 1910, when a barge, turning in the river, was lost with its entire load of produce. The property passed to Cecil Robb of Woodside, but he had no children, never lived there, and the house lay empty. It continued to do so for many years. The Waughs bought it in 1944 but did not live there either. The present occupier took it on, as an improving tenant, in 1969. It is now in pretty fair order.

Photograph: Michael O'Connell.
Situation: 51, Derrycarne Road, Derrybrughas, Portadown; td, Derrybrughas; Parish, Drumcree; District Council, Craigavon; Grid ref. H 013 583.
References: Listed B (14/1/16). VAL 1B/226A, p 130, and VAL 2B/2/18, p 77, in PRONI; G A Bennett, OSM, 1835, Armagh, I, p 39; Oram, 'Craigavon', UAHS, 1971, pt III, p 12; information from occupiers.

Derryhale House, Battlehill (or Bottlehill), Portadown

138. A handsome foursquare house of red brick, copiously clad in ivy, cotoneaster and creepers. It is two-storey, three bays wide and deep, with a modest return and a walled yard. The doorcase has a segmental fanlight and Tuscan columns; Georgian glazing-bars complete. No house of this size appears in the Valuation book of 1837-8; yet it might, or might not, be the house shown as "Dobbin's Bridge House" in Derryhale townland on the Ordnance Survey map of 1835. The plausible idea that it might have been a clergy house in connection with St Saviour's church nearby (40) seems not to hold water: the only clergyman to have lived in the house, and then not for long, was Rev. Charles King-Irwin. It looks as if the house, valued at £20 in 1864, was built as an investment for letting, so numerous are the changes of occupier. It seems probable that it was built by one David Waugh; in 1892 it was occupied by John Waugh; in 1893 by Samuel Gilmore; in 1898 by Isabella Corbett; the present owner bought in 1980 from a Mr Preston, who had acquired it subject to the tenancy of a Mrs Waugh.

Photograph: Michael O'Connell.
Situation: 1, Vicarage Road, Derryhale; td, Derryhale; Parish, St Saviour's; District Council, Armagh; Grid ref. H 981 580.
References: Listed B1 (15/4/5). OS map, 1835; VAL 12B/10/37A-D, in PRONI.

Mount Caulfield House, Bessbrook

139. A most puzzling house: Bence-Jones, without citing authorities, says: "A house of two storeys with a dormered attic, a gabled projection at one end of its front and a curvilinear gable at the other; probably a C19 rebuilding of a C18 house. 7 bay front, plus the gabled projection: window surrounds with blocking. Charming wooden porch, in the Chinese taste. In 1814, the residence of William Duff". The listers say "1839, extended 1867. Two-storey mansion with attics. Originally symmetrical with Dutch gables and other generally 17th century detail. The southern bay has been extended with canted bays". A stucco house with diamond patterned slates, and no lack of knops and gablets. The Mount Caulfield bleach green (but not the house) was advertised in the Newry Telegraph on 9 September 1820 "To be set for 6 months, Mount Caulfield Bleach Green lately in the possession of William Duff".

It is suggested, from the name, that this was originally a property of the Caulfeild family which subsequently passed to the Pollocks, or the Nicholsons. Blum says that "A family named Pollock had a modest woollen industry at Bessbrook at the end of the" (18th) "century, and owned the lands of the immediate vicinity. Mr Joseph Nicholson succeeded the Pollocks by purchase, and erected the first power flax spinning mill in Ireland. It was destroyed by fire in 1845 ... A few scattered houses and the residence of Mr J Nicholson, then represented Bessbrook. It was not classed among the villages of the county". This does not seem to be quite right: McCutcheon records that Nicholson was already operating a power mill in Bessbrook in 1806. He must have lived somewhere else before moving into Mount Caulfield House, possibly at some time after 1820.

The Valuation book of 18 March 1836 shows Joseph Nicholson as occupier of what seems to have been then a single-storey dwelling, measuring 61 feet by 32 feet by 10 feet 6 inches high: valued at £19. 9. 11: with the interesting note that he "spins 3 tons of flax in the week", and employs "154 girls and 49 men". However, the mill burned down in 1839 and remained unoccupied until 1845; Joseph Nicholson had retired in 1842 and removed to Crannagael House (140) near Loughgall.

In 1845, the Nicholsons sold to the Richardsons of Lisburn; John Grubb Richardson was the sole owner of the Bessbrook Mill from 1863 until 1878, when it passed to the Bessbrook Spinning Company Limited. By 1862, the house was in the occupation of Sara Richardson, and valued at the large sum of £56. It then passed to James N Richardson, who, at the age of 21, in 1867 married Sophia Malcomson. "The young people's home was Mount Caulfield, a house standing on an eminence above the mills; the grounds had been planted and laid out for him by his father, with conspicuous taste". It was probably at this period that the house was enlarged. His first wife having died, he remarried in 1893. He was the author of two long and facetious poems, 'The Quakri at Lurgan and Grange', and an account of his family (and Friends). He himself died in 1921, and his widow lived on in the house until 1945. His biographer says, in 1925, "It was quite characteristic that, although he installed electric light in the village as early as 1911, his own house, Mount Caulfield, still continues the use of lamps and candles".

The house was requisitioned during the second World War; and thereafter subdivided into three flats. It now has a rather inappropriate modern porch; the Chinese one has gone. According to notes in the MBR, it has, since 1996, been "at serious risk"; with leaking roof, and ceilings on the top floor collapsed; though the exterior still looks all right.

Crannagael House, Loughgall

140. There have been Nicholsons living here, or at Taul-bridge nearby, since 1620, when the Rev. William Nicholson, who had come from Cumbria in 1588, was appointed rector of Derrybrughas. He and his eldest son John both died violent deaths. His grandson William, "the Quaker", was more fortunate, and died in his bed, having rebuilt Taulbridge House after its destruction in 1641. (Once a very handsome listed house, it has in recent years been sadly spoiled, and so does not rate a mention in this book). A two-storey house at Crannagael was begun around 1760, finished around 1763, by James Nicholson, a grandson of William the Quaker. Parts of this are incorporated in the existing house, which seems to have taken on its present form and appearance about 1842.

This was the year when Joseph Nicholson, flax spinner, of Mount Caulfield (139), Bessbrook, retired aged 56, the mill having burned down in 1839; the property at Bessbrook he sold to the Richardsons soon after, in 1845. Although he lived on until 1875, it is likely that the house was enlarged and recast much earlier; in 1837, the house was valued at only £10, increased to £32 by 1862. It is a two-storey, three-bay, house of great character, with sandstone quoins, rendered walls, high parapet, roof topped by four large chimney-stacks, and a square porch: this last, and the frieze and cornice, may be additions made later than 1842. After an outbreak of dry rot, the house has recently received an extensive (and expensive) overhaul.

In 1875, the property passed to Charles James Nicholson, who died in 1891, and who is credited with introducing the Bramley apple to Ireland, and then to his brother Henry Joseph. The latter's elder son Henry Percy, a consulting engineer, died in 1928, and was succeeded by his younger brother George who had emigrated to Canada, but returned to take up residence and lived on here until 1944. The house is now owned and occupied by his grandson.

Photograph: Michael O'Connell.

Situation: Off Ardress Road, Cranagill; td, Cranagill; Parish, Tartaraghan; District Council, Armagh; Grid ref. H 923 563.

References: Listed B1 (15/2/41); Rocque, map, 1763; VAL 1B/233A, p 37, VAL 2B/2/21A, Bk 2, p 1, map of 1826 by J Winterside, T 1864/1-9 and deeds in T 2289/1-20, all in PRONI; Bassett, 'Armagh', 1888, p 184; Pierce and Coey, 'Taken for granted,' 1984, p 124; Nicholson, 'Nicholson', 1996, pp 244-6, 258, 260.

◁

Photograph: W A Green, Ulster Folk Museum WAG 2539.

Situation: 21, 23, 25, Green Road, Bessbrook; td, Clogharevan; Parish, Bessbrook; District Council, Newry & Mourne; Grid ref. J 047 281.

References: Listed B1 (16/22/24); just outside conservation area. VAL 1B/244B, p 96, VAL 12B/15/4A, p 2, and VAL 12B/15/6J, p 42, all in PRONI; advertisement in 'Newry Telegraph', 9/9/1820, in T G F Paterson Manuscript Collection, No 56, Vol 4, in Armagh County Museum; Lewis, TD, 1847, I, p 237; Bassett, Armagh, 1888, pp 236, 239; Smith, 'James N. Richardson', 1925, pp 43, 51; Blum, 'Bessbrook Spinning Company Ltd', [1945], passim; Bence-Jones, 'Burke's guide', 1978, p 212; McCutcheon, 'Industrial archaeology', 1980, p 259; notes in MBR.

Kinnegoe House, Lurgan

141. A late-Georgian five-bay (though the listers erro-neously say three-bay) two-storey farmhouse of the grander kind, now encased in unpainted smooth grey ren-der below and roughcast above, with vermiculated quoins and detailing around the broad doorcase; metal fanlight (a good replacement of 1988), sidelights, and wooden pilasters; Georgian glazing complete. A chimney-stack at each gable. Set back in a nicely-enclosed garden con-tained within rendered walls, with knops on the gate-pil-lars: to the right of the house, a large enclosed yard entered through a tall segmental-headed archway. A good deal of the original woodwork of doors and shutters sur-vives inside, although there have been many alterations over the years. Oram accords it an A; not so the listers, who just say "Early 19th century" - "Mid-Georgian detail-ing", whatever one is meant to understand by that.

The present owner acquired the property in 1980 from the Ormeau Bakery, which had bought it in 1963 from the Greacen family; who had bought it from a family called Doagh; who seem to have bought it from John Green, a coal merchant who conducted his business from the Kinnego cut. In 1888, Bassett writes: "A cut from Lough Neagh, at Kinnego, is nearly 300 yards in length. It was made about the year 1863. In winter it has a depth of from 12 to 15 feet of water, and in summer from 7 to 8 feet.

Lighters, from 60 to 100 tons burden, come in here with coal. Mr William John Green owns 4 vessels of this class. The captains, as a rule, live on board with their families. After paying all expenses, Mr Green divides the net prof-its with them. The lighters are towed from Ellis's Cut, the Lagan Canal connection with Lough Neagh, at a fixed rate of 6s. each, with cargo, and 3s. light. The toll on ves-sels from Belfast to Kinnego, is 9d per ton cargo; nothing on register. Coal and grain are the principal freights".

Oral tradition has it that the house was built by two Campbell brothers who subsequently built and managed the pub at Milltown nearby. The Valuation books confirm that a Robert Campbell was the occupier, under a 31 year lease from Lord Lurgan of 1857, from 1864 until at least 1874; the value was £17, but "house too close to road". It is doubtful whether this is the same house as that occupied in 1836 by William Burns, valued at £17.12.5, from which however "deduct £5 7 5 for unsuitableness".

Photograph: Michael O'Connell.
Situation: 78, Annesborough Road, Lurgan; td, Kinnegoe; Parish, Seagoe; District Council, Craigavon; Grid ref. J 066 612.
References: Listed B1 (14/3/4). VAL 1B/222, p 60, VAL 2B/2/19A, p 16, and VAL 12B/14/3A, p 69, all in PRONI; Bassett, 'Armagh', 1888, pp 343, 371; Oram, 'Craigavon', UAHS, 1971, pt III, p 13.

Kilbodagh, Drumbanagher, Poyntzpass

142. Originally built by the Close family of Drumbanagher (now demolished save for its porte-cochère - 212), whether as dower-house or agent's house is uncertain: the present owner thinks the latter, despite the fact that the listers assign this function to another house, attributed by them to Playfair, within the demesne wall. A curiously hybrid house, apparently of about the 1850s: in the upper storey, five traditionally-proportioned Georgian-glazed windows; below, two very wide three-light Victorian windows with a sort of label moulding over each, flanking an uncommonly large stucco porch with lions' masks. Hipped roof; granite quoins; the walls pebble-dashed, with creepers. It is quite likely that the house is older than it looks, for the back parts and out-buildings incorporate some details which would indicate an 18th-century date. The listers, however, rather surprisingly describe it as "Large two-storey villa with outbuildings. A complete contemporaneous grouping of a dwelling and out-offices relatively unaltered".

The present owners bought in 1994 from two sisters, Rose Russell and Mary Murphy, who had owned the house since 1968; before that, numerous changes of ownership seem to have taken place since the property left the ownership of the Close family, though it was occupied for many years in the 19th century by one Peter Quinn; valued at £45.

Photograph: Michael O'Connell.
Situation: 138, Tandragee Road, Poyntzpass; td, Drumbanagher; Parish, formerly Killevy, now Drumbanagher; District Council, Newry and Mourne; Grid ref. J 061 349.
References: Listed B1 (16/21/18). VAL 12B/15/23 A-E, in PRONI; OS map, 1861.

Glenanne House, Markethill

143. A mid-19th-century mill-master's house (the rear section of the main house possibly much older), with a large mid-Victorian conservatory and extensive outbuildings, walled garden, and very fine mature trees. The front, three-bay with three-light windows at each side of a wide porch: very wide oversailing eaves: Regency glazing-pattern: walls roughcast, with pebbles, painted ochre. The rear section has a slated gable with a Georgian-glazed window without reveals.

Bassett is informative about Glenanne: he illustrates the extensive mill buildings of George Gray & Sons, Linen Manufacturers, Bleachers and Finishers, but not the house. "Shaw's Lake, a body of water forty acres in extent, with a depth of about thirty feet, is the reservoir for power purposes. It impounds the Tate river and other smaller streams, and lets out from day to day sufficient of its store to drive six breast wheels and one Macadam turbine, aggregating 200 horse. Three steam engines, aggregating 180 horse, are used as an auxiliary. With these appliances 316 looms are kept at work weaving, and 34 engines beetle-finishing linen of all grades from coarse to fine. Messrs George Gray & Sons bleach as well as finish the products of their looms, having plenty of spread ground available in the limits of a property embracing 250 acres. From 400 to 500 people are employed in the various departments ... Bleach greens were established in the Glen at an early period, and about the year 1818, the late Mr. William Atkinson settled at Glenanne and erected extensive cotton spinning and weaving mills. In 1841 Mr. George Gray

acquired possession of the mills and premises ... The firm consists of Mr. George Gray, J P , Mr. Joseph H Gray, J P, and Mr. Wm B Gray". Both the first and the last-named are shown as residing in Glenanne House in 1888.

In 1836, the house and offices occupied by William Atkinson, measuring 57 feet 6 inches by 21 feet 6 inches by 22 feet 6 inches were valued at £31.13.0; in the later Valuation books, between 1866 and 1894, the house, offices, weaving factory, beetling mill, and land, were all (contrary to custom) lumped together in a single omnibus valuation of £277. In 1894, the house was valued separately again, at a figure of £55. This is not very helpful, but it seems likely that the front part of the house dates from the Gray family's acquisition of the concern in 1841. The 1847 edition of Samuel Lewis's Topographical Dictionary describes it as "an elegant residence", a term not likely to have been used of the older house. The Grays remained there until the second World War; for the past twenty years the house has been vacant, and is now in poor repair, but not beyond restoration: the grounds and garden could quite easily be made delightful once again.

Photograph: Michael O'Connell.
Situation: Glenanne, Markethill; td, Lisdrumchor Lower; Parish, Loughgilly; District Council, Armagh; Grid ref. H 982 339.
References: Listed B2 (15/7/81). VAL 1B/212, p 54, and VAL 12B/10/34A, in PRONI; Lewis, TD, 1847, II, p 277; Bassett, 'Armagh', 1888, pp 157 -160.

Plate IX *(overleaf)*:   Woodville House, Lurgan (110)
Plate X: a. The Argory, Derrycaw (66); b. Derrymore House, Bessbrook (106)
Plate XI *(opposite)*:   a. Raughlan House, Derryadd (57); b. Ardress, Loughgall (60)

Plate XIV: a. Dunlarg House, Keady (125); b. Mullaghbane Folk Museum, Forkhill (164)
Plate XV *(opposite)*: Tassagh railway viaduct and Callan River, Keady (200)
Plate XVI *(overleaf)*: Moneypenny's Lock, Brackagh, Portadown (60)

Derry Lodge, Lurgan

144. A very pleasant single-storey house, originally of smooth stucco with coupled pilasters at every corner but the stucco now roughcast, with complex graduated-slate roof and uncommonly long windows. Oram describes it as "handsome single-storey dwelling on outskirts of town, apparently c 1820, set back from road behind a pleasant garden court". It appears neither in the Valuation book nor in the Ordnance Survey map or memoir of 1836; the listers date it to 1854, whilst describing it as "late Georgian". This date is derived from the title deeds, from which it appears that Joseph Wilson, in view of his impending marriage, took a 2,000 year building lease in 1852 from Lord Lurgan.

The Valuation book of June 1862 is unusually informative: there is a good layout sketch of the house and its extensive outbuildings, classified 1A, valued at the considerable sum of £60, with the comment: "A very neat cottage, with handsome grounds attached - a very large area of roofing and leadwork".

The house has been tentatively attributed to Thomas Jackson, architect, of Belfast, and the attribution seems by no means implausible - he was in mid-career at this date and had recently designed the Friends' Meeting House in Lisburn. Moreover, the interior detailing is of the highest quality. The rooms, the doors, the windows and the shutters are all splendidly tall; the central roof-lit corridor has massive full entablatures around each side-doorcase, and jewel-like coloured glass in the internal doorways at either end. Drawing-room, dining-room and breakfast-room are handsomely proportioned and richly detailed. If only the all-pervading single-storey bungalow type had evolved along these lines!

In 1888, this was the residence, presumably rented, of Mr McGeagh, managing director of the Lurgan Weaving Company. After the death in 1911 of Joseph Wilson's widow, it was bought by William Waite, who died in 1952; it was for some years used as a school, but was lying empty and neglected when the present owner and her husband acquired it from a Mr Little in 1953. At the date of writing, though modern housing has encroached on the former grounds, it remains quite private and most attractive.

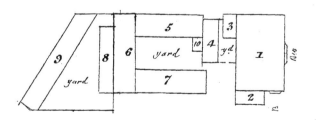

Photograph: Michael O'Connell. Plan: PRONI.

Situation: 29, Lough Road, Lurgan; td, Derry; Parish, Shankill; District Council, Craigavon; Grid ref. J 076 592.

References: Listed B1 (14/20/3). VAL 2B/2/20A, p 52, in PRONI; Bassett, 'Armagh', 1888, p 363; Oram, 'Craigavon', UAHS, 1971, pt II, p 10; H Dixon, notes, and photographs in MBR; and information from the owner.

Lurgana, Whitecross, Ballymoyer

145. In the late seventeenth century, the Synnott family leased from the see of Armagh eight townlands in and around Ballymoyer: and proceeded to prosper. The principal branch of the family lived in Ballymoyer House, now demolished; a subsidiary branch occupied the, originally very modest, house at Lurgana, supported by the nearby scutching-mill. Part of the oldest, single-storey house is still standing, and may be seen at the extreme right of the photograph; to it was added a four-bay two-storey Georgian-glazed extension, which must have been the Ballymoyer Cottage referred to by Lewis in 1837 as occupied by W Reid, likewise still standing; for the Valuation book of 1838 shows William Reid Esqre as occupier of a dwelling in Lurgana townland, in category 1B, measuring 71 feet by 21 feet by 12 feet, which, with numerous outbuildings, was valued at £31.14.11, plus £20 for corn mill and kilns. To these Parker George Synnott added a large and somewhat ungainly stucco Victorian mansion between 1862 and 1865, when it was valued at £55. The funds may have come from his well-off English wife, or may have come from the linen boom following the American Civil War. After his death, his widow auctioned the property in 1901, and it was bought by John King, grandfather of the present owner, who bought the place out under the Land Acts; but it had evidently somewhat deteriorated at this time, for the valuation fell from £55 to £40.

The house is in an Italianate style and is faced in stucco, the ground floor with channelled rustication and vermiculated quoins, the upper floor with plain quoins and block modillions at the eaves; the original plate-glass in the original sashes being today somewhat incongruously subdivided into compartments by plastic strips. The interior of the Victorian section has very tall rooms; the big windows make them light and airy. There are excellent and extensive stone outbuildings. Surrounded by mature trees and garden, this is a considerably more interesting and attractive house than appears from a glimpse of it through the trees from the road. It is a pity that the architect is not known: it does not look like the work of any of the architects employed by the Synnotts at Ballymoyer church (41).

Photograph: Michael O'Connell.
Situation: 4, Lurgana Road, Whitecross; td, Lurgana; Parish, Ballymoyer; District Council, Newry & Mourne; Grid ref. H 979 311.
References: Not listed . VAL 1B/239, and VAL 12B/15/2A-C, in PRONI; Lewis, TD, 1837, I, p 154; information from owner.

Drumalane House, Newry

146. Built at the same time as Drumalane Mill (189) next door, or possibly a little earlier: in 1866, valued at £50 and occupied by Hill Irvine, owner and builder of the mill, which he sold in 1876. Thereafter, it was occupied by a succession of mill managers, rather than mill-owners: Thomas Hoey was the first of many. This is, for County Armagh, a fairly rare example of a late 19th-century mill-owner's house; most were built earlier, and rather less grand; it is a product of the boom in linen resulting from the shortage of cotton following the American Civil War.

George Bassett, in 1886, writes: "Mr. Hoey's place, Dromalane House, has a park of 6¹/₄ acres, in which some of the loveliest effects of landscape gardening are visible. There are grottoes, open rock-work, a cascade, and two trout ponds fed by a sparkling brook, and shaded by large trees which have captivated the hearts of a colony of rooks. Dromalane House is near the Dromalane Spinning Mill, and was the residence of its original owner, the late Mr. Hill Irvine. It occupies the site of the birthplace of John Mitchel, and he died in it. Mr. Irvine was married to one of Mr. Mitchel's sisters: John Martin, also a brother-in-law of Mr. Mitchel's, caught cold while attending the funeral of the latter, and died in the same house". Gordon Wheeler comments: "The Young Irelanders, John Mitchel and John Martin, may well have died in the house in 1875, but Mitchel was actually born in Dungiven, County Londonderry (pace Bassett!)".

Very similar in style to the mill, a kind of Victorian delayed-Georgian, but the granite stonework is even more showy than that of the mill: in particular, the uprights dividing the canted bay windows are made from enormous monoliths.

The house is two-storey on (concealed) basement; five-bay; of squared granite; with hipped roof, carried on stone modillions; Georgian glazing-bars upstairs, a canted bay window, Victorian-glazed, on each side of the front door. Four fine big granite steps lead up to a doorcase with rectangular fanlight, sidelights, and carved stone console brackets. There is rather florid plasterwork in the hallway. A fine house, but unfortunately its external appearance today has been spoiled by the disgraceful amputation of its chimney-stacks, and internally, it has been sadly institutionalised. It now forms the centre-piece of a complex of healthcare buildings; the grounds have still good trees, and (perhaps) rooks, but the trout and the cascades are gone.

Photograph: Michael O'Connell.
Situation: Off Drumalane Road, Newry; td, Drumalane; Parish, Killevy; District Council, Newry & Mourne; Grid ref. J 084 255.
References: Listed B2 (16/29/7). VAL 12B/15/1 A-F, in PRONI; Bassett, 'Down', 1886, p 103.

20 - 23 Church Place, Lurgan

147. A tall terrace of four dignified very-late-Georgian-style three-bay three-storey houses (now offices), of painted stucco, with rustication on the ground floor, window aedicules at first floor, and dripstones above that; five yellow-brick chimney-stacks, with several protuberant television aerials, and more vegetation than is common; and most curious yellow-brick round-headed doorcases with pseudo-Norman dog-tooth detailing. Inside the porches, very attractive inner doorways with handsome coloured glass sidelights and fanlight. The houses are numbered from right to left; the two right-hand houses are later, and narrower, than the left-hand pair; also their façades are laid out at a slight angle, which leads to a peculiar convergence of the back yards and long returns. As can be seen from the photograph, No 23 turns the corner rather eccentrically.

Built in 1885 by Arthur Donnelly (plaque on front wall), a prosperous nationalist spirit grocer who himself lived in No 23; where Parnell once stayed the night, and played a game of chess with his host in the L-shaped drawing-room. "The late Arthur (Attie) Donnelly set up business in a small shop in Church Place (where Cafolla's is now) in 1839 and by dint of hard work and thrift eventually amassed a fortune. Seemingly he was assisted by a very thrifty wife, née Margaret Murray of Kinnego. He died a very rich man and one of the most extensive property owners in the town. A lot of his money came from a spirit-grocery business at 50 Church Place. He is said to have met more than a fair share of opposition and hostility in his day, but to have met it head on and frequently outwitted it!" His memorial in the Dougher graveyard records his death on 11 November, 1886, "an ardent supporter of the national cause / who fearlessly withstood / the local bigots of his time". Two years later, the Bassett's directory of 1888 shows Sarah J Donnelly of 50 Church Place as "Family Grocer, Provision Curer, Tea, Wine and Spirit Merchant, Tobacconist, etc.; Mild-Cured Hams and Bacon a Speciality"; and A Donnelly & Co., Church Place, as grocers and dealers in hardware.

In more recent times, the mantle of Attie Donnelly and his son Andrew has devolved upon the well-known Deeny family; of whom it has been remarked that, if Lurgan is (by metropolitan standards) a one-horse town, at any rate it is the Deenys who own the horse. Tallon enthusiastically describes this group as "one of the best and most impressive examples of Old Lurgan architecture still standing in the town". Certainly it closes with dignity one side of the open space surrounding the parish church.

Photograph: Michael O'Connell.
Situation: 20-23, Church Place, Lurgan; td, and Parish, Shankill; District Council, Craigavon; Grid ref. J 079 584.
References: 20, listed B, 21-23, listed B1 (14/21/4). Bassett, 'Armagh', 1888, pp 332, 375; Tallon, 'Memories of old Lurgan', 1987, p 36; Tallon, 'Fireside gleanings', 1988, p 59; information from owner.

CHAPTER SIX

SMALL HOUSES
AND COTTAGES

County Armagh is not as rich as it used to be in small houses, or cottages, of charm or architectural merit. For the most part, they have by now been knocked down - or fallen down - to make way for unsympathetic bungalows. In the past, the prosperity of large parts of the county rested, first, on linen; then, on apples. Today it seems to rest largely on mushrooms and smuggling: which of these has been responsible for the larger proportion of the bungalows I cannot say. I suspect that police overtime payments, too, have contributed their proportion. However that may be, the appearance of the modest, vernacular, houses and cottages of the county has deteriorated very sharply over the years since 1945, assisted also by the philistine farm improvement programmes of the old Ministry of Agriculture.

In 1998, my companion volume, Buildings of County Antrim, was sharply criticised, in an otherwise gratifyingly complimentary review, by Dr Philip Robinson of the Ulster Folk Museum: "almost entirely missing are the true vernacular cottages, farm houses and mills which express so much of the personality of County Antrim's built heritage".[1] I think this comment a little unfair, since I have throughout sought to use aesthetic merit as the highest of my criteria for selection. But I tried hard to respond, and to improve my performance, in County Armagh. Alas, I have not been very successful: this chapter on small houses and cottages is even shorter than that in my County Antrim book.

The truth is that there are now only three categories of thatched buildings remaining in the county. The first is the smartened-up, newly white-washed, rethatched (almost always with English reeds), and almost always enlarged in the interests of habitability, showcase, surrounded by agricultural antiques, pumps, lamp standards, and such like memorabilia. It is often charming, in a cloyingly chocolate-box manner, but it is too seldom genuinely authentic. The second, sprinkled all over the countryside, is unfortunately the decrepit, collapsing, wreck, with thatch falling in and mud walls fast disintegrating, used (if at all) only for storage, and quite devoid of visual attractions. The third is the flagrantly bogus, sometimes even enjoyably vulgar, contemporary reproduction. This last gives employment to thatchers, and pleasure to its owners (if not always to passers-by): but does not, in the absence of some endearing eccentricity, qualify for inclusion in this chapter.

Reference: 1. P Robinson, in 'Carrickfergus and district historical journal', IX, 1998, p 55.

Interior of weaver's cottage. Photograph: W A Green, Ulster Folk Museum WAG 282

Charlemont Cottage

148. This delightful small stone house is clearly shown, and in its present form, as "Store Keeper's House" in a "Plan of the Ordnance Establishment drawn to accompany the Inspectional Return for March 1811". (Next door, now in different ownership, there survive, in poorish order, parts of the Artillery Driver Barracks, Ordnance Stables, Forage Shed and Yards. The Hospital was to the rear; the Gun Carriage yard across the road). The listers suggest 1810. There is a datestone for 1806 above the doorway, so unless the front section was a later addition, this cannot be the "stone house for Barrack Master" for which, with an infirmary, an estimate of £93.6.6 in 1760 was quoted by J J Marshall.

In 1858, the government sold Charlemont Fort (15) in its entirety to Lord Charlemont, presumably including the Store Keeper's House which seems then to have been the residence of a Mrs Chambers, the housekeeper who looked after the officers. For many years the home of a veterinary surgeon, Mr Hobson, whose surgery was in the basement; then of a Mr and Mrs Elliott, from whom the present owner bought it in 1996.

The front section is of well-cut ashlar, one storey on basement, with an advancing pedimented central bay embracing doorcase and radial fanlight, and two tall Georgian-glazed windows on each side; the hipped roof topped by a well-detailed set of chimney-stacks. There is a wide central hall, with an unusual vaulted ceiling, with drawing room and dining room to left and right: behind these, a spine corridor, with a series of excellent rooms opening off it. The rear section, wider by two bays on each side, is now rendered. Dixon suggests that this early example of bungalow living may be an import from the military administration of India; adding "Among the most mature examples of the single-storey, spread-plan, late Georgian houses in the county - Derrymore" (106) "is more self-conscious and picturesque, but less compact".

Photograph: Michael O'Connell.
Situation: 16, Portadown Road, Charlemont; td, Charlemont; Parish, Loughgall; District Council, Armagh; Grid ref. H 855 557.
References: Listed B1 (15/1/23). Datestone; T 755, Vol 3, p 83, 1796, T 3407/3/11, 1811, T 3407/3/14, 1815, all in PRONI; Marshall, 'History of Charlemont', 1921, pp 53, 54; notes by H Dixon in MBR; information from owner.

Summer Hill, Navan, Armagh

149. Set on top of a drumlin, close to Navan Fort, and surrounded by fine trees, a little house of pomp and circumstance disproportionate to its size. Although really just a five-bay single-storey cottage, it has a tremendous doorcase, with three wide stone steps, elaborate radial fanlight and sidelights, inner and outer columns, and pediment. This splendid doorcase is recessed within a finely detailed segmental archway flanked by engaged Tuscan columns. The crude and cumbersome pediment and its out of scale supporting columns may be a comparatively recent addition. The house is roughcast; the pediment rendered; the entablature of the pediment cuts across the top of the doorcase arch; the finial is quite unsuitable; all very odd, but not unendearing.

There are two tall windows, recessed, on each side of the central entrance; no less than twenty panes in each sash, including marginal glazing, in the manner fashionable in the mid-1840s. Formerly these lit two fine large

rooms, drawing room and dining room respectively, and the rest of the accommodation was contained in a two-storey return; but this has quite recently been demolished, a lean-to single-storey return substituted, and the room to the left of the hall subdivided.

The listers describe it as "early 19th century single storey farmhouse", and cite its appearance on the Ordnance Survey map of 1833; but I suspect that the house only acquired its present appearance at a later date than that. A part of the Charlemont estate, for many years occupied by a family named Menary, from whom it descended to the Leemon family of Rosebrook, from whom the present owner bought it.

Photograph: Michael O'Connell.
Situation: Killylea Road, Armagh; td, Navan; Parish, and District Council, Armagh; Grid ref. H 834 446.
References: Listed B1 (15/14/18). OS map, 1833.

Linen Hill House, Milford

150. A formal hill-top late-Regency five-bay house, shown on the Ordnance Survey map of 1837. In appearance it is, from the front, one-storey, save for a single central pointed dormer; but in fact there are pairs of upstairs windows in each gable. There are granite quoins both at the corners of the house, and at the corners of the central projection. The walls are of stucco, painted an agreeable light green, with linked label mouldings above the ground floor windows, and a single one over the doorcase. There are Georgian glazing bars in all but the narrow central window above the front door, and wavy ornamental bargeboards. Regrettably, the four original tall stone chimneystacks have been removed. The house is set amongst good trees some way back from the road.

Like Ballyards Castle (75) and Beech Hill House (122), both in the same townland, this was originally a property of the Simpson family: "Margaret Simpson wife of Thomas Simpson of Linen Hill departed this life" in 1796; "John Simpson MD of Linen Hill" died in 1821; but I think the present house here must be a little later, conceivably as early as 1822, the date incised in the gateposts

of the next-door farm. The name is said to derive from the fact that linen was laid out to bleach on the fields here on the hill-top, and certainly, the Simpsons derived their substantial fortune from linen; though the family seems now to have died out without trace in this neighbourhood.

This appears to be the single-storey house occupied by Thomas Davison (so spelled) in 1836, held with 65 acres, and valued at £11.14.3. Bassett shows J W Davidson as the occupier in 1888: and indeed, successive members of the Davidson family - John, James Andrew, and James - occupied the house at least from 1864 until 1929. It was then bought from the Davidsons by Robert Herron, from whose son it was acquired by the present owners in 1972.

Photograph: Michael O'Connell.
Situation: 58, Ballyards Road, Milford; td, Ballyards; Parish, Lisnadill; District Council, Armagh; Grid ref. H 861 423.
References: Not listed (why not?). OS map, 1837; VAL 1B/27, p 45, and VAL 12B/10/9A-E, in PRONI; Bassett, 'Armagh', 1888, p 144; information from owners.

Annaclare House, Armagh

151. Although this has the air of a Regency cottage orné, only a very much smaller farm-house appears on the Ordnance Survey map of 1837; so this most attractive little house seems to date from about 1840. Tradition has it that it was built by a retired colonel in the Indian army (of whom there seem to have been many in the county). The house first appears in the Valuation book of 1866, valued at £35, and occupied by George Scott, whose family continued to live there, carrying on a substantial fruit farm, until at least 1911. Thereafter, the property passed to a Mr Bradford, from whom it was acquired by the present owners in 1955.

Set amidst exceptionally fine trees, lawns and outbuildings, it is a one-storey-and-attic house whose geometry is unconventional. Two canted bays flank the central doorcase, with pretty ironwork in the rectangular fanlight and sidelights. The roof sweeps down to embrace the bays and the gap between them, which is bridged by a segmental-headed arch supported on two slim octagonal columns, so providing a sort of recessed portico. The house is very well painted, with glazing bars complete, even in the attic windows in the gables. There is a modest and seemly single storey extension to one side. The outbuildings in the two yards appear to be original, and are in immaculate order.

Photograph: Michael O'Connell.
Situation: 76, Portadown Road, Armagh; td, Annaclare; Parish, Grange; District Council, Armagh; Grid ref. H 899 470.
References: Listed B2 (only?) (15/3/22). VAL12B/10/23A-E, in PRONI.

Sharp's House, Gosford Demesne, Markethill

152. A pleasing little house, white-painted roughcast over rubblestone, within the boundaries of the Gosford Castle demesne. Part single-storey, part two-storey, with a handsome two-storey bay or bow very similar in its detailing to that found in Whaley's Buildings, Armagh (107), which can be dated with confidence to the 1770s. Although estate maps going back to 1754 show a variety of houses on or near this site, it is not possible to say which is which. The single-storey part seems to be earlier than the rest.

It seems that a Mr Sharp lived in the house for many years, and so gave it its name. The house had been unoccupied, and deteriorating, for a considerable period when the HEARTH Revolving Fund negotiated a long lease from the Department of Agriculture. Extensive restoration was then undertaken, and the leasehold interest sold on to the present owner in 1996 subject to covenants for the future conservation of the building. Its surroundings have been admirably landscaped; and since it sits snugly inside the Gosford Forest Park, it constitutes an uncommonly attractive home on an uncommonly attractive site.

Photograph: Michael O'Connell.

Situation: Inside the walls of Gosford Forest Park, Markethill; td, Gosford Demesne; Parish, Mullaghbrack; District Council, Armagh; Grid ref. H 963 405.

References: Listed B (15/7/28). Sale particulars, HEARTH Revolving Fund, 1996.

147 Crosskeys Road, Keady

153. A very modest, but delightful, small low farmhouse, dating from before 1834, the central section two-storey, a single-storey extension to each side (but of differing heights), these all slated; the contiguous out-houses roofed with red-painted corrugated iron. The two-storey mid-section has half-doors, in a gabled porch with pretty barge-boards, and unevenly-spaced Georgian-glazed windows. The upper sashes in each window are two panes deep, the lower, only one pane deep. The walls are harled and lime-washed, with green trim and black splashband.

Very well painted and kept. The home of the O'Hagan family, who may well have built it, for very many years; and who restored it, extremely well, in 1997.

Photograph: Michael O'Connell.

Situation: 147, Crosskeys Road, Keady (in fact just off that road); td, Knockraven; Parish, Derrynoose; District Council, Armagh; Grid ref. H 827 357.

References: Listed B1/V (15/10/21); OS map, 1834; notes in MBR.

Manor House Lodges and Gates, Loughgall

154. An astounding extravagance of frilly ironwork and stonework, framing the access vista to the rather dull Manor House, the latter apparently designed by Frederick A Butler of Dublin for Mrs Cope about 1875. The gates themselves are, helpfully, signed and dated "R. Marshall Caledon 1842"; on this evidence, Dean considers all to have been commissioned before the death of Arthur Cope, without issue, at the age of thirty in 1844 . The Ordnance Survey map of 1834 shows a beginning made on a new avenue, but no house and no lodges; nor do they appear in the Valuation book of 1837; but in the Valuation book of 1863 there is a note "very ornamental gate entrance cost about £3,000", the lodges valued at £15.

For a very thorough description, the reader is referred

to Dean: rather than paraphrase his words, the following quotations will convey the flavour of this exotic outcrop: "a most striking Neo-Jacobean extravaganza ... Unfortunately the fine overthrow was toppled by a lorry in the 1960s and has not been replaced despite promises which have proved empty. The identical porters' lodges facing each other across the avenue are lavishly embellished, disguising simple two roomed single storey L plans ... The apex finials were originally a variety of wild animals, a lion and a bear identifiable, but all now removed ..." Despite the high gradings accorded by the listers, the Ministry (now Department) of Agriculture has not proved a very sympathetic custodian.

Finally, to quote Dean again, "The late T G F Paterson speculated that all may have been the work of William Murray with considerable assistance from Italian craftsmen who were already employed in building nearby Roxborough House, Moy, Co Tyrone, for Lord Charlemont. No corroborating evidence has come to light". This attribution does not seem convincing to me.

Photographs: Michael O'Connell (see also colour plate XIIIa); before the lorry struck, postcard in SELB Local Studies Library, Armagh.
Situation: Main Street, Loughgal; td, Levalleglish; Parish, Loughgall; District Council, Armagh; Grid ref. H 909 521.
References: Gates and screen listed A (15/2/2); gate lodges listed B1 (15/2/3); in conservation area. D 3727/E/40/7, 10, 11, 13, 20, and VAL 2B/2/28C, p 28, in PRONI; conservation area booklet, 1993; Dean, 'Gate lodges', UAHS, 1994, pp 39, 40; Reilly, 'Loughgall', 1995, p 31.

Summer Island Gate Lodges, Loughgall

155. "The prettiest pair of surviving Georgian Gothick porters' lodges in the Province" says Dean, and he is absolutely right. I cannot improve upon his description either, so (by his leave) quote it in full: "Situated to the back of a segmental lay-by approach, they rather contrarily have bow-fronted elevations. Each three bay, basically single storey, the two ground floor rooms giving ladder access to loft bedspace over. Gabled with slate roofs perhaps originally thatched. In whitewashed harled walls, the windows have high cills, their pointed heads forming "lancettes" with typical Y tracery. The sheeted doors arched to match. Brick dentil course to eaves. Some fifty yards distant a detached privy. The cottages flank four square Classical pillars contrastingly refined in ashlar stone, V-jointed with moulded cornices and a shallow concave capping. Built by the Clarke family as an introduction to their elegant Classical villa. Though now empty they are well maintained as popular cotoneaster-clad follies".

The listers suggest 1810 for the lodges; Dean suggests circa 1820; however, both lodges are clearly shown on William Kigan's map of June, 1794 - see the entry for Summer Island (63). I am told that a very experienced builder reported that, although the exteriors appear identical, the internal timber-work of the roofs differs markedly: certainly the work of different craftsmen; and probably, therefore, of different dates. This raises the probability that one of the pair was deliberately built, at a later date, to match and complement the original single lodge. It seems that the left-hand cottage is the better constructed of the two; but does this suggest that it is the earlier, or the later, of the pair?

Photograph: Michael O'Connell.
Situation: 30, Summer Island Road, Loughgall; td, Anasamry; Parish, Loughgall; District Council, Armagh; Grid ref. H 880 546.
References: Listed B+ (15/1/1). Map of 1794, T 2431 in PRONI; Dean, 'Gate lodges', UAHS, 1994, p 42; information from Mr Ralph Cowdy.

Hawthorn Hill Gate Lodge, Meigh

156. A neat stone gate-lodge of about 1845, with pyramidal roof surmounted by well-detailed chimney, set back from the road in a curved exedra opposite the front drive to Hawthorn Hill, one-time seat of the Chambré family, itself now blocked up; though its extensive outbuildings have been attractively restored to provide a courtyard centre with tourist and conference facilities. The gate lodge, still inhabited, has been very discreetly enlarged at the rear.

As Dean correctly says, "Distinctive chiefly for very pretty geometric patterned cast iron glazing bars to windows".

Photograph: Michael O'Connell.
Situation: 188, Dromintee Road, Killevy; td, Aghadavoyle; Parish, Killevy; District Council, Newry & Mourne; Grid ref. J 045 191.
References: Not listed. Dean, 'Gate lodges', UAHS, 1994, p 38.

Castle Gate Lodge, Tynan Abbey

157. Dean dates this lodge, and the central part of Tynan Abbey itself (64), to 1817, "architect probably John Nash", on the somewhat tenuous basis of drawings (destroyed) of a design for a mansion (unexecuted) signed by A C Pugin, of Nash's office; and on the undoubted fact that Nash worked at Caledon nearby. But there exists no evidence of any payment, and Nash was not the man to offer his services free. One may take leave to wonder, whilst wholeheartedly adopting his admirable description:

"The gate is in the form of a double "portcullis" in a Tudor archway recessed below machicolations. All framed by a tall 23' ... high screen wall, L-shaped 55' ... x 50' ... and located on a rightangle bend on the Middletown Road. Flanked by a square turret and an octagonal tower on the extremities, the latter housed the gatekeeper's accommodation. All in random squared uncoursed quarry-faced limestone, crowned by Irish crenellations with "arrowloops". The solidity of the whole composition is increased by battering of the wall base. The porter's room is approached up a flight of steps from the forecourt. Lit by two windows, with segmentally-pointed heads, from one of which he could overlook the distant gate. His spartan accommodation was supplemented some time later by an additional building against the ramparts".

Sir James Matthew Stronge, second baronet, was, as his mother-in-law remarked, "very near-sighted, and I should tremble at being drove by him". Dean suggests that it "must have been in deference to his eyesight that he conceived such a powerful Romantic castellated Gothick set-piece".

Photograph: Michael O'Connell.
Situation: Coolkill Road, Tynan; td, Corfehan; Parish, Tynan; District Council, Armagh; Grid ref. H 762 419.
References: Listed B+ (15/11/2). OS map, 1835; Dean, 'Gate lodges', UAHS, 1994, p 43.

Laurel Cottage, Tartaraghan

158. A handsome four-bay single-storey cottage, rough-cast and whitewashed, Georgian glazing-pattern intact; its slated hipped roof unfortunately topped by two redbrick chimneys neither roughcast nor painted to match the walls. Built as accommodation for the sexton of St Paul's Church, Tartaraghan (31), of 1816, and so probably not much later than the church, to which it bears the same relationship as a gate-lodge does to a mansion-house: there is even a faintly ecclesiastical air to the stone gate pillars and the clipped yews in the little garden.

Photograph: Michael O'Connell.
Situation: 34, Clantilew Road, Tartaraghan; td, Breagh; Parish, Tartaraghan; District Council, Craigavon; Grid ref. H 944 585.
References: Listed B (14/1/20).

7 Aughlish Cottages, Scarva

159. The least-altered of a row of twelve-plus-one (so as not to be thirteen) weavers' cottages, with distinctive tall very steeply-pitched roofs and gable windows which lit the weaving-lofts. Colloquially known as "Pot Stick Row". Very similar to, if not identical with, the three Manchester Estate cottages in Portadown identified by Dick Oram and dated by him to the early 1850s. Almost all the other houses in this group have been mercilessly "modernised": this one retains its white-painted roughcast with grey trim, circlets at the porch, Victorian glazing-pattern, and original paired chimneys; and its owner and his architect, much to their credit, say that they intend to keep it so.

Photograph: Michael O'Connell.
Situation: 7, Aughlish Cottages, Scarva; td, Aughlish; Parish, Mullaghglass; District Council, Armagh; Grid ref. J 057 437.
References: Not listed. Oram, 'Craigavon', UAHS, 1971, pt I, p 6; McCutcheon, 'Industrial archaeology', 1980, pl 93.2.

2 Creeveroe Road, Navan, Armagh

160. An unusual cottage with a concave angled front wall shaped to accommodate the curve of the road onto which it faces. Of whitewashed rubble, covered in climbing roses; door to the left, then three low Georgian-glazed windows; corrugated iron roof. It seems that, on a windless summer day in 1955, the former thatched roof suddenly fell in with a great puff - the roof-tree had completely rotted away from old age. It is possible that this cottage, unlike most others, goes back to the 18th century. Occupied from the 1860s by the Mallon family; on the death of John Mallon in 1963 at the age of 83, it passed to the present owner.

Photograph: Michael O'Connell.
Situation: 2, Creeveroe Road, Navan; td, Creeveroe; Parish, and District Council, Armagh; Grid ref. H 837 457.
References: Not listed. Information from owner.

Crabtree Cottage, Crabtreelane, Portadown

161. At right angles to the Farlough Road, only a couple of hundred yards from the parallel motorway, a very spruce and trim whitewashed six-bay single-storey thatched cottage, with porch and half-door projecting and the thatch carried up into a hump above them, and a separate outbuilding at right angles likewise thatched. Charming, but just a little self-conscious, like a schoolboy with face newly washed and hair newly brushed; but no doubt this will wear off.

In 1835, Lt G A Bennett remarked "Derryall, proprietor Mr Wallace, Captain Acheson of Portnorris middle landlord, who sublets it very high. Houses mud." This house is built not of mud but of brick beneath the plaster and whitewash. Oral tradition locally has it that the house was built by a person named Litters (apparently the anglicisation of a Huguenot name), that he worked in a claypit or brickworks in the vicinity (possibly Derrybrughas, 137) and may have been part-paid in bricks. A cottage here appears on the Ordnance Survey map of 1837, but it is impossible to be sure that is the same one. The Litters family lived on in their working farm until 1974; it was by then in poor order, and was extensively restored by one Ian Dickie. He was followed about 1990 by George Topping, a thatcher by trade and inclined towards advertising his skills: the wheat-straw thatching accordingly incorporates some fancy adornments more in the English than the Irish tradition - but not the less attractive for that. Pierce and Coey describe it as "An early 19th century Ulster weaver's thatched house and barn".

Photograph: Michael O'Connell.

Situation: 50, Farlough Road, Portadown; td., Derryall; Parish, Drumcree; District Council, Craigavon; Grid ref. H 984 599.

References: Listed B1/ Q (14/1/27). G A Bennett, OSM, 1835, Armagh, I, p 39; OS map, 1835; Pierce and Coey, 'Taken for granted', 1984, p 68.

Bilbrooke Cottage, 9 Bluestone Road, Portadown

162. A fine seven-bay thatched roadside cottage, and out-buildings, still a working farm, whitewashed, with two brick chimneys; a thatched extension at right angles, and, at the right-hand gable, another extension, slated, partly of rubblestone and partly of brick. Difficult to date: perhaps mid-19th century? Vested by the Craigavon Development Commission, and then declared surplus to requirements. Bought back by the present owner, and most carefully and conscientiously restored by him between 1992 and 1996. All very trim, and now, thanks to his efforts, pretty as a picture.

Photograph: Michael O'Connell.
Situation: 9, Bluestone Road, Portadown; td, Lisnamintry; Parish, Drum-cree; District Council, Craigavon; Grid ref. J 046 547.
References: Listed B1/Q (14/4/10); Oram, 'Craigavon', UAHS, 1971, pt III, p 8.

30 Bluestone Road, Portadown

163. A seven-bay thatched, whitewashed and perhaps mud-walled cottage, shown on the first Ordnance Survey map, so earlier than 1835. The listers describe it as "vernacular weaver's cottage of harled field stones and thatched". Two small square cemented chimney-stacks project over the thatch. The cottage has nice gate-pillars and boundary walls to the road, and a black-painted splash-band. For "many generations" the home of the Robinson family, it was vested by the Craigavon Development Commission, and bought back in 1994 by its previous owner. Rethatched in 1992; awaiting another rethatching, especially around the chimney-stacks; but for the present, in pretty good shape.

Photograph: Michael O'Connell.
Situation: 30, Bluestone Road, Portadown; td, Crossmacahilly; Parish, Drumcree; District Council, Craigavon; Grid ref. J 049 551.
References: Listed B1/Q (14/4/1). OS map, 1835; Oram, 'Craigavon', UAHS, 1971, pt III, p 8; notes in MBR.

Mullaghbane Folk Museum, Forkhill

164. A small two-bay single-storey two-roomed thatched and whitewashed cottage, believed to be two hundred years old, sensitively restored in 1971 by the Mullach Ban Folklore and Historical Society. Inhabited for many generations by members of the extended Murtagh family; eventually, by an elderly bachelor of the same name (though no relation) who could not be bothered to put the ashes of his fire out of the house; when, at length, the thatched roof fell in upon the mess inside, the parish priest took mercy on him, and allowed him to live in the caretaker's rooms at the parochial hall. In gratitude, he presented his tumbledown cottage to the parish, which in turn presented it to the Society, which has turned it into a tiny roadside showpiece.

Built of rubblestone, white-washed, in the traditional vernacular manner, it has two tiny windows and a half-door painted green, and a chimney at each gable. Perhaps a little regrettably, it has been (very well) rethatched, not in the straw traditional in the locality, but in imported reeds. There are old-fashioned rambling roses at either side of the doorway; and appropriate outbuildings, including a lean-to accommodating a nicely-faded farm cart. Inside, the original kitchen fireplace survives, with crane and bellows, and a rich jumble of miscellaneous furnishings provided by contributions from the residents of the parish. How welcome it would be if every parish were to follow this example of enlightened local initiative!

Photograph: Michael O'Connell (see also colour-plate XIVb).
Situation: Corran Road, Redmond's Cross; td, Tullymacreeve; Parish, Forkhill; District Council, Newry & Mourne; Grid ref. H 983 215.
References: Listed B2 (16/19/6). Records of the Society; notes by R Oram in MBR; information from Mrs Norah B McCoy.

Leo's Cottage, Meigh

165. An attractive vernacular cottage, of uncertain date, very lovingly restored by its owner, Mr Sean Callaghan, after the death of its last occupier, Leo Jordan, who left in 1994. Of five bays, whitewashed walls, green trim, black splash-band; traditional glazing-bars; and a beautifully-thatched roof with four straw birds on the ridge - trade mark of the thatcher, Tom O'Byrne from Navan, County Meath. The interior now contains all mod. cons, as well as a traditional kitchen and a good deal of furniture given by Miss Bell from the near-by Killevy Castle (70). It is presently leased to the Dromintee/Jonesborough Senior Citizens and Handicapped Club. The gardens and surroundings are beautifully laid out and cared for: a real showpiece, and a labour of love. Not, however, open to the general public except by special arrangement.

Photograph: Michael O'Connell.
Situation: Low Road, Meigh; td, Adavoyle; Parish, Killevy; District Council, Newry & Mourne; Grid ref. J 062 198.
References: Not listed. Photographs and documents on display in the cottage; information from owner.

180 Mullalelish Road, Richhill

166 (left). A modest cottage dating from before 1834, the central section thatched, the outbuildings at either end slated, all attractively whitewashed, and the trim painted bright blue. Although it is not permanently occupied, it seems that the owner has put it in order to provide accommodation for guests. Rethatched in 1994.

For many years, owned and occupied by a Mrs Boyd who died aged 93 in 1993, leaving the place to the neighbour who had looked after her. In a note of 1989 in the MBR, Oram reports "The building is in great order inside and out. The windows are home-made, without any parting slips, all in Russian pine. The old hearth has been fitted with a late Victorian grate but the old surround, brackets, mantel etc are all intact & the cranes etc are in the outhouse. Over the fire is a half-loft, the rest of the ceiling has been sheeted in t[ongued] and g[rooved]. The barn is an old Belfast roof-truss job - the standards, all but one, have been replaced in steel (railway lines mostly) but the roof is intact".

Photograph: Michael O'Connell.
Situation: 180, Mullalelish Road, Richhill; td, Mullalelish; Parish, Richhill; District Council, Armagh; Grid ref. H 984 490.
References: Listed B1/Q/V (15/4/13); OS map, 1834; notes in MBR.

Charles Sheils's Institution, Armagh

167. A fine L-shaped sandstone range of Victorian alms-houses, completed in 1868, by Lanyon & Lynn, more or less to a standard design employed also, with variations, in Killough, Carrickfergus, Stillorgan, and Dungannon. Williams says: "Armagh is one of their simplest designs but with splayed layout to follow the contours of the hill". As I suggest in Buildings of County Antrim, this seems likely to have been the work of John Lanyon, "too fussy to be that of his father, too cheerfully unscholarly to be that of W H Lynn". The warden's house has a formal Gothic doorway and clock-tower, somewhat less elaborate than that at Carrickfergus. "The style of the building is Gothic Revival in the Lombardic form made popular through the writings of Ruskin" (UAHS). Originally, twenty-five quite spacious terrace houses, including that of the superintendent; with a detached later wing of 1912 in the same style, by Young & Mackenzie. "Each adult inmate receives £10 a year, children between 10 and 15 years old, £5, and under that age £2 10 0. The design of the founder was to help persons of small income, who have seen better days"

(Bassett). His manner of doing so was strikingly enlightened for the period. Charles Sheils, born in Killough, made a fortune in Liverpool. His rules stipulated that "No religious disputes of any description will be tolerated". Each institution was to be managed by a committee comprising four members of the Church of Ireland, four of the Roman Catholic Church, and four of the Presbyterian Church.

It is unfortunate that much of the original five acres of communal garden on Tower Hill had to be sold off for development in order to finance the modernisation of the buildings.

Photograph: Michael O'Connell.
Situation: Off Tower Hill; td, Killuney; Parish, and District Council, Armagh; Grid ref. H 880 455.
References: Listed B (15/17/46); outside conservation area. Bassett, 'Armagh', 1888, p 111; 'Buildings of Armagh', UAHS, 1992, p 200; Williams, 'Architecture in Ireland', 1994, p 12; Brett, 'Buildings of County Antrim', UAHS, 1996, p 231.

CHAPTER SEVEN

PUBLIC BUILDINGS, COMMERCIAL, ETC.

The grandest public buildings of the county are still those with which Archbishop Robinson endowed it in the 18th century: the Library (176), the Royal School (171), the Observatory (178); closely followed by the slightly later Court House (169), County Museum (173), Savings Bank (191), and the earlier range of St Luke's Hospital (179); all in Armagh city itself. Communications provide many fine structures sprinkled through the countryside: road bridges (some of the most modest and rustic being the most delightful); railway bridges and viaducts; canals, locks, lock-houses, and aqueducts.

Of the once flourishing industrial archaeology of the linen industry, little now remains. Those former mills which have not been dismantled, or converted to other uses, are mostly semi-derelict, used now only for agricultural storage. Here and there stand the chimneys of abandoned mills, often elegant round, octagonal, or square structures of brick or stone, now without function: but it is too much trouble to take them down. Presumably, eventually they will all just fall of their own accord, like elderly trees in a gale, causing considerable inconvenience (or

worse) to those in their neighbourhood at the wrong moment. There are a few relics on the banks of the Callan River, and traces of past falls and flumes, but the other principal souce of water-power, the Camlough River, is now a mere piped trickle. Fruit farming seems to have produced no very characteristic building forms, though there a number of farm-houses with extensive apple-stores in their farmyards. The present-day mushroom houses are not things of beauty - plastic successors to the ubiquitous war-time Nissen huts.

The centres of the larger towns and villages have suffered so severely from thirty years of bombing that there are few shops, pubs, hotels, banks, or commercial buildings of much historic or architectural significance left: though a handful have survived undamaged, or have been laboriously restored, and are accordingly here recorded

It is pleasing, in this chapter, to be able to record a contemporary building, of 1999, which I can whole-heartedly admire: the Cardinal O Fiaich Library (177) in the city by Paul Mongan and Peadar Murphy, of P & B Gregory, architects, Belfast.

Shopfront of former Post Office, Russell Street, Armagh (186). Photograph: Michael O'Connell

Court (or Market) House, Loughgall

168. J C Innes of the Ordnance Survey, writing about 1837, gives a succinct description: "The court house, situated at the north-east end of the town of Loughgall, is a plain stone building, roughcast, whitewashed and slated, 52 feet long and 29 broad, built in 1746. The upper part of the building is used as a court house and the under as a market house". Valued at £14. 8. 8 in 1837; from 1863 onwards, reduced to a nominal £6. Lewis says "There is a large and handsome market-house, but the market, and also four fairs which were previously held, have been discontinued ... a manorial court is held monthly before the seneschal".

It is an attractive four-bay two-storey hipped-roofed building, whose speckled rubble stonework (of an unusually light colour) is no longer, perhaps regrettably, roughcast and whitewashed; that is a matter of taste. Four very tall windows in the south-west facing front, with nine panes in the upper sash and six in the lower, light the large and airy court-room, which is reached by a ramp and half-arch of stone. The market hall below originally had four open arches on each side, and one at each end, but these are now blocked up, by wooden doors in the main façade. The building has good quality cut-stone eaves course and window-sills but, perhaps rather surprisingly, no quoins.

Restored in 1996 for the owner, under the supervision of Dawson Stelfox and Marcus Patton of HEARTH, to provide three commercial units below, and a large well-lit workspace above; untenanted at the time of writing.

Photograph: Michael O'Connell.
Situation: 77, Main Street, Loughgall; td, and Parish, Loughgall; District Council, Armagh; Grid ref. H 909 522.
References: Listed B1 (15/2/7); in conservation area. VAL 1B/230, p 54, and VAL 2B/2/28C, p 23, in PRONI; J C Innes, OSM, nd, Armagh, I, p 76; Lewis, TD, 1837, II, p 313; Brett, 'Court houses and market houses', UAHS, 1973, p 40; conservation area booklet, 1993; information from owner.

Court House, Armagh

169. "The County Court House is deemed very inconvenient and an estimate of a new and grand edifice, to the amount of £6000 for this purpose, is now" (1803) "before the Grand Jury" (Coote). "The building, which was erected in the year 1809, is situated a little to the north-west of the public walks, now" (1819) "denominated "The Mall". Thus situated, it is seen to considerable advantage, and has a striking effect. It is built with hewn limestone, with a handsome portico in front" (Stuart). "A set piece that is the major focus of the Mall ... This controlled, symmetric, classical composition, clearly and simply proclaims order and the rule of law to all the populace" (UAHS). Alas, that proclamation has been disregarded by the bombers on more than one occasion, though the building has been laboriously restored.

On its very prominent site, this must be the best-known work by Francis Johnston in Armagh; but its appearance is by no means as he wished it to be. In 1820, he wrote: "I sent a plan for the new Session House (erected there about seven years ago) but it has not been followed, the Managers (an Attorney and others) were prevailed upon by some of the workmen to reduce the diameter of the columns (I suppose for the greater convenience of getting the stones of which they are composed) and have thereby ruined the portico". As Goslin puts it, "Indeed, the columns and responding pilasters do taper dramatically and this gives the court house a quirky lightness rather than the solemn grandeur a Roman styled temple court house should effect."

This seems to have been one of Johnston's first jobs after his appointment, in 1806, as architect to the Board of Works in Dublin; in the following year, he was paid £27.6.0 for a second plan and elevation. In 1973, I wrote "Its learned and idiosyncratic classicism is slightly marred by two defects: first, the elongated thin-ness of the columns, and still more the pilasters, of the portico; ... and second, the double-humped arrangement of the roof - invisible from close up, where the pediment masks the central valley, but disturbing from a distance. Nevertheless ... it is a building of much charm and distinction".

"The pedimented portico stands on a plinth of seven steps; the tall Doric columns and pilasters taper sharply ... Within the portico, the central doorway is at the head of four further steps, and crowned by a large round-headed window with fanlight. The subsidiary doors on either side are inscribed "Record Court" and "Crown Court"; above the lintels are round-headed niches with shell fluting. There are triple guttae, an odd idiosyncracy of Johnston's, at the imposts of each arch. The frieze has mutules and, here, full sets of guttae. The stonework of the central block is clean-dressed, that of the side bays slightly pecked to simulate vermiculation. Each side bay has quoins, and a single tall round-headed window with fanlight, inset in a rectangular recess; here too the imposts have triple guttae" (Brett). "This relationship of planes is resolved in a very strange manner at the extreme corners, where, instead of the more usual projection, the wall face in fact recedes before the composition is resolved by the staggered rusticated quoinstones ... There is no parapet, instead the roof drains directly into a gutter cut into the top of the cornice" (UAHS).

"Alone amongst the court houses of Ulster, that at Armagh has an interior of as much merit and interest as its exterior. The central hall is not, in fact, central; it is (by several feet) off-centre. It contains two scrolly porticos leading to the court-rooms; each interior doorcase, of severely paired Doric pilasters, is contained within a tall arch supported on fluted pilasters - swelling strangely in exaggerated entasis - with oak-leaf capitals. The cornice and frieze incorporate guttae, mutules, and swags; the central circular roof-light has finely-moulded floral plasterwork" ... "The inner hall contains a fine divided staircase. Here, the corners of the cornice have been coved, the curves carried elegantly on bunches of feathers; the roof-lantern is similar to that in the front hall. At the head of the staircase, a wide central segmental arch gives access to the Grand Jury corridor: at either side is a scalloped niche with good plaster detailing - consoles, oak and olive leaves. In the centre of this gallery is a circular lunette incorporating a cadaverous bust, carved by J K Jones, of Edward Tickell KC, assistant barrister for Co Armagh from 1830 to 1858" ... "The two large Grand Jury rooms ... have tent-like coved ceilings, with delicate plasterwork, incorporating in the former, arrows and scales of justice; in the latter, cornucopiae and festoons: in each case, surrounded by entwined sprays of oak and olive. Each room has a plain marble chimney-piece, and a good chandelier. Of the courtrooms, each has tall arched windows framed in fluted pilasters; each has a very strongly-carved anthemion-console canopy over the judge's chair: that in the Crown court is surmounted by a fine crude gaily-painted wooden lion and unicorn, supporting the royal arms, and has also a jury-gallery with corkscrew balusters" (Brett). Dr McParland points out the resemblance to some of the interior features of Johnston's work at the Bank of Ireland in Dublin, Charlemont Forest, and Townley Hall, and suggests that "Such details show Johnston's peculiar attachment to certain motifs, as if, in the feathers, the acorns, the open fan motifs in window reveals, and the Greek Doric profiles, he wished to leave an unobtrusive signature of his presence".

Since 1809 the building's history has been somewhat chequered. A major internal remodelling took place between 1860 and 1863 under the supervision of Thomas Turner, but apparently to plans prepared by John Davidson, the county surveyor. In July 1860, "the fittings in the present courts are all to be pulled down, and the barristers' pews placed in front of the dock so as to face the judge; ... accommodation for the juries in waiting, and the public; cells under the court for the prisoners, a room for the Grand Jury witnesses, a room for the attorneys, and considerable sanitary improvements. Both courts are to be lighted at night by sunburners" (Rogers). In the mid-1960s it was selected by Captain Terence O'Neill, then Minister of Finance, as the sole court house to be retained and restored as a historic building; and a fairly drastic, if by present-day standards rather unsophisticated, programme of rehabilitation was carried out between 1965 and 1971 by Albert Neill. This included the removal of the original woodwork, and the introduction of tiled ceilings and inappropriate light fittings. Subsequently, the building suffered bomb damage on several occasions, most recently, and most disastrously, on 3 September 1993. A very extensive programme of reconstruction and enlargement, at vast expense, has followed, under the supervision of Stephen Leighton. The work has been careful and conscientious, but the precautions against another bomb are intrusive, and the new woodwork naturally lacks the glow and patina of polished Georgian mahogany. The building is, at the time of writing, back in use, though now surrounded by high security railings and ancillary defences of a kind which would have made Francis Johnston gasp.

Photograph: Michael O'Connell. Elevation drawing: Francis Johnston, IAA.
Situation: The Mall; td, Corporation; Parish, and District Council, Armagh; Grid ref. H875 455.
References: Listed A (15/16/1); in conservation area. Drawings in Murray collection, IAA; D 1905/2/147C, GJ 1805, 1807, 1835, 1859-63, all in PRONI; Coote, 'Armagh', 1804, p 321; Black drawing 25/50, in Armagh County Museum; Stuart, 'City of Armagh', 1819, p 529; Rogers, 'Record', 1861, p 31; T G F Paterson, Armachiana, IV, p 65, in Armagh County Museum; F Johnston, letter of 29 February 1820, reprinted in IGS 'Quarterly bulletin', VI, 1963, p 3; McParland 'Francis Johnston', 1969, p 127; Brett, 'Court houses and market houses', UAHS, 1973, p 37; B Goslin, unpublished Catalogue of Murray Collection, 1990, p 44, in IAA; 'Buildings of Armagh', UAHS, 1992, pp 10, 153.

Former Court House, Lurgan

170. Turner & Williamson, architects, of Derry, designed the new court house in 1873, at a cost of £4,000; it had been hotly opposed by the ratepayers of Portadown, who wished it to be sited there. Williams regards it as "A forerunner ... for their Magherafelt courthouse in 1874, designed ... in what has also been called their 'frontier' manner".

"An original and interesting building in the polychrome brick manner of William Butterfield, making ingenious use of a triangular corner site between William Street and Charles Street. The main front to William Street is of four bays and two storeys, plus a tall gabled roof with very tall arch-coupled chimneys at each end, and a prominent ventilator in between. The porch extends the length of the building and incorporates two broad round-headed arches, strongly reminiscent of the market house tradition, despite their squat Romanesque columns. These are flanked by slim windows. There is an addendum to the west, pedimented, with a curious brick mini-oculus in the tympanum, and two round-headed windows below. The gable-end of the main block is treated like a pediment, with another brick oculus; below, a large apse-like projection, with round-headed windows,

topped by a demi-conical slate roof, fills the triangle of the pavement. All this is carried out in yellow brick, with ornamental bands of red brick. The result is masculine, robust and colourful" (Brett, in 1973).

Soon after these words were written, the court house was rendered superfluous by the completion of the new crown court in Craigavon. Many proposals were considered, but none came to anything; until, at the last moment, it was acquired by the owners of the nearby Ashburn Hotel, and "restored" in 1996 as a public house to the designs of Michael Doyle of Dublin. The exterior now looks extremely well, apart from unavoidable security grilles and blanked-out windows: happily, the shutters which seal off the arched openings are retractable and disappear from sight when not in use. The interior comes as quite a surprise. Almost everything is new, except for the royal coat of arms, the ceiling, and some of the fireplaces. A stuffed judge, red-robed and bewigged, life-size, now adjudicates in a kind of pulpit above the door; he looks across the room at a stuffed prisoner, hand-cuffed and sinister, likewise life-sized, in a dock attached to the upstairs bar. The furnishings, the detailing, above all the clever use of books and book-cases, are all effective: and altogether, the interior makes excellent fun of the majesty of the law.

Much as I detest theme pubs in general, and stuffed dummies in particular, I must concede that this is an unusually successful and enjoyable conversion of a building which might easily, without it, have been lost.

Photographs: Postcard, SELB Local Studies Library, Armagh; Michael O'Connell.
Situation: William Street, Lurgan; td, Derry; Parish, Shankill; District Council, Craigavon; Grid ref. J 078 587.
References: Listed B (14/21/8). D1928/O/4, and GJ 1872-5, in PRONI; IB, XIV, 1872, p177, and XV, 1873, p29; Oram, 'Craigavon', UAHS, 1971, pt I, p 9; Brett, 'Court houses and market houses', UAHS, 1973, p 40; Williams, 'Architecture in Ireland', 1994, p 14.

Royal School, Armagh

171. "The buildings belonging to the institution, which were completed in the year 1774, cost £5,078, of which £3,000 were advanced by Primate Robinson, and £2,078 by the reverend and venerable Dr Grueber, DD. They are extensive and well adapted to academical purposes; but as the dwelling houses front each other and are, in a great measure, concealed from view by the portico and school-house, those parts which are visible in the adjacent country, are seen at a great disadvantage. It is, indeed, difficult to find edifices so well constructed and so extensive, which excite so little interest in the mind of the spectator, when merely considered as architectural objects" (Stuart).

And: "The present school-house is situated a little southward of the Observatory. It is separated from the great Castledillon road by a quadrangular court, in front of which a portico of considerable extent extends along the highway, and communicates with two distinct, convenient and roomy dwelling-houses, appropriated to the use

of the master, his family and the students. Thus the court is completely enclosed by these dwelling houses, the portico and the school-house itself, in the rear of which there is a spacious playground surrounded by a well-built wall of considerable height"... And: "The schoolroom is 56 feet by 28 feet, and the dining room and dormitories are spacious and well ventilated. One hundred boarders can be comfortably accommodated in this seminary" (Stuart).

The original buildings of rubble stone, designed by Thomas Cooley as part of Archbishop Robinson's ambitious schemes for the improvement of Armagh, have of course been added to and enlarged many times over the years. "The principal buildings are grouped in a traditionally collegiate form to create the four sides of a quadrangle". "The armorial bearings of George III adorn the south wall of the quadrangle between the escutcheons of Primates Robinson and Beresford ... The proportions of the buildings are classical while Gothick dressings give an added air of scholastic respectability. All the parapets that face College Hill are crenellated, the entrance doorways from the street and the cloister arcade have Tudor Gothick dressings and the windows of the south block have label mouldings in the same style" (UAHS). The cloister lies immediately behind the entrance screen.

In 1849 the original single-storey library in the south range was raised by a further storey; in 1872 a large schoolroom and other classrooms, and a sanatorium, were added; more recent extensions, including the new headmaster's house, have been built to the sympathetic designs of Major W A Johnston.

Arthur Young much admired the establishment in 1776: "admirably adapted for its purpose: a more convenient or a better contrived one is nowhere to be seen"... "It is a spacious, regular and handsome edifice; admirably contrived for its purpose ... During the incumbency of Dr Carpendale, who was appointed to its preceptorship by the founder, the institution was regarded as the Eton or Westminster of Ireland" (PG). Surprisingly, considering its antecedents, it lacks, and has always lacked, a chapel.

A number of Cooley's original plans, elevations and details survive in Archbishop Robinson's Library; the ground plan is inscribed "General Plan of the New School at Armagh showing the Master's Apartments - the Publick School and Offices and the Play Ground for the Boys. September 28th 1775. Thomas Cooley."

Photographs: Michael O'Connell; postcard, SELB Local Studies Library, Armagh. Engraving: from Stuart.
Situation: College Hill, Armagh; td, Corporation; Parish, and District Council, Armagh; Grid ref. H 878 458.
References: Listed B+ (15/17/38); in conservation area. Drawings in Armagh Public Library, and in IAA; Young, 'Tour', 1780, p 104; Stuart, 'City of Armagh', 1819, pp 440, 543, and plate facing p 366; PG, I, 1845, p 80; Pierce and Coey, 'Taken for granted', 1984, p 45; 'Buildings of Armagh', UAHS, 1992, p 83.

Maddan Schoolhouse, Derrynoose

172. "The late Mr Smith gave the ground whereon the schoolhouse is built": apparently this was Rev. Nathaniel Smith, rector of Derrynoose from 1812 till 1823. Most unusually for a two-storey building, there are no stairs or other means of communication between the upper and the lower storey, short of walking round the outside of the building. It is dug back into the hillside, so that the lower floor is entered from the playground, facing the road, whilst the upper rooms are entered from a porch carried over the area at the rear. It is five bays long; the front has no less than three doorways, one with curly barge-boards on its small porch. The walls are of once-white-washed roughcast over fieldstone; the roof is hipped; the glazing-bars are still intact.

"The school was a large one for the period, with the 1826 Education Report recording that it cost £160 to build and could accommodate 150 scholars": but "despite its grand size, it could only entice fifty-three students (18 Established Church, 23 Presbyterian and 12 Roman Catholic) ... The school was clearly not viable and seems to have soon gone out of business ... It subsequently came back into use as Maddan National School and later as a

parish hall before it again fell into disuse", about 1986 (Hossack). Now deteriorating, but not yet quite beyond rescue: although it appears that the vestry, to whom the building still belongs, in 1997 turned down a very reasonable offer from a prospective restoring purchaser as "a bit of a joke": and expressed the intention of repairing it as a parish hall. However, to date of writing, nothing has been done, the building has continued to deteriorate, and any joke there may be about the matter appears to be in very poor taste.

An improbable notice on one gate-pillar announces "presented by Mrs M J Hughes to commemorate her 100th birthday, 1935": but is unclear what it was that she presented, or to whom!

Photographs: Michael O'Connell.
Situation: On road from Keady to Tamlaght; td, Maddan; parish, Derrynoose; District Council, Armagh; Grid ref. H 810 366.
References: Listed B2 (15/14/12). Commissioners on Education in Ireland, 'Second report', Appendix 22, 1826; H Hossack, in 'Buildings at risk', III, UAHS, 1996, p 35; file in MBR.

Former Schoolhouse (now County Museum), The Mall, Armagh

173. Originally, the Charlemont Place National School-house of 1834: an extremely grand little building, attributed to William Murray. "A two-storey building with three tall arched windows behind the ashlar limestone tetrastyle Ionic portico and matching doorways in screen walls at each side of the portico" (UAHS). "A group of local people subscribed to build and run it" (Weatherup); the lease was transferred in 1856 by the school trustees, of whom Lord Charlemont was one, to the Armagh Natural History and Philosophical Society: "which has since, through the liberality of his Grace the Lord Primate and that of the nobility and gentry of the neighbourhood, as well as the inhabitants of the city, been considerably improved. Within the Society's house are a reading room, library, lecture and committee rooms, curator's residence, and a museum" (Rogers). The old single-storey schoolroom was divided into two ground floor rooms and a balcony by the local architect Edward Gardner.

The building was gradually extended backward over the outbuildings and playground. In 1891 an art school and studio were established behind it under the auspices of the Science and Art Department, South Kensington. It was taken over by Armagh County Council in 1931 to serve as Library Headquarters and County Museum. The brick return was added in 1957; the whole building has recently undergone a thorough-going refurbishment; and the institution flourishes as an out-station of the Ulster Museum in Belfast. Successive curators have made notable contributions to the local history of the county, and have greatly eased the task of this researcher.

Photograph: Michael O'Connell.
Situation: 6, Charlemont Place, The Mall; td, Corporation; Parish, and District Council, Armagh; Grid ref. H 875 455.
References: Listed A, (17/17/1); in conservation area. Rogers, 'Record', 1861, p 32; D R M Weatherup, in 'Irish booklore', II, 1972/6, pp44-53; Weatherup, 'Armagh', 1990, p 40; 'Buildings of Armagh', UAHS, 1992, p 133.

Former Schoolhouse, Bessbrook

174. The original schoolhouse was of 1853, "a neat cottage construction, well ventilated, with a sufficiency of light ... with eight desks each eight feet long. In 1853 19 boys and 33 girls attended" (MacNeice). It was considerably enlarged, to cope with the increased population of the village, in 1875, and owes its present appearance to that enlargement: though in style and spirit, like much else in Bessbrook, it has a surprisingly Regency flavour for so late a date. The listers describe it as "Single storey symmetrical picturesque composition with decorative roof trim and recessed central bay. Strongly expressed chimneys. Stone walled playground and decorative railings." And add that it " faces the Institute" (182) "across a formal garden at the head of College Square".

Badly bomb damaged in the 1970s; now a disabled adults' resource centre. The necessary adaptations have been carried out with discretion: apart from the very regrettable amputation of the chimney-stacks. Though the original lattice windows were replaced in the 1920s, this is still a very attractive and nicely-painted building, five bays deep, school-room for boys on one side, for girls on the other, linked by over-sailing eaves carried on cast-iron columns; stucco; Tudoresque label mouldings; quoins; lancet niches above the side windows.

Photograph: Michael O'Connell.
Situation: College Square West, Bessbrook; td, Clogharevan; Parish, Camlough; District Council, Newry & Mourne; Grid ref. J 047 287.
References: Listed B (16/22/16); in conservation area. D A MacNeice, Factory workers' housing, QUB thesis, 1981, p 69; conservation area booklet, 1983.

Convent of Mercy, Newry

175. A large, very fine, eleven-bay three-storey-on-basement range of dressed granite; glazing-bars complete. The two bays at each end, with double quoins, break forward, and have narrower paired windows. All the windows on the ground floor are round-headed, those in the centre of the upper storeys are square but with chamfered corners, set in round-headed or segmental-headed recesses. Good pilasters at the doorcase; nice iron railings and overthrow. The roof is topped by a ventilator grille surmounted by a cross.

Bassett says "The Convent of the Sacred Heart, presided over by the Sisters of Mercy, runs from Catherine-street to Canal Street. Broad sunny corridors, adorned with pictures and mottoes, are thorough between both streets ... Not the least of the attractive features are beautiful terraced gardens with ample conservatory and statuary embellishments. A department in which are about 350 children, is taught under the authority of the National Board of Education, and there is a sewing school of about 70 ... This convent was founded in Canal-street by the Rev. Mother Mary O'Connor, in 1855, and was a branch from Kinsale. The extension to Catherine-street was made in 1863."

This is the impressive work, completed in 1861, of John Bourke, a prolific Dublin architect who specialised in the design of churches, convents and related schools and institutions. Between 1855 and 1861 he was architect of the Mater Misericordiae Hospital in Eccles Street, Dublin; in 1858 had built the Sacré Coeur convent and schools in Armagh; and in 1868, was to build St Clare convent schools in Newry.

No longer used as a school, it is now occupied only by a small number of nuns, most of whom teach at Our Lady's modern school on the other side of Catherine Street. I have wondered whether a convent should be classified as a "clergy house" or as a "public building"; but, since nuns are not (yet?) classified as "clergy", have with some reluctance classified this very fine piece of work as a "public building", the more willingly since it was also a school.

Photograph: Michael O'Connell.
Situation: Catherine Street, Newry; td, Lisdrumgullion; Parish, Newry; District Council, Newry & Mourne; Grid ref. J 083 269.
References: Listed B1 (16/25/1). 'Dublin Builder', 1st April, 1860, p 240; Bassett, 'Down', 1886, p 99; information from IAA Index of Irish architects.

Archbishop Robinson's Library, Armagh

176. Every time I pass by, I am enchanted over again by the eccentricity of the Greek inscription on the façade of this building: ψυχηζ ιατρειον, meaning "psychiatry" or "the healing of the spirit", long before the birth of Sigmund Freud in 1855. In fact, before the building was refaced in 1846, the Greek inscription was slightly longer; but I much prefer the simpler version.

"One of the most perfect architectural set pieces in the City, built to designs by Thomas Cooley in 1771; it was extended by adding a bay to each end by John Monsarrat" (sic) "in 1845" (UAHS). The library was formally constituted by an Act of the Irish Parliament of 1773. Both Act and library were modelled on Archbishop Marsh's Library in Dublin of 1707; the layout of the reading-room follows the precedents set at Trinity College, Dublin in 1732 and at Christ Church, Oxford (Archbishop Robinson's own college) in 1739. Robinson spent £3000 on his building and placed within it, as its foundation book collection, his own personal library.

"The building contains a suite of convenient and excellent apartments for the accommodation of the librarian and his family. The room in which the books are chiefly arranged is 45 feet in length, 25 feet in breadth and 20 in height. It is light, airy, commodious, and in every respect well adapted to the object in view. There is also a gallery, which contains many valuable works" (Stuart in 1819). But Lewis says that "In 1820, an additional staircase was erected, as an entrance at the west end, which has in a great measure destroyed the uniformity and impaired the beauty of the building". However, the Parliamentary Gazetteer of 1845 takes the view that it "presents a very handsome appearance; contains spacious and neat accommodation for a large collection of books, and an elegant suite of apartments for the librarian". Bassett, in 1888, notes "there are at present in it about

17,000 books ... also a small collection of antiquities ... the public library continues to this day one of the chief attractions of the city".

In fact, it seems that between 1845 and 1848 Cooley's original cube was enlarged and refaced to provide, at the east end, a completely new hall, staircase and façade to Cathedral Hill, and, at the west end, a balancing extension, all to the designs of a mysterious John(?) Monserrat, "of whom" writes Hugh Dixon "nothing else is known". The Governors advertised for a plan to extend the Library in 1844 and offered a premium of £20 which was duly won by Monserrat in that same year. The evidence is plain to see in the Library's minute book: 11 February 1844, "that a sum of not exceeding Thirteen hundred pounds be expended in completing the library according to Mr Monserrat's plan and specification"; 3 October 1845, "Ordered that Mr Monserrat's plan for the alteration of the original plan for the enlargement of the library be adopted". But how to interpret this? Is the building as it now stands, with its very polished and accomplished exterior, really the work of Monserrat, not Cooley? Or did Monserrat re-use or adapt Cooley's designs? Or, as Dr Simms speculated, did Monserrat execute plans prepared years earlier by Francis Johnston for the enlargement of Cooley's original design? Exasperatingly, Edward Rogers, who as Deputy Librarian must have known the true facts, merely says that "In 1847 the Governors expended upwards of £3,000 in enlarging the Armagh library, and its present appearance differs materially from that which is given in a medal struck by order of the founder to commemorate its erection". (In fact, the contract cost came to £2141. 11. 0; Rogers's figure includes for fittings and external railings). It is a real puzzle; but there can be no doubt that, altered or not, the library deserves the "A" awarded it by the listers.

I cannot improve upon the description of the UAHS listers, and will not attempt to do so. "The entire building is in ashlar limestone; the ground floor is rusticated and the remainder smooth. The elevation facing the cathedral is three bays wide and unified by a subdued order carried up through both storeys. The parapet balustrade rises above a deep cornice overhang supported by modillion brackets. The rest of the entablature is only expressed in the central bay. This bay is slightly advanced and is topped by a pediment ... The two flanking bays have blind attic panels. All three bays contain recesses with semi-circular heads rising through two storeys and broken at mid height by a string course. The central bay has an arched niche at first floor level which is protected by a segmental pedimented hood on console brackets. Below this is the main entrance which has a straight hood mould also supported by consoles. In the flanking bays there are windows; at first floor these have triangular pedimented hoods and moulded stone architraves; at ground floor level there are only architraves. The elevation facing Cathedral Close has five bays. The design is similar to the entrance elevation except that the first floor windows have semi-circular heads and there are no hoods of any kind".

Gordon Wheeler, who has made a particular study of this library, adds "Monserrat's extensions lengthened the bookroom by twenty three feet six inches and provided a continuous gallery on all four sides of the room ... The Library as designed by Cooley originally had to be entered through the apartments of the Keeper whose staircase gave access both to the bookroom and to the gallery on its inner side. The 1820 staircase partially remedied this but was replaced by Monserrat's work at the east end."

I remain in doubt whether to regard this admirable

building as a fine and characteristic example of Thomas Cooley's work of 1771, or as Mr Monserrat's flash-in-the-pan masterpiece of 1845.

Photographs: Michael O'Connell; MBR.
Situation: Abbey Street, Armagh; td, Corporation; Parish, and District Council, Armagh; Grid ref. H 875 455.
References: Listed A (15/20/8); in conservation area. Drawing 74 in RIAI Murray Collection, IAA; Drawings in shelf Z XIX D, one dated October 5, 1785, in Archbishop Robinson's Library; medal in Armagh County Museum; DIO/4/22/7, 3 and 4, in PRONI; minute book of Governors, 1795 - 1941, S 13, pp 88, 93, in Library; Coote, ' Armagh', 1804, p 313; Stuart, 'City of Armagh', 1819, pp 536-539; Lewis, TD, 1837, I, p 68; PG, I, 1845, p 80; Rogers, 'Record', 1861, p 24; Reeves, 'Memoir', 1886, pp9-11; Bassett, 'Armagh', 1888, p 85; G O Simms, in 'Irish booklore', I, 1971, p 140; DRM Weatherup, in 'Irish booklore' II, 1972/76, pp 268-299; Pierce and Coey, 'Taken for granted', 1984, p 8; B Goslin, unpublished Catalogue of Murray Collection, 1990, p 59, in IAA; 'Buildings of Armagh', UAHS, 1992, pp 38-40.

Cardinal O Fiaich Memorial Library, Armagh

177. A strikingly successful and polished example of public architecture of a quality extremely rare in the county, by Paul Mongan and Peadar Murphy of P and B Gregory, architects, of Belfast. (Whether Armagh really needed another library in addition to at least three excellent existing ones, is perhaps questionable; but let that pass). The site is a windy hillside between the Moy Road below, and the rear of Ara Coeli (92) above. In 1996, the project was

accorded grant aid from the National Lottery and, as the architects themselves say in the articles cited below: "This ensured not only the overall viability of the project, but that a much higher standard of finish and quality of materials than had originally been envisaged would be used". The building is a very straightforward, uncluttered rectangle of glass and blue Roscommon limestone, with hipped lead roof. Two contrasting textures of stone have

been sensitively juxtaposed. The stone panels are divided, on the front elevation, by tall vertical windows, and topped by a continuous horizontal clerestory below the oversailing eaves. There is also a continous rooflight running from one end of the building to the other. A massive stone porch, with heavy bronze doors, projects from the front wall of the building. This is not a clamant or aggressive building; its authors have had the good sense, and good taste, to let its merits speak for themselves without trying to compete with the cathedral buildings on the hill-top. An oddity is that the Cardinal's name is incised to the left of the main door, but sideways, as though he were standing on his ear: a posture not inconceivable for that endearingly unpompous Prince of the Church.

The interior is very simple and subdued, divided into three clearly-demarcated areas: the public reading room and a meeting room to the front; rooflit offices for librarian, archivist and staff in the spine of the building; and document and book storage at the windowless rear. "The materials are limited to ensure that a clean modern interior is possible and one that will both contrast with, and complement the exterior".

And: "The fact that the building is free-standing and clearly visible from all sides is quite unusual, and we were faced with the task of having to design each of the four elevations as equal individual elements in their own right, which would integrate to create a complete and balanced built form". In my view, the architects have been entirely successful in this; and are to be congratulated on the best piece of contemporary public architecture in Ulster since Liam McCormick's church at Burt, County Donegal.

Photographs: Michael O'Connell (see also colour-plate VIIa). Elevation drawings: P Mongan and P Murphy, P & B Gregory, Architects.

Situation: 15, Moy Road, Armagh; td, Corporation; Parish, and District Council, Armagh; Grid ref. H 287 346.

References: Not listed (yet); outside conservation area. 'Seanchas Ardmhacha' XVII, 1998, pp167, 168; 'Irish architect', No 144, February 1999, p 31-34; 'Perspective', VII, No 4, March-April 1999, p 46.

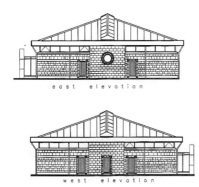

east elevation

west elevation

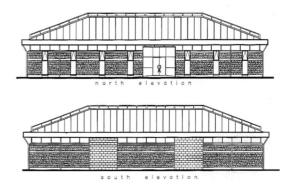

north elevation

south elevation

Observatory, Armagh

178. "The last public building erected by Primate Robinson was the Observatory in 1793", according to Rogers. But in fact, work began, to the designs of Francis Johnston, in 1789, and was "nearly completed" by April 1790. "Of very elegant appearance" thought Sir Charles Coote. "It is furnished with a complete astronomical apparatus, and contains very convenient accommodation for a professor" (Stuart). "The Observatory stands on one of the hills, north by east from the ancient cathedral, and by its green domes becomes a most striking feature in the view of Armagh from many points" (Bassett). "The south front displays, in great neatness of architecture, an elevation of two storeys, with a large circular turret in the centre, surmounted by a dome" (PG). "Primate Robinson dying before the internal arrangements were completed, the establishment remained in an unfinished state till 1825" (Lewis). A second circular tower was built in 1827, and a square two-storey tower, with the arms of Primate Beresford, in 1841.

"The buildings are stone with conglomerate rubble for

the main walling and ashlar limestone for the dressings. The proportions are classical, the decoration is minimal; the architectural effect is achieved by the subtle relationships of solid to void ... The main elevation is three-bay, the entrance is central and approached by a fanned flight of seven stone steps ... The main feature of the south face is the circular telescope tower which bears ... " the inscription 'The heavens declare the glory of God'. "Approximately two-thirds of the bulk of the tower projects beyond the body of the building and the observation room at the top creates an attic storey. The whole feature is capped by a hemispherical, copper-clad dome. The telescope is supported on a central limestone pillar rising through the full height of the tower and braced against the outer wall by the stone treads of the spiral stairway" (UAHS).

The same authority describes the interior detail as "restrained and minimal"; yet there is an astonishing wealth of elegant craftsmanship in stone, wood, plaster and metal. Beadings; flutings; chair-rails and skirtings; curved chimney-breasts and cupboards; arches; gates and mantelpieces; even miniature peacock-shaped bell-pulls: combine to constitute a magnificent, and living, museum of Francis Johnston's best work. The valuable collection of clocks and astronomical instruments is admirably displayed. The gardens and grounds are beautifully laid out and maintained. The only matter for regret is the intrusion of a stuffed-dummy astronomer.

Photographs: Michael O'Connell; MBR.
Situation: College Hill, Armagh; td, Corporation; Parish, and District Council, Armagh; Grid ref. H 877 458.
References: Listed A (15/16/3); outside conservation area. Coote, 'Armagh', 1804, p 88; Stuart, 'City of Armagh', 1819, pp 450 and 523-527; Lewis, TD, 1837, I, p 68; PG, I, 1845, p 80; Rogers, 'Record', 1861, p27; Bassett, 'Armagh', 1888, p 89; Moore, 'Armagh Observatory', 1967, passim; Butler, 'Seeing stars', 1990, passim; Bennett, 'Church, State and astronomy', 1990, passim; 'Buildings of Armagh', UAHS, 1992, pp 85-88.

St Luke's Hospital, Armagh

179. The hospital, originally built for the "lunatic poor", consists of two separate and impressive stone ranges, known as "The Hill" and "The Hollow" respectively; and a number of free-standing smaller buildings, including Protestant and Roman Catholic chapels, and a very chapel-like morgue.

The central block and cell wings of the Hollow were built at a cost of £20,900 between 1820 and 1825 (when the first patients were admitted) to designs by Francis Johnston, who entrusted the supervision of the work to his nephew William Murray. They are built of limestone ashlar and limestone squared rubble, originally 33 bays wide, now no less than 55 bays wide, two storeys and basement, with a cupola and clock (with weather vane dated 1824) marking the central canted entrance bay. At either side of the central block is a forward-projecting wing, topped by a pediment, and incorporating a wide and emphatic recessed panel. Everything is austere, classical, and symmetrical, except for the prominent water-tower at the left-hand of the range, built of stone in the style of an Italian

ELEVATION.OF.THE.LUNATIC.ASYLUM.

campanile in 1875. There have been changes over the years; the fenestration appears not to be original; segmental-headed windows may have taken the place of rectangular windows; the canted bay seems to be an addition. The buildings were variously extended in 1841, 1863, and 1875, and modernised by G P & R H Bell in 1979. But, as the UAHS listers justly remark: "It is to the credit of all those who, through time, have been given the responsibility to alter or add to this fine building that, in almost every case, they respected the work of Francis Johnston. The result is that today the building presents a satisfying unity overall".

The Hill building was built in 1901 by the County

Surveyor, Chudley Dorman, and is an unexpectedly accomplished building for an official whose duties were usually, one supposes, much more limited. (Plans in the Armagh County Museum are, however, signed "R H Dorman", and dated 1904). To quote the UAHS listers again, it "is a very imposing addition to the group. It is sited at the top of a rise overlooking the main asylum but, by being set at right angles, does not attempt to compete visually with it. The symmetrical design is in the French Renaissance style and has steeply pitched and mansarded roofs. The silhouette is enlivened by decorative iron crestings, copper clad ventilating cupolas and massive stone chimneys; the central unit has two storeys and an attic decorated by a tower". Now used for administrative purposes.

Altogether, a remarkably impressive and coherent group.

Photographs: Michael O'Connell. Elevation drawing: Francis Johnston, IAA.

Situation: Loughgall Road, Armagh; td, Mullynure; Parish, and District Council, Armagh; Grid ref. H 865 467.

References: The Hollow, Listed B+; The Hill, Listed B (The Hollow, 15/16/9; The Hill, 15/16/10); outside conservation area. Drawings in Armagh County Museum and in IAA; 'Buildings of Armagh', UAHS, 1992, p 193; information from Mr Dan Thompson.

Fever Hospital, Middletown

180. "The fever hospital is a neat edifice, built in 1834, containing 4 wards with accommodation for 16 patients; and the dispensary, with a residence for the physician, is a handsome building in the Elizabethan style" (Lewis). "A large handsome building, stone finished and well situated on the slope of the hill close to the western end of the village" (OSM). According to the parish history, "A fever hospital, capable of accommodating 12 or 14 patients, was built in Middletown in 1832 by the trustees of Bishop Sterne's Charities at an expense of £500. A dispensary with surgeon's house attached was also built at a cost of £700". However, a plaque in the wall of the former hospital is inscribed "Elizabethan House / Built 1834". Cholera was severe in Middletown in the 1830s: of 81 cases, 35 were fatal. The resident doctor, David Smith, died in 1847, aged only 35, "of fever caught in the discharge of his arduous professional duties" (probaby typhoid). At this time, the house was enlarged to double the number of beds: eventually, there were eighteen beds in each of the upper and lower wards. There was a roomy morgue at the rear, and the doctor's residence and dispensary were next door, where the police station now stands.

At some date after 1854, the infirmary was closed and converted into a Church of Ireland school. When the new primary school was built at Drumhillery soon after the second World War, the school in turn was closed, but the teacher, Mrs Gray, and her husband lived on here; it has been used as a dwelling ever since. Being so close both to the police station and the border, the building suffered many vicissitudes: it is recalled that Mr Gray could on occasion be seen picking bullets out of its walls with a pen-knife. After his death in about 1988 it was acquired by the present owner, who has put it into excellent order. A large, rambling, two-storey structure, with white-painted rough-cast walls, and grey-painted long-and-short cut-stone surrounds to doors and windows; a single column supporting the roof of the porch. The plastic windows and door are regrettable, but they do not much spoil the handsome appearance of the building from the busy road nearby.

Photograph: Michael O'Connell.
Situation: 51, Monaghan Road, Middletown; td, Tullybrick Hamilton; Parish, Tynan; District Council, Armagh; Grid ref. H 751 388.
References: Not listed. Lewis, TD, 1837, II, p 368; E A Williamson, OSM, 1838, Armagh, I, p 131; 'Historical sketches of Tynan and Middletown', 1995, pp 108, 115, 121.

Former Masonic Hall, The Mall, Armagh

181. Built as a Masonic Hall (set square and dividers still in evidence) in 1884, at a cost of £1,400, by the local architect James Fullerton, but now used as a gospel hall. Bassett says: "It is in the early Gothic style. The principal gable faces the Mall, next to the First Presbyterian Church, and is flanked on one side by a tower and spire, and on the other by a circular-ended staircase with steep conical roof. The largest lodge room is 40 feet by 20. Full accommodation is provided for the four lodges ... which indicate the flourishing condition of Masonry in Armagh". The masons moved elsewhere in 1946.

"Enchanting toytown gothic extravaganza in a vaguely Venetian Gothic style, all in polychrome brickwork. The main entrance consists of twin doors set inside pointed arches carried on short, banded columns on high pedestals and framed by a larger pointed arch supported on similar columns. Above this arch is a large, interesting plate rose window centred on the main gable of the hall which is decorated by stepped parapets and diagonal latticework patterning in the apex. On the right hand side of the centre gable there is a squat square campanile tower

with high level arcading below the steep brick eaves corbelling. The tower supports the tall four-sided spire, each side pierced by a lucarne. On the left hand side of the main gable is, first, a buttress, and then, at the corner, a low half round staircase tower with small pointed window openings following the line of the steps and a steep conical roof carried on steep corbelled eaves as on the campanile" (UAHS listers).

"... Flaunting its red and yellow brick and lively silhouette against the sober grandeur of its Presbyterian neighbour ... Trefoil-shaped timber-vaulted chapel on the upper floor" (Williams). Altogether, a surprisingly exotic creature to find in the staid context of the Mall.

Photograph: Michael O'Connell (see also colour-plate Va).

Situation: The Mall West; td, Parkmore; Parish, and District Council, Armagh; Grid ref. H 877 453.

References: Listed B (15/17/19); in conservation area; 'IB, XXVI', 1 April 1884; Bassett, 'Armagh', 1888, p 109; 'Buildings of Armagh', UAHS, 1992, pp 14, 144, 146; Williams, 'Architecture in Ireland', 1994, p 11.

The Institute, Bessbrook

182. A dignified two-storey building of locally-quarried granite, deliberately asymmetrical, of considerable merit: in a sort of sub-Ruskinian style, with more than a whiff of Venetian Gothic; clock in the gable; triangular dormers containing ogee lucarnes; fine, upstanding chimney-stacks. "The Institute, built 1886-7, is a handsome building, containing one of the largest halls in the county, and bears the motto 'In essentials Unity, in non-essentials Liberty, in all things Charity' "(Blum). "Built by the Company's employees under the supervision of William J. Watson, Newry, 5 October 1885, John G. Richardson presiding" (plaque). "In 1885 a Town Hall was built at an expense of £2600 from a design by Mr. W. J. Watson, Architect, Newry. It is a handsome granite structure, and has a spacious assembly room and reading room and library. The working people elect their own committee of control, and appear to enjoy the benefits of the institution" (Bassett). "A community centre had also been erected by the firm ... and here, in addition to a large hall capable of seating nearly one thousand persons, were a library, billiard room, lecture room and newsroom, well supplied with papers and periodicals" (Camblin).

Williams writes: "The most prominent building in the village is not a church but the town hall, now known as the community centre. Designed by the local Gothic Revival architect William Watson, it was built in 1886. Two parallel ranges, the front containing the meeting rooms; the rear the hall. The architectural idiom is that of William Barre, but without his brio". This last comment seems to me unduly disparaging.

This was one of the last of the Richardson family's benefactions to their workers: the mill village had been laid out beteen 1845 and 1855, just before the boom caused by the American Civil War. The extremely large hall, with its complex timber roof and pointed arches, is exceptionally fine. The mill finally closed in 1972, and during the years of the Troubles was gradually turned into an extensive army base with the busiest helicopter-pad in Europe. The Institute itself suffered bomb damage in the 1970s - that is why the clock does not work - and fell into deep disrepair, but was extremely well refurbished and restored in 1998 as a multi-purpose community centre, with lottery support, to designs by T Gilsenan, architect. It is, at the time of writing, generally in excellent order; generally known locally as "the Town Hall" which, in the ordinary sense, it is not.

Although generous, the Richardsons had a reputation for strictness; the Institute was built at the request of the workers, who signed a carved wooden "round robin" in the form of a circular plaque with their names around the perimeter, in order to disguise the identity of the originators!

Photograph: W A Green, Ulster Folk Museum WAG2531.
Situation: College Square East, Bessbrook; td, Clogharevan; Parish, Camlough; District Council, Newry & Mourne; Grid ref. J 049 287.
References: Listed B1 (16/22/9). Bassett, 'Armagh', 1888, p 237; Blum,'Bessbrook Spinning Company Ltd', [1945], passim; Camblin, 'Town in Ulster', 1951, pp 99-101, and pl 60; D A MacNeice, Factory workers' housing, QUB thesis, 1981, p 69; Williams, 'Architecture in Ireland', 1994, p 12.

Cricket Pavilion, Royal School, Armagh

183. The listers say: "A largely single storey flat-roofed symmetrical pavilion with a first floor observatory-like room of octagonal plan cantilevered out over the front entrance. Ground floor walls are rendered, with large corner glazed windows of small panes, while the first floor room is timber boarded and has a clock face. Designed by Philip Bell, this is a good and unspoiled example of "Modern Movement" design." Built by subscription as a memorial to those old boys of the school who served and fell in the second World War. Listed in 1994 following a survey of post-1914 buildings of significance.

The listers have got it exactly right. This delightful little building does credit to the firm of G P & R H Bell: it should not be forgotten that G P Bell was an extremely effective planning officer for Armagh, as well as being a founder member, and second chairman, of the Ulster Architectural Heritage Society.

Photograph: Michael O'Connell.
Situation: College Hill, Armagh; td, Corporation; Parish, and District Council, Armagh; Grid ref. H 880 455.
References: Listed B (15/17/67); outside conservation area.

Head o' the Road Inn, Tartaraghan

184. A traditional building, long, low roughcast and whitewashed, slated, and Georgian-glazed. Its origins, like the reason for its unexpected name, are lost in the mists of antiquity; it is said to have been a public-house for around two hundred years, and looks to be of about 1810. Though originally single-storey and only three bays long, at some unknown date, two additional bays were added, as was the upper storey. In 1932, when the father of the present owner acquired it, it was still a spirit grocery, with the bar at the right-hand end, the grocery in the middle, and the owner's living room and kitchen at the left-hand end.

Recently reslated and repainted, now in excellent order; it is just a pity that the four cement-rendered chimney-stacks on the roof-ridge were not roughcast and white-painted to match the walls; but that would not be too hard to remedy. Rural County Armagh does not seem to be rich in authentic and unmodernised old inns or public houses; so this is something of a find.

Photograph: Michael O'Connell.
Situation: Lawson's Bar, Clantilew Road; td, Breagh; Parish, Tartaraghan; District Council, Craigavon; Grid ref. H 944 585.
References: Listed B1 (14/1/7). Oram, 'Craigavon', UAHS, 1971, pt III, p 11; information from owner.

Gildea's Pub, Hamiltonsbawn

185. At the cross-roads at the heart of the village of Hamiltonsbawn, a simple two-storey-and-attic building, stucco with quoins, combining public house and dwelling under one roof, very possibly before that an inn. The main front is of 8 bays upstairs, 5 (irregularly spaced) below, and has a magnificent Gibbsian doorcase with rectangular geometrical fanlight, suggesting a date of around 1780. In the gable is set a Hamilton "coat of arms", which is believed by local historians to have been brought here from Hamilton's

old bawn, spoken of as "the Castle". (The latter building, erected in 1619 by J Hamilton Esq and much damaged in 1641, came into possession of the Achesons of Gosford (65), and Bassett quotes Dean Swift's poem 'The grand question debated whether Hamilton's Bawn shall be turned into a Barrack or a Malt-house'. As Taylor and Skinner confirm, it was in fact converted into a barracks; but, again according to Bassett, "Mr. McRoberts, by permission of Lord Gosford, removed the fortifications for improvement purposes"). Below the coat of arms is a more modern wide window engraved with the legend "J Gildea / Wines & Spirits / Old Bushmills Whiskey".

In 1838, according to J Heming Tait of the Ordnance Survey, Hamiltonsbawn contained "38 cabins and 23 two-storey houses. The trades are 6 grocers and publicans, 2 carpenters, 3 shoemakers, and 1 smith. There is no place of worship nor police force nor magistrate". This appears to be the house, valued in category 1B, for which in 1836 Hugh Quinn, publican, paid £12 yearly to a Mr McParland, but did not have a lease. In 1864, it was occupied by Michael O'Connell, who was followed, in turn, by Bernard and James McConnell, from whom it was acquired by Peter Gildea in 1929: in whose family it remains.

Photographs: Michael O'Connell.
Situation: 2, Main Street, Hamiltonsbawn; td, Drumorgan; Parish, Mullaghbrack; District Council, Armagh; Grid ref. H 948 447.
References: Listed B1 (15/13/34). Taylor and Skinner, 'Roads', 1778; VAL 1B/213, p 132, and VAL 12B/10/24A-D, in PRONI; Lewis, TD, 1837, II, p 2; J H Tait, OSM, 1838, Armagh, I, p 97; Bassett, 'Armagh', 1888, p 162; information from owner.

6 and 8 Russell Street, Armagh

186. So full and clear is the description given by the UAHS listers that, with their permission, I cannot do better than quote it in full: "c 1840. Three-bay, two-storey terrace, originally a group of three single-bay houses. Red brick in Flemish bond with ashlar quoins to corner; smooth render to ground floor. Original windows with glazing bars to first and second floors". "The ground floor of no. 6 is superbly embellished by an ornate entablature consisting of the original door with delicate Gothick fanlight and ground floor window with marginal glazing bars set between clustered columns with foliage capitals supporting cornice and nameboard, surmounted by extravagantly carved leaves and flowers, inside a rococo shaped frame. In the centre is a block bracket, probably to take a bust or vase. This unique little structure, with two columns missing and a third crudely replaced, just survives and the building (once a post office) awaits restoration". And: "No. 8 has a rectangular fanlight with marginal glazing and original door. The shop window and fascia have recently received minimal restoration - more is needed. The side elevation with three gable windows and a small attic window results from the step-back in the frontage line" (1992).

Happily, since the foregoing descriptions were written, this splendid little group has been very well restored, as solicitor's offices, and four apartments (known as "Porter's Lodge", as No 8 seems to have been called in the past) in the course of 1996-8, under the supervision of Ian Donaldson, architect. It now looks exceedingly well, with its curlicues ('Victorian baroque'?) painted in a very appropriate shade of ice-cream pink In 1860, Robert Birch, the town's postmaster, transferred his office into No 6. In 1882, his successor John Williams moved the Post Office to the opposite side of the street: the building subsequently became the solicitor's offices of Monroe and Anderson, whose successor, having acquired both practice and premises, carries on the business under his own name. It contains many pleasing mementos of 19th-century postal, or legal, practice, and has been restored with great taste and skill. Next door, in No 8, lived for many years the late Mr T G F Paterson, that notable local historian, antiquarian, and first curator of the Armagh County Museum: who averred that he shared the premises with the ghost of an 18th-century (or earlier) archbishop. A blue plaque in memory of Mr Paterson, if not of his companion, would not come amiss.

Photograph: Michael O'Connell.
Situation: 6 and 8, Russell Street, Armagh; td, Parkmore; Parish, and District Council, Armagh; Grid ref. H 876 453.
References: Listed B (15/17/32A & B); in conservation area. T G F Paterson, Armachiana, IV, p 29, in Armagh County Musueum; O'Neill, 'Armagh Post Office', [1984], pp 6 - 9; 'Buildings of Armagh', UAHS, 1992, p 181; 'Belfast Telegraph', 15/2/1997.

Shops and former Hotel, Bessbrook

187. Bessbrook acquired, and deserved, a degree of fame for its philanthropic layout and arrangements; although, sadly, its charms have much deteriorated in recent years, as a result partly of helicopters and partly of consequential double-glazing with plastic windows. "The carefully planned lay-out of the open spaces and the impressive scale of the community buildings were sufficient to rank the village with such famous English examples as Saltaire, Bourneville and Port Sunlight" (MacNeice). However, "As a Quaker," (Richardson) "was inspired by William Penn's scheme for the colony of Pennsylvania and was less concerned with village planning than with the ideals of the temperance movement" (Conservation area booklet). "The shops at the corner of Charlemont Square terminated in a temperance hotel where teachers, clerks and travellers could stay". But there was to be no public-house, pawnshop, or policeman in this Quaker-owned mill village: John Grubb Richardson, and his son James Nicholson Richardson (distant cousins of mine several times removed: my maternal grandmother was a Quaker Richardson from Lambeg) saw to that. The shops comprised General Store, Butcher's Shop, and Dairy, all owned by the Bessbrook Spinning Company.

As James N Richardson (see also 139) expressed it in his parody of Macaulay's Lays of Ancient Rome, The Quakri at Lurgan, of 1902:

> "From far-famed model Bessbrook,
> Where Bacchus is unknown,
> Where lack of public-houses
> Hath starved him of his throne
> (Police, pawn-shop nor publican
> Come nigh this realm of ease,
> The envious call it in their wrath
> "The City of Three P's")".

These tall stone buildings, old-fashioned for their date with their Regency glazing-bars, lend considerable charm to the heart of Bessbrook. Charlemont Square was the original heart of the planned village (see 174 and 182). As MacNeice remarks, "It is not clear if an architect was employed to design this layout or the house plans, but John Hardy, a civil engineer, was employed as the company architect in 1881, though he may have been associated with the construction of the larger mill buildings. The building work on the houses was carried out by masons and joiners employed by the firm and stone was obtained from the quarries nearby". Built of local granite, with various colours of brick for dressings, two-and-a-half-storey with dormers, two of the frilly dormer barge-boards still surviving; delightful segmental-headed shop windows; chamfered corner; and clock: all facing onto the grassy central square.

The group was built between 1862 and 1866. No 1 (now the Post Office) was perhaps more of a lodging-house than a hotel (though it was labelled "Hotel" in the Valuation book): let in 1866 to James Weir, and valued at the large sum of £25. No 2 was let to John Wilson, and valued at £15. No 3 was let to Michael Boyle, and valued at £12; the same value was placed on No 4, let to James Henderson; but No 5, then and now apparently not a shop but a rather grand private house, was valued at £20 and let to Thomas Sinton.

This particular terrace is now in pretty good shape, though unfortunately the coherence of both Charlemont Square and College Square has been largely lost by regrettable and inconsistent alterations, especially to the windows. No 16 College Square West, now derelict and apparently unoccupied, seems to be the only two-storey private house in either square to retain its original glazing pattern: a pity, given so large a grouping of such uncommon quality, and even of international importance.

Photograph: Michael O'Connell.

Situation: 1 - 5, Charlemont Square East, Bessbrook; td, Cloughareevan; Parish, Camlough; District Council, Newry & Mourne; Grid ref. J 046 285.

References: Listed B (16/22/1A-E); in conservation area. VAL 12B/15/6A-C in PRONI; Richardson, 'Quakri', 1899, p 16; Fell Smith, 'James N. Richardson of Bessbrook', 1925, passim; D A MacNeice, Factory workers' housing, QUB thesis, 1981, pp 42, 69, 86; conservation area booklet, 1983, passim.

42 - 46 High Street, Lurgan

188. A pair of stout three-storey town houses, one of stone and one of brick, unified not only by their black and grey paintwork but also by a horizontal band of ornate rusticated stucco, with eight three-dimensional heads: a lion's over the coach arch (illustrated on page 288); perhaps Britannia; a man with a flowing beard and a look of Lytton Strachey (perhaps St Patrick); Shakespeare; perhaps Homer; perhaps Queen Boadicea; a mustachio'ed man in a helmet (perhaps King Arthur?); and the youthful Queen Victoria; which at any rate proves that the figures cannot have been applied to the façade before, at earliest, 1837.

"John Ross of High Street - prominent in the linen trade at the turn of the century ... were world famous business folks, and the ornate array of sculptured heads which

adorn the facade of the High Street premises is a lasting memorial to their good taste" (Tallon). In 1854, John Ross appears in the street directory as "Linen and cotton yarn and grain merchant, in Main Street"; in 1863 he has two entries, both in High Street, as "Cambric and cambric handkerchief manufacturer" and as "linen yarn merchant"; for the rest of the century, the firm appears as "hemstitch factory, High Street". In the Valuation books, the left-hand house was described in 1862 as "a strong blackstone house". In 1896, the name of John Ross is struck out, and the names of Thomas Ross and W R Ross substituted.

In 1971, Oram described this as "a splendid blackstone three-storey block of c. 1810, 44" (now 46) "perhaps later

... and with excellent crisp stucco mouldings upstairs. The ground floor stuccoed ... at some later date, perhaps c. 1850"; classified A; and illustrated. Gordon Wheeler suggests that, as Ross moved in at some time between 1854 and 1863, he may have unified the buildings with his stucco ground floor, in the course of adapting it for shop and factory purposes. In 1981, the block was listed. But unhappily a large car-bomb on 4 March 1992 deprived these houses of their four stout chimney-stacks, their original window-sashes, and most of their doors. Now in multiple occupation, defaced by regrettable (if no doubt necessary) grilles, doors and security shutters, as well as some unsuitable signs. The group well deserves a thorough overhaul.

Photographs: Michael O'Connell.
Situation: 42, 44, 46, High Street, Lurgan; td, Lurgan; Parish, Shankill; District Council, Craigavon; Grid ref. J 845 582.
References: Listed B (14/24/27). OS maps, 1835, 1859; VAL 2B/2/20D, pp 100, 102, in PRONI; Belfast and Ulster street directories; Oram, 'Craigavon', UAHS, 1971, Pt I, p 9; Tallon, 'Fireside gatherings', 1988, p 59.

Drumalane Mill, Newry

189. A very large, imposing, Victorian spinning mill, in excellent condition and almost entirely unaltered, except for the removal of all the machinery, and some later additions. The mill-owner's home, Drumalane House (146), of around the same date, is just next door, though not in the same townland. The mill was conveniently accessible by road, rail, tram and canal: it now looks out over the vast car-park at the back of Sainsbury's new store.

Bassett, in 1886, who seems to have thought it to be in county Down, gave a very thorough description: "It is situated in the Clanrye Valley, near the Canal, river and railway, and although inferior in size to the mills at Bessbrook, is fully equal to them in perfection of outline and structural solidity. Indeed there is good reason to believe that Bessbrook was the model from which the builder took his plans. At the time of the American War the popular impression in Ulster was that the high road to fortune lay through the portals of every mill devoted to the manufacture of flax. The late Mr. Hill Irvine, a well known and wealthy resident of Newry, became a convert to this idea, and without having had any previous experience, spent about £40,000 in the erection of the Dromalane Mill.

The walls are composed of native granite, the window dressings being of red brick. The stairs are also granite, and the building throughout is in almost every respect fire-proof. Mr. Irvine began to use the mill for flax spinning about the year 1866. The Dromalane Spinning Company, Limited, succeeded by purchase in 1876, but owing to a depression in trade, did not make it a profitable undertaking. In 1882, the Bessbrook Spinning Company bought it, and it has since been continued at its full capacity as a spinning mill. Certain important changes were made in the machinery. There are 7,200 spindles worked by steam, and employment is given to from 300 to 400 people. Bessbrook has telephonic communication with Dromalane, and is partly connected with it by means of the electric tramway, the principal owners of which are the Bessbrook Spinning Company. The yarns spun at Dromalane are all sent to Bessbrook ... Through all the periods of depression in the linen trade this Company has maintained the even tenor of its way, demonstrating by kindly practical methods that a large population of working people, representing nearly every religion known in Ireland, may live" (eheu fugaces!) " in peace and comfort

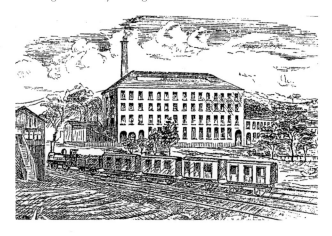

without the expenditure of a penny for police protection."

It was designed by Mr Hill Irvine's cousin, William Mitchel. In 1867, it was valued at £270, with a note in the Valuation book "the first floor of this mill is about a quarter occupied with machinery, second floor half ditto, third floor all ditto. Forty horse power steam engine". The valuation eventually reached £390. The main block is a massive four-storey fifteen-bay granite building, with an external iron fire escape, the floors supported by internal cast-iron columns. At its rear stand boiler-house and the very tall, tapering, octagonal brick chimney. The L-shaped office block has Georgian glazing. There are various other subsidiary buildings, for the most part quite congruous. Spinning ceased in the 1960s: the buildings are now part empty, part used by Timber and Tile Products Ltd.

Photograph: Michael O'Connell. Wood-engraving: from Bassett.
Situation: Off Drumalane Road, Newry; td, Lisdrumliske; Parish, Killevy; District Council, Newry & Mourne; Grid ref. J 085 255.
References: Listed B1/IA (16/29/16). VAL 12B/15/1A-G, in PRONI; Bassett, 'Down', 1886, p 87; notes by F W Hamond of 1992 in MBR.

Chimney, Darkley Mill, Keady

190. An extraordinary tall, tapering, octagon of brick, flared out gracefully at the top, held together by iron straps every few feet, towering above the main street of the mill-workers' village of Darkley (left): its effect accentuated by the fact that it stands quite high up on the hillside, not on the valley floor. This is a particularly fine example of its kind: these great mill chimneys, still not uncommon in Ulster, called for great skill and craftsmanship on the part of designer and bricklayers alike.

This one was part of the achievement of William Kirk, from Larne (for whose memorial in Keady, see 215). "There are 200 power looms and beetling works at different points on the Callan river, extending for six miles ... The extensive buildings at Darkley ... were erected by Mr William Kirk, in conjunction with his son, Mr William M Kirk, and are devoted to flax spinning and linen weaving. The mill contains 8,000 spindles, and the factory 200 power looms" (Bassett). Kirk began his career in the district in 1840, "using one small building", and no doubt relying exclusively on the water power of the Callan; it seems likely that the two chimneys on the site were erected during the boom in flax spinning of the 1860s, possibly to augment the existing water power by the use of steam engines, or perhaps to keep the cogwheels turning at times of low water in summer or ice in winter.

At the foot of the chimney, facing the street, a remarkably small brick-arched fire-place, no larger than that to be found in a parlour house; immediately to one side, a rectangular mill-dam and the layd that fed it; on the other side, a blocked up building with an incongruous notice declaring this an alcohol-free zone. It is not easy to visualise how the chimney functioned in its prime; but an unsigned article on Factory Chimneys in the 11th edition of the Encyclopaedia Britannica helps a bit: "Chimneys, besides removing the products of combustion, also serve to provide the fire with the air requisite for burning the fuel. The hot air in the shaft, being lighter than the cold air outside it, tends to rise, and as it does so air flows in at the bottom to take its place. An ascending current is thus established in the chimney, its velocity, other things being equal, varying as the square root of the height of the shaft above the grate ... In designing a chimney the dimensions ... have to be so proportioned to the amount of fuel to be burnt in the various furnaces connected with it ... Ordinary factory chimneys do not in general exceed 180 or 200 ft. in height ... In section they are round, octagonal or square. The circular form offers the least resistance to wind pressure, and ... requires less material to secure stability than the octagonal and still less than the square; on the other hand, there is more liability to cracking."

Photograph: Michael O'Connell. Lithograph: in private ownership.
Situation: In main street of Darkley village; td, Darkley; Parish, Armagh-breague ; District Council, Armagh; Grid ref. H 860 312.
References: Surprisingly, not listed. Lewis, TD, 1837, II, p 34; Bassett, 'Armagh', 1888, p 169; 'Encyclopaedia Britannica', 11th ed, VI, 1910, p 165; McCutcheon, 'Industrial archaeology', 1980, p 298, and pl 92.4.

Savings (now First Trust) Bank, Armagh

191. A handsome foursquare building on a peninsular site fronting Gaol Square, but in fact No 1, Victoria Street, with a subsidiary frontage to Barrack Hill. The building was designed by William Murray in 1837, and two years later the Savings Bank moved here from the Tontine Rooms in English Street. "It is two storeys in height and beautifully built of ashlar stone with deeply recessed blockwork to the ground floor. The building originally provided for a banking hall, offices and a manager's residence" (UAHS). The principal façade has an imposing tetrastyle Ionic portico, with the words "SAVINGS BANK" incised in the entablature; the same words, this time raised in a recessed panel, appear prominently in the parapet of the advancing central bay. The window above the porch has an elegant little triangular pediment, the windows at either side have only hood mouldings.

The Victoria Street elevation has four bays, with the street name incised in the stonework, and wreaths above the first-floor windows; and the words "SAVINGS BANK" once again in the parapet. The Barrack Hill frontage is similar to the entrance façade.

Thomas Bradshaw, in 1819, remarks that "a short time since, a Savings Bank was established, under the most respectable gentlemen in the neighbourhood". Bassett, in 1888, observes: "There is probably no place in Ireland of the size that has so many banking establishments." (Armagh) "has branches of the Bank of Ireland, Provincial, Ulster, Belfast, Northern and Hibernian banks, and one of the old-style institutions for savings (the Armagh Savings Bank), managed by Mr Thomas Smith. This was founded in 1818, chiefly to encourage small depositors, but large ones also use it. The limit is £200 for one depositor. There were 4,031 depositors in November 1887, and the amount of their deposits was £190,435. 4s. 11d." Now First Trust bank, as the public is informed by an unduly obtrusive notice-board which consorts ill with the admirable modern railings and with the classical façade.

Photograph: Michael O'Connell

Situation: 1, Victoria Street, Armagh; td, Corporation; Parish, and District Council, Armagh; Grid ref. H 881 452.

References: Listed B+ (15/17/42); in conservation area. Bradshaw, 'General directory', 1819, p 61; Stewart, 'RHA index of exhibitors', I, 1985, 1838/192; Bassett, 'Armagh', 1888, p 113; T G F Paterson, Armachiana, IV, p 99, in Armagh County Museum; 'Buildings of Armagh', UAHS, 1992, p 204.

Former Belfast Bank, Armagh

192. A remarkably strong and robust façade, "(1851); built for the Belfast Banking Company to designs by Charlees Lanyon" (UAHS). Apart from the building's appearance on the map of 1851, the evidence shows that the bank was open for business at this address by July, 1850, under the management of Thomas Kidd who until then had carried on business from his home in Upper English Street. I know of no evidence that this bank was designed by Lanyon, and the UAHS listers cite no authority for their attribution (Dixon is not so bold), but it seems reasonably likely. It now forms one element in St Patrick's Trian, a visitors' centre providing a home for many stuffed dummies, which cost nearly £4 million, and was opened by Jacques Delors of the European Economic Union. Armagh Council deserves great credit for rescuing this splendid building in 1990 on its abandonment as a bank; but, unfortunately, deserves almost equal discredit for keeping so distinguished a façade permanently disfigured by horrible hanging banners.

Dixon associates this style of building with the wealthy bankers of 15th and 16th century Italy: "The ornate stone front of the Belfast Bank at Armagh is an exceptionally vigorous example, with full-height rustication, lively sculpture, and heavy dominating cornice. The design might derive from Florence or Rome".

Unusually for Armagh, it is built of imported reddish sandstone. The heavily rusticated façade is divided into three bays, each incorporating a recessed round-headed arch: those at the sides with very tall windows; the central arch containing doorway, pediment, and in the tympanum an extraordinarily large and energetic carving of the arms of the City of Belfast (evidently appropriated, with or without leave, by the Belfast Bank), including, as supporters, wolf and sea-horse. One would have liked to know who carved these, as also the heads adorning the keystones above the windows.

The manager's house, of about 1800, stood in the concealed courtyard at the rear, reached through a fine stone archway to the right and connected to the bank by a tunnel; now containing restaurant, craft unit and crypt gallery, its formerly very handsome entrance shamefully spoiled.

Photograph: Michael O'Connell.
Situation: 40, English Street, Armagh.; td, Corporation; Parish, and District Council, Armagh; Grid ref. H 875 454.
References: Listed B+ (15/20/15); in conservation area. 'Armagh Guardian', 1/7/1850; J O'Hagan, map, 1851; Dixon, 'Introduction', 1975, p 61; 'Buildings of Armagh', UAHS, 1992, p 112.

Ulster Bank, Lurgan

193. An excellent stone banking-house designed by Vincent Craig, architect, of Belfast, not long before he was obliged to leave Belfast and live abroad for reasons of health. Opened for business on 23 July 1911. One of his last and, in my view, most accomplished works. According to the contemporary report in the Irish Builder, the lower front is of Aberdeen granite, the upper part Mount Charles stone: the former is grey, the latter slightly yellowish, like butterscotch.

This is a five-bay three-storey building, with an interesting central shallow five-light oriel. The stonework is elegant and ingenious; particularly so the jointing of the voussoirs over the coach-arch. The sundry modern ground-floor intrusions have been well-handled and are unobtrusive. All seems in excellent order. The building is taller than its neighbours, and in consequence its red-brick gable walls and chimneys, perhaps a little unfortunately, expose the fact that the handsome stonework is only skin-deep.

Photograph: Michael O'Connell.
Situation: 14-16, Market Street, Lurgan; td, Lurgan; Parish, Shankill; District Council, Craigavon; Grid ref. J 081 584.
References: Listed B (14/24/28). Plans, N54-58, in Ulster Bank premises department; IB, LIII, 1911, p 146.

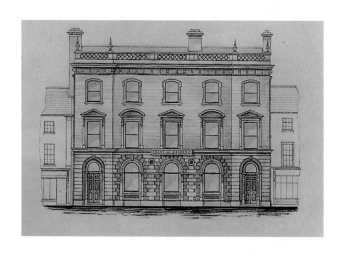

Bank of Ireland, Portadown

194. A massive five-bay three-storey granite building of 1868, by Sandham Symes of Dublin. The ground floor has three round-headed windows in the centre, flanked by a pair of tall round-headed doorways, each outlined by a cable moulding and topped by a Herculean keystone head. The first floor windows are rectangular but with rounded upper corners, enclosed in aedicules with alternate triangular and segmental pediments. The top floor has five segmental-headed windows with moulded architraves. Above, the parapet masking the roof contains, surprisingly, a balustrade of white-painted iron railings. The chimney stack and gable-end have been rendered.

The skill with which the granite carving is handled is considerable: especially in the two heads (one crowned, one uncrowned) and the strange squiggly vermiculation of the rusticated areas of the ground floor. The building was severely damaged by the large bomb of 22nd May 1993, but the damage has been made good externally, and the interior completely refashioned to designs by Robinson and Patterson, architects. As originally designed, this banking house contained accommodation both for manager and assistant manager.

Photograph: Michael O'Connell. Elevation drawing and plan: Sandham
   Symes, IAA.
Situation: High Street, Portadown; td, Corcrain; Parish, Drumcree;
   District Council, Craigavon; Grid ref. J 011 538.
References: Listed B (14/10/1). Oram, 'Craigavon', UAHS, 1971, pt I, p 4;
   'Ulster architect', March/April, 1997.

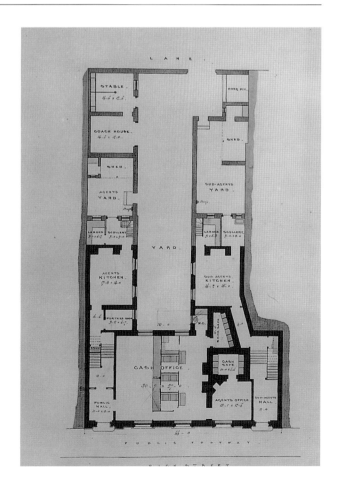

Cusher Bridge, Clare, Tandragee

195. The listers, rather dryly, describe this charming little bridge, whch carries a country road over the Cusher river, as "probably 17th century: the bridge comprises five equi-sized segmental arches in random rubble. The piers have angled cutwaters on both up and down sides which extend to form pedestrian refuges at parapet level. The carriage-way has a slight hump-back, and dog-leg approaches ... Good example of 17th century bridge design, and a strong landscape feature". Its antiquity is borne out by Samuel Lewis's comment: "the village is situated on the river Cusher, over which is an ancient stone bridge" (1837).

This, to me, is a delightful piece of vernacular engi-neering, with its complex variety of curves and angles, in a charming rustic setting. Lt G A Bennett of the Ordnance Survey does not seem to have shared my view: "Bridges over the Cusher river are 5 in number and 3 wooden bridges for the convenience of the proprietors of mills. None of these bridges deserve particular note".

Photographs: Michael O'Connell.
Situation: Between Harrybrook House and the entrance to the village of Clare; tds, Clare and Ballyshielbeg; Parish, Ballymore; District Council, Armagh; Grid ref. J 012 430.
References: Listed B+/IA (15/6/4). Bridge here shown on Herman Moll's map of Ireland, 1714; G A Bennett, OSM, 1835, Armagh, I, p 10; Lewis, TD, 1837, I, p 329; notes by F Hamond in MBR.

Carrickrovaddy (or Tuscan Pass) Bridge, Jerrettspass

196. The listers, quoting Hamond, say: "Single elliptical span in rubble Silurian masonry with dressed sandstone voussoirs and out-splayed parapets ending in rounded pillars. Towpath carried through West side of arch. Designed by John Brownrigg and built by John Chebsey, it is the only one of Brownrigg's bridges along the canal to survive unaltered." McCutcheon explains that John Brownrigg reported in October 1801 "giving details of the poor condition of the Newry Canal at that time"; and that "the inland section of the canal was thoroughly overhauled - one might almost say rebuilt - during the first decade of the 19th century".

Rodney Green says "Beyond the seventh lock, ... built with granite ashlar, is Jerrettspass bridge which was designed by Brownrigg in 1802 to take the place of an earlier bridge broken down by the military in 1798. It is a graceful little bridge, built of rubble masonry with cut-stone voussoirs and coping to the parapet walls which curve outwards to terminate in three-quarter pillars. There were dates on the key blocks of the arch, but that on the S. side is now" (1963) "indecipherable. On the N. side the date

1808 clearly appears as well as a name which is now too faint to be read. The bridge has a towpath 5 ft. 9 in. wide. John Chebsey signed a contract for the building of Tuscan Pass bridge, as it was then known, in June 1804". Gould says that Brownrigg was "apparently of Scots origin. He is believed to have built (or rebuilt) several bridges but only that at Jerrettspass is definitely ascribed to him (1808). It is very unusual in the way in which the parapet rises straight from a raised round column at each end to a point in the centre. Unusual, that is, for Ireland ... The design is, however, quite common in parts of Scotland".

An exceptional and attractive bridge: the council has restored the towpath from this point to Newry.

Photograph: Michael O'Connell.
Situation: The bridge carries the Carrickrovaddy Road over the Newry Canal; td, Carrickrovaddy; Parish, Jerretspass; District Council, Newry & Mourne; Grid ref. J 064 332.
References: Listed B1/IA (16/21/84). Datestone; Green, 'Industrial archaeology', 1963, p 69 and pl 26; McCutcheon, 'Industrial archaeology', 1980, pp 76, 77 and pl 13,6. M Gould, in 'Ulster architect', April/May 1997, p 6.

Ummeracam Bridge, Cullyhanna

river with a smaller stream. The listers consider it to be mid-19th century since it makes its first appearance on the Ordnance Survey map of 1860, but it looks as if it might be older. They solemnly describe it as "Two skewed semicircular spans over the Ummeracam River with asymmetric canted cutwater. Rubble limestone with ashlar dressings": and add the dry comment, "The valuable feature and the real interest of this bridge is the way the difficulties of a skewed span have been so cleverly resolved using the simplest of materials and techniques". A more romantically-minded viewer, such as me, might think that the value and interest of this bridge resided in the aesthetic beauty and elegance of its complex curves.

Photograph: Michael O'Connell.
Situation: Td, Dorsy; Parish, Cullyhanna; District Council, Newry & Mourne; Grid ref. H 953 201.
References: Listed B2 (16/19/16); OS map, 1860.

197. A delightful little twisty two-arch stone road-bridge, with cutwater, just at the confluence of the Ummeracam

Craigmore Railway Viaduct and

198, 199. Of the former, Huband Smith, writing just after its opening, says "it [the railway from Drogheda] traverses the great Craigmore Viaduct, a prodigious work, carrying the railway across a deep valley. This viaduct was completed about twelve months ago and on the 13th May, 1852, the first locomotive engine passed over it. The extreme length of the work, from end to end, is 1,400 feet; its greatest height over the surface of the ground is 150 ft.; and the width of the roadway at top 28 ft. It consists of 18 semi-circular arches, each 60 ft. span, resting on piers 7 ft. 6 ins. thick at the level from which the arches spring. The structure is composed entirely of a superior description of granite, in which the surrounding country abounds. The cost of the entire works was about £50,000. Several of the piers and abutments were excavated to a depth of 40 ft. below the surface, in order to commence the work on the solid rock upon which the whole viaduct is built. There were about 120,000 tons of stone used in the construction of the work, which was completed in two years from its commencement."

Dr McCutcheon remarks: "The great viaduct in Craigmore-Mullaghglass ... is one of the most impressive railway structures in Ireland ... It is a graceful curved viaduct of eighteen arches, ... built by William Dargan for the Dublin & Belfast Junction Railway Company to a design by their engineer, Sir John Macneill, in 1851-2, at a cost of about £50,000". "There is nothing in Ireland to be compared to

the Egyptian Arch, Bessbrook

it for size" The Builder commented on its completion.

Half a mile away "the railway crosses the Newry-Camlough road on the striking and unusual 'Egyptian Arch' ... which was also the result of collaboration between Macneill and Dargan" and was built in 1851: "the arch reflects the growing popularity of the Egyptian idiom in public architecture of the day. In Ireland the only other railway structure of note built in this style was the Broadstone terminus" in Dublin, designed by J S Mulvany (McCutcheon). Unfortunately, the original parapets have been altered, and recurrent bomb damage has not helped.

The completion of the final railway link between Drogheda and Portadown was no mean feat, especially as the line from Dublin to Drogheda had been laid to a gauge of 5 feet 2 inches, whilst that from Belfast to Portadown had been laid to the earlier recommended gauge of 6 feet 2 inches. The Ulster Railway Company had to give way, and re-lay its track in 1847 at a cost of almost £20,000.

Photographs: Viaduct, Michael O'Connell; Egyptian Arch, postcard before its mutilation, Local Studies Library, Armagh; Michael O'Connell.

Location: Viaduct, Derrybeg/Craigmore/Mullaghglass tds; Parish, Camlough; District Council, Newry & Mourne; Grid refs. Viaduct J 06 28, Arch J 070 275.

References: Viaduct, listed A (16/24/4); Arch, listed B+/IA (16/23/1). 'Builder', VIII, 1850, p 424, and X, 1852, p 599; Smith, 'Belfast and its environs', 1853, pp 10, 11; W A McCutcheon, in UJA, 3rd series, XXVII, 1964, p 155, and pls xxivA and B; McCutcheon, 'Industrial Archaeology', 1980, pp 106, 109, 160, 192,193, and pl 27.

Tassagh Railway Viaduct, Keady

200. The branch line from Armagh to Castleblayney was constructed between 1903 and 1910 by the euphoniously named "Castleblayney, Keady and Armagh Railway Company", with the purpose of "keeping the ambitious Midland Great Western out of the zealously guarded territory" of the Great Northern Railway. The engineer was Sir Benjamin Baker. The original contractor was Robert Worthington, but he was superseded in 1908 by George Mills. The section from Armagh to Keady was opened on 31 May 1909, and remained open until 1957; but the Keady-Castleblayney section was forced to close in 1923, making it "one of the shortest-lived railways in Ireland" (Morton). This viaduct over the valley of the Callan River is extraordinarily impressive.

McCutcheon remarks that "the railway architecture and civil engineering along this line are worthy of attention because of its late date of construction ... reflected in the use of building materials in vogue at that time and, less obviously, in the overall appearance of the buildings and structures ... at Tassagh ... the large, 11-arch viaduct has concrete piers, with brick facings on each of the arches, and brick vaulting ... Altogether the Tassagh viaduct is a lighter structure than the two great early masonry viaducts in the province - at Craigmore, near Newry"

(198) "and at Randalstown - and though the use of stone, brick and concrete has been quite skilful, the overall result is less solid. As the railway here finally closed down to goods traffic in 1957 and the general economic justification for the line was very doubtful, with the withdrawal of regular passenger services as early as 1932, the durability of the structure was not really put to the test". McKee says it stands more than 70 feet high, and some 570 feet long, each arch having a span of 45 feet: "in all an estimated 485,000 bricks were used in the construction of the arches".

Today it stands, gaunt and imposing, blocked off at each end, and absolutely useless: as impressive and pointless a piece of engineering as the Pyramids or the Pont du Gard, but aesthetically nearly as exciting.

Photograph: Michael O'Connell (see also frontispiece and colour-plate XV).

Situation: Glen Road, Keady; tds, Tassagh and Ballynagalliagh; Parish, Keady; District Council, Armagh; Grid ref. H 861 383.

References: Listed B /IA, (15/14/1). McCutcheon, 'Industrial archaeology', 1980, p 162, and pl 22; Pierce and Coey, 'Taken for granted', 1984, p 176; Morton, 'Railways in Ulster', 1989, pp 24-26; McKee, 'Railways', 1990; Allison, 'Way we were', 1993, p 76.

The Trough Aqueduct, Terryhoogan, Scarva

201. A fine ten-arch rubblestone bridge, known as the Trough, carrying a canal feeder leading water from the Cusher River into the Newry Navigation. Lieutenant Bennett of the Ordnance Survey says, of the townland of Terryhoogan, "The Newry Canal runs to the east end of it, on which are 2 locks and a wooden bridge. The canal feeder already mentioned in Cargans runs through this townland and enters the canal at the Wash bridge". But his notes for Cargans, alas, seem to have gone missing.

The listers suggest that this imposing structure predates the opening of the canal in 1742; but McCutcheon, in the caption to his photograph, prefers the view that it was built in the early 19th century to augment the flow through a feeder watercourse running three and three-quarter miles cross country into the summit level of the canal.

Green notes John Brownrigg's report, in 1801, on "a rotted wooden trough to carry the feeder from the Cusher river"; and "There is an aqueduct of ten arches on this feeder, known as the Trough and built by Brownrigg to replace a wooden structure which had fallen into decay" before 1811.

The arches carry the water across a valley, but only a very minor rivulet runs below.

Photograph: Michael O'Connell.
Situation: Tds, Terryhoogan and Cargans; Parish, Ballymore; District Council, Armagh; Grid ref. J 053 446.
References: Listed B+/IA (15/5/5); G A Bennett, OSM, 1835, Armagh, I, p 18; Green, 'Industrial archaeology', 1963, pp 66, 69, and pl 26; McCutcheon, 'Industrial archaeology', 1980, p 84, and pl 13.2.

Moneypenny's Lock, Brackagh, Portadown

202. An astonishing group of great charm, tucked away in near-invisibility. Turn off the Horseshoe Lane down a smaller lane at the gable-end of a farmhouse; carefully closing the gates, traverse the planked level-crossing over the main Belfast to Dublin railway line; carry on till the lane rises to cross the river by the first of several stone bridges; turn left along the towpath between the river and the old Newry Canal and then, tucked away between wooded banks, across another (iron) bridge you will find first the stone-faced lock (a pity the gates are gone) and then the charming little white-washed two-storey lock-house,

the older part with its gable facing the canal and narrow Georgian-glazed windows above and below, next door the early 19th-century cottage, modest enough in truth, with brown-painted trim, porch and bargeboards. The two-storey granite bothy, standing a few yards away, contained a warehouse, stabling for eight canal horses, and lodgings for the lightermen. The cottage is framed on one side by a very large old Irish yew tree, on the other by a somewhat younger weeping willow.

This lock is shown as 'Truman's' on Walter Harris's map of 1743; by 1800, known as Freeman's Lock after the

family which lived in Brackagh House nearby; Stephen Moneypenny was at that time the lock-keeper and "his family continued as lock-keepers through several generations until the canal was abandoned as a waterway".

McCutcheon describes the Newry Navigation as "the first true summit-level canal in the British Isles, antedating both the Sankey Cut at St Helen's and the Bridge-water Canal at Manchester" ... "a considerable feat of engineering". This humble group of rustic buildings has surprising connections with some of the great names of architecture: Sir Edward Lovett Pearce, appointed Surveyor-General in 1730 with responsibility for canal building, had as assistant the architect Richard Castles, who was in sole charge of the Newry Canal between 1733 and 1736. An authority on continental canals, he was originally a specialist in navigation works, "probably built the first stone lock chamber in Ireland", and the predecessor of this may well have been one of his. The work took from 1731 until 1742; the intention of the Irish Parliament was to supply "means by which coal from east Tyrone could be speedily and cheaply transported to Dublin". It was to be transshipped at Newry, having made its way through the orchards of county Armagh in horse-drawn barges.

The original lock was "pulled down and completely removed and taken away" in 1804: on 8 June of that year John Chebsey of Newry, architect, contracted for the complete rebuilding (and enlargement to 62 feet by 14 feet 6 inches) of this, and other works, for the considerable sum of £4,150. 16. 0, all to be completed by 1st December 1804. The contract contains extremely detailed specifications for the structure, materials and detailing to be employed; but unfortunately nothing about the buildings which, according to McCutcheon, are of about the same date. Green says: "The fourteenth and last lock of the canal is built of granite ashlar with a stone sill and floor as specified in Chebsey's contract of 1804 ... A bridge of Brownrigg's typical design with an iron span is built across the N. end of the lock. On the S. side of the E. abutment

of the bridge is an oval stone plaque inscribed 'John Brownrigg / Esqr. / Engineer / 1805'".

This delightful little group was bought by the National Trust from Mr W C Moneypenny in 1982, restored, and confided to the care of Craigavon Council, the exhibits displayed there contributed by the Craigavon Historical Society. It is open on summer weekend afternoons: but worth a voyage of discovery at any time.

Photographs: Michael O'Connell (see also colour-plate XVI).
Situation: 30, Horseshoe Lane, Brackagh, Portadown; td Brackagh; Parish, Kilmore; District Council, Craigavon; Grid ref. J 033 531.
References: Listed B1 (14/2/13). Contract book, 1801-1805, OPW 1/5/7/1, in National Archives, Dublin; Green, 'Industrial archaeology', 1963, p 70; McCutcheon, 'Industrial archaeology', 1980, pp 53, 54, 84; A Wilson, in 'Craigavon Historical Society review', VI, 1988-9, p 4; Pierce and Coey, 'Taken for granted', 1984, pp 68, 69, with good colour photo; file in MBR; information from Philip B Wilson.

Victoria Lock, Fathom, Newry

203. Often referred to as "Victoria Locks": however, although there are two lock-gates, there is only one lock, 220 feet long and 50 feet wide. This impressive structure was built in the 1840s by William Dargan under the direction of Sir John Rennie. Rodney Green gives a very detailed account of it: "With the exception of the iron-sheeted outer gates installed in the nineteen-thirties, Victoria Lock ... has changed little in appearance since it was completed to Sir John Rennie's design. The ashlar masonry of the lock is of Carlingford limestone except for the quoins of the gate recesses which are of Mourne granite. The masonry is V-jointed and the seaward side of the lock has a bold rounded profile ... the intention was to have three pairs of gates so as to economise with water. The original gates had English oak frames and were planked with Baltic timber."

And, as to its construction: "work began with blasting and dredging at Narrow Water in 1830. The channel was deepened 3-4 ft., upstream as far as Squire's Point and all the way down to Warrenpoint. Rubble guide walls were built of a total length of one and a quarter miles. This work was done at a cost of £48,000 and continued for nearly twelve years. Work on the extension of the canal did not begin until 1842, again a prolonged task which was not finished until 1850 ... The contract for the work was for £40,000, and it was to have been completed by 1846, but unexpected difficulties were encountered with making the embankmemt which rested on slob and apparently sank as much as 30 ft. in places. All was at last completed in April 1850, and twenty-one vessels, including three steamers each of over 500 tons, sailed up the canal to Newry. The appropriate names of Victoria Lock and Albert Basin were given to the new works. No less than £170,000 had been spent" ... Rennie " was proud to claim that this was 'the largest canal in Great Britain, or in any other country, with the exception of the great canal from Amsterdam to the Helder'."

McCutcheon remarks, of Ulster's canals in general, "Only the Lagan and Newry Navigation enjoyed any degree of commercial success and even with the latter prosperity was due largely to the success of the ship canal, more especially after its extension to Upper Fathom, near Narrow Water, and the erection of the great Victoria Lock." Extensive (and expensive) improvement works were carried between 1931 and 1935; but the last commercial traffic passed through the lock in 1936. It has been disused since 1974, but was well tidied up by the District Council in 1989, and specially reopened for a flotilla of tall ships in 1999. It is still much appreciated by fishermen and picnickers, with its fine squared-granite walls, bollards both granite and cast-iron, chains, wheels and other paraphernalia of a ship canal. But it would be useful to have an explanatory notice-board showing how the various, rather puzzling, mechanisms actually work.

Photograph: Michael O'Connell.
Situation: Td, Fathom (Upper); Parish, Killevy; District Council, Newry & Mourne; Grid ref. J 109 207.
References: Apparently not listed: why ever not? Green, 'Industrial archaeology', 1963, pp 67, 68, and pl 23; McCutcheon, 'Industrial archaeology', 1980, p 76, and pl 14.6.

CHAPTER EIGHT

FOLLIES, MONUMENTS
AND MEMORIALS

Perhaps surprisingly, County Armagh seems to be a more serious and sober place than the canny Scottish County Antrim. It is not rich in follies or eccentricities; certainly, it has nothing to rival the bizarre surrealism of the Carey monuments in and around Toome.[1] And I have not been able to find much else with which to adorn this concluding chapter, apart from a brace of 18th-century obelisks (208, 209), a brace of 18th-century meridian marks (207), a brace of 18th-century gateways (210, 211), and a miscellany of odds and ends. But it should be remarked that many churches around the county contain funerary memorials, and sculpture, of interest and importance: the best examples being in Mullaghbrack church (34) and Armagh Church of Ireland Cathedral (39).

References: 1. Brett, 'Buildings of County Antrim', UAHS, 1996, pp 293-295.

Roubiliac's statue of Sir Thomas Molyneux in St Patrick's (C of I) Cathedral, Armagh (39). Photograph: MBR

Cockhill Windmill, Tartaraghan

204. Classified as an example of industrial archaeology, but since it lacks machinery, sails and rudder, it now (as altered) seems to me to count rather as an ornamental eye-catcher. Its name derives from an inn named "The Cock" which stood here on the highest hill-top in the parish, some 168 feet above sea-level. Its history is exceptionally well documented, thanks to the researches of Canon Fleming and Fred Hamond.

It was evidently built by a Mr Edward Hoope between 1706, when he acquired the site, and 1723, when he mentions the mill in his will. In 1749, Thomas Hoope leased it to George Hutchinson. In June 1778, John Wesley preached "at the bottom of the garden" at Cockhill; "the table was placed under a tree, and most of the people sat on the grass before it". In 1793, the Rev. W Hutchinson leased it to Joseph Atkinson, who a month later sold on to Alexander McKittrick the "wind mill, horse mill, malt kiln, dwelling house, and miller's house" at Cockhill. Then, clearly, a very flourishing establishment, it seems to have deteriorated thereafter; in 1837 Thomas Atkinson leased it to Thomas McClelland, smith and carpenter, on

condition that he would repair it and have it finished by 1st September 1838; which however he failed to do. In 1910, all the working parts were removed, a flat roof was substituted for the former conical cap, and a crenellated parapet built around the flat roof. Since the rubblestone walls have only a slight batter, the resulting near-vertical cylinder really does look like a fortification. Despite this, Hamond considers that all the evidence, including the small window-openings, favours an early date, rather than a rebuilding. Standing nearly forty feet high on its prominent hill-top, it is well-placed both to catch the passing breeze, and to catch the passer-by's eye; but, since apple trees have been planted all around it, not easy to photograph.

Photograph: Michael O'Connell.
Situation: Off Drumanphy Road; td, Drumanphy; Parish, Tartaraghan; District Council, Armagh; Grid ref. H 943 564.
References: Listed B1/ IA (15/2/39). VAL 1B/233A, VAL 2B/2/21A, VAL 12B/10/2A-E, D 604, all in PRONI; C Bailey, OSM, 1835, Armagh, I, p 120; W E C Fleming, in 'Craigavon Historical Society review', VI, 1988-9, p 7; Reilly, 'Loughgall', 1995, p 53; Fred Hamond, notes in MBR.

Brownlow Vault, Shankill Burial Ground, Lurgan

205. A most curious exercise in solid geometry, apparently dating (in its present form) from about 1740; now largely covered in rendering or Roman cement, but originally perhaps all of ashlar. "This vault was part of the original church erected in Lurgan by the Brownlows after they acquired the land in 1609 and when it had ceased to be used as a church; on the building of the present church, it was converted into the vault" … "The last burial was that of Lady Jane McNeill who was the second wife of the first Lord Lurgan" (Tallon); she died in 1878.

A carved stone flambeau stands, slightly askew, on top of a sizeable rendered cone; on top of a cut-stone entablature; surmounting a rendered cube, disfigured by the graffiti of many years, its plain walls pierced only by arrow-slit-like ventilators at back and sides, stout (padlocked) door, and two inset plaques above the door. The vault stands on a hummock near the centre of the attractive old graveyard, amidst mature trees, many of them yews; now, unhappily, subject to recurrent bouts of vandalism.

The principal inscription proclaims that "The remains of the family of Brownlow (not ignoble from its foundation) rest here. Elizabeth (of the most noble family of Abercorn) the illustrious widow of William, who died in 1737, took care to build this tomb as a monument of her affection. He did not require the honour of a tomb, who by his own design, and almost at his own expense, raised a grand temple dedicated to Christ, and was constantly present at public worship not as a guest of the Church, but as an inhabitant of the town …" and so forth. The subsidiary inscription records the renovation of the monument in 1859 by the fourth Lord Lurgan.

Photograph: Michael O'Connell.
Situation: Shankill Street, Lurgan; td, and Parish, Shankill; District Council, Craigavon; Grid ref. J 075 587.
References: Listed B (14/21/6). Oram, 'Craigavon', UAHS, 1971, pt II, p 8; Tallon, 'Fireside gleanings', 1988, p 156; correspondence in MBR, of 11 September 1986 and 26 August 1990.

Cross Pillar, Portnelligan, Middletown

206. The land at Portnelligan, near Middletown, was leased in 1731 by Robert Maxwell of Fellows Hall (74) to Richard Cross. Local tradition has it that this curious little monument commemorates the departure for the American colonies of a military member of the family. This may have been Lt Richard Cross of the 21st Regiment of Dragoons, who made his will in December 1796, "as being destined for foreign service abroad", leaving his half-share of Portnelligan to his brother Alexander, £10 a year to his brother John, £15 for the poor of Tynan, and his large violoncello to Mr Thomas Greir of the city of Armagh. Unhappily, the will was proved in April 1799; in the Canterbury Prerogative Court, so he must have died or been killed in the course of the Napoleonic wars.

To the east of the driveway to Portnelligan House (100),

some 100 yards short of it, stands this peculiar dressed limestone structure six feet high, consisting of a podium on a stepped plinth, with a shield on its north face bearing three heraldic flowers; a cornice block; and a block inscribed with the date "1774". Above this, an octagonal block, then an octagonal finial with a sort of vegetable top, conceivably a sort of three-dimensional fleur-de-lys. All most bizarre: and looking to be, in its present form, much later than 1774.

Photograph: Michael O'Connell.
Situation: In grounds of Portnelligan House, near Doogary Lough; td, Portnelligan; Parish, Tynan; District Council, Armagh; Grid ref. H 784 383.
References: Not separately listed. Deeds and documents in custody of owners; very detailed notes by H Dixon in MBR.

Meridian Marks, Tullyard and Ballyheridan, Armagh

207. Markers, due north and south of Armagh Observatory (178), for checking the accuracy of astronomical instruments. The North Meridian Mark at Tullyard stands within a railed enclosure high on a hillside some two miles from the Observatory. The group, locally known from its peculiar silhouette as "the IN", comprises an extraordinary set of standing stones, reminiscent of a mini-Stonehenge (two pinnacles, linked by an arch, incorporating slots, apertures and oval mouldings); and an iron obelisk. According to Dr Butler of the Observatory, upon whose description I cannot hope to improve, built "to provide a stable reference point on the horizon with which the instruments could be checked for any disturbance ... an arch-shaped structure surmounted by two pinnacles. These served to provide the initial alignment of the transit instrument, with finer adjustment provided by a small copper disk with a triangular hole in its centre ... built in or around the early 1790s and were almost certainly the work of Francis Johnston ... Adjacent to the northern stone mark stands a cast iron obelisk in the Egyptian style. It is the work of Gardner's foundry at Armagh and was erected in 1864 when the Jones Mural Circle was converted by" (Romney) "Robinson to serve as a meridian circle ... The fine adjustment of the instrument relied on an adjustable pointer which is hidden in the apex of the obelisk, so that it was visible from the Observatory,

but not to the vandals that so frequently tried Robinson's patience. Both of the northern markers have been recently restored by the Department of the Environment."

"A second, southern meridian mark, which still survives, was built at Ballyheridan just beyond the southern extremity of the Palace Wall. It is a square neo-classical column and is probably also the work of Francis Johnston ... those at Armagh are the only ones known to survive in Ireland. In Great Britain about a dozen examples have been recorded, most of them associated with observatories in Scotland which have themselves, long since, disappeared." Very oddly shaped and rather inelegant, the south marker consists of an ashlar column on a tall plinth of rubblestone, at which the mice seem to have been nibbling; there is a carved star in each face; a lozenge at each corner; and an extraordinary open pediment with curving horns: all topped by "a moulded cap supporting an iron sighting marker".

Photograph of north marker: Michael O'Connell.
Situation: North marker, td Tullyard, Parish Grange, District Council Armagh, Grid ref. H 877 478; south marker, td Ballyheridan, Parish and District Council Armagh, Grid ref. H 879 427.
References: North marker, B+ (15/3/2); South marker B (15/15/2). J Butler, in 'Buildings of Armagh', UAHS, 1992, pp 24, 25.

Volunteers' Obelisk, Castle Dillon, Kilmore

Photograph: Robert French, NLI WL 5893.

Situation: Td, Turcarra; Parish, Kilmore; District Council, Armagh; Grid ref. H 909 494.

References: For some absurd reason, not listed, but, despite its date, an ancient monument in state care (8/31). Wilson, 'Post-chaise companion',

208. Sir Charles Coote, in 1804, says: "The late Sir Capel Molyneux erected an obelisk, just adjoining the demesne, to commemorate the services of the Volunteers of Ireland; being situated on very elevated ground, it is now a noted landmark. This pillar is sixty feet high, and the base twelve feet square. On a black slab in front is the following inscription:

'This Obelisk was erected by the Right Hon. Sir Capel Molyneux, of Castle Dillon, Bart, in the year 1782, to commemorate the glorious revolution, which took place in favour of the constitution of the Kingdom, under the auspices of the volunteers of Ireland.'"

And Sir William adds: "This same gentleman, whose patriotism was so well known, erected another obelisk, to commemorate the establishment of the Order of the Knights of St. Patrick in Ireland": but of this latter, I can find no trace. Lewis also attributes both obelisks to Sir Capel, but the Post-Chaise Companion of 1803 describes "a most cultivated and wooded landscape, to whose beauty two conspicuous obelisks contribute not a little. They were erected by the late Lord Rokeby and Sir Capel Molyneux: the first, to commemorate the Order of St Patrick; the latter, in honour of the Volunteers of Ireland. In fine, the park-gate and offices are in the first style of architecture and elegance, and a suitable mansion-house, in the room of the present old one, would render this seat one of the most agreeable in the kingdom". The house was, in fact, rebuilt in 1842 (72); the gate-lodges and pillars, somewhat surprisingly, have been attributed to Sir William Chambers and are now in a state of dilapidation.

The base of the obelisk stands at a height of 260 feet above sea level, on the summit of Cannon Hill. It is "a tapering shaft built of quite small pieces of local grey stone" on a tall base with plinth and capital courses. "A programme of crack-checking, pointing and replacement of deteriorating stone must be contemplated in the middle term" according to an unsigned and undated memorandum in the MBR. There seems little likelihood of this: the field in which it stands is ferociously plastered with "keep out" notices.

Howley, comparing the Castle Dillon obelisk to the Ross monument in Rostrevor, considers it "similarly engaging, more by virtue of its location than its design ... [it] stands with great prominence on a small hill and serves as a useful landmark for much of the surrounding countryside. This obelisk was erected by Sir Capel Molyneux, third baronet and MP, to commemorate the winning of independence by the Irish Parliament in 1782" - perhaps a slight over-simplification?

The Volunteers have gone; the Irish Parliament has gone; the Molyneux family of Armagh have gone; Castle Dillon is now a nursing home; the obelisk remains.

1803, p 64; Coote, 'Armagh', 1804, p 345; Lewis, TD, 1837, II, p 514; Leslie, 'Armagh clergy', 1911, p 307; Bence-Jones, 'Burke's guide', 1978, p 66; Howley, 'Follies', 1993, p 15; Dean, 'Gate lodges', UAHS, 1994, p 35; notes in MBR, AR 8/27.

Archbishop Robinson's Obelisk, Armagh

209. "In the primate's demesne a very elegant obelisk was erected by Lord Rokeby, in compliment to the late Duke of Northumberland, his Lordship's friend and patron, on which is inscribed a suitable inscription: this pillar is very ornamental, and cost above £1,000" (Coote).

"On Knox's Hill, in the demesne lands, south of the palace, his Grace erected, in the year 1783, a superb obelisk built with the same kind of elegant stone" (as the palace) "and 114 feet in height. On the pedestal, which is decorated with carved mouldings, are the King's arms, and those of the Duke of Northumberland, in basso relievo, which occupy two of its sides. The other two are covered with Latin inscriptions, in raised letters, indicating that the obelisk was erected by Richard Armagh, Baron Rokeby, in the year 1782, &c. Its object was to commemorate the friendship which subsisted betwixt the Primate and his patron the Duke of Northumberland. On the shaft are two shields of arms - one representing that of the see of Armagh, surmounted by the mitre, the other his Grace's family arms, with the baronial coronet - Motto - 'Non nobis solum sed toti mundo nati'" (Stuart).

Edward McParland and Mark Bence-Jones both say that the obelisk was by Francis Johnston. In an important letter of 1820, printed in full in the Irish Georgian Society Bulletin for 1963, Johnston expressly states that "In the early part of the year 1784 my Master Mr. Thomas Cooley ... died and I was in consequence appointed by the late Lord Primate Robinson, Architect to his buildings at Armagh, where I erected the present tower to the Cathedral in that city, completed the inside of the chapel attached to his Grace's palace, and an obelisk which stands on Knox's Hill in the demesne ..."

Sir Howard Colvin, however, attributes it to John Carr of York on the strength of an ink sketch drawn, upside down, on the reverse of the back fly-leaf of Carr's copy of Robert Morris's Select Architecture in Sir John Soane's Museum, and inscribed "design'd pr J.C. and built by the Ld primate of all Ireland 1782." The drawing gives measurements, apparently showing the overall height as 119 feet; and the proportions and elevations are approximately as executed, though showing a non-existent doorway in the (differently rusticated) plinth, and giving no indication of either the recessed panels containing lettering or the projecting panels bearing enwreathed armorials. The attribution to Carr is said to be corroborated by the initials JC carved on the monument, but I have not been able to find them. Although I know of no other instance at Armagh where Robinson employed an English rather than an Irish architect (Cooley, though English by birth, adopted Irish residence), the Archbishop originally came from (and also derived the title of his peerage from) Rokeby in the North Riding of Yorkshire, and before coming to Ireland had been a prebendary of York Minster, of which Carr carried out a survey between 1770 and 1773. It seems to me most probable that both attributions are right and that the design was furnished by Carr, but its

execution entrusted to Johnston, who interpreted Carr's designs with some freedom.

Bassett remarks of the obelisk "it is due to Dr. Robinson's memory to say that its erection was suggested as a means of honourable employment for the people of Armagh during a time of severe distress". Opinions seem to differ as to its height as built: Inglis says "it is 157 feet high, and of chaste proportions and decorations". The UAHS listers point out that "its base is set just below the horizon as perceived from the south face of the palace. The siting is axial on the palace, the clear geometry is in marked contrast with the conscious informality of the rest of the landscape" Now marooned in the middle of the city's golf course, and not readily accessible to members of the non-golfing public.

Photograph: Michael O'Connell. Drawing: John Carr, Sir John Soane's Museum, London.

Situation: In the middle of the County Armagh Golf Club course; access from Markethill Road; td, Parkmore (or Demesne); Parish, and District Council, Armagh; Grid ref. H 881 435.

References: Listed B+ (15/18/21); outside conservation area. Carr's drawing and legend, Sir John Soane's Museum, ref AL 39A, Vol 10; Coote, 'Armagh', 1804, p 323; Stuart, 'City of Armagh', 1819, p 447; Inglis, 'Ireland', II, 1835, p 356; Bassett, 'Armagh', 1888, p 91; IGS quarterly bulletin, VI, 1963, pp 1, 5, McParland, 'Francis Johnston', 1969, p 94; Bence-Jones, 'Burke's guide', 1978, p 12; 'Buildings of Armagh', UAHS, 1992, p 174; Colvin, 'Dictionary', 1995, p 226.

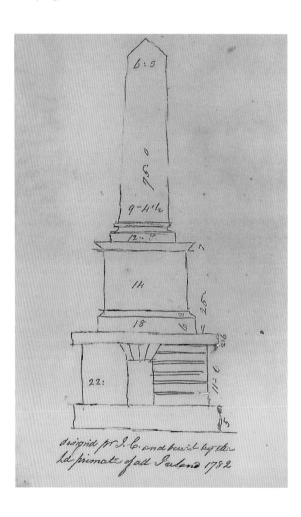

Archbishop's Gate Pillars, Cathedral Close, Armagh

210. Designed by Thomas Cooley, Dean says in 1771, the UAHS 1780; as the old Palace (80) was of 1770, the former seems more likely. In their present position they are misleadingly promising. Dean, who treats the piers as if they were honorary gate lodges, says: "The drawing which survives was executed almost in its entirety. The four grand piers were built from grey limestone quarried at the southern end of the demesne and carried two flanking timber wicket gates and double wrought iron carriage gates with spear tops". The UAHS listers say "two tall piers of blocked ashlar limestone embellished with Greek key pattern banding above which is a frieze with carved stone swags, heavy cornices and ball finials on stem pedestals. Two side gates and side piers join the high curved stone walls of the sweep in. The fine iron gates are probably nineteenth century or later. Originally sited on the Newry Road at the principal entrance to the Primate's Palace, the gates framed the building which had a most impressive approach with a curving drive. The present gateway to the Palace was then a service entrance to Dobbin Street Lane. The gates were removed when the R.U.C. barracks were built in 1963 and re-erected in Cathedral Close".

It would be hard to conceive of a greater architectural contrast between the grandeur of this entrance and the

ordinariness of the See House (94) to which they afford access. The modern concrete tubs and bollards are in the highest degree inappropriate.

Photograph: Michael O'Connell. Drawing: Thomas Cooley, IAA.

Situation: At entrance to See House, off Cathedral Close; td, Corporation; Parish, and District Council, Armagh; Grid ref. H 873 453.

References: Strangely, not listed, although in conservation area. Drawing in IAA; T G F Paterson, Armachiana, IV, p 47, in Armagh County Museum; 'Buildings of Armagh', UAHS, 1992, pp 67, 176; Dean, 'Gate lodges', UAHS, 1994, p 33.

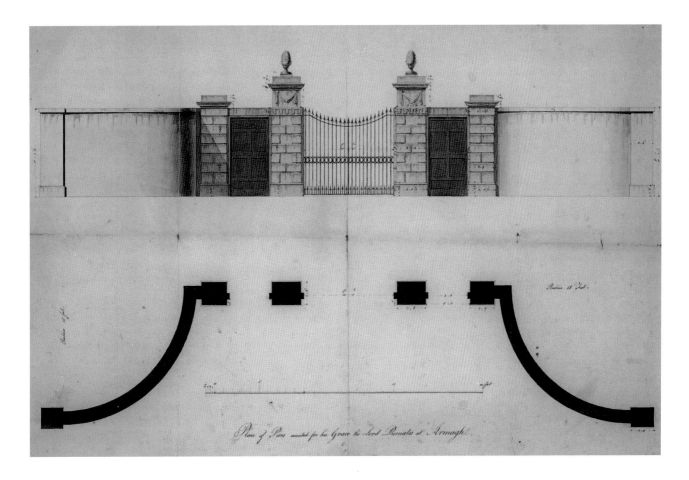

East Gate, Ulster White Linen Hall, Newry

211. A sophisticated classical archway of 1783, now standing in isolation in a small railed tarmac playground at the edge of a housing estate. "This disused barracks was originally built as a white linen hall for the town of Newry. The walled area encloses over six acres. On the W. side, fronting on the canal, is an impressive granite entrance arch. A spinning wheel and harp and crown are carved in relief on the piers. The cornice of the piers and of the pedimented top of the arch have Greek key decoration. The linen hall was built...to develop the direct export of linen from the north of Ireland without using the services of the Dublin factors. The building of the Belfast white linen hall rendered the Newry hall superfluous, and at any rate the bleachers preferred to trade direct with their customers in Britain" (E R R Green).

Thomas Bradshaw, in 1819, remarked "The present barrack was built by a company of gentlemen, originally for a white linen-hall. The design not having succeeded, the concern was offered to government for about one-third of what it had cost, which was about £14,000. The buildings are remarkably well adapted to the uses to which they are at present applied ... They are equal to the accommodation of 1,144 men".

In 1966, the authors of the Archaeological Survey, who seem like the late Rodney Green to have been under the impression that it was in County Down, described it as follows: "It is built of finely wrought granite, with wide semi-circular arched opening, the head of which rises into a triangular open bed-mould pediment, supported on square piers. The piers have moulded bases, fluted imposts and entablature with moulded cornice, fret-enriched frieze and deep architrave; the architrave has inset panels, on the S. pier carved with a spinning wheel and on the N. pier with a harp" - and vice versa inside the gateway. The Lawrence photographs reproduced by F H Bell show that the archway was slightly modified for barracks use (but it is now back in its original form), and that it was contained in a screen wall with postern doors with Gibbsian surrounds to either side. Since then, all the stone barrack buildings - except for this archway - have been demolished to make space for a housing estate, on the edge of which the ornate gateway looks out of place. Could not something be done to improve its surroundings? This is an architectural set-piece of high quality, despite the fact that its architect is not known.

Photograph: Michael O'Connell.

Situation: "Linenhall Square", Newry; td, Lisdrumgullion; Parish, Newry; District Council, Newry & Mourne; Grid ref. J 086 271.

References: Listed (surprisingly, only) B2 (16/25/19). Bradshaw, 'General directory', 1819, p xix; Green, 'Industrial archaeology', 1963, p 34 and pl 10; 'Archaeological survey of County Down', 1966, p 430 and pl 206; Lawrence, 'Newry, Warrenpoint & Rostrevor', 1989, pp 14, 15.

Porte-cochère, Drumbanagher House, Poyntzpass

212. Not really either a folly; nor a monument; nor a memorial - but how else to categorise this astonishingly eccentric solitary survivor, all that remains of W H Playfair's enormous Italianate masterpiece, Drumbanagher House? Lewis mentions the "large portico", but Bence-Jones, more correctly, refers to it as "a vast arched porte-cochère": for its openings, on three sides, are tall and wide enough to accommodate a coach and four, whose passengers could debouch at the front door in comfort, sheltered from the weather. The wide doorcase, now devoid of its door, stands at the top of three broad steps: it is an eerie experience to step through the opening, not into a welcoming hall, but into - a bed of nettles. For all the rest of

the great house has been carted away, and much of the demesne is now planted out in forestry.

The stonework is of the highest quality, with crisply carved Close and Maxwell armorial bearings: the strange, hollow, surviving structure resembles a Roman Arc de Triomphe. Now the ivy is encroaching on the stonework, and if it is not cut back soon, will take over: a kind of northern *seges ubi Roma fuit*. The relationship of the porte-cochère to the rest of the house is demonstrated in Playfair's surviving drawings in Edinburgh University library; a detailed account of its construction and furnishing is given by Gow, who remarks: "Playfair was Scotland's most fastidious and exacting architect and 'Close's Castle'

271

was one of his grandest private houses." Designed in 1829 for Maxwell Close and his wife Anna (née Brownlow), begun in the following year, and completed around 1837, at a cost of £80,000 (see also Brownlow House - 69). And Gow records: "When the Closes suggested that" (the porte-cochère) "might have been executed more cheaply with a cement rather than a carved stone vault and have a slate rather than a lead roof, they were firmly rebuffed by their architect who countered that as the 'principal' feature of his design, visitors' first impression of a house, to which he devoted so much care and expense would be a false impression."

John Heather of the Ordnance Survey wrote in March, 1838: " Drumdannaher House," (sic) "the seat of Colonel Close, who commenced the building of it about 6 years ago. The house has a humble appearance" (!). "It has no massy architecture about it. All seems light, spacious and neat ... There is a great profusion of cut stone about it and the pleasure grounds. The stones have all been got in Scotland and brought over in a rough state".

R M Young says "The Close family is of Yorkshire origin, the first member to settle in Ireland being Richard Close ... who held a commission in the army despatched to Ireland in 1640 by Charles I ... His grandson, the Rev. Samuel Close, married a daughter of Lady Maxwell, of Elm Park, Co Armagh, and their son succeeded to the Elm Park estates."

It was occupied first by the British army, then by the Americans, during the second World War, which perhaps did not much conduce to its welfare; in 1951 the fixtures and fittings were auctioned off, and the big house was demolished, the materials being sold off, while the descendants of the original owner moved into a modern house built just in front of the porte-cochère, or into the land steward's house in the stable yard. In 1962, the father-in-law of the present owner told the Belfast Telegraph: "No mortal could have afforded to keep the castle going. So I had it demolished. Death duties, upkeep and financial difficulties meant I just had to get rid of it ... It was perfectly sound and in good order when it was demolished ... Now it looks like something hit by a nuclear bomb".

Photograph: Michael O'Connell. Wood-engraving: from Byrne.
Situation: 7 Drumbanagher Wall, off the Poyntzpass - Newry road; td, Killybodagh; Parish, formerly Killevy now Drumbanagher; District Council, Newry & Mourne; Grid ref. J 058 355.
References: Listed B1 (16/21/27). Playfair drawings, in Edinburgh University library (elevation AR 22/1.2); VAL 1B 217, and VAL 12B/15/23 A-E, in PRONI; Lewis, TD, 1837, II, p 472; Heather, OSM, 1838, Armagh, I, 1838, p 52; Byrne, 'Carlingford Bay', 1846, p 210; Young, 'Belfast and province of Ulster', 1909, p 246; 'Belfast Telegraph', 2/4/1962; Bence-Jones, 'Burke's guide', 1978, p112; 'Gate lodges', UAHS, 1994, p 36; I Gow, in 'Irish arts review', 1998, p 57.

DRUMBANAGHER CASTLE—SEAT OF COLONEL CLOSE.

Belvedere (Ruins), Fathom, Newry

213. High up on the hillside of Fathom Mountain, looking out northwards over the Clanrye valley, very difficult of access in an overgrown Benson's Glen, an extraordinarily large and impressive folly, totally undocumented so far as I can discover. Local tradition has it that it was an O'Neill castle; perhaps such a castle once existed on, or near, this site; but it seems more likely that it was an

extravagance of that branch of the Needham family, Earls of Kilmorey, who seemed to have built Fathom Park (now Fathom House - 96); or just possibly of their successors, the Bensons, after whom the glen is named. Some structure is shown on the 1834 Ordnance Survey map. However, there is a weathered datestone set into the northern wall reading "J Ferguson 1885", so perhaps it is more modern than it looks, or is locally reputed to be.

Octagonal, with the staircase in the wall facing the steep hillside at the rear; seven large windows in each of three storeys, the top storey now much decayed, looking out over seven magnificent, and very carefully chosen, views; of cutstone, which cannot have been easily raised to the site. Now roofless, floorless, and derelict: but still a surprising and impressive survival. Perhaps access to it could be restored, perhaps it might even yet be turned by some entrepreneur into a fashionable tea-room, as part of the tourism initiatives now on foot for the regeneration of South Armagh?

Photographs: Anthony Cranney.
Situation: Benson's Glen, Fathom Mountain; td, Fathom (Lower); Parish, Killevy; District Council, Newry & Mourne; Grid ref. J 095 228.
References: Listed B2 (16/13/29); OS map, 1834.

Thomas Millar Memorial, Lurgan

214. A delightful prickly memorial, just outside the former Lurgan court house, very well restored in 1998, with an octagonal spire, and gablets, carried on a central ashlar column surrounded by eight marble columns: executed by John Robinson of Belfast. The inscriptions record that the Rev. Thomas Millar was in 1842, most surprisingly, "ordained a missionary to the South of Ireland" (where the heathens lived?, can he have been a "souper"?); installed in Lurgan 1844; "By Pulpit and the Press, By his Doctrine and Example, He laboured to win souls"; "Died 10th May 1858 aged 39 years" in the Trent railway disaster according to the listers; "Erected by a grateful public sensible of their deep obligation and desirous to perpetuate the memory of a good citizen an affectionate friend and a faithful Minister of the Gospel".

Photograph: Michael O'Connell.
Situation: William Street / Charles Street corner, Lurgan; td, and Parish, Lurgan; District Council, Craigavon; Grid ref. J 078 587.
References: Listed B (14/21/7); O S map, 1859; Oram, 'Craigavon', UAHS, 1971, pt I, p 9.

William Kirk Memorial, Keady

215. Born in Larne in 1795; Member of Parliament for the constituency from 1852 to 1859 and again from 1868 until his death in 1871; as the inscriptions on the four sides of his monument proclaim "For 40 years he was the mainspring of the industrial activity and social progress of this town and district ... A man of strong intellect, uniting energy and sterling honour, he was withal of humble spirit for he feared God and served him...So rare a combination of qualities merited this memorial of one, who was eminent as a merchant, a magistrate, and a senator ... Erected by many friends in remembrance of William Kirk MP 1871". (See also 102 and 190, Darkley House and Darkley Mill Chimney.) Williams describes this as "Forceful Gothic octagonal spire ascending from a massive drinking fountain to commemorate the philanthropic exertions of the local MP."

A most curious High Victorian monument, very evidently the work of an engineer rather than an architect, the bastard offspring of an illegitimate union between a pyramid and an obelisk. Its proportions are squat and unimpressive; it has an un-classical flying buttress at each corner carrying a subsidiary pinnacle, except that one of

the four has gone missing. Yet it provides a fitting and formal central feature for the rather sprawling and undistinguished little town of Keady, and, as well as commemorating that rather forbidding entrepreneur William Kirk, provides a fitting memorial to the eccentric Fitzgibbon Louch, civil engineer, who had the endearing quirk of signing his work in mirror-writing, as at the market house of 1870 which used to stand just opposite, until it was bombed. He practised in Dublin, Derry and Belfast as architect and engineer, and was author of Lough Eske Castle, County Donegal, and Ballynacrea House, County Antrim. The memorial was restored in 1993 under the supervision of John Morrison Associates.

Photograph: Michael O'Connell.
Situation: The Diamond, Keady; td, Crossmore; Parish, Keady; District Council, Armagh; Grid ref. H 844 340.
References: Listed B1 (15/9/3). IB, XIII, 1871, p 288; Brett, 'Court houses and market houses', UAHS, 1973, pp 22, 38; 'Keady & District Historical Society journal,' 1992, p 32; Williams, 'Architecture in Ireland', 1994, p 13.

COLONEL·THE·RIGHT·HONOURABLE
EDWARD·JAMES·SAUNDERSON
M·P·FOR·NORTH·ARMAGH
FROM·1885·TO·1906
LEADER·OF·THE·IRISH·UNIONIST
PARTY·FROM·1886·TO·1906
BORN·1837·DIED·1906

A·DEVOTED·SERVANT
OF·HIS·COUNTRY·AND·HIS·GOD

Edward Saunderson Memorial, Portadown

216. A strikingly energetic bronze statue, on a handsome granite plinth, prominently sited in the centre of Portadown, of a local worthy, landlord and politician. The inscription records that Colonel the Right Honourable Edward James Saunderson was MP for North Armagh from 1885 to 1906; leader of the Irish Unionist Party from 1886 to 1906; "A devoted servant of his country and his God"; born 1837, died 1906. A very successful exercise in the realist style, signed by W Goscombe John RA, and erected in 1908.

Colonel Saunderson was a choleric Unionist and Deputy Grand Master of the Orange Order who led the opposition to Mr Gladstone's Land Acts and Home Rule Bills alike. With his bald head and mutton-chop mustachios, he was eminently caricaturable: a kind of predecessor of Colonel Blimp, he was often caricatured in the Nationalist press. This is certainly not a caricature; it is obviously a good likeness; and yet, a smile is raised by the sweep and clarity with which the sculptor represents frock-coat, watch-chain, whiskers and waistcoat buttons; all the more so when the statue is seasonably decorated with a long, old-fashioned, Orange sash, the bottom attached to a trouser-leg with string.

Photographs: Michael O'Connell; postcard, SELB Local Studies Library, Armagh.
Situation: Market Square, Portadown; td, Tavanagh; Parish, Drumcree; District Council, Craigavon; Grid ref. H 009 537.
References: Listed B (14/16/2). Oram, 'Craigavon', UAHS, 1971, pt I, p 4.

W. & G. BAIRD, LTD.   COPYRIGHT.
THE LATE COLONEL SAUNDERSON, M.P.
FROM PHOTO TAKEN SEPT. 29, 1906.

Crimean War Memorial, The Mall, Armagh

217. "Sir William Verner wrote Lord Panmure with regard to Crimean trophies for Armagh, and had a reply dated July 13, 1857 stating that the municipal authorities of Armagh should make direct application to the Government"; which they did; but then found themselves "unable to expend rates for setting it up". In the end, Archbishop Beresford bore the costs of installing it. The gun itself is believed to have been one of those captured at the siege of Sebastopol; the mounting is more ornamental than business-like. (A similar cannon on an identical mounting was presented by the War Office to Newry). "One of the guns captured during the war with Russia, 1854, mounted on its carriage, occupies such a conspicuous place, that while reminding of strife, it also helps thoughtful persons to appreciate the advantages of peace" (Bassett). Originally it stood where the Boer War memorial now stands. It was for many years flanked by two German field guns from the first World War, removed as salvage (like so many gates and railings) in 1940 (Weatherup).

It does indeed still occupy a very prominent position in the centre of the Mall, itself rightly described by the UAHS listers as "one of Ireland's most attractive urban parks". The head of the Mall is presided over by Francis Johnston's court house (169); at its foot stands the gaol, a building more distinguished for its contribution to the streetscape than for architectural elegance (it was rather coarsely refronted in the late 19th century); and a considerable number of notable buildings line its east and west flanks. Formerly the town race-course, in 1797 what is now the Mall was leased by the Archbishop to the burgesses to provide "a public walk for the people". The trees then planted had, by 1888, attained what Bassett describes as "majestic proportions".

Photograph: Michael O'Connell.
Situation: To the south of the White Walk crossing the Mall; td, Corporation; Parish, and District Council, Armagh; Grid ref. H 877 455.
References: Not listed; in conservation area. 'Newry Telegraph', 7/7/ and 28/8/1857; Bassett, 'Armagh', 1888, p 91; T G F Paterson, Armachiana, IV, p 121, in Armagh County Museum; Lawrence, 'Newry, Warrenpoint & Rostrevor', 1989, p 11; Weatherup, 'Armagh', 1990, pp 22-24; 'Buildings of Armagh', UAHS, 1992, p 129.

BIBLIOGRAPHY

This bibliography relates only to printed books. Citations from newspapers and journals; particulars of maps, guides to individual buildings, deeds, documents, letters, private papers and unpublished material, will be found in the references appended to the entries for the buildings concerned. Where no such particulars are given, it may be assumed that the authority in question is in private hands and unavailable for public access.

Allison, H.T. *The way we were: historic Armagh photographs from the Allison Collection.* Compiled by J.D.Fitzgerald and D.R.M.Weatherup. Belfast, 1993

An archaeological survey of County Down. Ed by E.M.Jope. Belfast, 1966

Bassett, G.H. *The book of County Armagh.* Dublin, 1888

Bassett, G.H. *County Down guide and directory, including the borough of Newry,* Dublin, 1886

Beaufort, Daniel *Memoir of a map of Ireland,* Dublin, 1792

Bence-Jones, Mark *Burke's guide to country houses, Vol. I: Ireland,* London, 1978; 1988

Bennett, J.A. *Church, State and astronomy in Ireland: 200 years of Armagh Observatory,* Armagh, 1990

Binns, Jonathan *Miseries and beauties of Ireland,* London, 2 vols, 1837

Blum, R.H. *Bessbrook: a record of industry in a Northern Ireland village community,* Belfast, [1945]

Bradshaw, Thomas *The general directory of Newry, Armagh ... Portadown, Tandragee, Lurgan ... for 1820,* Newry, 1819

Brett, C.E.B. *Buildings of County Antrim,* UAHS, Belfast, 1996

Brett, C.E.B. *Court houses and market houses of the province of Ulster,* UAHS, Belfast, 1973

Buildings at risk: a catalogue of historic buildings at risk in Northern Ireland, UAHS, Belfast, 1 - , 1993 -

The buildings of Armagh. Ed. by Primrose Wilson. UAHS, Belfast, 1992

Burke, Sir Bernard, *A visitation of seats and arms of the noblemen of Great Britain and Ireland,* 2nd series, 2 vols, London, 1854, 1855

Burke's Irish family records, London, 1976

Burke's landed gentry, 2 vols, London, 1886

Burke's landed gentry of Ireland, London, 1912; 1958

Butler, John *Seeing stars: two hundred years of astronomy in Armagh 1790-1990,* Armagh, 1990

Byrne, P.A. *A picturesque handbook to Carlingford Bay and the watering places in its vicinity,* Newry, 1846

Calendar of State papers relating to Ireland, 11 vols, London, 1860-1912

Calvert, Hon. Frances, *An Irish beauty of the Regency. Compiled from ... the unpublished journals,* London, 1911

Camlin, Gilbert *The town in Ulster,* Belfast, 1951

Carville, Geraldine *Creggan: a Celtic Christian site. Tangible links with St. Jarlath, 3rd archbishop of Armagh,* Dundalk, 1996

A century for Christ: centenary of First Presbyterian Church, Portadown, 1858-1958, Portadown, 1958

Clarkson, L.A. and Crawford, E.M. *Ways to wealth: the Cust family of eighteenth century Armagh,* Belfast, 1985

Clendinning, K.M. *The Parish of Shankill: a brief ecclesiastical history,* Lurgan, 1983

Clergy of Down and Dromore. Ed. and with brief parish histories by Fred Rankin, Belfast, 1996

Cloake, John *Templer, tiger of Malaya: the life of Field Marshall Sir Gerald Templer,* London, 1985

Clow, W.M. *The centenary book of the First Presbyterian Church, Portadown, 1822-1922,* Portadown, 1922

Colvin, Sir Howard *A biographical dictionary of British architects, 1600-1840,* 3rd ed., London, 1995

Collins, D. *Ardmore Parish Church,* [n.p.], 1995

Commissioners of Inquiry on Education in Ireland, *Second report,* London, 1826 [HC 1826/27(12)xii]

The complete peerage, 13 vols, London, 1910-1959

Coote, Sir Charles *A statistical survey of the county of Armagh, with observations on the means of improvement,* Dublin, 1804

Cordner, William *Brownlow House: a short guide,* Lurgan, 1993

Craig, Maurice *The architecture of Ireland from the earliest times to 1880,* London, 1982

Craig, Maurice *Classic Irish houses of the middle size,* London, 1976

Craig, Maurice *Dublin 1660-1860: a social and architectural history,* Dublin, 1952

Craig, Maurice and The Knight of Glin *Ireland observed: a handbook to the buildings and antiquities,* Cork, 1970

Curl, J.S. *Classical churches in Ulster,* UAHS, Belfast, 1980

Curran, C.P. *Dublin decorative plasterwork of the seventeenth and eighteenth centuries,* London, 1967

Davin, Dan *Closing times,* London, 1975

Dean, J.A.K. *The gate lodges of Ulster: a gazetteer,* UAHS, Belfast, 1994

Deane, C.D. *The Ulster countryside,* Belfast, 1983

Dixon, Hugh *An introduction to Ulster architecture,* UAHS, Belfast, 1975

Dixon, Hugh *Ulster architecture 1800-1900,* UAHS, Belfast, 1972

Donaldson, John *A historical & statistical account of the Barony of Upper Fews in the county of Armagh, 1838,* Dundalk, 1923

Doyle, J.B. *Tours in Ulster: a handbook to the antiquities and scenery of the north of Ireland,* Dublin, 1854

The Drennan letters, 1776-1819. Ed. by D.A.Chart, Belfast, 1931

Dunlop, Durham *Life of W.J.Barre,* Belfast, 1868

Encyclopaedia Britannica, 11th ed., 29 vols, London, 1910-1911

Evans, E.E. *Prehistoric and Early Christian Ireland: a guide,* London, 1966

From the isles of the North: early medieval art in Ireland and Britain. Ed. by Cormac Bourke, Belfast, 1995

Gallagher, Lyn and Rogers, Dick *Castle, coast and cottage: the National Trust in Northern Ireland,* Belfast, 1986; 1992

Gallogly, John *The history of St. Patrick's Cathedral, Armagh,* Dublin, 1880

Galloway, Peter *The cathedrals of Ireland,* Belfast, 1992

Glin, *Knight of,* Griffin, D.J. and Robinson, N.K. *Vanishing country houses of Ireland,* Dublin, 1988

Green, E.R.R. *The industrial archaeology of County Down,* Belfast, 1963

Green, W.J. *Methodism in Portadown,* [Belfast], 1960

Gregory, Augusta, *Lady, Cuchulain of Muirthemne: the story of the men of the Red Branch of Ulster,* London, 1902

Gwynn, Aubrey and Hadcock, R.N. *Medieval religious houses: Ireland,* London, 1970

Gwynn, Stephen *The fair hills of Ireland,* Dublin, 1906

Harbison, Peter *The High Crosses of Ireland: an iconographical and photographic survey,* 2 vols, Bonn, 1992

Hayes-McCoy, G.A. *Ulster and other Irish maps, c. 1600,* Dublin, 1964

HEARTH: a review of projects completed 1978-1993, Belfast, 1994

Henderson, Isobel *St. Mark's, Killylea 1832-1982: a short history of Killylea Parish, its church and people,* [Killylea], 1982

Hewitt, John *John Luke (1906-1975),* Belfast, 1978

Historic monuments of Northern Ireland. Ed. by Ann Hamlin, Belfast, 1983

Historical sketches of the Parish of Tynan and Middletown. Ed. by Seamus Mallon, Tynan, 1995

Hogg, M.B. *Short history of Keady Parish, its church & people,* Armagh, 1928

Howley, James *Follies and garden buildings of Ireland,* New Haven, 1993

Hughes, Thomas *The history of Tynan Parish, County Armagh,* Dublin, 1910

Inglis, H.D. *Ireland in 1834: a journey,* 2 vols, London, 1834, 1835

Ireland, Denis *Statues round the City Hall,* London, 1939

Jenkins, *Dame* Jennifer and James, Patrick *From acorn to oak tree,* London, 1994

Jupp, Belinda *Heritage gardens inventory 1992,* Belfast, 1992

Keane, Marcus *The towers and temples of ancient Ireland: their origin and history discussed,* Dublin, 1867

Kerr, W.G. *The Parish of Mullabrack,* [? Markethill], 1953

King's Inns admission papers 1607-1867. Ed. by Edward Keane, Dublin, 1982

Knox, W.J. *Decades of the Ulster Bank, 1836-1964,* Belfast, 1965

Larmour, Paul *Belfast: an illustrated architectural guide,* Belfast, 1987

Lawrence, W.M. *Newry, Warrenpoint & Rostrevor: early photographs from the Lawrence collection 1865-80.* Compiled by Fergus Hanna Bell, Belfast, 1989

Leslie, J.B. *Armagh clergy and parishes,* Dundalk, 1911; *Supplement,* Dundalk, 1948

Lewis, Samuel *A topographical dictionary of Ireland,* 3 vols, London, 1837; 1840; 1847

Lockington, J.W. *A history of the Mall Presbyterian Church, Armagh, 1837-1987,* Belfast, 1987

Loeber, Rolf *A biographical dictionary of architects in Ireland 1600-1720,* London, 1981

Love, H.W. *Records of the archbishops of Armagh: being an indexed catalogue of manuscripts, documents and books in the archiepiscopal Registry of Armagh,* Dundalk, 1965

Lundie, G.T. *First Armagh Presbyterian Church, 1673-1973,* Armagh, 1973

Lyons, Mary C. *Illustrated incumbered estates: Ireland, 1850-1905,* Whitegate, 1993

McAleenan, C. and Crilly, J. *In the shadow of Slieve Gullion,* [n.p.], 1990

Macalister, R.A.S. *Corpus inscriptionum insularum celticarum,* 2 vols, Dublin, 1945, 1949

McCarthy, R.B. *The Trinity College estates 1800-1923: corporate management in an age of reform,* Dundalk, 1992

McCutcheon, W.A. *The industrial archaeology of Northern Ireland,* Belfast, 1980

McDonnell, Joseph *Irish eighteenth-century stuccowork and its European sources,* Dublin, 1991

McHugh, M. *Houses upon the glebe: a short history of rectories in the Parish of Mullabrack and Kilcluney,* [? Armagh, c 1985]

McKee, Eddie *Railways around County Armagh,* Bessbrook, 1990

McMinn, Joseph *Jonathan's travels: Swift in Ireland,* Belfast, 1994

McParland, Edward *Francis Johnston, architect, 1760-1829,* Celbridge, 1969 (Quarterly bulletin of the IGS, XII, Nos 3/4)

Malcomson, A.P.W. *Isaac Corry, 1775-1813: an adventurer in the field of politics,* Belfast, 1974

Mallory, J.P. and McNeill, T.E. *The archaeology of Ulster,* Belfast, 1991

Manchester, W.A.D.M., *9th Duke of, My candid recollections,* London, 1932

Mankowitz, Wolf *Wedgwood,* London, 1953

Mansbridge, Michael *John Nash: a complete catalogue,* London, 1991

Marshall, J.J. *History of Charlemont Fort and Borough in the county of Armagh, and of Mountjoy Fort in the county of Tyrone,* Dungannon, 1921

Marshall, J.J. *History of the Parish of Tynan in the county of Armagh. With notices of the O'Neill, Hovenden, Stronge and other families connected with the district,* Dungannon, 1932

Mason, W.S. *A statistical account, or parochial survey of Ireland,* 3 vols, Dublin, 1814, 1816, 1819

Meyer, Kuno *Selections from ancient Irish poetry,* 2nd ed., London, 1928

Mills, J.F. *The noble dwellings of Ireland,* London, 1987

Molyneux, N.Z.R. *History genealogical and biographical of the Molyneux families,* New York, 1904

Moore, Patrick *Armagh Observatory: a history, 1790-1967,* Armagh, 1967

Morton, Grenfell *Railways in Ulster: historic photographs from the age of steam,* Belfast, 1989

Moryson, Fynes *An itinerary ... through ... Germany, Bohmerland ... France, England, Scotland, and Ireland,* London, 1617

National Trust *Penrhyn Castle, Gwynedd,* London, 1991

Needham, Richard *Battling for peace,* Belfast, 1998

New perspectives: studies in art history in honour of Anne Crookshank. Ed. by Jane Fenlon [and others], Blackrock, 1987

Nicholson, N. *Nicholson,* Cranleigh, 1996

O'Brien, Darcy *W.R.Rodgers (1906-1969),* Lewisburg, 1970

O'Donovan, John *Letters containing information relative to the antiquities of the counties of Armagh and Monaghan collected during the progress of the Ordnance Survey in 1835.* Ed. by Michael O'Flanagan, Bray, 1927

O'Dwyer, Frederick *The architecture of Deane and Woodward,* Cork, 1997

O Fiaich, Tomás *St. Patrick's Cathedral Armagh,* Dublin, 1987

O'Kane, Louis *Lower Killevy - Ireland: outlines of their history,* Newry, [1955]

Old families of Newry & district from gravestone inscriptions, wills and biographical notes. Ed. by R.S.J. Clarke, Belfast, 1998 (Gravestone inscriptions, County Down, XXI)

O'Neill, C.P. and O'Neill, S.P. *Armagh Post Office: its history & postmarks.* [Armagh, 1984]

Oram, Richard *Craigavon,* UAHS, Belfast, 1971

Ordnance Survey memoirs of Ireland. Ed. by Angélique Day, 40 vols, Belfast, 1990-1998

The parliamentary gazetteer of Ireland, 3 vols, Dublin, 1845-1846

Pierce, Richard and Coey, Alastair *Taken for granted,* Belfast, 1984

Pigot, J. *City of Dublin and Hibernian provincial directory,* Dublin, 1824

Planning Service *Planning, archaeology and the built heritage,* Belfast, 1999 (PPS6)

Potterton, Homan *Irish church monuments 1570-1880,* UAHS, Belfast, 1975

Powell, Anthony *Faces in my time,* London, 1980

A preliminary survey of the ancient monuments of Northern Ireland. Ed. by D.A.Chart, Belfast, 1940

Reeves, William *A memoir of the Public Library of Armagh,* London, 1886

Reilly, Pat *Loughgall: a Plantation parish,* [Armagh], 1995

Richardson, E.M. *Next door neighbours at 9 and 10 Grafton Street, W,* London, [1926]

Richardson, J.N. *The Quakri at Lurgan & Grange,* Bessbrook, 1877; [1899]

Rodgers, W.R. *Collected poems,* London, 1971

Rogers, Edward *Memoir of Armagh Cathedral with an account of the ancient City,* Belfast, 1876

Rogers, Edward *Record of the City of Armagh,* Armagh, 1861

Rogers, Edward *Topographical sketches in Armagh and Tyrone,* 2nd ed., Armagh, 1874

St. Francis Church, Annaghmore, 1856-1956: centenary ... souvenir booklet, Belfast, [1956]

St. Saviour's Church, Portadown, centenary year book 1858-1958, [Portadown, 1958]

Shaffrey, Patrick and Shaffrey, Maura *Irish countryside buildings: everyday architecture in the rural landscape,* Dublin, 1985

Sheehy, Jeanne *J.J.McCarthy and the Gothic Revival in Ireland,* UAHS, Belfast, 1977

Sleater, Matthew, *Introductory essay to a new system of civil and ecclesiastical topography, and itinerary of counties of Ireland,* Dublin, 1806

Smith, C.F. *James Nicholson Richardson of Bessbrook,* London, 1925

Smith, J.H. *Belfast and its environs, with a tour to the Giant's Causeway,* Dublin, 1853

Stewart, A.M. *Royal Hibernian Academy of Arts: index of exhibitors and their works, 1826 to 1979,* 2 vols, Dublin, 1985,1986

Stokes, William *The life and labours in art and archaeology of George Petrie,* London, 1868

Stuart, James *Historical memoirs of the City of Armagh,* Newry, 1819; New ed. by Ambrose Coleman, Dublin, 1900

Studies in building history in memory of B.H. St J. O'Neil. Ed. by E.M.Jope, London, 1961

Tallon, Alfie *Fireside gleanings,* Lurgan, 1988

Tallon, Alfie *Memories of old Lurgan,* Lurgan, 1987

Taylor, George and Skinner, Andrew *Maps of the roads of Ireland,* London, 1778; 1783

Thompson, Paul *William Butterfield,* London, 1971

Tonna, Charlotte Elizabeth *Letters from Ireland in 1837,* London, 1838

Waterman, D.M. and Lynn, C.J. *Excavations at Navan Fort 1961-71,* Belfast, 1997

Weatherup, D.R.M. *Armagh: historic photographs of the primatial city,* Belfast, [1990]

Williams, Jeremy *Architecture in Ireland, 1837-1921,* Dublin, 1994

Wilson, William *The post-chaise companion ... through Ireland,* Dublin, 1784; 1786; 1803; 1813

Wright, G.N. *Scenes in Ireland. With historical illustrations, legend, and biographical notices,* London, 1834

Young, Arthur *A tour in Ireland in the years 1776 ...[to] ... 1779,* London, 1780

Young, R.M. *Belfast and the province of Ulster in the twentieth century,* Brighton, 1909

Gates at Richhill House (56), before their removal to Hillsborough Castle in 1936.
Photograph: AR Hogg, Ulster Museum

INDEX

(to page numbers)

The Argory Lion (66)
Photograph: Michael O'Connell

The Lurgan Lion (188)
Photograph: Michael O'Connell

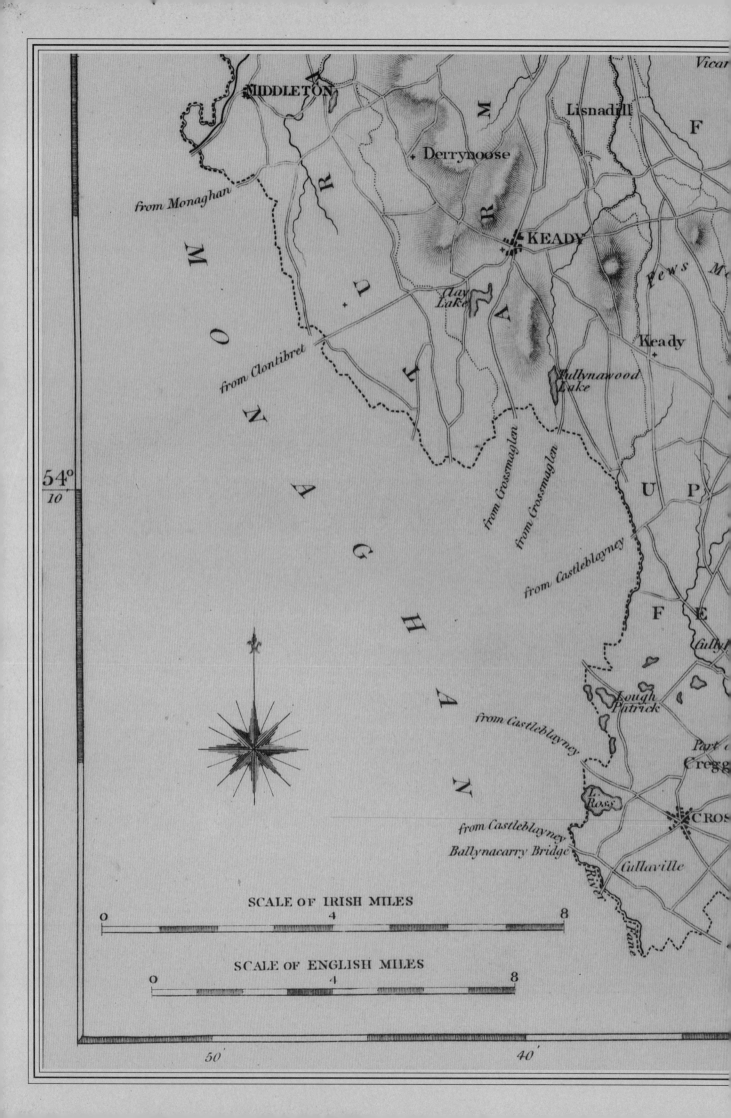

MIDDLETON

from Monaghan

M O N A G H A N

from Clontibret

54°
10'

SCALE OF IRISH MILES

0   4   8

SCALE OF ENGLISH MILES

0   4   8

Vicar

Lisnadill

F

Derrynoose

M
R
R

KEADY

Clay
Lake

A

Pews M

Keady

Tullynawood
Lake

T

from Grossmaglen

from Grossmaglen

U P

from Castleblayney

F E

Cully

Lough
Patrick

Part o
Cregg

from Castleblayney

L.
Ross

CROS

from Castleblayney
Ballynacarry Bridge

Cullaville

River Fane

50'

40'